A Pilot's Life
Hump Pilot & Crop Duster

by

Kenneth Babcock

Casablanca—December 1944

Hump Pilot Kenneth Babcock

© 2006 Kenneth Babcock
All rights reserved.

First Published 2006
Penman Publishing, Inc.
200 West 38th Street
Chattanooga, Tennessee 37410

Pictures and quotes appearing in this publication are used with permission of photographer, owner, or writer.

A Pilot's Life

Hump Pilot & Crop Duster

by KENNETH BABCOCK

ISBN: 1-932496-49-1

Manufactured in the United States of America.

Printed by Penman Publishing, Inc.
Reprinted November 2007
by Penman Publishers

Kenneth Babcock Visiting in the Home of Max & Edna Chennault

Behind Ken on the Wall
Is a Display
Of
Gen. Claire Chennault
Memorabilia

Dedication and Acknowledgements

To Blanche for her love, encouragement, patience and help

To my daughter, Sherry, who in her early years was without her father

To my many friends in the Fayette Writers Guild and Toastmasters Club

To my three roommates and others who died for our freedom.

Table of Contents

Chapter   **Page No.**

Ken in Casablanca (*Humphrey Bogart* picture) ii
Dedication & Acknowledgments v
Curtiss C-46D Commando (picture and specifications) ix
List of Photographs .... x-xi
Maps of China .... xii - xiii

1   **A Terrible Storm in China** 1
2   **Early Beginnings** 6
         • First Memories of Colorado 9
3   **Life in the 1920s** 11
         • About the Taylors 13
         • The Famous Indian Scout and Trail Driver 13
           Colonel Charles Goodnight
         • And Now to School, Still in the Twenties 15
         • The So Called Comforts of the Twenties 18
         • I Dream Of Flying 20
         • My First Track Meet 24
4   **Our New Home Is Built** 26
         • Real Snow For Christmas 28
         • Gertrude Goes To College 28
         • Life in the Thirties 30
         • I Become a Boy Scout 32
5   **Terlingua, Adventures, Climbing Mountains** 35
         • Another Mountain to Climb: Mitre Peak 37
         • Mud Hole, Spanking 38
         • High School and Studying Piano 39
         • All Guns Are Loaded Guns 40
         • Music 41
         • Summer On a Ranch 43
         • Jayter and His Jack Rabbit 45
         • Doctor Jay Shurley, Specialist in Psychiatry and Psychoanalysis 46
6   **From the Boy Scouts to Flight Instructor** 49
         • Boy Scout Trip to Yellowstone 49
         • Attending the University of Texas 51
         • Still Having It Tough 52
         • The Dropout Goes to Work in McCamey, Texas 53
         • The Rattlesnake Derby 54
         • I Was My own Boss Until I Got Married 55
         • I Learn To Fly 56
         • Preparing to Instruct Army Air Corps Cadets 58
         • Western Hospitality 60
7   **I Begin My Career as Flight Instructor: Teaching Army Cadets** 61
         • Settling Down to Home Life in Fort Stockton 62
         • The Inevitable Happens 64
         • An Unusual Weather Phenomenon 65

8	**Army Air Force Career Begins** **67**	
	• Assigned To Air Transport Command, Ferry Command 69	
	• Ferrying the Martin B-26 Bomber and Other Planes 70	
	• Army Air Force Shenanigans 75	
9	**Leaving the United States** **78**	
	• Puerto Rico 78	
	• To Belem, Brazil, and Across the Amazon Jungle 79	
	• Ascension Island 80	
	• Temporary Assignment to Casablanca Airfield 84	
	• Cairo, Egypt 85	
	• Pietsch Re-Assigned 88	
	• Lalminar Hat, Bengal, India, My New Assignment 90	
10	**China, the End of the Road** **92**	
	• Transfer To Luliang 97	
	• Life of the Chinese 101	
	• Unusual Stories of Flying In China 102	
	• An All Day Walk Across the Valley 103	
	• More Flying 103	
	• St. Elmo's Fire 104	
	• Check Out By Pilot Bill Miegel 105	
	• Playing Bridge 107	
	• First Pilot At Last 107	
	• Three Strikes and You're Out 109	
	• The Missionary Gets to His Mission 110	
	• My Friend, Gordon Wendell, and Crew Bail Out 110	
	• A Special Mission 111	
	• Sergeant Buys a Chinese Wife 111	
	• Single Engine 113	
	• Crashes and Accidents 114	
	• Setting a Record of Cargo Over the Hump 116	
	• Theft of a Gun 118	
	• More About the Local Chinese 119	
	• An Extremely Rare Phenomenon 119	
	• Researcher Photographs Rare Form of Lightning 120	
	• End of WW II in Sight 120	
	• Going Home 124	
	• Next Stop – New York, New York, USA 126	
11	**A Civilian Again and In Business** **132**	
	• Back to Flight Instructor Again 133	
	• Post War Housing Problems 134	
	• Flying in West Texas Weather 134	
12	**Thirty Years of Crop Dusting** **141**	
	• I Buy My First Crop Dusting Airplane 142	
	• Strange Air Currents 143	
	• Preparing For Dispensing Liquid Fertilizer 145	
	• Tractor Application of Fertilizer 146	
	• Lloyd McKinney – Foreman 147	
	• Cashes W. Taylor 148	
	• A Close Call – Forced Landing at Airport 148	

- DDT and Toxaphene Removed From Insect Control
  Now We Had To Use Dangerous Chemicals 149
- Some Aspects of Crop Dusting 151
- A Hurricane and Cold Front Collide
  Cause Heaviest Rains in Recorded Texas History 156
- Another New Airplane 157
- Another Summer Spraying Crops 159
- God Working Overtime to Keep Me Alive 160
- More About Flight Instructing 162
- A Vacation Above Ruidoso, New Mexico 162
- Another Interlude of Teaching Flying 164
- I Buy Another Spray Airplane 166

13 **God Takes Over My Life** 168
14 **More Brush Spraying** 171
- Flying Stearmans For Gardner Brothers 172
- Punching a Time Clock 176

15 **I Go to Work For the Baker, Inc.** 179
- Some Contract Flying 181
- Dr. Ernie Sandidge, M.D. 181
- Riding Bicycles 182

16 **My Family** 185
- Hump Pilot Reunions 186
- Mount St. Helen and Its Devastation 189
- Sightseeing and Visiting Relatives on the Road Home 189
- Yellowstone and Teton Mountains 190
- My Aunt Kathryn Babcock 191
- Visiting Faegene's Aunt, Mrs. Roy Eddleman 192

17 **Don't Even Try to Guess What the Future Holds** 193
- Major Changes in My Life 196
- Faegene Ill With Leukemia 196
- Faegene dies 198
- Hip Surgery 198
- On the Road Again 200
- A Double Knee Replacement 205
- The Wedding of Chris and Kristen 207
- Reminiscing About the Past 208

18 **A New Beginning** 209
- Wedding Bells Are Ringing, For Me and My Gal 211

19 **Back to China, Year of 2000** 214
- There's No Place Like Home, and Love Makes the Home 223
- Work on house in Sonora and Taylor Reunions 226
- HUMP Pilot Reunions (later years) 227

Epilogue (to sum up my life) 229

Index of People Mentioned 231

Built for the "Hump"

Curtiss C-46 D "Commando"

During WWII, the AAF accepted 3,144 C-46s for hauling cargo and personnel and for towing gliders. The aircraft gained its greatest fame in airlifting supplies over the "Hump" (the Himalaya Mountains) in the China-Burma-India Theater in World War II. The C-46 could carry more payload than the C-47, and it offered better high-altitude performance, which was one of the reasons it was used so extensively in the CBI. C-46 crews began flying the hazardous air route over the Himalayas in 1943 after the Japanese closed the Burma Road. However, as a result of the CBI's harsh conditions, the type had a relatively high loss rate, and maintenance was a problem.

General Characteristics of the C-46A

1. The primary function is transport.
2. The power plant is two Pratt & Whitney R-2800-51 Double Wasp 18-cyclinder, twin-row radials engines.
3. Thrust is 2x 2,000 HP
4. Wingspan is 108 ft.
5. Length is 76.3 ft.
6. Contractors - Curtiss-Wright Corp Higgins Aircraft Co.
7. Height is 21.7 ft.
8. Wing area is 1,360 sq ft.
9. Weight, when is empty is 30,000 lb. Weight maximum load was up to 52,000 lb. in the CBI.
10. Speed is 270 mph.
11. Ceiling is 24, 510 ft.
12. Range is 3,150 miles
13. Freight - 10,000 lb. or 40 seats
14. A Crew of four.
15. First flight was March 26, 1940
16. Date deployed was 1943.
17. Cost of $233,000.
18. Number built was 3,182

List of Photographs

Pic #	Picture Name	Chap #	Page #
1	Very Fashionably Dressed Ladies	1	4
2	My Mother, Edith Stella Knoll Babcock	1	4
3	Kenneth on goat with mother	1	5
4	Ken crawling through grandmother's door screen - 1920	1	5
5	Ken and mother at Colorado farm	1	5
6	Ken in front yard - 1922	1	5
7	Ken at age six	1	5
8	OST Filling Station - Sonora, Texas - 1928	3	12
9	Old picture of Tourist Court	3	13
10	Filling Station and Tourist Court	3	13
11	Amateur Spelunkers – Felton Cave	3	21
12	Babcock Spelunkers – Felton Cave	3	21
13 - 16	The O. G. Babcock Family	3	22
17	Track picture and newspaper article	3	24
18	Gertrude Babcock – Painting Mural Texas A&M	4	29
19	Eagle Boy Scout and newspaper article	4	34
20	Scouts on rail train at Salt Lake Flats	4	34
21	Mitre Peak	5	37
22	Marie Watkins	5	39
23	San Angelo Symphony Orchestra, 1929-1930	5	41
24	Charter flight and Dr. J. T. Shurley	5	47
25	"Jayter" at South Pole Research Station, Antarctica	5	47
26	Old friends – Ken and Dr. J. T. Shurley	5	47
27	Boy Scouts Trip to Yellowstone - 1935	5	48
28 - 29	Amateur Photographer	6	52
30 - 32	Army Flight Instructor, Commander, Flight Officer - 1942 - 1946	6	60
33	Sign post in Casablanca	9	86
34	Arab selling Potatoes	9	86
35 - 36	On the streets of Casablanca	9	87
37 - 38	Pietsch and Kenneth – Casablanca - December 1944	9	87
39	Curtiss C-46 Commando	9	87
40 - 41	George Yost in Luiliang	10	98
42	Suez Canal	10	128
43	Captain from Fort Worth	10	128

Pic #	Picture Name	Chap #	Page #
44 - 45	Home at Last with Faegene and Sherry	10	131
46	Ken in his Television and Radio Repair Shop	11	140
47 - 48	Our First Airplane, Pop, My Family	12	144
49	Kenneth, Freddie and Lloyd McKinney	12	147
50	Cashes W. Taylor	12	148
51	Result of the Severe Drought in the 1950's	12	153
52 - 53	Pecos River Flood, Spring 1954	12	154
54 - 55	More devastation from Pecos River Flood	12	155
56	Ken's Call-Aire Crop Dusting Airplane	12	157
57	Crop Dusting	12	158
58	Bob & Bobby McKinney / pilots standing by airplane	12	161
59 - 62	Ken Babcock Bicycling	15	183
63	Grandpa and Aunt Kathryn Babcock	16	191
64	Kenneth and Faegene Babcock – 50th Anniversary	17	198
65 - 66	Ken and Blanche's Wedding	18	212
67	Memorial Ceremony at Hump Monument (China, 2000)	19	215
68	Terra Cotta Warriors and Horses	19	215
69	Chinese Ingenuity	19	215
70	The Great Wall	19	215
71	The new airport in Diquing (Shangri-La)	19	216
72	The group on the Great Wall	19	216
73	Ken's Recital	19	224
74	Volunteering at Christian City	19	225
75	Toastmasters	19	225

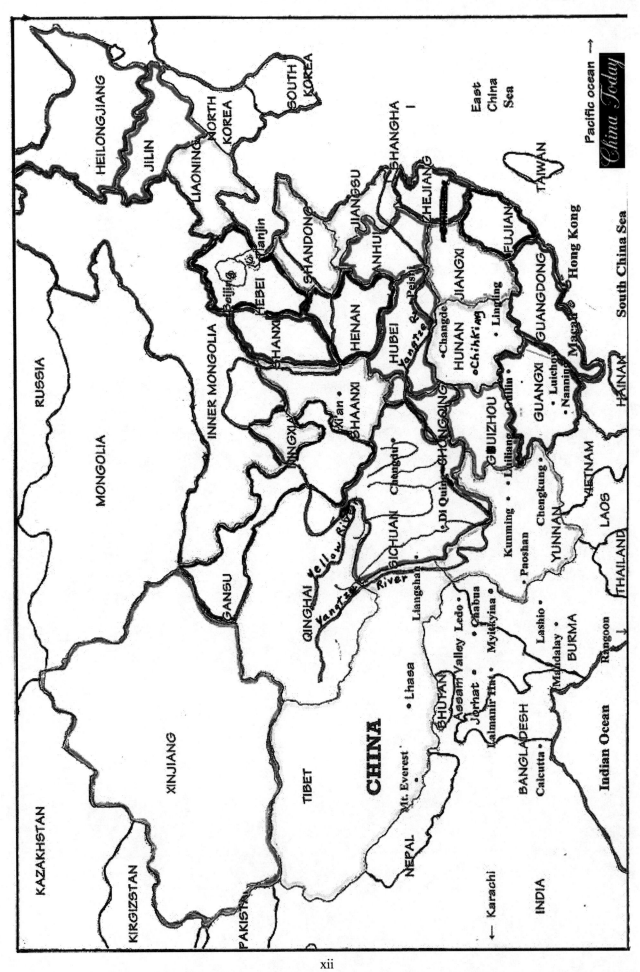

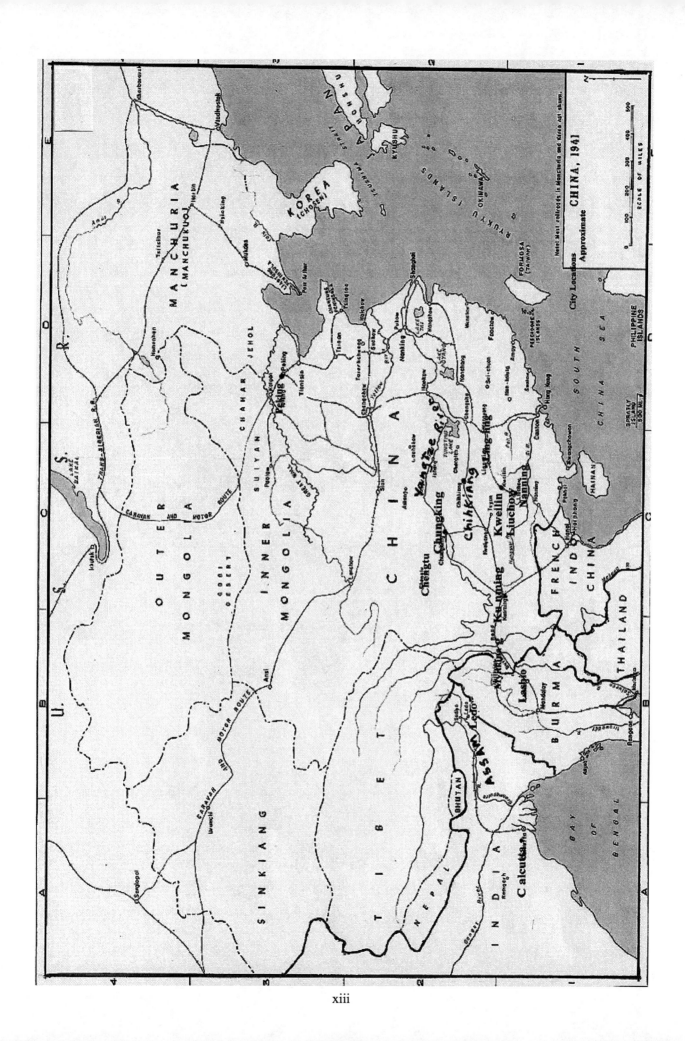

Kenneth Babcock
World War II Army Air Force Pilot
China-Burma-India Theater of War - 1944-1945

Chapter 1

A Terrible Storm in China

One beautiful starlit night, after delivering thirty drums of fuel to the fighter base in Chihkiang, China, we were flying back to our home base of Luliang. It was June 1945, and I was flying a Curtis Commando C-46. The air was smooth, the music from Tokyo Rose beautiful and the steady humming of the engines soothing and relaxing. We were looking forward to getting home and into the "sack." The only light in the cockpit was the glowing red of the instruments. We were leaning back in our seats, catching glimpses through the windows of ghost-like mountains slipping by beneath us.

About twenty minutes from Luliang I lazily reached for the microphone and contacted Approach Control for instructions to enter their traffic pattern. We had been flying at 10,000 feet, expecting a straight-in approach. Luliang replied: "Roger. Report reaching eighteen-five." (18,500 feet). That report jolted us wide-awake—a thunderstorm right on top of our home base, Luliang? What in the world? We hadn't seen a cloud all night. There was nothing to do but get up there as quickly as possible, so we began an immediate climb. We donned our oxygen masks and anxiously anticipated entering a thunderstorm.

With only 500 feet vertical separation during instrument holding patterns, there had to be thirteen airplanes in their holding patterns already, waiting their turn to land. This meant it would be over an hour before we could. Shortly after reaching our assigned altitude we flew right into the thunderstorm even before we saw it. It had to be sitting right on top of the airfield. Suddenly all hell broke loose. The storm buffeted and jerked us around, then dropped us at 2,000 feet per minute. I went to full throttle and pulled up the nose trying to slow our decent. Suddenly an updraft grabbed us; we were sent upwards at 1500 feet per minute. An immediate throttle reduction, full flaps, and lowered gear slowed the upward thrust somewhat. I had lost and gained about 300 feet in a matter of seconds. My intention was to keep the assigned altitude as close to 18,500 feet as possible.

Another powerful column of air hit us and down we went again. Full power was again applied, twenty degrees of flaps was also quickly applied for more lift and we raised the landing gear. This slowed the descent somewhat. I asked the co-pilot for engine cowl flaps to reduce excess engine temperatures. Too high a temperature is hard on engines. I had glanced at the instruments and noticed the temperature was still climbing. The co-pilot did not know what to do or where to find the controls. I needed help fast. I told the crew chief to take over the co-pilot's seat and job. Apparently the co-pilot was newly arrived and untrained for these conditions. Again the wind currents switched; we were shooting upwards at 2500 feet per minute. Again I called for full flaps, gear down, and I closed the throttles. I noticed the crew chief had closed cowl flaps and lowered flaps and gear as directed, yet our flying speed reached 160 miles an hour with no power.

Then "Wham!" Down we went, the seat belt keeping us from banging our heads against the top of the cockpit or being thrown out of our seats. Again we were riding this enormous roller coaster. Back to full power, gear and flaps down to twenty degrees. Our speed was low, but we were barely holding flying speed. Cowl flaps were opened again to control cylinder head temperatures. Then our vertical momentum reversed itself. We were being pushed rapidly upward yet again by the powerful column of rising air. I closed the throttles and was fighting constantly to control altitude, making procedure flight patterns, timing my turns, and timing pattern legs. I was keeping our altitude as close as possible to 18,500 feet. Glancing at the temperature gauges I noticed the air intake and cylinder head temperatures were just right, and breathed a sigh of relief for a good crew chief. With cylinder head temperatures too low or too high the engines could fail. I certainly didn't want that to happen.

Thoughts flashed across my mind as my eyes again swept across the gauges, seeing my back-up attitude flight emergency system (needle and ball) was pegging back and forth, of no use to me at all. The artificial horizon would just have to keep working.

We were unable to receive radio messages, only static on all radios. This situation was fast becoming desperate. We had completely lost radio contact with the station two miles directly below us. I told the radio operator to keep trying. We had a high frequency radio, which was supposed to work in the static of a thunderstorm, but it didn't that night. I was fighting for all I was worth to maintain my assigned altitude (there could be another airplane flying holding patterns only 500 feet below and another 500 feet above). It was also necessary to pull my oxygen mask aside for a short time when communicating.

The crew was standing behind me, hanging onto any handholds they could find. Suddenly our attitude instrument (artificial horizon) tumbled, leaving us helpless to maintain control. I yelled to the others to get their parachutes on. I knew we couldn't fly by the needle and ball. With no artificial horizon we didn't have a chance. I thought we'd "bought the farm" (burial plot). I scanned the instruments again, and spotted the small, normally unreliable, artificial horizon mounted down low on the pedestal, a part of the automatic pilot, working perfectly. Although low on the pedestal I could see it well enough to fly by. The crew hollered back to me that they couldn't catch the parachutes. I hollered back and said "That's OK, we're getting out of here," and I turned the airplane to a heading for Kunming. That small horizon kept working fine, even though in some of the diving turns the little airplane in it went out of sight. I was still able to keep the airplane relatively level, hoping the unreliable horizon would "hang in there and keep on working."

The storm was still giving us all the hell it could. It was about ten minutes before we began to ease out of it. I began reducing power to lower our altitude and the right engine propeller RPMs remained the same. That right hand automatic propeller control had "gone out" sometime during the storm. No problem. I used the manual toggle switch to adjust that propeller to the proper RPMs, and continued our slow descent, coming out into the nice smooth air of the night. What a contrast. I was now able to re-set the regular artificial horizon.

I re-seated the co-pilot and had him contact Roger Queen (RQ-the call sign for Kunming) to relay our position and new destination. They notified us Item Mike (Luliang) had listed us as "missing" for the past 30 minutes. Had we been in that storm that long? I guess I was so busy I didn't notice the time. I'd never been busier.

Then it really hit me. Our lives had depended upon one small unreliable gyro artificial horizon. Had it not been for that little unreliable gyro horizon we would have all been dead. We'd had a close call. Thank you again, God.

I had flown through many rough thunderstorms, mostly over the "Hump," fought icing, snow and hail, but this had to have been the mother of all storms. Flying through a thunderstorm was one thing; trying to maintain altitude and a holding pattern in the extreme turbulence was quite another.

We'll never know how many pilots flew into storms like this one, and were not lucky as we were. It would be doubtful that a pilot with little experience in instrument flying could have even maintained control in such turbulence for long with the instruments all working. With no gyro instruments operating and in reasonable weather, perhaps they could have bailed out. We couldn't. I wonder if a lost gyroscope horizon may have caused some of the many crashes in some terrible storm on the Hump. That would certainly be possible, and even probable.

Our chance to catch, put on, and jump with the parachutes would have been virtually impossible and downright dangerous. Just imagine swinging violently under a parachute in such violence, and then landing in the dark in that same extreme turbulence. One could even have been carried upward to thirty or forty thousand feet, or dropped at a fast rate of speed down to the ground. One of my buddies had bailed out in a similar storm was carried in a makeshift stretcher about twenty miles to our field because of his broken back. I'm not sure how his back was broken, parachuting down, or being thrown against the ground.

It is comforting to know the new instruments designed in the 1950s do not tumble in rough air. They continue working, even if upside down.

Having our own crew chief flying with us was handy that night, as he went right to work replacing that defective propeller control. We always kept two crew chiefs assigned to each of our airplanes so that one could always fly with his airplane. They did a great job keeping those airplanes airworthy.

My life had flashed before my eyes that night. Still having much life left to live, I begin my memoir at birth, ignorant and naked.

Prelude to Chapters 2 — 6

The Early Years

The next few chapters are of my life growing up in the 1920s and 1930s. This is a historical section of those times as I lived them, a prelude to my flying career, which begins in Chapter six.

Fashionably Dressed Ladies in 1915
Lady on the left is Ken's mother—Mrs. O.G. Babcock

Mother, Kenneth and Gertrude

Ken on goat, being held by his mother

Ken crawling through screen Grandma's kitchen door, 1920

Ken and mother at the Colorado farm

Ken in front yard - 1922
1021 S. Crockett, Sonora, TX

Ken at age six

Chapter 2

Early Beginnings

Why write a book? (see epilogue, page 229)

To a certain extent we tend to live in the past, but isn't the past a part of the present? Beginning immediately, doesn't the future become the present, so aren't the past and future close to us at all times? Here I go getting philosophical, which seems to be one of my traits. At some time in my youth I decided that my health and happiness should be among my first concerns, and that thought is still in my mind today. This may be apparent in my writing. I try to be clever and funny, seeking the humor in most situations. Although I can be serious, I tend to temper that seriousness with humor. As I look back it seems I've had a fantastic life. I certainly did not dream I'd ever be flying a huge transport airplane in China in a terrible thunderstorm. We just don't know the future, do we?

I was born in a red brick house in Dallas, Texas, on November 1, 1918, ten days before World War I Armistice Day. About two years later we moved into a wooden clapboard house in the small west Texas ranch town of Sonora. I have been told I crawled out the front door and sat down in the yard on a red-ant bed. Those ants must have been stinging me all over.

When I was about two my mother, Edith Stella Babcock, took me by train to Berthoud, Colorado, to visit my grandmother. When my bedtime came on the train Mother asked the porter to lift me into the upper bunk. Being picked up by the black porter must have scared me as this is my first memory in this life, and I remember I bawled. The porter was nice and gentle, placing me in the upper bunk, with me crying like mad. Mother then stood on the lower bunk, leaning on the upper bunk with her arms around me and comforted me, all of which I remember. I was apparently becoming aware of life around me.

I was told much later that I crawled through the kitchen screen door of my grandmother's house at her farm near Berthoud, Colorado. I remember it only as it was told to me, and have a picture of me doing just that. I don't really remember anything else about that early trip to Colorado. I was told many years later that I'd had a strong allergic reaction to the fresh alfalfa in the cows' milk and was quite sick for a short time.

We had some wonderful neighbors in Sonora, the Ridleys. They were ranch people with three sons. Kenneth was about my age. Chilton and Floyd were the two older boys. They taught me to peel pecans with my pocketknife. Being only a six-year-old boy it was a difficult operation for me, and the pecans in those days were mostly native and hard-shelled. Somehow I managed to peel some.

One morning Gertrude, my twelve-year-old sister, was swinging our one and a half year old baby sister, Edith May, in her little baby swing on the front porch. We liked to hear Edith May laugh as we were swinging her, higher and higher. Suddenly the swing unhooked and Edith May fell about seven feet, landing on her little bottom. This knocked her breathless. We hollered for Mother who came running, scooped her up in her arms and ran swiftly to Mrs. Ridley. Gertrude and I stayed on the porch, full of remorse. It seemed like a long time before Mother came home carrying Edith May. She told us our little sister was all right. The fall had only knocked the breath out of her. We didn't know what happened over at the Ridleys, but we figured Mrs. Ridley must have saved our little sister's life.

I was about seven years old when the Ridleys moved to a ranch near Rocksprings. I visited with them for ten days that summer. What a grand time they showed me. Kenneth and I rode horses every day. One day the old retired racehorse I was riding decided to race when I urged him into a lope. I couldn't slow him up, try as I might. He finally decided to stop, almost sliding into a closed gate. This was my first "cowboying." In later years I got to ride more horses than I really wanted to.

Our first house in Sonora was located at 1021 South Crockett at the south edge of town. There was a nice front porch, three rooms and no back porch, only a door. A wire fence surrounded the property, and there was a wire gate in the back yard wide enough to accommodate an automobile of the early 1920s. There was a chicken roost in one end of the little barn in the back yard with enough room for the few goats and sheep, which Daddy occasionally brought in for observation. Closing the barn door provided protection for the chickens from the elements, the raccoons and foxes.

Like most young boys, I climbed on any and over everything and fell off the barn, cutting my forehead on some rusty tin. This caused blood poisoning, so Dr. Blanton, the only doctor within sixty-seven miles, treated me. There are still a few little scars on my forehead.

Our house, like most houses in Sonora at that time, had an outdoor privy. Paper was furnished courtesy of Montgomery Ward and Sears-Roebuck Catalogues. When the weather was quite cold or raining, an indoor bathroom would have been pure luxury. We bathed in a #2 washtub in the kitchen, the warmest room of our three-room house.

Being an entomologist with the Federal Government, my father, O. G. Babcock, needed animals where he could observe them for various parasites. He spent most of his workweek about thirty-five miles south of town at the Texas Experiment Sub-Station to Texas A&M College, where he had some animal pens. Robert Eli Taylor, a prominent rancher in Sutton County at that time, had been instrumental in obtaining the building of the Experiment Station in 1919. Because of this Sub-Station my father had been sent to Sonora in 1920 to coordinate his work with that of the Texas Agriculture Experiment Station.

While Daddy was away at work, which was most of the time, Mother, Gertrude and I fed the animals. We gathered the chicken eggs and kept water pans full. The goats loved to lower their heads and butt the closest target. They would chase me the minute I turned my back to them and butt me unless I turned around. They were always butting each other, or about anything else that moved. One morning Mother bent over to pick up some clothes to hang on the line. She didn't notice the goat behind her, and believe you me, when Mother got up off the ground, she was mad. That weekend when Daddy came home he quickly built another pen. With the goats fenced in our chores were made easier and safer, especially for me and certainly for Mother.

One day Daddy brought a goose home. It became our job to feed that pest. He'd try to get behind me and pinch me on the "you know where." I was sure glad when we decided to have him for dinner one Sunday. I then learned how hard it was to pluck the down from a goose, but it was worth it: mother made me a nice goose-down pillow. She also made feather pillows, and I have wanted a feather pillow to sleep with under my head ever since.

Did you ever dream the same nightmare several times? I did. One dream was of a wolf chasing me through the back fence gate and into the back door, where I would get halfway in and then "freeze." I'd wake up quite scared. I had this same dream several times. How odd.

When we were six years old, Jack Rape and I played together about every day. I always knew when it was time to go home for dinner because Mrs. Rape would send me. Jack and I played marbles, ante-over (throwing a ball over the house for the boy on the other side to return it), and explored the hills around us. We tried to make marbles out of what we thought was clay. It didn't work, of course, but it was fun trying. Jack had several sisters who were usually busy helping their mother. I have known those girls most of my life, and cherish their friendship. Wanda is the only one still living in Sonora.

When in the third grade, Jack managed to get hold of some animal traps and we began running our trap line early each morning, re-setting them as we went along. We would catch a skunk or two, bring them home, skin and stretch the hide on a board. We then sold these stretched skunk hides to Elmo Johnson for fifty cents each. A fox hide in good shape would have brought five dollars, but we never caught one.

After running our trap line we would take a good bath, scrubbing ourselves thoroughly and dress in fresh clothes. It didn't work, though. Everyone knew what we'd been doing. One morning we caught a skunk in a shin-oak thicket. I was about ten feet away when he turned his back on me, raised his tail, and let loose with "Eau de skunk," straight into my left eye. I can feel it yet. We had no water to wash my eye with. It burned every step of the way home. Believe me, a skunk can protect himself with accuracy. That eye has been a wee bit weaker ever since. Well, that event ended our trapping.

One older boy pulled a trick on the school by taking an odor sack from a skunk, tying it shut with a string. He brought it to school and released the string letting it roll down the aisle on the wooden floor. That room had to be ventilated for a whole year.

All boys like to throw rocks, and there were plenty around to throw. The Saunders boys, who lived about two blocks away, threw rocks at me sometimes when I was passing by their house. The older brother Harold would sometimes force me into a wrestling match with Richard. I learned a few things about wrestling, like it or not. Alan, the youngest, is a retired Army Air Force colonel and a fellow pilot. He was stationed in India in the China-Burma-India Theater of World War ll. Richard and Alan and families live west of San Antonio in the hill country.

I wonder if it is natural for most boys to want to fight. I never did so; I learned to avoid a fight as much as possible. I was sometimes forced to fight, though. George Archer would catch me and make me box with his younger brother, Francis. Francis had longer arms than me and hit me with ease. Jack Dempsey, the world champion boxer and hero to would-be boxers, probably caused the interest in boxing among the kids at that time, but not for me. I avoided getting into boxing matches. Being able to run fast I avoided some fighting. It wasn't long until I could out-run them all. I don't know how many times I dreaded starting home after school, knowing "they" would be waiting for me. A few years later my running speed paid off in high school track.

I began to enjoy running and ran up and down the hills and across the valleys. I usually ran the one-and-a-half miles to town and back. Thirty years later I asked one old timer in Sonora if he remembered me. He answered, "Sure, you're that kid who was always running."

When I was five years old, Mother asked me to hold the heavy lid of the chest type icebox while she was lifting something out of it. I got tired and let it fall on her head. I distinctly remember her holding her head and asking me, "Why did you do that?" I know it must have really hurt, as there were tears in her eyes. I realized how selfish and inconsiderate I had been and still feel badly about having done that.

In those early years of my life there were many winter nights when Mother stayed up, trying to alleviate my painful earaches. She applied hot dishtowels heated above the wood stove, or rags heated in hot water. Neither did much good, but my wonderful Mother tried her best. Quinine was about the only earache medicine available or known in those days; it helped very little and made my ears ring.

Mother would sit patiently, holding her hand on my forehead and holding my hand. Her presence helped me tolerate the pain. When I would finally go to sleep, then, and only then, would she go to bed. Apparently those earaches were caused by inner ear infections as I had colds often, perhaps caused by our drafty house. These earaches must have contributed to my hearing loss in future years. I have read that quinine was also damaging to your hearing. In those early years we used quinine for just about every illness, as it seemed to be about the only medicine the doctors had available. I wonder if everyone believed it must be good for you because it tasted so awful.

I am now more aware that my hearing loss began in my early years and affected my life in many ways. While attending the University of Texas during 1936-1940, my hearing loss was a definite handicap. Most of my larger classes were in large lecture halls. As I had difficulty understanding what the teachers said, I tried, somewhat unsuccessfully, to supplement lectures with studying the books. My study habits were apparently insufficient as I still had trouble making my grades. I feel that I learned a lot from attending college, although my grades generally didn't show it. Many years later I took some night college classes to learn more mathematics, and made the Deans' Honor Roll the two semesters I attended. I must have learned to study.

In the 1920s and early 1930s grass didn't grow on the Sonora School playground. My sister Gertrude came home every day scratched and bruised after playing basketball on the gravelly outdoor court. There was no gymnasium, only a three-story rock schoolhouse with a bell tower on top and a large gravel playground.

Some of my memories of school are of the bell ringing at 8:00 a.m. each weekday morning. The auditorium was on the second floor, where we assembled and held plays on the stage. That was where one stood to recite "The Village Smithy" poem. The stage was also our band and orchestra practice hall in 1929. There was a small room up in the bell tower, which served as the piano teacher's room to which I climbed so many times.

At five years of age I was taking piano lessons from Miss Wiggington in that little room in the bell tower. The only thing I remember about those lessons is getting rapped on my knuckles by a pointer when I hit a wrong note. Gertrude was taking piano also, and became a good pianist. She even got paid to play for the silent picture shows of the late 1920s. Gertrude was fortunate that she didn't hurt her fingers playing basketball on that outdoor court. She did get her nose smashed playing the rotating game where players grab a handle on the end of chains fastened to the top of a central vertical pipe like a Maypole.

All players, except the one who was "It", would grab a handle and start running the same direction around the pole and under the one who was "It." This time she was the one who stayed back. She held her chain above all the others, letting them wind up. Then she got spun around faster and faster, lost her grip and went flying off, landing on her face. I saw her coming home crying and bleeding around the nose. Of course I was scared that she was badly hurt, but she wasn't. Years later I mentioned it to her and she'd forgotten it.

- First Memories of Colorado

In 1924 Mother took Gertrude and me to visit Grandmother Sussana Bashor Knoll again on her farm near Berthoud, Colorado. I would wander around the barns that housed the huge Percheron farm horses. Going past the pens I remembered the scent of the different animals and smelling the dust from freshly plowed fields as well as all the odors unique to a farm. Then away I'd go to the little pond of clear spring water, breathing in the fragrance of fresh cut alfalfa and spying the orchard of ripening red cherries just waiting to be eaten. How exhilarating this was. I noticed the honeybee hives were not far from the cherry trees, but there was plenty of alfalfa for the bees to use for making their honey.

One day Gertrude and I were in the orchard eating ripe cherries, enjoying the tart but sweet taste that lingered on our tongues. I had climbed into the tree to find the ripest, sweetest cherries. I ate some and passed some down to Gertrude. All of a sudden Gertrude started screaming and ran back toward the house. I hurriedly climbed down and ran after her, wondering what in the world was wrong. When I got to the house, there she was, sitting in Grandma Knoll's lap, crying, while mother was searching through Gertrude's kinky hair. She found a honeybee entangled in her hair and carefully eased the curls apart and out flew the honeybee. After that incident, I couldn't get Gertrude to go to the cherry orchard anymore.

When I stood beside that little pond, I remembered the stories mother had told me about her childhood on the farm. How much fun they had in the winter when the pond froze and they could skate on the ice. Also her four brothers would saw blocks of ice and haul them to the "Ice Barn." The "Ice Barn" was designed with cork walls and plenty of straw for separation and insulation between the blocks of ice stacked in layers. The ice would stay frozen all summer. When I saw all that ice stacked in the ice barn, I asked if we could make some ice cream. Sure enough, we made some and they let me sit on top of the freezer to keep the churn from moving around while they churned. The hot, fresh, homemade cherry pie, with ice cream melting on top, made memories that have lasted a lifetime.

After work one afternoon, I saw my uncles all chewing tobacco while enjoying the cool breeze under the tall trees in front of the farmhouse. It looked appetizing to me so I chased them begging for some. They just laughed and dodged me. Someone finally gave me some chewing gum, though, and that made me happy.

One favorite memory of the farm in Colorado is my being lifted up onto my favorite Percheron draft-mare at the end of the work day, then riding her back to the barn. That horse was so broad I could have laid down on her, but I just held on to her long mane. I felt like I was on top of the world.

My horse Daisy looked odd to me next summer when we visited Colorado. She had no tail. It had been caught in the thrasher and jerked out. It bothered me a lot that such a thing happened, especially to "my" Daisy.

Mother told me how she and her sister used to ride a draft-horse the several miles to school when the snow was deep. They would stake her out to forage for grass until school was out. Then they rode her home.

Mother also told me there were times they could skate most of the way to school on the big frozen irrigation ditch.

Chapter 3

Life In the 1920s

In my first year of school my playmates caught the mumps. Since there was no one to play with, I told my mother I wished I had the mumps too. She answered: "I don't think you would like that." Well, I did get the mumps, on both sides. I got to stay home from school and remembered what my mother told me. She was right. I'd much rather have been in school. It seemed afterwards that I caught all the usual childhood diseases as fast as they came around. We didn't receive vaccination shots in those days.

When I was quite young, the T.L. Millers lived across the street. Lamont was about my age. When the Millers moved to Big Lake, Florene, and then Dolphe were born. Later Garnet, another girl, came along.

T.L. Miller was a well-known jeweler in that part of Texas. He advertised by painting a big black lettered sign "T.L. MILLER, JEWELER" on every stock water tank in sight of every road in this part of West Texas. I renewed my friendship with the Miller family years later when I moved to McCamey. They were actually living in Odessa where T.L. owned a Jewelry Store, one in McCamey and Big Lake until 1940 when he auctioned off both stores. Dolphe became good friends with Faegene and me.

T.L. was as well known in the Sonora area as was Bob Ward, who had a tailoring business in San Angelo. Bob advertised by putting signs along all the principal roads in the area, one word at a time, reading "BOB - WARD - HAS - FITS". All I knew about Bob Ward was that he had "fits." We loved to call out the words as we drove by them.

Florene Miller became an airplane pilot and instructor in 1941. T.L. (Miller) also passed his private license test. The rest of the Miller family became active during WW II in supporting the Army Air Force. Florene became a Ferry Pilot early in WW II, one of the first women to do so. She was placed in charge of the women pilots at the Love Field Air Transport Base at Dallas. Later on the women pilots were known as WASPS. Florene Miller Watson is well known today and is called upon to give talks about the early days of women aviators and her experiences in the Ferry Command. In 2003 she was honored during the "Santa Rita" Days Celebration at Big Lake, Texas, (where she had lived years earlier) and in Texon. The field is now known as the Florene Miller Watson Airport. A monument in her honor was recently erected at the Airport.

After the T.L. Millers moved from Sonora, Mr. Brantley, a mechanic, moved his family into the house the Millers had left. Their son, W.B. and I became friends and playmates. The Brantleys moved to McCamey a few years later as McCamey's oil boom heyday furnished jobs during the depression years of the 1930s.

Ted Gilmore was a good friend when we were about five years old. We smoked cigarettes (candy) together and played cowboys and Indians. As we both wanted to be the Indian we compromised and both played Indians and had our own Indian suits. We would hide and pretend to ambush and kill pioneers and cowboys with our toy pistols. It seems my friends eventually all moved away. Ted and his family moved to Fort Worth about 1932.

In 1935 or 1936 I visited Ted in Ft. Worth, Texas, and we attended the big Texas Centennial Celebration together. We attended the Casa Mañana extravaganza. We visited other shows, of course, but especially Sally Rand performing her famous "Fan Dance," and also the Sally

Rand's Nude ranch. The only livestock Sally had on her ranch were pretty cowgirls dressed only in holster, guns and boots.

Five years later Ted joined the army, and fought in the Iwo Jima invasion during WW II, fighting the Japanese instead of Pioneers. Our early training must have been helpful, as he came through WW II virtually unscathed.

There were two Tourist Courts in Sonora in the twenties: Beulah Pfiester owned the "3 in 1" on the Highway in the east part of town. The "OST" (Old Spanish Trail) was owned and operated by Fred Jungk and his wife, Zola, on the west side. There were five suppliers of fuel in town by 1930, and gasoline at first sold as low as 16 cents per gallon.

Mr. Fred Jungk was born in Germany in 1895 and grew up in America. He joined the U.S. Calvary and served about three years in the Philippines. Returning to the States he then served in the Calvary stationed at Marfa at Fort Clark. This was the time our Calvary was kept busy with Poncho Villa's raids into Texas. When things quieted down Mr. Jungk left the Calvary and married a young lady named Zola in 1918, moving to Sonora, Texas.

He began building his Service Station and in 1925 had the first in Sonora, adding some tourist courts about 1928 he called the "OST Tourist Courts" (Old Spanish Trail). It became "Zola's Courts" three years later under her management. Pat Jungk, Zola's son, was born March 20, 1930 and is now operating the courts with his wife, Dorthy. The OST Courts have been modernized in recent years and are still owned and operated under the same family that built them, nearly eighty years ago.

OST Filling Station - Sonora, Texas
Owned and operated by Zola and Fred Jungk - About 1928

The following article appeared on the front page of
The Devil's River News, October 25, 1935, Vol. XLV, No. 51

A five-week campaign urging motorists to change oil in their motorcars to a grade suited for winter driving begins in this week's issue of the News as a result of the cooperative efforts of Sutton County handlers of Texas Company products.
   Sixteen-inch advertisements are to be used in each issue. The cost of the advertisement is shared by the wholesale agent, Ernest Carroll, and the following retailers:
   Fred Junk, operator of OST Tourist Camp;
   Floyd Dugan, operator of a company station near Lowry Draw;
   Mrs. Beula Pheister, operator of 3-in-1 Tourist Camp; H.C. Carson, owner of City Motor Co

I remember buying a burro for quarter when I was about seven. That was a lot of money for a seven-year-old in those days and I was sure proud to be her owner. After riding her for several days she apparently tired of me. Trotting right up to a prickly pear cactus, she ducked her head and stopped. I slid right over her head into that prickly pear cactus patch. After pulling all the thorns from my skin and clothing, I sold that "blankety blank" burro for twenty cents. I'd have taken less. I really didn't need a burro anyway.

- About the Taylors

When the Eli Taylor family moved to within three blocks of our house, I was glad to have some new friends to play with. There was a daughter my age, Cora Belle, and Jimmie and Basil who were a couple of years younger. There were 10 children in the Taylor family, but all were grown except Cora Belle, Jimmie and Basil. Mrs. Taylor passed away about a year after moving into town leaving Papa Taylor (Robert Eli) with the smaller children still at home. We kids were still able to play together until Jimmie and Basil moved in with their older brother, Cashes Taylor and his wife, Nancy, about a mile away.
   Cora Belle and I started to school together. Later on Jimmie was in Boy Scouts and came out for track and basketball, as well as football, so we became good friends. In the future the Taylor family became quite important to my life.

- The Famous Indian Scout and Trail Driver, Colonel Charles Goodnight

In December of 1924 the government sent Daddy to the Goodnight ranch in the Panhandle Region of the state of Texas to check for parasites on buffalos and Cattalos. Cattalo was a tentative name Colonel Goodnight had for the cross breeding of cattle with buffalo. The buffalo and cattalos were put in pens and Daddy went to work examining these animals for parasites and insects.

I had just turned six years old and my sister Gertrude was twelve. Daddy took us with him by train. Four hundred miles on dirt roads in a Model T Ford in 1924 would have been quite a trip.

Colonel Goodnight looked impressive with his whitish whiskers stained brown in spots by tobacco juice, and rather small in stature. (He was then in his 90s). He had a huge buffalo robe on the floor. I heard him instructing his foreman Cleo Hubbard to arrange a buggy ride for "the little 'uns." What fun that turned out to be.

We rode around the canyon viewing rock cliffs and spires along the broad valley of the Palo Duro canyon. Seeing buffalo roaming the fields was exciting for us. We were told there had been a cloudburst not long before we came, and we could see where the road was washed out.

There is a museum in Canyon, Texas, honoring Colonel Goodnight and his ranch headquarters. Colonel Goodnight was quite famous in the late 1800s as a scout and Texas Ranger. About the end of the Civil War he and Mr. Loving established some cattle trails to move cattle to New Mexico and Colorado. Later, when he started ranching, the colonel became an important leader and was highly respected by all, including those in the State Capitol. My daddy and the colonel became good friends in 1924 and corresponded by letter until the colonel died about four years later. Mrs. Goodnight died in 1925.

Along with Mr. Loving, Colonel Goodnight was well known for establishing the Cattle Trails to New Mexico and Colorado from San Angelo, Texas. They were called the "Goodnight-Loving Trails," over which he and Mr. Loving drove cattle to markets from central and western Texas to New Mexico and Colorado. These trails were created during the last thirty years of the 1800s. They went west from Fort Concho (now San Angelo, Texas) through Centralia Draw north of what is now Mertzon, then on to the west passing north of Big Lake and then through Castle Gap, some 13 miles north of McCamey, Texas. Horse Head Crossing on the Pecos River was still another 12 miles west from Castle Gap. From Horse Head Crossing, the trail continued on west and then north, following the Pecos River into New Mexico, where it branched toward Colorado. This trail avoided the Staked Plains of Northwest Texas where there were untold numbers of unfriendly Indians and open prairie.

The Comanches and Apaches frequently came down from their camps in the New Mexico mountains and raided the the plains of of Texas and New Mexico. It was on one of these raids that the Comanche Indians killed Mr. Loving, catching him and a cowboy scouting ahead of a trail herd, where the Pecos River crosses the Texas-New Mexico line. Mr. Loving had an arrow in him and couldn't travel, so the cowboy went for help the only way he could, by floating down the river at night. He reached Colonel Goodnight and his crew, but too late to save Mr. Loving's life. There is a town called Loving in New Mexico only a few miles east of where Mr. Loving was killed.

When Colonel Goodnight retired from trail driving, he established his famous ranch inside the Palo Duro Canyon. He fenced the canyon in the south and in the north, effectively keeping the cattle and some of the buffalo within his ranch. The cliffs and steep canyon walls served as fences on both sides. Some of the buffalo herd that ranged wild within the canyon were later given to the National Park Service. He developed his ranch into one of the larger and more successful ranches in Texas, and became a leader in the ranching business. Time after time he traveled to Austin on behalf of the cattle ranchers of Texas.

- And to School, still in the Twenties

I joined the "going to school" crowd in the fall of 1925. Although we all thought we hated school, secretly we looked forward to the renewing of friendships with our playmates. After vacations and weekends we would groan and fuss about having to go back to school. We were like the little boy sitting on the back porch steps crying at the end of the school year. His mother asked him why he was crying. He answered, "Because in only three months I'll have to go back to school."

Being a normal boy I also wanted to be like the rest and wear a skullcap. The skullcap merely fitted down over your head and had no brim. I begged mother to make one for me, but she refused. I guess she just didn't like the way they looked. One day she decided to save the quarter it cost for my haircut. She got out the scissors and went to work. That turned out to be the last time she tried that, for in about 20 minutes she was making me a skullcap to wear. She told me not to take it off, either, until my hair grew back.

One Halloween some older boys got a little wild. They put a milk cow up in the bell tower of the school (three stories of steps), and pushed over several outdoor privies (outhouse toilets) of which there were many in those days. The crowning trick was carrying School Superintendent Britt's new model "T" touring car to the top of the steep 200-foot hill behind the schoolhouse. There had to be several strong boys to take down the fence and maneuver over and around the large rocks guarding the rim at the top of that steep hill.

It was startling and unbelievable to see that black Ford Touring car of Superintendent Britt's, sitting in full sight on top of that hill. There were no roads up there, either. Well, Mr. Britt somehow guessed who was behind that and made them carry it back down.

The younger kids usually had a party after the trick or treating, with plenty of popcorn, hot chocolate and maybe some homemade taffy to pull. Our costumes were mainly of ghosts because we could use an old bed sheet with holes cut out for arms and eyes. There was little danger from cars as there were very few in the 1920s. As we grew older we would sometimes have a party or a dance.

I learned in my first year of school that you could get into trouble running around with the wrong crowd. One of my older playmates found an unlocked window in the schoolhouse one Saturday, and in we went, helping ourselves to pencils and some odds and ends. We got found out, of course. I knew it was wrong. Bad company is bad news.

Although I wasn't physically punished, my conscience has never let me down again. We returned all we had taken.

Life in the early 1920s was much like it was during the first of the century. My sisters and I were fortunate that both our parents had earned college degrees, Daddy in 1910 and Mother in 1912, so they were able to help us with our studies. However, Daddy was gone most of the time doing his research at the Texas A&M Experiment Station. Mother saw that we studied.

As the Experiment Station was thirty-five miles south of town, the government either furnished Daddy with a car (Model T Ford) or paid him car expenses. With roads unpaved and poorly maintained the model T would sometimes take hours to drive those 35 miles. There were gates that had to be opened and closed, ruts in the roads to contend with, etc. It was just easier for Daddy to stay at the Experiment Station, only coming home once or twice a month, especially if it rained.

Daddy being gone much of the time meant I had to be the "man of the house." At least that's what my mother told me. I was given the job of taking care of the chickens, the wood fires, and whatever else came up. I admit at first I was little help because I was so young. As

I grew older and stronger I was able to take over all chores such as feeding the chickens, gathering the eggs, watering whatever animals we had at the time and cleaning up the back yard. This included seeing that the large billy goat had feed and water in his little pen.

Sometimes Daddy took me to the Experiment Station with him. The memory of opening all those gates makes me realize Daddy must have been quite happy to take me along. Have you ever had to open and close your own gates when driving alone? The Experiment Station installed a "Bumper Gate." Daddy learned to ease through the right side, gunning the car at just the right speed so the other end of the gate would swing halfway around. The bumper gate idea began "catching on" and several of the ranchers installed them. This reduced the need for us gate openers.

At the Experiment Station I stayed with Daddy in the "Big House," a two story concrete house where Experiment Station Superintendent Dameron and his family lived. The house was large in order to accommodate the many visitors. I loved to explore the buildings and pens scattered around the area and play with the other children.

That two-story house had a unique odor of concrete, which wooden houses didn't have. It was fun climbing up and down the stairs and playing with the smaller Dameron children. One late afternoon, we went over to Mr. Carpenter's (the cowboy) home. We were really impressed when a black cowboy joined us and played his banjo. What fun it was to listen to the lively music.

When Daddy brought me home my chores would begin again. By the way, did you ever gather fresh eggs from under a hen? Nearly every chicken decides from time to time to hatch her eggs. She objects quite vigorously to anyone who reaches under her to gather her eggs. She punishes you by pecking your hand, and "boy," that hurts. Sometimes we replaced her eggs with plastic ones and she wouldn't know the difference. Cleaning the chicken house was always a big chore for me, but it was necessary in order to kill the parasites. Of course I didn't do this until I was older, about eight.

Our schoolhouse in Sonora was an old two-story rock building having the first grade and the rest rooms in the large basement. The first grade room was later turned into a cafeteria that my mother was hired to manage. All eleven grades were taught in that rock building until the new high school was finished in 1932. The new high school building was two stories, with athletic rooms and central steam heating from a furnace in the basement. A separate one story Home Economics building was also erected.

Mother's maiden name was "Knoll," and she was a member of the Shaker Church of Hygiene, Colorado as she grew up. Our Knoll ancestors may have brought that denomination with them from Alsace Loraine when they moved to America. During 1997 my cousin Dean Knoll, took me to visit the Shaker Church our parents had attended in Hygiene, Colorado. There were several headstones with the Knoll name; all were ancestors of ours.

I pictured in my mind the Knoll family riding from the farm the several miles to the Shaker Church, in a horse drawn wagon or carriage, in all kinds of weather. Mother was certainly a devout Christian. She saw to it we children were exposed to Christianity, and she chose the Methodist Church of Sonora to be our church, there not being a Shaker Church in the Sonora area.

When we were able we went to church every Sunday, having to walk about a mile when Daddy was not there. I was always given a nickel for Sunday school collection. One Sunday while walking to church by myself, I let temptation creep into my head and spent that nickel for an ice cream cone. Guess what. My teacher must have told my mother I didn't put my nickel in the collection. I wasn't spanked, but I think I would have preferred it. Mother was terribly disappointed in me. I never again failed to give my nickel. I also charged some candy one time at the grocery store, but never did it again after mother received the grocery bill.

We saved some of our wood stove ashes for making laundry soap. We made the soap in a big iron pot in the back yard. This homemade soap was quite effective when used on the clothes, especially with the water heated by a fire under the pot. The soap was made in that same iron pot, with ashes and lard (bacon grease) and a little lye. When washing clothes, my job was to stir the clothes using an old mop handle. The best way to do this was by raising and lowering the clothes with the mop handle leveraging on the pot rim. We would let the fire die down after the clothes boiled a little while, then lift the clean, hot, clothes out one by one with the mop handle, into a tub of cold rinse water. After a little rinsing in each of two tubs, and some hand wringing, they were then hung out by mother to dry on our clothesline. Mother took care of the starching and bluing before she hung them.

The next year we bought a double tub, on legs, with a wringer installed between the tubs. We felt we were really getting "up-town" then. I transferred the hot washed clothes into the first tub, rinsed the clothes, and then I put them through the wringer, using both hands to turn the handle of the wringer. I was unable to twist the clothes by hand, but with a run back through the wringer they were ready to be hung up by mother on the clothesline to dry.

Have you ever milked a cow? For those of you who haven't, this is the procedure: first put feed in front of the cow and turn the calf in with its mother. When the calf gets the milk coming down, take the calf away from her and tie it up. You then wash off the cow bag and teats, sit down on a milking stool, bury your head in the cows' flank and get busy squeezing the teats, squirting the milk into the milk pail. Putting your head right up in the cows flank is important as the cow has the desire to swish her tail to keep the flies off. That tail can really sting. I heard of one man who tied a brick to the end of the cows' tail and really got "clobbered". One important point: be careful not to let the cow step on your foot. It is nearly impossible to push on her and get her to move.

I preferred to use a single legged stool when milking that let me shift positions easily, allowing me to reach each teat. Mother was always better at milking than I was. She must have had a lot of practice when she was growing up. I was never able to milk a Jersey cow, as their teats are shorter and smaller. Mother, with her smaller and stronger hands, could get twice the milk from the Jersey cow than I could. The Jersey's milk, incidentally, is richer and creamier than any other cows we had.

In the 1920s before we built our new home we would drive our Model "T" Ford to the nearest big town, San Angelo, to shop for items we couldn't get in Sonora. Until Sonora had a dentist we drove to one in San Angelo, some seventy miles of dirt road. The model T Ford took most of a day to get there, so we spent the next two nights in a small two-story hotel to give our parents time to go shopping.

During the next day or so the grown-ups shopped and the children were safely playing in the hotel. The Hotel Manager's little girl, Janelle, was my age, and we played together like five year olds do, running up and down the stairs and hiding behind a steam radiator on a landing between the floors. Janelle was my first girl friend. I'd already kissed one girl but that hadn't lasted long. It had happened one day when I was four years old and sitting in the second row in the Church of Christ, watching a wedding taking place. When the groom kissed the bride, I kissed the girl beside me. Our romance only lasted through the kiss, but we were applauded.

Usually we would leave San Angelo for home after two days and nights. We tried to avoid traveling when the ground was wet as the dirt roads turned to mud even from a light rain. One time we were in San Angelo when it rained hard, and had to go home through the mud. There was a big mud-hole some 12 miles north of Sonora. All we could do was wait our turn to get pulled through that mud hole by a team of mules. A farmer charged a dollar for each vehicle he pulled through. The 1920 vintage cars had small tires, so the only way to handle muddy roads was with mud-chains on the tires or by being pulled through. Those chains were hard to install, especially in the mud and rain.

As I grew a little older, we played marbles (Keepers). This is a game that if you knocked the others players' marbles out of the ring they belonged to you. "Cowboys and Indians" was another fun game for us, as was "follow the leader," "ante over," and "Hide and seek." "Ante over" was played with a rubber ball. One player would yell "ante-over" and throw the ball over the house. The other would then reciprocate. Still another game, played more by girls, was called "jacks." It was played by bouncing a rubber ball and picking up the jacks one by one. If you didn't "miss," the next round you picked up two at a time, etc. until all were gone or until you missed. Another game was jump rope.

Pretending to be cowboys was fun for us, especially when Hoot Gibson was shown on the local movie theater. Then there came Tom Mix in the movies and cowboying became our daily fun. We could do the quick draw with our toy pistols, and were perfect shooters as well as being very fast. Our stick horses could run a long way.

Somebody discovered how to put a wire through the top of a two cans so we could walk on the cans like stilts holding a wire coming up to our hands from the top of the cans. Then along came the idea of a tight string stretched from tin can to tin can so we could talk through and around a corner.

At Christmas we made popcorn and strung it up all inside the house. Mother always made candy and hot chocolate ready for us on Christmas morning.

- The So-Called Comforts of the Twenties

In the 1920s and on into the 1930s the rural homemade phone lines were strung on wooden poles along the country roads going to the scattered ranch homes. We knew how many rings for each ranch: it would be a combination of short and long rings. Being party lines, it was sometimes necessary to request of anyone talking on the line to let us use the line in an emergency. There was always one person at least that liked to "listen in" on your personal conversations.

We kept our cooler on the back porch. Cooler? Yes. A cooler was an enclosed shelving covered over with long dish towels which were kept wet by absorbing water from the pan of water on top, the towels resting in that water. The air passing through the damp towels created some evaporation, which cooled the inside air. This kept food and milk fresh for several days. This worked better in dry West Texas than it would in a more humid climate.

Just "around the corner" from the "good old days" came the 1930's. Some of the big changes were a few paved streets and roads, electric radios, refrigerators, bigger and better automobiles and improved phone service. A Butane gas tank buried in your back yard supplied fuel gas to stoves that replaced the old wood burners. It was amazing to see this much progress during the "Great Depression" of the 1930's.

It was still necessary to keep the milk in scalded glazed jars to help prevent spoilage. The cream would settle on top of our fresh whole milk overnight. Next morning we could skim off the cream for use on cereal or cooking. Sometimes we let the whole milk get slightly sour before churning, improving the flavor and speeding the time of churning the milk into butter.

One of my first jobs as a small boy was making butter by turning the churn wheel. This took a long time for a small boy. As a reward Mrs. Wilson, for whom I often churned, would make me some real whipped cream, flavored with vanilla and sugar. Mother usually rewarded me with some fresh buttered piecrust, toasted with sugar and cinnamon. Incidentally, the butter kept really well in the cooler.

Clabber, cottage cheese, and buttermilk were by-products made by letting the milk sour. The clabber could be eaten as is or put in a porous bag, squeezed and hung up to drain, leaving cottage cheese in the bag. Those things were all quite healthy and inexpensive. I loved clabber with a little sugar. It was quite delicious. Homemade cornbread in buttermilk was another tasty treat.

When home delivery of ice became available, we bought an insulated wooden icebox, with a metal compartment at the top for the ice. The cold air naturally went downward into the storage chambers. A small tube drained water from the melting ice into a pan under the box. This had to be emptied every day. Each customer was given a cardboard sign by the ice company, with the numerals 15, 25, 50 and 100 printed consecutively on the corners. This card was then put in the front window of the house and rotated so that the amount of ice wanted was in the top corner. The delivery boy would read the window card, chop that size off a big block, and carry it inside the backdoor and put it into the icebox. The commercial ice came in 100 pound blocks, easily chopped up with an ice pick where the ice was pre-sawed part way through in different sizes. This ice kept perishables better than the cooler, but in only a few more years the refrigerator became available.

We then bought a General Electric refrigerator with the compressor mounted on top. We could even keep ice cream frozen within the ice compartment. We made some ice in it, too. It is likely the ice making in the new refrigerators eventually spelled the end of many commercial ice plants of those days.

In designing our new home in the days before air conditioning, cross ventilation planning meant windows, windows, and more windows. There were thirty-three of them in our new house. Years later I had to paint around those panes in those windows. What a chore that was, as all of them were multiple panes inside and out. The cross-ventilation, however, served to keep us somewhat less hot in the summer time if there was even a slight breeze present.

It was about 1933 when the Ritz Theater in San Antonio, Texas, installed a "washed-air" unit, which cooled the theater with huge fans blowing or sucking air through big straw panels having water dripping through them. There were little lights in the ceiling of the theater, imitating stars. This made us feel as if we were sitting outside under the stars in the cool breezes. Every summer when we went to San Antonio, we went to the picture show at the Ritz.

As far as I knew there were no car heaters until the late 1930s, when a gasoline heater was designed to fit inside the car. Sounds dangerous, doesn't it. There were no air conditioners in the cars that I know of until the late 1940s and early 1950s. The passengers in the old Model T Fords were "heated" by hot bricks or rocks heated on the stove, wrapped in newspapers and put on the floorboards of the cars. You then covered up with blankets draped down over those hot bricks and rocks.

Many were the time we drove in the Model T with heated bricks and stones wrapped up in paper. We covered ourselves with heavy blankets for the three-hour drive to attend concerts in the Concert Hall in San Angelo. It was really cold coming home as the bricks and rocks had cooled off. The curtains would pop and sway, helping to keep out some of the cold air. Daddy bought season tickets for these concerts each year, and we weren't going to waste those tickets just because the weather was cold. We heard the finest classical concert artists of the world during the late 20s and early 30s. It was worth going through some discomfort to hear them.

- I Dream of Flying

During the late 1920s I had found some "pulp magazines" (cheap paper books) full of stories of WWI airplane "dog fights." I read about the French Quadrille (whatever that was), and about the Spads and Sopwith Camels and other airplanes of that day. I read that pilots wore a white scarf and polished high-top boots, drank wine, and were popular with the girls. I fell in love with flying airplanes from all that fiction I was reading.

About the time I was reading about the WW I flying, along came an old WW I flying machine over the house in Sonora. Gertrude and I saw it come in for a landing only three blocks behind our house. We hurriedly walked to the small open spot in which the plane landed. Gertrude asked if I wanted to go up in the plane. I answered, "I don't have any money." She said, "Well, I have some, come on." We walked up to the old bi-plane and the pilot met us, took Gertrude's money and strapped us in. My dreams were about to become true.

With the engine starting to roar, the wind began blowing hard into our faces. I dodged down behind the little windshield. Suddenly we were off the ground climbing over some high lines and flying higher and swinging to the right. I looked down and saw we were circling the town, passing right by Eaton's Hill. The vista on houses below opened to our view when the pilot lowered the left wing in a turn. The beautiful sight of streets and homes all neatly lined up in squares spread out below us. What a thrill to be looking down on it all. The pilot put the plane in a little dive, giving us quite a thrill. Then another little dive and another thrill tickled our stomachs. He then landed the plane. The thrill of my young lifetime was over too quickly but would never be forgotten. I knew even then, that some day I would be a pilot.

As I think back to times long ago, memories just "Keep Coming Back like a Song" (A popular ballad of the era) and become clear in my mind. Gertrude was a loving sister who influenced my life in so many ways. Taking me flying is only one example. She encouraged me to play the piano, even playing duets with me. Teaching me to dance was another wonderful gift. Though only twelve years old, I had confidence and the know-how, so I began going to the community dances. Bob Wills and the Texas Playboys played often, as well as Jack Teagarden and even Lawrence Welk and his Orchestra. Dancing became a fun thing for me and I was allowed to attend almost every dance.

Gertrude even taught me to drive the Model 'T' Ford. When you turned a corner you turn the wheel hard. Well, I turned it hard all right, causing us to cut over and across the corner curb and sidewalk of our next-door neighbor, Mrs. Sim (Bertha) Glasscock. There was no damage done other than to my pride. I scared us both. It had happened so quickly.

Although I loved Gertrude I teased her, sometimes calling her "Gertie." I knew I could outrun her. It was fun for me. Boys seem to be that way, though, probably just wanting attention.

We usually had a dog. The first little dog was Edith May's, named "Muffie." She was fluffy, white and "protected" us from all the delivery boys, especially Less (Leslie) Fambrough, who brought us the groceries. (Yes, they did deliver groceries in those days). I accused him of making her mad by kicking at her and yelling at her, but of course, we were at fault not keeping her tied up when Less was coming with his armload of groceries. He had to deliver them all the way to the back of the house and onto the back porch and was always in a hurry. Muffie was frantic when Mr. Fambrough drove up. Sometimes I would catch her and hold her.

When Daddy was home, she was not allowed inside the house, but Mother let us bring her in sometimes when he was away. Muffie was a lot of company for us, running and always ready to play. After Muffie died we had a funeral for her. I was later given a dog named "Tip," named after a spot of white on the end of his tail. My Coach, Ted White, talked me into giving Tip to him. I'm still wondering why I let him talk me out of my dog. Maybe I had another. Coach told me he was a good dog.

Edith May was growing up, slowly, it seemed to me. She was about seven when she came down with a contagious fever, so all the family except Mother and Edith May moved out of our house for a week. We brought food and other necessities to the back window. She was quite ill for a couple of weeks, but recovered completely.

Amateur Spelunkers - Led by O. G. Babcock
Felton Cave - Sonora, Texas, November 7, 1927
All Spelunkers were schoolteachers,
except for Mr. O. G. Babcock's family.

Kenneth Babcock, Miss, Haley, Miss Moore, Miss Wray, Miss Draper, Miss Groom, Miss Ball, T. M. White, and seven unidentified people.

Mrs. O. G. Babcock, Gertrude Babcock, Kenneth K. Babcock, Edith May Babcock, and four unidentified people—Felton Cave—Spelunking in West Texas

Gertrude, Kenneth, Daddy, Mother & Edith May

Kenneth, his sisters and Muffle

Kenneth's daughter, Sherry, Kenneth,
Edith May, Gertrude, Mother & Daddy

Mr. & Mrs. Orville Babcock - 1927
Children: Gertrude, Kenneth & Edith May

Daddy was sent out from time to time for special expeditions related to his job, such as the trip to Colonel Goodnight's ranch. On another such trip he was sent to the Carlsbad Caverns to collect insects found within the cave. This was just after the U. S. Park Service purchased the cave, and several years before it was opened to the public. Daddy brought all our family on this trip.

Daddy and Dr. L. H. Bailey were commissioned by the National Geographic Society to do a study of life in the caverns. Daddy did the insect phase of the study and Mr. Bailey examined mammalian life. Daddy took all our family with him and we had a cabin to stay in at the entrance to the Cavern. Mr. White, finder and explorer, was in charge of the cave and was serving as guide to the group of scientists sent to go through the cave. This tour in the cave lasted most of three continuous days and included the lower caverns, which was larger than the upper cavern. Only the top cavern is opened to the public today.

The rough rocky road going up the mountains was too steep for our Model T Ford. Sometimes a Model T could be backed up such steep roads, but this road was too rocky. You see there were no fuel pumps in model T's. It only had gravity flow from the tank in front of the windshield. Consequently, we had to wait at the bottom of the steep hill for Mr. White to come down for us in his big Buick passenger car, which did have a fuel pump.

It was exciting to ride in that big car, the biggest I'd ever been in. We arrived at the cave entrance where there were several houses, one of which we stayed in. Mr. White Sr. was left in charge of everything while his son was in the cave.

The entrance to the cave was a big hole going straight down about 60 feet with a wire ladder hanging down along one side of the opening. There was a ridge, then another long wire ladder. We watched Daddy leave with the group of scientists, led by Mr. White Jr., going down the ladder into that huge hole and out of sight.

In the meantime I was busy being a seven-year old boy, throwing rocks, wandering around and being bored. On the second day Mr. White, Sr. caught me throwing rocks down into the cave. Boy did I get a chewing out. Of course I was wrong to be throwing rocks down into the cave, but I guess I resented being corrected.

The trip was successful and they went through both the upper and lower cave. Daddy found several insects and bugs in the cave. They spent three days in the cave. I believe this experience of cave exploration got him interested in spelunking, as we later explored several other caves of which most were in the Sutton County area where we lived.

The Felton cave, as it was called at the time, was thoroughly explored by my Father. It became a favorite cave for introducing others to the sport of spelunking. Since our family took in two lady schoolteachers to room and board each year, we felt it was of importance to entertain them, so we took them to the Felton cave. The cave had residents such as bats and "Daddy long-leg" spiders. The ladies naturally screamed when bumped by a bat or when rubbed against a stack of pulsating Daddy Long Leg spiders, adding to my fun. Another thrill was entering the cave when clambering over the large rocks at the entrance of the cave. Rattlesnakes under the large rocks became disturbed and would begin rattling under us. That was scary for me as well as for the others.

During the late "20s" we explored the cave just outside Sonora. Today this cave is known as the Caverns of Sonora. We could only go about 1500 feet into the cave as a room fifty feet deep stopped us. In 1956 two spelunkers managed to traverse that deep room, enlarge a hole in the far wall and enter the fabulous Caverns of Sonora.

Finances were supplied in promoting the new Caverns of Sonora by a small group of local men, and the two spelunkers began developing the first parts of the cave to open to the public. They even slept in the cave, digging depressions for their hips. In about two years they managed to cut a cave exit close to the main building. The company hired to cut the exit spent several months working with a huge circular bit, eight feet in diameter. This new opening enabled the tour through the cave to be continuous through the exit, eliminating having to return back through the entrance.

These caverns are known to be one of the most beautiful sites in the world and visitors come from all over to see them. As yet, it is still privately owned, although the State of Texas reportedly has tried to buy it.

- Running Track

Kenneth Babcock's time of 2 minutes, 14.9 seconds in the half-mile run at Veribest Saturday was only .9 of a second more than the record in that event for boys over fifteen.

While I was in seventh grade the coach gathered up a few of us to take to Rocksprings, Texas, to participate in a track meet. I was always running, so I guessed I could win something. Well, I did win. I won all six events I entered. From that time on I was inspired to be a track star, and trained nearly every day, running wherever and whenever I could.

In the San Angelo Standard Times in the early spring of 1935 was an article about the Sonora track team going to a meet at Veribest, Texas. I was a junior in high school that year. The following is a copy of the write-up:

Sonora boys under fifteen years of age bested the track teams of fourteen other West Texas schools in Veribest Saturday, while Babcock, entered in the meet for older boys, romped home to the tape first in the half-mile event.

Babcock defeated Hensley of Melvin, Day of Melvin and Jobe of San Angelo to win his event in the senior boys' competition.

Vernon Morris, son of Mr. and Mrs. H. V. Morris, accounted for 9.5 points of the Sonora boys 18 points in the junior meet. He won first in the 100-yard dash, second in the 50-yard dash and was a member of the relay team winning first in the 440-yard event.

Hurling his body five feet, two inches in the air was the feat of Jim Taylor, son of R. E. Taylor, who won the high jump from Mann of Brady, Adams of Mertzon and Jones of San Angelo. Thirty-one boys were eliminated by Taylor.

No training had been given the Sonora boys in high jumping, Coach Adams said this week. For that reason Taylor's work is especially commendable.

The Sonora and Brady teams were "nip and tuck," according to Coach Adams, throughout most of the meet. Thirty-two boys were entered in the high jump; all but four went out when the bar reached the five-foot height. Taylor then jumped five feet and two inches, winning first to put the Sonora team ahead of Brady.

The Sonora relay team made up of S. H. Stokes, O. B. Higgins, Taylor and Morris, made the distance in 52 seconds, six-tenths of a second better than the Brady team's time. A silver figure mounted on an attractive base and nine medals were brought to Sonora by the victorious team. The boys get to keep the medals and the school will retain the silver figure indicating the team's triumph.

In my senior year I was confident I could win the 880-yard (1/2 mile) race at the State Meet. However, after qualifying in the Regional Meet we received no notice there would be preliminary 880-yard qualifying trials at Austin on Friday. The finals then, as usual, were to be run on Saturday. We had planned to run the 880-yard race only on Saturday, as in the past. Clyde Littlefield, the man in charge, refused to let me run in the finals of the 880, since we had arrived too late for the preliminaries. Although I had recorded the best time in the state of Texas in the 880-yard run that year, that made no difference.

Coach Littlefield did let me enter the mile run, as that race had required no preliminary. I had never run in a one-mile race before, and had no idea how to pace myself, but I ran and was pleased to at least place sixth with the time of four minutes and forty-one seconds. Even though that time was considered pretty good time in those days I still felt like I had "let down" my supporters.

It was also a big let down for me, as I had dreamed and planned for two years of winning first place in the 880. Today I wonder, had I run and won that half-mile race, what effect it would have had on my life. I had some satisfaction that my coach timed me on the dirt track (slower than the track at Austin) in 1:55.8, faster than the 880-yard winner at the State meet that year and the fastest recorded time in any high school in Texas that year. Had I qualified for even a small scholarship, would it have been helpful to me in any way? Who knows? Things have a way of working out, though, don't they? Perhaps things worked out the best for me. You just don't know the future.

Chapter 4

Our New Home Is Built

My father had been working some time making blueprints and plans for our future home. He presented his plans to purchase material, location and prices to the banker, Roy Aldwell. Agreement on the loan was reached between them, and they shook hands. No papers were signed. That sure wouldn't happen today.

Daddy was ready to build, ordered material and hired some competent workmen. Work was begun on our new baked tile home at 908 S. Crockett St, Sonora, Texas. This gave me a new place to explore and play, also an opportunity to do odd jobs such as picking up wooden blocks and nails. When the laying of tile began I took on the job of carrying the tile to the scaffold for the bricklayer. One day I worked too hard, too fast and loaded the scaffold with too many tile. Down came scaffold, tile and bricklayer. No one was hurt. I remember the concern shown by the bricklayer. He was afraid I was hurt. I assured him I was fine and continued the job, but I had learned not to be over-eager. I was barely nine years old, so I still had a lot to learn.

As work continued a load of granite sand had been piled up in the back and became my mountain. I built mountain roads for my cars (blocks of wood). Most kids were lucky to have a small sand box, and never a whole mountain like mine. In my memories today I picture myself crawling on my knees pushing my "cars" up and around the curves of "my mountain." No wonder I had to replace my knees in 1997.

The house was put on a solid concrete foundation under every wall including the inside walls.

I found out later that Daddy buried all water pipes and sewage pipe at least 30 inches deep. That depth would keep the water from freezing in Colorado where he had come from, but it was never that cold in West Texas. I found out years later how deeply the pipe was buried, when I decided to replace all of the initial plumbing. We had to spend several days digging that old pipe out.

Daddy planted a pecan tree in the back yard, just after we moved into our new home, in 1927. It was called a "Texas Prolific". The tree was trimmed to seven feet tall and really lived up to its name. In most years it produced more pecans than any of the other four pecan trees we had. It is still fulfilling its name in the year 2002, and shades an area of about 800 square feet. This seventy-foot tree has a trunk about two and ½ feet in diameter. One year, about 1950, I went home and helped harvest all those pecans by hand. We sold the surplus of 600 pounds.

Finally the house was finished enough to move in, and what a thrill it was. We accepted Ruth Tipton as a roomer and border. She was a new teacher in the fall semester of school. Gertrude was a senior in high school, planning to go to the College of Industrial Arts (CIA), at Denton, Texas. Later on Ruth married Edgar Shurley, a rancher. In 1941, Gertrude married Ruth's brother, E. D. Tipton, ten years later. Having Ruth with us was to me like having another older sister. I already had a younger sister, and my older sister Gertrude was soon to be away in college.

Daddy was still spending much of his time at the Experiment Station, leaving me to do all the chores. I chopped up the wood supplying both the cook stove in the kitchen and the stove in the Dining Room. I carried out the ashes, fed the chickens, gathered the eggs and cleaned the chicken house each week. I killed and dressed the fryer chickens, watered and weeded the garden and cut the grass. As I write this I realize it sounds like a lot for a boy to do. It really wasn't. I did get an allowance of a quarter a week. That was enough money for a ten-year old boy, in those days. Daddy had a good job then, earning him one hundred twenty five dollars a month.

Having a nice big back yard gave my mother an idea. She ordered an extra 50 fryer white-leghorn fryer chicks from the hatchery at Comfort, Texas, so I could sell some as fryers. That idea worked out just fine for me and I went through the neighborhood taking orders for dressed fryers, at twenty-five cents each. Mother didn't charge me for them, and paid for all the chicken feed. What I sold was all profit for me. We also had plenty of chicken to eat and I made some spending money. Nothing tasted better than those little fried chickens.

We brought our wood cook-stove with us to the new house. It had a reservoir for hot water, so we kept the stove hot most of the time. We would heat water in pans on the top of the stove when more was needed. Mother would wake me up early each day so I could finish in the bathroom and have all the stoves working so she could cook breakfast early to have time to eat before going to school. Our new kitchen was large, with a nice nook set four feet out on the north side, enough room for our breakfast table.

There was a fireplace in the living room where we kept the piano. Sometimes it was too cold to practice, so then I had to build a fire in the fireplace. The dining room was large enough to easily place eight persons around the table. The back porch was large enough for me to curtain off a small room for my very own. The master bedroom wall joined my room and was large enough to also hold a small bed for Edith May.

Mother loved to invite new schoolteachers over for Sunday dinner each fall. She liked to invite teachers who were known to dislike goat meat. She could make goat taste like the best beef. After Sunday dinner the teacher usually complimented mother for her excellent beef roast, and the teacher was always shocked to find she'd actually been eating goat. We always got a kick out of doing that. I wonder if not liking goat meat was a way to get an excellent Sunday Dinner for them. If so, that was fine with us as we always enjoyed their company and we knew the teachers were struggling along on short pay.

Another trick we played on one of the teachers at a Sunday Dinner (we picked one with a good sense of humor) was by placing her in the chair that had a slow air leak in the cushion. The "sssss" it made when sitting down on it would cause everyone to look at her. We'd quickly turn away, acting embarrassed, which embarrassed her all the more. As I mentioned, she had to have a good sense of humor but she had a great dinner too. We all got a big laugh.

In our small community, though somewhat isolated, we sometimes went to extremes to liven things up. We all loved a good prank. One example occurred during an air-show put on one Fourth of July. The announcer covered the act from take-off of the airplane until the parachuter "jumped" out of the highflying airplane. Actually, the "parachuter" was a dummy that resembled a man. The jump was announced, and the announcer began "following the "man" down all the way. He became quite excited when no parachute was opened. I could see the horror on the faces of the onlookers as the announcer screamed "Oh my God." This looked quite realistic, as if the *main* chute failed to open. There were screams and other vocal sounds from the crowd. Finally, as the dummy was near the ground, it was seen that it was all a trick. I observed this incident and felt at the time it was rather extreme.

Another of my playmates was Roberta Holland, whose mother and mine were close friends. I liked her Daddy, who was a pastries cook. He always gave me an oatmeal cookie when we went to see them. Mr. Holland had rented a bakery in El Dorado, Texas, only 21 miles from Sonora. Sadly the Great Depression of the thirties, along with the drought, was really beginning in earnest, and this caused Mr. Holland's bakery to be shut down. He now had no job.

He finally was hired as a ranch hand some twenty miles east of Fort Stockton, Texas. He and his family moved into a small adobe ranch house on the ranch to be the caretaker. This was 100 miles west of Sonora, and was a very lonesome area, having no neighbors.

One day we drove out and visited them. The rough hilly country had few trees, and it was hot and windy at that ranch. There were no trees or grass at all around the house, just dry creosote and black brush. I'd like to have stayed longer as there were tall rocky hills that tempted me to climb them.

I've never understood why these tragic things happened, but within a year after we visited them, Mr. Holland was found dead in the pasture a mile from the house with both wrists cut. We felt so sorry for the Holland family.

Mr. Holland's death was the third death of persons I knew well. In the first grade one little girl had died of Appendicitis. Her classmates were convinced it was caused by Miss Green, the teacher, as she had paddled the girls' hands the day before the girl became sick. About two years later another classmate and close friend died from appendicitis. His name was Emma Lee Logan, twin to Emma Lou. His family was such a fine Christian family. This puzzled me that God didn't prevent this from happening. This seems to be an eternal problem for all people, I think. We hear the preachers tell us what the scriptures says about death and how we all will go to heaven if we are good. We seek a more understandable answer. I can only observe today that the surest thing about life is death itself. Life continues and is the most precious gift from God. Of course we know He promised us a better life to come.

- Real Snow for Christmas.

We usually remember unusual weather, and I certainly remember an eight-inch snow at Christmas time in 1928 in Sonora. I think that snow was one of the deepest snows in Sonora in the twentieth century.

Because the snow was so deep, I felt I could drag in a big cedar Christmas tree. Sure enough I found a nice big cedar tree on top of a nearby hill. I cut it down with my little hatchet and started dragging it in. Even a fence failed to stop me.

I laid the tree on the front porch and sawed the bottom of the trunk flat, ready for the wooden base I would make. Before I put it on the stand I thought I'd better check the height. Boy, was it big! It was over two feet too tall even in the eight-foot ceiling. I cut more of the tree off and put the tree on the stand in the living room, the top touching the ceiling. I was proud of the biggest Christmas tree we'd had. We had to pop extra popcorn for enough popcorn ropes to go around it. Being close to the fireplace we could easily burn the Christmas wrappings in the fireplace.

The pleasing odor of fresh Cedar permeated the house, and there was plenty of room on this big tree for presents. The greatest thing about Christmas, of course, is the happiness of giving. Mother always saw to it we each had gifts to give. Christmas was certainly a special time of the year for us. Even as I reached adulthood and had our own family Christmas tree, I still missed the odor of Cedar, and the wonderful feelings of Christmas as a child. Don't we all?

That same year we built a giant snowman with sticks for arms and a carrot nose. It was fun to run and play in the deep snow, wrapping tow sacks around our shoes and ankles for warmth. Snow in West Texas was rare, so we made the most of it, nearly freezing our feet, hands, ears and nose. There were lots of snowmen all over town that year.

When I was just twelve Edith May was barely seven. She was old enough for her to follow me around and play with me some. When I turned twelve years old I began another segment of my life, I joined the Boy Scouts of America. I kept busy working to advance in ratings as a Boy Scout. She wanted to come along with me, and I sometimes took her. However, I loved to run everywhere I went and couldn't do so when she went along.

Edith May took piano lessons and was active in her Sunday-School class. When in high school she became Editor of the "Sonora High School Bronco" newspaper. I saw one of her productions nearly fifty years later, and I was proud of her work as editor. I was always proud of her, especially when she graduated from College.

As WW II had separated our family for several years I was surprised when I returned and found that Edith May had been one of the candidates for "A&M Sweethearts". She later married Bob Kokernot, an Aggie. I missed seeing her during her college days.

- Gertrude Goes To College

My Sister Gertrude Babcock
Painting the Mural at Texas A. M. University

Gertrude left to attend the College of Industrial Arts in Denton, Texas in 1931. She was a natural artist, as she could draw all sorts of things quickly and quite well even as a child. Four years later our family attended her Graduation Ceremony at CIA, in Denton, Texas. After the graduation ceremony, the Dean spoke to me, asking what I planned to study when I went to college. I told him "Geology." He complemented me highly, and said: "Few people study Theology today." I'm afraid I disappointed him when I repeated that it was Geology, not Theology. He said "Oh" and walked away.

Now that she was a Commercial artist, Gertrude found a job in Dallas designing glass containers for cosmetics. That just wasn't her "cup of tea." She came home and found a job teaching in the Mexican school. In those days our schools were not yet desegregated. Her students loved her, and she told me years later how much she enjoyed teaching there. Many years later as I visited Sonora, several of her former students came up to me to ask about her and told me how much they thought of her. After teaching two years, she went to Mexico City to study Mexican art.

She came home after about three months and opened an art studio in the top floor of our two-story garage. Daddy had fixed up the studio for her. She taught and did some painting of her own.

Gertrude bid on a major panoramic scene for the Agriculture building of Texas A&M University, and won the bid. She was to paint a life-size mural from wall to wall behind the stage, depicting agriculture from early America to the present (1935). She worked full time on the mural and when she finished we were so proud of her. It was just beautiful. Those oxen pulling the Prairie Schooner stood out so life-like. This panorama can still be seen in the Agriculture Lecture Auditorium at A&M University of Texas, at College Station, Texas.

- Life in the Thirties

The economy was quite depressed all through the 1930s, with money and jobs scarce and men working seven days a week for as little as $10.00. (You were lucky to find any kind of job).

A few more of the changes from the 1920s to the 1940s were credit cards, ball point pens, pantyhose, dishwashers, clothes dyers, electric blankets, seal beam headlights, hydraulic brakes, and, I believe, brassieres, etc. In those days we got married first and then lived together.

This era was the beginning of what we now call "fast foods." Fried shrimp was becoming a delicacy and was always excellent, large and not too expensive. It was my favorite food. Still is.

Woolworth's was our favorite store. Their prices were all 5 to 15 cents. They did a big business in those depression days.

In the year 2000 I asked our grandson, Zachary, how many ice cream cones he thought twenty dollars would have bought when I was his age. He studied a little and said "20?" I laughed and told him at .05 each, it would have been 400. What a difference in buying power the last 70 years have made. Today an ice cream cone is $1.30 (plus tax). Of course there is much more money in circulation today as compared with those early days of the last century. In Shanghai at the end of WW II, in 1945 I converted a $50.00 U.S. Gold bill into the Japanese script then being used at that time in Shanghai, and received a pile of large bills, close to a million dollars. My supper cost me $50,000. That was the first and last time I have been a millionaire. Two days later I was broke.

The economy became more depressed all through the 1930s. Money and jobs became scarce with men working seven days a week. Food was much cheaper than today. We ate pinto beans, chicken, homegrown vegetables, potatoes, and sometimes goat meat. Sundays, we sometimes had roast beef. Potatoes were popular as they were fairly inexpensive, tasted good, and filled us up, especially when we also had cream gravy. We bought flour by the sack. Mother told me the first fight she and Daddy had was over not making gravy for the potatoes. Daddy was quite upset when there was no gravy for the potatoes. He informed mother that if you had potatoes you always had gravy. From then on, there was gravy when we had potatoes.

My sisters and I were raised in a happy and busy environment, which I believe is influential in reducing aggression between children. I believe parents today have more problems raising their children than our parents had. There are so many diversions today. With the availability of automobiles temptations we never dreamed of are commonplace today. We could and did kill ourselves with the cars of the 1930s just as today, even with such light traffic. I believe parental supervision may have been stronger in our days. During the 1920s there was alcohol if you had the money. Bootlegging was a popular business then, as prohibition still existed.

Somehow we got through the prohibition days pretty well. In recovering the whisky bottles thrown out along the roads, I realized a lot of people in our town must drink a good bit of whisky. I made spending money selling those empty bottles to the bootlegger. I have the faith that the young people of today may build themselves more character and resistance to temptation, just as steel becomes stronger by exposure to fire. We can at least hope so, can't we?

In Sonora, still quite a pioneer western ranch community, with a bit of the old west lingering on, there was still some resentment to authority. One boy, in the 1920s, was somewhat older than his classmates. He had to work to help support his family, going to school only part-time. He was giving his teacher some problems so she sent him to the principal for punishment. The boy objected and, being almost as large as the principal, jumped over and around the paddle. He then left school and came back the next day. Again he was sent in to see the principal. "You ain't goin' to 'whup' me," he said, when the principal reached for his paddle. The boy pulled a six-shooter from his pocket. He didn't get spanked, and didn't get to finish his education in school, either. The time of carrying six shooters had ended only a few years before, but some people were apparently slow to adjust.

When Texas A&M College moved Dr. I. B. Boughton to the Sonora Experiment Station as Veterinarian, our families became good friends. Dr. Boughton had a strong personality, was always positive, and drove a red "Flying Reo" passenger car like he was driving a racecar. He had a mustache and a grin like Clark Gable. His wife was a beautiful French lady. They had lived in Haiti, and had three children; Rique, the oldest, eight years old; Josette, age 5, who was the same age as my sister, Edith May; and the youngest, Alain, age six.

When Daddy came in one day he announced Dr. Boughton had been driving too fast and burned up his car. I quickly got on my bicycle and rode out to see it, as it was only five miles from town. Well, I didn't understand. It was not burned up at all. I rode home and reported that and was told it was the engine that was burned up. In my mind I pictured the engine all melted down. At the age of thirteen, words sometimes had only one meaning. Some people had "farplaces" while we had a fireplace. I at least figured that one out.

One day I was asked to baby-sit Edith May and the Boughton children. Before I agreed I requested permission to spank Rique if I thought it necessary. Dr. Boughton agreed to my terms. I had observed the little "devil" as being quite spoiled. Sure enough, Rique became uncontrollable. I guess I thought I was the upcoming "Dr. Spock" and took him over my knees and gave him a good "hand" spanking. That was a spanking "heard around the world." He did behave after that and I forgot all about it, but Rique didn't. Fifty years later I saw him at a Sonora School Reunion. The first thing he said as he saw me was: "You spanked me when I was little." I was surprised, as I'd completely forgotten it.

"Well, Rique," I answered, "It must have been effective if you still remember it." I was glad to hear him laugh.

Late one night Daddy answered the telephone, and announced he had to go help an Odd Fellow whose car was broken down on the highway. I wanted to know what this odd fellow looked like. As it turned out he was a member of the "Odd Fellows" organization of which I had never heard. I had pictured in my mind Odd Fellows surely must have looked odd. Isn't that odd that they named an organization: "The Odd Fellows?"

I was fourteen years old when Mr. Penick, who distributed cold drinks in Sonora, hired another Boy Scout and myself to sell cold drinks at a barbeque and dance held at Camp Allison, thirty-five miles east of Sonora. This was a free barbeque to promote Tom Connelly for Governor against Lyndon Johnson. Tom was tall, good looking and wore the proverbial "ten gallon hat" of a Texan. He was a fine speaker, and quite popular in West Texas. The free barbecue brought a big crowd. His opponent, Lynden B. Johnson, was not very popular in our part of West Texas, and I don't think he was invited.

We were kept busy selling cold drinks in our hastily erected drink stand. Close by was the large barbecue pit dug in the ground, where a young cowboy was doing the barbecuing. The pit was enclosed inside a wooden counter. My co-worker and I noticed Ikey Kring, a young cowboy from Sonora, trying to sample the barbecue. The cook had been working all day in the pit, and was quite irritable about anyone sampling the barbecue. When Ikey began climbing the barrier to get a sample, the cook came out over it, and all hell broke loose. Other

...up and pulled the cook off Ikey in time to prevent him from getting his eyes ... That cook was one tough "hombre." No one else tried tasting the barbeque ... ook said, "come and get it."

...yed busy selling pop until after midnight, when the dance ended. We crawled ... edrolls on the ground beside our drink stand, tired and sleepy. When I awoke next mor... I picked up a piece of paper lying on the ground beside me. It was a folded $20.00 bill. Boy. That was like finding $200 today. I put it in the bank along with my pay from Mr. Penick, to add to my future college funds.

In the summer of 1935 I went to work for Joseph Trainer's Department Store and Dry Cleaners. I'd worked there about a month when the State Engineer for the DOT came over and talked to Mr. Trainer about hiring me. Mr. Trainer graciously agreed.

In only a short time I was working on the surveying crew. That was fun. We were outdoors all day preparing for construction of ten miles of new highway toward Ozona. I spent that summer helping to survey and setting marker posts, then checking truckloads of caliche for the roadbed.

I usually ate lunch with the laborers working in my area and traded fruit to them for their homemade burritos. I practiced my Spanish by conversing with them. I liked my work, although it lasted from daylight to dark.

There was much responsibility on me, and I took it seriously. When a load of caliche was short for any reason, I had to turn it down. The truck drivers owned their trucks and were paid only for the full load they delivered to the work site after hauling it over ten miles of rough road. Caliche is softened powdered rock occurring extensively in West Texas. One truck lost a quarter of his load on the truck's right side when a catch tripped before reaching the unloading site. I had to turn down his load. That meant he would not get paid for that load he had hauled 10 miles.

The driver was quite angry. He would need to dump the remaining caliche somewhere else than on the road, before returning the ten miles for another load. He drove off, stopped on a deeply banked curve on the old road, with the right side high on the incline. Not thinking, he emptied the full bin on the right side, same side of the empty bin. The weight of the fully loaded left side then caused the truck to flop over on its side. The driver came walking up to the coffee shop, cussing and saying he was going to whip that kid (me). Thank goodness he didn't try.

- I Become a Boy Scout

The day I reached twelve, November 1, 1930, I joined Boy Scout Troop 19, of Sonora, Texas. I was focused upon being the best Boy Scout I could. One of the first requirements of a Boy Scout was to do a good turn daily. This became a daily effort for me. One of my first good turns daily was riding on my bicycle to a store and buying a box of raisins for a boy who was hitchhiking to Houston from California. His appreciation cemented my desire to continue doing a good turn daily. I had learned how good it felt to help other people.

John Eaton was the Scout Master, and did a wonderful job leading me into the scout work. I owe that man all the respect and appreciation I can muster up. John was able to inspire us all to a higher plane of excellence. We won about all the troop contests such as knot tying, signaling, first aid, etc., due to John's ability to lead us. These contests were on the required abilities for advancement toward the ultimate Eagle badge.

If we came to the Boy Scout meetings early we'd sometimes played ante-over until time for the meeting. In the regular meeting we would compete between patrols in the scouting activities. I always looked forward eagerly to those weekly meetings.

During our summer scout camp the activities at Camp Louis Farr were somewhat different than camp activities of today. First we were expected to earn the money required for the week's camping. We needed to make a list of items to take, including special items for special badges we planned to work on. There were councilors available at camp.

Our transportation usually consisted of a truck onto which we scouts loaded ourselves and our baggage. When we arrived at camp we were assigned a tent area. After raising the tent and tying it down to the stakes, we dug the drainage ditches, lined the walkways with rocks, and dug out our Citronella to use as mosquito repellant. We put up our cots and fitted our sheets and blanket.

We would then be ready for inspection and were graded on how neat and clean we made and kept our living area. We were graded every day on neatness and cleanliness. The reward was a painted emblem on our scout belt.

Mr. Draper, the Concho Valley Council head Counselor, was in charge of the camp, and really kept things rolling. We could sign up for archery, weaving, stringing beads, not speaking for 24 hours, etc. Not talking for 24 hours. Talk about difficult. I made it, but only in my second attempt. Even then I was quite proud of myself.

There were Red Cross Life Saving classes at the swimming hole, and councilors to help us earn merit badges. Keeping tent site neat and clean, K-P duty, and other interesting things kept us busy. We were awarded a stencil on our Boy Scout belt for each successful completion.

We did a lot of singing when we gathered together for each meal, and were supervised to be sure we were eating three prunes a meal. One of the songs I remember was in a foreign language. The words were, "O Whah tah foo Siam." to be sung rapidly.

An infraction of almost any rule resulted in getting swatted on our backside with a wicked-looking paddle. This paddling was always performed in front of all. The paddle was split and about 6 inches wide. I believe every one received a few swats. It didn't hurt much, if any, but sounded like it did. You couldn't get away with doing that today, could you? It was effective then, though, being done in fun and fairness to all.

Our dining area was a large, closed, room with screens across all open areas. One end of the large building was a huge rock fireplace, made with volunteer scout help one summer. Some of us had previously spent a week in summer carrying rock and helping to build that enormous fireplace. That supper we had all taken turns cooking, and I was asked to cook biscuits. I had never cooked them before and, knowing no better, fried them in a skillet on top of the stove. From then on everyone wanted me to cook those delicious biscuits every day.

I continued in my scout work as Junior Assistant Scoutmaster until I went off to college. I received my Eagle Badge in 1935 and was surprised that I was the first Eagle Scout in Sutton County. At that time I was selected to be assistant Scoutmaster.

When I moved to McCamey in 1940, I volunteered to be assistant Scoutmaster. When the scoutmaster, "Spider" Webb, moved I took over as Scoutmaster for five months until I moved to Fort Stockton. I believe Elmo Mitchell was Scoutmaster in McCamey when I left for Fort Stockton. In Fort Stockton, as in McCamey, we scouts worked on first aid contests, flag signaling, tying knots, fire building and hiking. It was fun and educational for the boys, and I took them on several hikes. I was proud to have contributed to the scouting movement in the short time I had available. I acted as Scoutmaster in Fort Stockton until the Army Air Corps Flight Cadets arrived when I became too busy to be a scouter. I remember one of the scout's mothers brought cookies and lemonade to our meetings. I included her crippled scout on our hike, and gave him extra consideration due to his being crippled. His mother was very appreciative that I had done so. She had tears in her eyes when I had to step down as Scoutmaster.

Eagle Scout Ken Babcock

Excellence in Scout craft, as indicated by the earning of many merit badges, has won for Kenneth Babcock, son of Mr. and Mrs. O. G. Babcock, the coveted rank of Eagle Scout. He is a member of Troop 19, Sonora, and was recently made a junior assistant Scoutmaster. The picture to the left appeared in the San Angelo Morning Times Wednesday, November 6, 1935.

Three Boy Scouts from the Ranch district of the Concho Valley Council, Kenneth Babcock of Troop 19 at Sonora and J. T. Ballew and M.C. Laird, Troop 18, at Eldorado achieved the highest rank in Scouting during October, records show. Scout Babcock, the oldest of the three, 16 years of age, joined the Boy Scouts in December 1931. He has 26 merit badges. Only 21 are required. Ballew and Laird came into Scouting in July 1933, and are both 15 years of age. Babcock and Laird were both chosen to attend the National Jamboree this summer also.

Note: The National Jamboree scheduled for Washington D.C. was cancelled due to the Polio outbreak. The groups of scouts were taken instead to Yellowstone National Park

Scouts on rail train at Salt Lake Flats in Utah

Chapter 5

Terlingua, Climbing Mountains

I loved the outdoors, climbing hills and mountains, exploring. My family planned a Thanksgiving outing in 1933 in the Chisos Mountains, located in the center of what is now the Big Bend National Park. It was then open range. The one hundred and thirteen mile road from Alpine to Terlingua, the only town in the area, was being graded for the first time ever. We were in our new 1932 Desoto, and the alkali dust (the opposite of acidic soil) was about 10 to 12 inches thick some 90 miles south of Alpine, due to the roadwork.

All of a sudden our engine stopped running. Out of gas. We found that a rock or root had broken the drain plug out of the bottom of the gas tank. There we were, nearly a hundred miles from civilization, in extremely wild desert country. A work crew pulled us into Terlingua, a town of small Mexican rock houses, and a Mine-operated commissary, which only offered bare essentials for living. They left us with our car at the gate of the Terlingua Mercury Mine. The mine, one of the largest in the world, was a haven for wild donkeys, cougars, bear and deer.

We had to wait for help from the mine company, the only help available within 113 miles. There was no place for us to camp but in the street. The Terlingua Mine Company wasn't interested. However, they finally agreed to repair the gas tank for us, just to get us out of their way. They took the car inside the gate and took two days repairing it. We were told they had to take the tank off and fill it with water before they could weld it up.

We had spent two days and two nights on the dirty street watching the Mexican families come and go, getting provisions and water (the only available water) and carrying it home by hand or by burro. At the time there must have been about 70 Mexican families living in those small, primitive rock houses. What a movie it would have made, showing those workers or their wives coming in to trade at the one store, and making the trek back to their tiny rock houses. This area is deep in the Chihuahuan Desert and the nights were cold as this was Thanksgiving week. Sleeping between Mr. Cory and my Daddy was like sleeping under a tent without a cover. When they came to bed, the covers rose about a foot above me. I nearly froze.

Finally, we were able to continue the twenty miles or so to the Chisos Mountains, where Elmo Johnson had obtained permission from the owner for our visit. After checking in with the rancher we were sent several miles on a ranch road to our camping destination. We made our camp on a fairly level place right beside a draw. We gathered dandelions and vines for padding under our tarps, and then added the blankets. This was at least going to be much better than sleeping on the hard, dirty street in Terlingua.

As we were finishing breakfast, the sun peeked from the top of 8,000-foot Mt. Emory. We then began walking up the canyon toward the base of the mountains, on the well-traveled trail. This trail had been in use by Indians for hundreds of years, and is now being used by ranch vehicles and animals, and anyone walking from Mexico such as "wet-backs" (illegal Mexicans who swam across the Rio Grande.). As we walked along we saw some small deer with huge milk-white tails. These were Chisos Fan Tail deer, uniquely small and rare, only found living in the Chisos Mountains and in the Mountains just across the Rio Grande in Old Mexico, about 8 miles away.

Mr. Victor Cory, a "top notch Botanist" as my Dad called him, wanted me to accompany him on a short cut over the top of Mt Emory. When we came to a small trail going to the left,

Mr. Cory thought it was the short cut. Away we went, right up that tiny trail. After reaching the peak at over 8000 feet, we would then join the rest of the party for Thanksgiving dinner down on the Indian Trail. Ah, the plans of mice and men.

We finally decided we had left the main trail too early, so knew we had some extra distance to cover. Mr. Cory was a little hefty while I was a thin fifteen-year old boy in top physical shape. Mr. Cory was carrying a round metal container for the plants he was collecting, and we both had one orange each. I was only carrying a twenty-two-caliber rifle. We were becoming rather warm. We were in a part of the Chihuahua Desert with daytime warm temperatures. Even at Thanksgiving it was warm climbing up that mountain. We replenished our canteens from a small bit of water found behind a small dam.

Entering a pine forest we were surprised to find a neglected log cabin. I learned later that it had been built and used by the U. S. Geodetic surveying party some twenty years earlier. This area had all been surveyed. What a job it must have been, surveying over 8,000 foot high Mount Emory.

I began carrying Mr. Cory's metal sample case for him along with my rifle, and we just climbed and climbed. By the middle of the afternoon we realized we were still far short of the peak and stopped to rest. Being rather hungry, we decided to eat our oranges. Boy, they were delicious. I even ate my peelings and Mr. Cory's orange peelings also.

I can still taste them. Delicious. We tried not to think of the Thanksgiving dinner awaiting us over the mountain peak on the Indian trail.

Mr. Cory never cursed, but had a saying that was unique. "I-gosh" he would say. On and on and on we went, finally reaching a narrow ridge of rocks piled up leading to the peak only some hundred yards away. Mr. Cory said, "I-gosh, we still have to climb over those rocks. Be careful." We were. There was about a thousand-foot drop or more on each side. The cold north wind was hitting us full blast as we were now exposed to the north slope, at an altitude of over 8,000 feet.

We reached the peak about an hour before the sun went down, and Mr. Cory said, "Well, I-gosh, we made it." There was a lot of paper there, including toilet paper, stuffed in jars, with the names of the many people that had preceded us in climbing this peak. We took time to add our names to the lists. In such a remote place we were surprised at the number who had climbed this Peak.

After a short rest, we continued over the crest with relatively easy walking down to the Indian trail that crossed the mountains. Not finding any signs of recent travel, we followed the trail back down the mountain watching for signs of the other party. Still no tracks. Half way down to the base of the mountain, we found Thanksgiving Dinner waiting for us, sitting on a big rock ledge.

The rest of our party had apparently gone back to the camp. That Thanksgiving supper tasted as good as any I've ever eaten. Skipping dinner and climbing over 8,000 feet over a mountain we sure appreciated the others for leaving us that food. We had begun our climb at an altitude of about 1500 feet above sea level. I don't know how far we had walked that day, but I do know we started at 5:30 in the morning and had climbed all day long. We still had at least five more miles to go when we got to the base of the mountain. I give my older, heavier companion a lot of credit as he never complained and stayed right with me. I continued to carry his metal collector's box of plants, but even so he was quite a man.

When we reached the floor of the canyon, there sat our coupe, parked on the trail with the keys in it. We quickly loaded the food that was left, in the car. Mr. Cory drove the coupe that last five miles. As we made our way back to camp in the car, I thought of my mother, my little sister Edith May, and Marie Watkins, none of whom were used to walking so far. It must have been hard on all of them. They had walked over ten miles that day. They were glad to see us, though.

Next day we broke camp and drove home through Alpine. Everyone was tired but full of wonderful memories. To Alpine was one hundred and twenty five miles of dirt road, and there were still another hundred and seventy miles of graveled road to our home in Sonora.

The Chisos Mountains and the rough, dry desolate area lay far from civilization. Even today relatively few people know of this land called "The Big Bend." Seven years later, in 1940, Texas designated this area a Texas Park, and in two more years the Federal Government made it into a National Park. Included in the National Park was the entire land inside the semi-circle made by the river changing directions before heading to the southeast again. The Rio Grande River had cut a 1700 foot deep canyon through the uplift. The river enters into the land surrounding the Chisos Mountains from the west. Santa Helena canyon had been formed the same way as the Grande Canyon of Arizona, the river cutting a canyon out of the gradual rising of the land.

The Rio Grande River made a huge bend in its direction of flow, from which the name "Big Bend" came. This is still wild country and sparsely populated.

- Another Mountain to Climb: Mitre Peak

Photo of Mitre Peak—1940
Taken and developed by Ken Babcock

The next spring our family drove to the Davis Mountains for a short vacation. This was some 130 miles north of the Chisos Mountains and 175 miles west of Sonora. We made our reservations ahead of time for the Mitre Peak Guest ranch, thirteen miles north of Alpine, Texas.

What a beautiful location this was, with cabins built in the mouth of a small canyon directly across a dry creek from the 6100-foot Mitre Peak.

Only a quarter mile behind the camp in the canyon there was a natural pool of water just big enough for swimming. While we were there we went swimming in it nearly every day.

I joined a group the next day after arriving, to climb Mitre Peak. Being fifteen years old and having had the recent experience of climbing the taller mount Emery of the Chisos Mountains, this climb looked like "duck soup," until we began climbing it. Some of our climbing became nearly vertical, and the peak seemed to be getting taller and steeper the more we climbed. When we reached the top, the reward was a breathtaking 360-degree panoramic view of canyons and peaks of the Davis Mountains.

We could view the Sul Ross College thirteen miles away, built on the side of a mountain in the east part of the city of Alpine.

Descending Mitre Peak was almost as difficult as the climb. We were all glad to arrive to the foot of the mountain before dark. We had left our cars part way up the mountain, and that last mile to camp was heaven to us tired mountain climbers. Although I was in good health and quite active and younger, I was just about as worn out as the older folks who had come along. There was a shared feeling of accomplishment.

The thrill of being on top of a tall mountain and being able to look far into the distance in all directions is a thrill I have never lost. I can appreciate how it could become an obsession for people to continue climbing higher and higher.

We spent several days at this beautiful Mitre Peak Guest Ranch, giving me time to climb the twenty to thirty foot cliffs on both sides of the small canyon behind the camp. It was fun to explore some of those lower mountains. There were many rattlesnakes in the area, too. We had heard one or two in close proximity to us while climbing Mitre Peak. I understand there was a young lady, about fifteen years old, who had survived a fall onto a slab of rock on the north face of Mitre Peak, just the year before. She had managed to catch herself on a ledge. By the time the rescuers reached her, she was dead from being bitten several times by a rattlesnake that was also on the ledge.

All this mountain climbing, hiking and running I was doing must have helped me to attain the success that I was having in school track meets. In those days being an athlete seldom helped you with a school scholarship or in getting a job, but it did give you personal satisfaction.

Mother had so much trouble with me catching colds and having earaches before we moved into our new home in 1927, that she purchased a whole basket of oranges one September. Every day when I came home from school, I'd sit down and eat oranges. I think I ate most of them all by myself. Mother later told me that I'd had no colds that winter. Eating oranges replaced my habit of eating Skinner's Raisin Bran after school until I ran out of oranges.

Staying healthy was getting more national interest at this time as Joe Lewis, a black man, was on the newsreels winning all his fights with knockouts. He was shown shadow boxing and training. We respected that black boxer. He said little but did lots. All the kids went around mimicking Joe's short one-two punch that floored his opponents.

- Mud Hole, Spanking

Just before noon one day and after some heavy fall rains, a car became stuck in the big mud hole in the dirt road in front of our house. I became engrossed in watching their effort to get the car out. Daddy had put in a cement curb, which held up some of the rainwater. That contributed to the mud hole. I think I loved mud holes, especially this one. I've told people all my life about the hardships I went through as a boy, and one was my having to walk to school every day, rain or shine. It was a whole block and a half, but I had to walk it. A little mud was really nothing to me. Ha ha.

Well, the people stuck in the mud in front of our house were having a tough time. I was so engrossed in watching them I hardly heard my mother calling me in for dinner. Then, a little later, I heard: "Son, come in for dinner right now." About five minutes later I heard, "Son, come into the house this instance." Believe you me I scooted into that house that time, followed by my dad. I went into the bathroom and locked the door. There was a firm knock on the door. Then I heard, "Son, unlock this door." I did so, quickly.

In came Daddy. He went straight to the razor strap that was hanging by the lavatory. Then I not only heard the razor strap hitting my backside, but I felt it, five or six times. Afterward I had to enter the dining room among averted eyes. The embarrassment hurt almost as much as the spanking.

- High School and Studying Piano

Marie Watkins
Piano and Voice Teacher—Sonora, Texas
1932 - 1940's

Miss Watkins roomed at my parents' home while she lived in Sonora and became a loved member of our household. She was a talented teacher of voice and piano and was responsible for my success as a piano player. When she moved to San Angelo, Texas sometime in the late 1930's, she continued to return to Sonora and teach music, staying in our house.

Track wasn't my only competition. Marie Watkins entered me in a national rating competition, to be held for our part of the country at San Angelo, Texas. This was held on Thursday afternoon, the day before I was to go to Austin for the State Track Meet. I competed in the top category requiring twenty classical piano solos by memory. They were to represent all the different ages of composition of classic piano compositions including modern classic.

One difficult number I played was a Mozart Sonata composed for piano and orchestra. I felt confident about playing it. I was rated a "1," highest given, in the advanced group. I was proud of that rating, and thankful for the competence of my teacher.

Going to high school was an exciting time in my life, as it should have been. One extra activity I participated in was being editor of the school newspaper. It was a challenge. When I went to the University of Texas in the fall of 1936, I edited the Methodist MYF paper on the "Drag" across the street from the University. A large active group of the university students always had several activities to report on in the paper. I had much help from the other students, and it was a fun thing for us to do.

I had made pretty good grades through high school, and enjoyed the classes and the friendship of my fellow students. In high school one amusing incident happened to me as a freshman: we boys were "hazed" by making us "run the gauntlet." Due to my track training I was very quick at starting, and fast, so when I was to run down between the two lines of boys with their belts in their hands, thankfully not a one was quick enough to hit me.

Many times at noon some of us high school boys would gather downstairs where a pipe crossed the hall just the right height for chinning. We started competing on the number of times we could "chin." I out-chinned everybody. Lacy Smith was a close second. About 60 years later I ran across Charley Ferris, one of these boys, and the first thing he mentioned was about my chinning. I had forgotten it, but he hadn't.

When I was in the 9th grade I had a roommate. Mother and I agreed to accept J. O. Mills as a boarder. J.O. had been home taught at the Roy Hudspeth Ranch through the eighth grade. They then had moved to a ranch west of town twenty miles away on dirt roads. Due to the unimproved county roads it became quite a hardship in wet weather for the ranchers to bring their children to town each day to attend school. Some ranchers were able to build or buy a home in town, but of course that was not always possible. Well, J. O. slept with me in my back-porch room and it was like having a brother. He joined the Boy Scouts, and was in my class at school. I went home with him to the ranch some weekends, rode horses, hunted coons, and in season hunted turkey.

Next year J.O.'s step-father, R.V. Sewell, built a service station on the new highway being built through his Sutton County ranch, and added a short order sandwich shop about six months later. Prohibition had just been voted out, and Mr. Sewell was selling 3.2% beer. Crockett County voted to stay "Dry". Ozona, the Crockett County seat, was only 16 miles from Mr. Sewell's Service Station and Café. Ranching had been a poor business during the drought and general depression. When "Ruff" Sewell opened his station and café the business boomed as some of the ranchers from Crockett County were financially well off and liked their beer, which was not available in their county.

On the weekends when I went home with J. O. he and I enjoyed helping at the cafe and Mr. Sewell welcomed our help. We sold beer as well as soda pop, and Mrs. Sewell sometimes cooked a ham enabling us to sell a lot of ham sandwiches. Most of those ranchers spent the whole day at the café drinking beer. One of them only drank ale, so Mr. Sewell kept an extra case cooled down just for him. This man could drink the whole case of ale in one day.

J.O. took piano lessons from Miss Watkins too and he and I played a few piano duets. We were able to study, go to Scouts and play games together. The year he stayed with us was a rainy winter, so he also spent several weekends with us. There was running water in the draws and plenty of mud when it rained.

When we were seniors in high school, J. O. drove a 1935 Ford coupe to school as most of the road out his way had been much improved and more bridges built. Although I missed him, there were times I'd go home with him on weekends for activities we enjoyed on the ranch. One night a panther crossed the road ahead of us, right by "Dead Man's watering hole." That was the first I'd ever seen. It looked to me as if the lion jumped clear across the highway. Wow!

- All Guns Are Loaded Guns

Hunting coons and rabbits was exciting for J.O. and me. It became more exciting one night when something ran in front of the car. As I quickly moved the shotgun around to line it up it went off, blowing out the windshield. Between the noise and broken glass flying it was several seconds before we realized what had happened. No other damage done, thank goodness, but I was mad at myself. How did I become so careless? I'm not sure, but hopefully I learned a good lesson.

Years later I borrowed a 343 rifle from Bob Teaff. Jack, my son-in-law, and I were hunting deer one day. I got out of the pickup to shoot at a deer standing just behind a thin bush. When I took off the safety the gun fired. There was something wrong. It was a gun Bob had traded for, and he didn't know it was defective. Thank goodness I had the gun outside the door before it happened. I had learned a lesson: to be more cautious. I had done a lot of dumb things, but I did learn never to trust a gun.

One accidental shooting occurred while three Boy Scouts were sitting around a table. Two of them were arguing about whether or not a twenty-two rifle was loaded. One was so positive the gun was unloaded he pointed it at the other boy's chest and fired, killing him. All three were friends of mine. What a terrible tragedy.

We were all given good safety training in Boy Scouts, making no excuse for the carelessness we sometimes displayed. A boy, not in my scout troop, was accidentally killed when he and a friend had been target shooting at a ranch. They were shooting at bottles on fence posts. One boy went over to replace a bottle and the other boy didn't see him rise up. He shot him when he rose, killing him. I practiced shooting often, and carried my twenty-two rifle with me while walking in the hills. I was careful where I aimed and kept in mind where that bullet would go if I missed. My shooting practice paid off, in a way, because I qualified as expert rifleman with an M-1 army carbine. I never had to use that skill, I'm glad to say.

I was glad to be carrying a side gun, though. I was walking alone down a short street in Casablanca, North Africa less than a year later, when I suddenly realized there was no one else on this street. But no, I saw movement at the end of the street. A group of men were converging there. I looked back, and the same thing was happening behind me. I quickly pulled out my 45 pistol, preparing to fire. Suddenly there were no people at either end of the street. I felt a little like I was in the old Wild West, for a moment. I fully intended to use that gun, if necessary. I had already talked with some of the M.P.s stationed in Casablanca and planned to take their advice: *Take no chances. They respect your gun. Use it if necessary.*

Many of the ranchers I knew kept their guns loaded and usually out of reach of children. Knowing the guns were loaded caused us to be careful around them.

- Music

My father loved playing his violin. He drove sixty-six miles to San Angelo about once a month, to take violin lessons from Mrs. Miller. He ordered himself a new violin back in the late 1920s, with Mrs. Miller's advice, from Chicago, on credit. He paid it off at fifteen dollars a month, saving all receipts. I found this out some fifty years later when I went through Daddy's files.

I went with my dad one night when he visited Grandpa John Ward to hear him fiddle. As a young man, Mr. Ward had worked as a cowboy in the wide-open range of the Big Bend country and was popular with the other cowboys because he played the fiddle. He was still the best fiddler in Sonora as he grew older, and I sure enjoyed hearing him play. Daddy played his violin with him, also, but he couldn't "fiddle" like Grandpapa Ward. Another night Daddy invited Cashes Taylor to our house and he and Daddy had fun doing some "fiddlin" together. Cashes had taught himself how to fiddle, and really had a good "feel" for fiddlin'.

In 1930 Daddy played the violin in the San Angelo Symphony Orchestra. My love of classical music has been inherited from my father, as Classical music is still the type of music I enjoy the most.

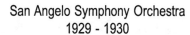

San Angelo Symphony Orchestra
1929 - 1930

(See captions identifying orchestra members on top of next page)

1st Violins	2nd Violins	Viola	Clarinet
J.T. Houston	Joe L. Mays	Ruth Rich	G.J. Kane
Mrs. Ivan Bell	John Tester	Violoncello	L. Harrison
Joe Haddon	O.G. Babcock	Mrs. W.C. Beesley	Trombone
Jean Benge	J.A. Meaders	J.A. Motley	Jim Hislop
Henri Rogers	Emmett Hughes	Contra-Bass	Piano
Eugenia Pool	J.B. White	Fred Wilson	Mrs. Dragoo Beall
Mrs. P.L. Bailey	Joe Miller	W.E. Albert	

As a young man Daddy was working in the Silver Plume Mine in Colorado about 1906. He earned a few extra dollars by playing his mandolin for the Irish miners in nearby Georgetown. He even demonstrated to me how he learned to "jig" like the Irishmen.

In order to play for the Georgetown miners it was necessary for him to walk from Silver Plume down the mountain to Georgetown, several miles in the mountain forest. One night he was attacked by a mountain lion. The lion jumped Daddy as he walked down the trail, taking a swipe at him in the dark, then ran off. Luckily Daddy was unhurt.

Daddy also worked in his dad's lead mine. Granddad sold the mine, built a mansion in University Park, Denver, only to have it partially gutted by a fire. Then, after being a philanthropist by giving land to the schools around Denver, his investment in lead hit rock-bottom and Granddad was broke. He still had a gold mine but the vein of gold ran into a vein of Iron Pyrite, which made it too expensive to mine the gold. Granddad had to go to work, finally ending up as janitor in a school located on land he had given them. He worked there until he retired, and lived until he was 96 years of age.

Jake Houston, the talented San Angelo first violinist (second cousin to Carlene Peeples Stacy), visited Sonora for performances at our high school. What a performance he always presented. As my dad would say, Jake was "Top-Notch." He suffered from heart trouble, which prevented him from performing professionally. There were times we had fun playing together, my dad, Jake Houston, both on violins, and me on cello. Sometimes we had a violist and/or pianist join us.

Scouting, school activities, and running kept me busy most of my high school years, but summers I spent a lot of my time reading and listening to classical music. My parents had purchased a Panatrope, a fancy "78 RPM" record player of the early 1930's. Daddy had purchased many records, both "10" and "12", of outstanding artists such as Fritz Kreisler, Madam Schumann Hienck, Caruso, Galli Curci (sp), Paderewski and others. The Panatrope played one record at a time, so I had to go change the record every two to three minutes. The Panatrope was in the dining room and I liked to lie on the couch in the living room reading. I had the volume turned up in order to hear the music, and when Daddy would come through the house, he'd go straight to the Panatrope and turn down the sound. After he left the house, I would go turn the volume up again. I got lots of exercise going to and from that Panatrope.

I read a lot since my parents had a good collection of books and magazines, such as the National Geographic. I really enjoyed those times listening to the music while reading.

Early in the summer of 1932 we made a trip to Colorado in our new DeSoto car. Our first stop in Colorado was Uncle Frank's farm, a few miles out of Del Norte, Colorado. Uncle Frank Babcock and his wife, Kay, had rented this farm to raise potatoes, but a lack of snow in the mountains had kept the valley dry that spring, and there was little water runoff from the mountains. Without sufficient water, the planted potatoes would not mature. Uncle Frank had to go to work in the mountains as a miner for money to support them, so we didn't get to see him. They had put some hogs in the field to dig and eat the potatoes. We stayed with Kay about 10 days helping her with the farm work and visiting.

I had learned to drive, so I drove her truck to the lettuce shipping sheds daily, obtaining truckloads of culled lettuce at Del Norte, to feed the hogs. Those hogs had to be pretty healthy; eating all that fresh lettuce and the raw potatoes they dug up.

One morning Kay received a phone call from a neighbor, offering her some of last years' potatoes stored in her cellar. "Sure, I'll get them." I volunteered. I took a pitchfork with me and boy did those potatoes stink. Although some were rotten I figured the hogs would eat them anyway. They did. I believe those hogs would have eaten anything.

On the second floor of the old farmhouse was an old pedal operated organ, and one piece of sheet music. I played that song "Baby Face" on that foot-pumping organ over and over, backwards and forward, and even cross ways, I think. It was fun, though.

When we returned home from Colorado, I resumed practicing and playing on the piano and cello. Mr. Schwiening and my father had been instrumental in promoting the music department in the Sonora schools. The school board hired a young man named "Heine" who had just graduated from music school in Germany to be a teacher and conductor. In those days and in a small West Texas ranch town, it was unusual to have an orchestra.

My father played the violin with us when he could, and I loved playing my Cello in the orchestra. Doing this encouraged me to practice more. In the band I played the piccolo and baritone Tuba

A few years later in college I played my cello in the Austin Symphony orchestra. We practiced every week, and performed several times a year. Colonel Hurt was our volunteer director, but his initial job was directing the "Band of the Southwest," the University of Texas Band. Colonel Hurt did a fabulous job with the Symphony, receiving fine reviews and complimentary write-ups in the "Austin Statesman" newspaper each time we gave a concert. I played as second cello and part of the time as first when the regular first cellist was not there.

I also played in a special orchestra for a light opera production put on by the University Of Texas Light Opera Company. The fine soprano soloist was student Val Jean Allred.

- Summer on a Ranch

During my first stay with J. T. Shurley on the Ira Shurley ranch, we were budding cowboys. The next summer, we were carpenters helpers assisting in remodeling around the ranch house, as well as being cowboys. That second summer I also became a dynamite man, digging a cesspool in solid rock. I learned how to crimp the fuse on the cord between my teeth, and how to tamp the dynamite lightly in the hole I had dug with a crowbar. I realize what a dangerous thing it was for a young boy to be doing, but I did it anyway. It was hard work and dangerous, but it was fun.

It is said that you are what you eat, but personally I think what you are depends upon how you think and learn through interaction with your environment and associating with people. You also learn through reading and keeping your eyes and ears open and your mouth shut, most of the time. Keeping my mouth shut has always been difficult for me.

We took care of the sheep by riding the pastures watching for "wormy" sheep (infected by screw-worms). These worms were the larvae of a "blow fly" that laid their eggs on any raw wound in any warm-blooded animal. The resulting maggots would kill an animal in only a few days if not treated with a tar concoction smeared on the wound. We first treated the wound with Benzene to kill the worms, then tied the sheep to a tree and came back for him, or put him on the saddle to carry in to our worm trap near the house. We had to treat each wound and apply tar repellant each day. I'm glad to say that the blowflies were pretty well eliminated in Texas and Northern Mexico some twenty years later. That is the reason there are so many more wild deer in Texas today.

Every person with whom you come in contact influences you in some way. I enjoy being with people and at other times also enjoy being alone. I loved to wander in the hills around Sonora by myself, dreaming and thinking and seeing. I have also been fortunate to have many "best" friends, and one of the most outstanding of these was J. T. Shurley. He influenced me in many ways, even in arranging a blind date for me with my future wife.

J. T. and I helped Mr. Shurley "pull" the water wells when they weren't producing water. J. T. did the tricky job of pulling with the Model T Truck, with long rope and pulley attached to lift the well rods and pump.

Mr. Shurley was quite proud of J. T. when we doped the sheep. He said J. T. would make a good doctor. We used a large syringe to inject the medicine down the sheep's throat, which required some skill.

Each Sunday one of us, J.T. or myself, went to town with Mr. Shurley, about thirty-five miles of country road. Transportation was a Model "A" Ford Coupe. One of us always had to stay at the ranch so that he could round up the wormies in the late afternoon to doctor them with the Benzene and fly repellant.

One Sunday I was left at the ranch and Mr. Shurley's horse was the only one available for me. Although no one but Mr. Shurley rode this horse, I decided I'd ride him. When I started loping out the gate into the trap the horse started taking longer and longer leaps and it dawned on me he was pitching. When I finally gained control, I had to ride back to pick up my hat. That horse liked to demonstrate his independence, it seemed.

Our relationship was good for both J. T. and me. He contributed the mentality and I contributed the physical workouts. He had a tremendous ability to concentrate and to remember. I was an athlete and had J.T. doing calisthenics and swimming every day.

His mother had told me how she helped him develop his ability to concentrate: she put him into a room each day with his toys or books, allowing no one, including herself, to disturb him, for one hour. This must have prepared him to learn, as he was an honor student all the way through medical school.

An example of his concentration was when we were roommates at the Little Campus Dormitory at the University of Texas. I tried to get his attention from his studying across the room. After calling to him several times, I finally picked up a tennis shoe and pitched it onto his head. That broke his concentration. Perhaps I shouldn't have done that, but it was about the only way I could break his concentration without getting up and walking over to shake him.

Our work on the sheep ranch was routine. One of our jobs was milking the cows morning and night. We were awakened each morning about 4:00 o'clock by the banging of pots and pans that, according to J.T., was his dad being upset because Jewel, his wife, wouldn't come out to the ranch and do the cooking. We would get up and quietly go out the front door in the dark (we slept on the screened-in front porch) and go on foot to bring in the milk cows from their small pasture. We had four cows to milk, two each.

This milk had to be attended to right after breakfast each day. After breakfast the scalding of the ceramic milk jars was done while washing the breakfast dishes. Then the fresh milk was put into the scalded ceramic jugs and placed in the cooler. Next morning we would skim the cream off, leaving the skimmed milk, a lot of which we drank. We churned butter whenever we had time, so we kept plenty of buttermilk, real cream and butter for our meals. The pan bread Mr. Shurley baked every day supplied us dessert when we added unlimited cool milk, fresh made butter and plenty of homemade wild plum jelly. We lived like kings.

One night I won a buttermilk drinking contest with J. T. and spent most of the night watching an eclipse of the moon from the open door of the out-house. That fresh buttermilk tasted great, and we usually drank some every night. The gallon and a half I drank was a bit too much for me.

We almost always had pinto beans cooking on the stove, to be ready to eat at noon or whenever we had the chance to eat. Every night we went swimming in the stock tank after supper. I would lead us in several exercises to keep J. T. in good physical shape, supplementing our other daily physical activities. He was tall and somewhat clumsy, so I was trying to get him in better muscular shape by exercising with him each night. He enjoyed doing so and appreciated me helping him.

- Jayter and His Jack Rabbit

An interesting sidelight before the times spent on the ranch was the time Mr. C.J. Jennings, game warden for our area of Texas, invited Jayter and myself to accompany him on an overnight trip to Menard. There was a river in Menard, a town 60 miles east of Sonora. He left us by the river near Menard for a few hours and we enjoyed swimming and fishing and we built a small fire to warm some food. It was nearly midnight when Mr. Jennings came back and picked us up. He took us to the Volunteer Fire Department where we bedded down for the night. He then left for the rest of the night. He told us next morning he had caught some poachers of deer.

After breakfast next morning, we left for Sonora on the dirt road down a lane fenced on both sides. When two baby jackrabbits ran across the road J.T. and I jumped out of the car and caught them.

I turned mine loose, but Jayter kept his and raised it as a house pet until after it was completely grown. How startling it was to visit the Shurleys and be greeted at the front door by a trained grown jackrabbit hibity-hopping up to you on its long legs.

Jayter had a lovely younger sister named Guyon, about two years younger than me. I remember a birthday dance Mother had for me, and Guyon came, wearing a pretty strapless dress, her first. I remember thinking that she had grown up awfully fast. She was just learning to dance and did quite well. She had a nice personality and a pretty smile. I never saw her upset at anything.

Guyon lived to graduate, get married, and a few short years later died from a brain tumor. This was really an unexpected shock.

Mrs. Shurley wanted her son to grow up receiving the best education she could give him. She recognized his capabilities. Moving to San Angelo, a larger town 67 miles from Sonora, enabled J. T. to graduate from a larger high school. He could then attend the San Angelo Junior College two years before entering the University of Texas in Austin. I missed them in Sonora those last two years of high school, but we kept in touch.

While I was a junior in high school, Jayter (J.T. is nicknamed Jayter) called me from San Angelo, inviting me to visit him in San Angelo the weekend of February 22, 1935. Jayter wanted us to double date with his girl and her best friend. I accepted the invitation and met Faegene Eddleman, the girl who five years later, on November 22, 1940, would become my wife. She and I hit it off from the very first. A few weeks later I had a second date with her and then announced to my mother I'd found the girl I was going to marry.

I continued taking piano while in high school, although the school orchestra was discontinued when Heinie left. Playing the piano must have helped my typing as I set a speed record of 95 words per minute. Years later I was amazed that record was not broken for 51 years.

I also tried some acting, playing a part in the senior play in a comedy entitled "The Poor Fish." I was the *Poor Fish*. That's all I remember of that. Hollywood's probably still waiting for me.

- Doctor Jay Shurley, Specialist in Psychiatry and Psychoanalysis

After 1940, when I left the University of Texas to go to work in McCamey, out in West Texas, Jayter went on to The University of Texas Medical School the next year at Galveston, graduating in 1942 with high honors as a physician, MD. He then interned for a year at the Indiana University Medical, Indianapolis, Indiana, and then took 3 years of Residency in Psychiatry at the Pennsylvania Hospital, Philadelphia, Pennsylvania. This qualified him, after a Board Examination, to call himself a specialist in Psychiatry.

After spending five years as a Candidate in Psychoanalysis in Philadelphia, he opened his own practice in Psychoanalysis and Psychiatry in Austin, Texas, June, 1951, with full acceptance of the Texas Psychoanalytic Society.

In 1944 during the war, my wife, Faegene, came to spend a few weeks with me while I was stationed in Wilmington, Delaware. We went by riverboat to visit Dr. Shurley in Philadelphia. Dr. Shurley (Jayter) took us out to visit the Liberty Bell and a few famous buildings. Later we dined in a Chinese restaurant, where I ate my first-ever Chinese food, Egg FooYung. We had stretched our time to the limit so we had to rush to catch our boat back to New Castle, Delaware. I'll never forget the sewer odor given off by that beautiful river. I hope it's been cleaned up by now.

What an effort it must have been for Jayter to study and work so long and hard for his specialty. He was quite successful in his studies, though, as he was appointed by the Veteran's Administration as their first (and only) Senior Medical Investigator in Psychiatry. He proceeded doing pioneer research on Human Isolation & Sensory Deprivation. This became a prime consideration in planning and executing long duration space flight, and in designing the International Space Station. Wow.

Later he pioneered medical and psychiatric research at the South Pole Station, Antarctica, regarding sleep and waking in adjustment to a circ annual dark and light cycle. This was dramatically different from the invariable 24-hour cycle we are adapted to. This was also information and knowledge needed for astronauts in orbital flight, or on a space station.

Dr. Jay told me he was a teacher of psychiatry even before he completed his residency, and rose to the rank of full Professor at 39 years of age. I am 86 years of age and have been a teacher of flying for nearly 50 years. I'm still not a professor of any kind.

It was 10 years later, in 1954, when I flew my airplane to San Antonio to visit with him a few days, where he served as an Army doctor. As he needed to go to Austin, I flew him over, a flight he thoroughly enjoyed. The high point for me was being treated with some delicious cheese blintzes in a delicatessen in Austin. It seems we were always eating when we got together.

His life has been rewarding and outstanding, and I'm proud to be one of his best friends. I loved to discuss philosophy with him when we got together.

Sadly Dr. Shurley passed away in Oklahoma on February 25, 2004. His life force remains with me and many others, but I'm sure he's in a better place now.

Piper Seneca Twin—about 1982
On Charter Flight—stopover in Oklahoma City, Oklahoma

"Jayter"
South Pole Research Station (Antarctica)

Old-time friend, Dr. Jay T. Shurley & Ken Babcock, Pilot

Boy Scout Trip to Yellowstone Park
Spring of 1935

- An overnight stay in a park just out of Salt Lake City, Utah

Note: Nelson's Camp Sign

Chapter 6

From the Boy Scouts to Flight Instructor

- Boy Scout Trip to Yellowstone

In the summer of 1935 the National Boy Scout Jamboree that was to be held at Washington, D. C. was cancelled due to the Infantile Paralyses epidemic of the thirties. The Concho Valley Boy Scout Council then replaced the National Jamboree trip with a never to be forgotten trip to Yellowstone National Park for those Scouts signed up for the National Scout Jamboree.

Two buses carried our tents, cooking material, and all the scouts. Most nights we camped out. The bus driver and owner of the buses, Reed Trotter of Water Valley, Texas, donated his time and buses for scouting trips as well as school functions. In later years, I discovered that Reed Trotter was Carlene Peeples Stacy's grandfather. Mr Trotter enjoyed cooking and may have been the man who also cooked for us. Our cook would have breakfast ready for us each morning. One morning I watched him throw in several pounds of bacon to cook at a time, as well as scrambling dozens of eggs. He cracked the eggs with both hands, and cooked hot biscuits. What a cook he was, and how appreciated. Two of the three men as our supervisors were Robbins and Bert Hague, from San Angelo.

The first high spot for me was a Sunday dinner in Boulder, Co. One of my cousins, Myrtle Metz, met me at the café for a short visit. I had corresponded with her since visiting in Colorado three years earlier. How nice it was to see her again. She was one of the first girls I had a "crush" on. The next time I saw her was sixty-two years later. She was then a widow living in an assisted living complex in Colorado Springs. She told me of her several children and grandchildren, and said she'd had a wonderful life. Life just goes on, doesn't it?

In Colorado Springs it was determined the bus couldn't make it up Pikes Peak. We were disappointed, but we passed through Denver and reached Thermopolis, Wyoming that evening, where we camped out. I went shopping and bought my first pocket watch with a silver dollar.

That night we went swimming in an indoor warm-water pool. The artesian well supplied the indoor swimming pool with warm water. What a thrill for us west Texans to swim in warm water at night. Most of us only had stock tanks with cold water to swim in. I still remember the feel of that warm water, and I felt as if I could swim faster in it. That was a high spot of our trip.

Next stop was Cody, Wyoming, where we visited the Buffalo Bill museum. I learned more about my hero, Buffalo Bill Cody. I'd read all the books I could find about him. This was the country I'd read about, and Wyoming was where Buffalo Bill actually grew up, close to the Indians.

That night we stopped and made camp, just inside Yellowstone Park. We put up our 2-man pup tents and shoveled out body contours for added comfort. I went to sleep dreaming of bears prowling about.

The next morning as we drove into the park there was a moose standing in a beautiful little stream of water. He had his head in the water, huge horns sticking out. When he stopped browsing in the water and raised his head, what a sight it was to our young eyes. There he stood, chewing a mouthful of watercress dripping water, belly deep in the stream, green grass and flowers all around. He just stood there contentedly chewing his watercress, completely unaware of watching eyes or anything else.

Driving through the park I couldn't believe the beauty we saw. Fifty-five years later Faegene and I visited Yellowstone, and the fire of the 80s had destroyed so much of that beauty. It was quite depressing to see it so, but I'm sure it will be beautiful again.

At Old Faithful we were assigned to cabins instead of our pup tents, because of the bears. The feeding of the bears took place in the late afternoon, and when I left my cabin I met a bear head-on. He was coming straight for me between the rows of cabins. I lost no time "shifting" quickly to the left between the cabins and as we say in West Texas, I "vamoosed" out of there.

The Geysers were terrific. Old Faithful erupted in all its beauty, splashing hot water high into the air. We toured the geysers and saw the natural hot spring "washing machine". That really was impressive. The guide dropped our handkerchiefs into the hot water, and they were sucked down out of sight. In about a minute here they came right back up, squeaky clean. That water was hot. They no longer allow anything to be dropped into the geysers today.

After leaving Yellowstone we went through some unpaved mountain roads, rather narrow and with one-way curves. Everyone honked their horns starting around those blind curves. One time the driver of our bus had to get out and drive a car around our buses, as the driver of the car was afraid to do it himself. There was quite a drop-off. Another time we found a car hanging over the edge of the road, two wheels off the road. We Scouts all got out, managed to get ropes on the car, and pulled the car back on the road by "Scout" power.

The Great Salt Lake. What a remarkable place that was. We stopped for an hour so we could go swimming in the salt water, which had receded nearly a mile due to the drought. As the water receded, rails had been laid on the dry salt bed and a small train carried us to the water. We quickly put on our bathing suits and rode the little train to the water and jumped right in. Surprise. We didn't sink. We waded out into the water walking on the solid salt crystals that had formed on the bottom, until we reached deeper water. It was deep enough to swim in, and we discovered that we couldn't sink. We just floated chest deep in the water. We couldn't believe it. We just bobbed around like corks. When we got out and dried off, we found fine salt crystals covering our bodies. That salt sure burned your eyes when it was splashed in them. Washing the salt out was impossible as there was no fresh water available. Years later the rains came and re-filled the lake, diluting the salt and reducing the buoyancy we had experienced in 1935.

Three months later, on September 3rd, only a few days after we went swimming, Sir Malcolm Campbell, of England, came to the Bonneville Salt Flats near where we had been, and broke the worlds speed record with his latest car, the "Bluebird." He became the first man to drive over 300 mph. It was clocked at 301.12 mph.

Sir Malcolm was born in England in 1885 with a desire for speed, beginning to race first on bicycles in 1900, switching to motorbikes two or three years later. He then learned to fly in 1909 and flew combat during WW I.

His first ground speed record was 146.16 mph. Finally, in a newly modified special built 28-foot long five-ton car powered by a Rolls Royce R-type 2500 horse power engine made the record in 1935 at 301.12 mph.

After visiting the Church of the Latter Days Saints and hearing the magnificent organ, we camped at a park not far from Salt Lake City. Can you imagine about 75 Boy Scouts lining up with regular park visitors to use the only bathroom? Yes, there was only one.

Traveling into Arizona we had our first view of the Grand Canyon. We were disappointed we couldn't stay longer. What a magnificent and unbelievable canyon this was. We sure wanted to walk down into it. Running short of time, however, we had to drive on to the Carlsbad Caverns.

Only a few years earlier, my father had spent three days in Carlsbad cavern. I wished he could see it now, and hear the men's quartet sing "Rock of Ages" after seating us on the formation called the Rock of Ages in the "Big Room." Lights were turned off and in absolute darkness the men began to sing "Rock of Ages" softly in harmony. Lights were progressively turned on as the music became increasingly louder. This gave us the impression the sound was approaching from far off. Chills ran up and down my spine. This part of the program in the Cave was discontinued later on as there was some damage to the delicate formations from the vibrations caused by the singing.

As we were tired and worn out by this terrific and unbelievable trip we continued on through Big Lake to let out one scout, then finished the trip in San Angelo.

- Attending the University Of Texas

When it became time for me to register at the University of Texas I had saved up about $140. That paid my tuition and covered the cost of my books, with twenty dollars left over. My family paid my room rent for the entire semester (only twenty-five dollars) and sent me twenty-five dollars expense money a month for the first semester. The record enrollment of over 9,000 students contributed to a scarcity of jobs for students.

Although my major was Geology, going to college was important to me in so many other ways than academics. I met people from other parts of the state and country, discovering how other people thought and lived. I learned how to get along with others who had different views from mine. I made many friends who were to become lawyers, engineers, and geologists, and discussed politics. One friend, John Connelly, became governor of Texas. His future wife, Ida Nell Brill, was an excellent dance partner. Jake Pickle, from Big Springs, got his law training and went into politics quite successfully.

I looked around Austin for a job of any kind, but found virtually none. There were some Government organizations such as the NRA, the CCC and possibly others, but I could find no way to even contact them. Once in a while I would find a short-time job, but none lasted over an hour or so. My family sent me fifteen dollars a month for living expenses during the second semester, in addition to the twenty-five dollars rent covering the second semester. Comparing those prices with today's would be ridiculous, but the thirty cents an hour was probably almost as useful as five dollars an hour today. After the first year I had virtually no help from home, except for an occasional five dollars my mother sent me, bless her heart. I know Daddy thought it would be good training for me to make my own way like he did, but our country was just beginning to recover from a deep depression and drought.

Mother earned the five dollars by reporting social events in Sonora to be printed in the San Angelo Standard Times Newspaper. I can't say enough good things about my mother. I never heard her raise her voice at anytime. She occasionally said she was "Put out." If I hurt her feelings, I felt badly. She sacrificed for me and was so good to write me letters. Wasn't I lucky to have a mother like that?

Both Mother and Daddy had worked their way through college, so things had not been easy for them either. Mother had worked at least one summer in the big new white hotel at Estes Park, Colorado. Daddy once wrote her a letter letting her know he did not think it proper for a lady to work outside the home. She lost no time in letting him know that was not any of his business. That settled that. She refused to marry Daddy until she finished school and had her diploma. Daddy had worked his way through college from 1905 to 1910, working in the gold and silver mines in Colorado during the summertime. There was one summer he spent working with a Paleontologist collecting fossils in the Bad Lands of Wyoming. What fun that must have been. He said it was hard and hot work, though. During the school terms he fired a furnace each morning in a green house.

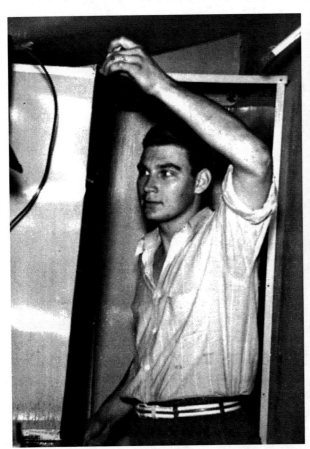 

Amateur Photography—A Hobby of Ken's—The University of Texas

- Still Having It Tough

The school cafeteria finally hired me to serve food at 30 cents an hour. I was able to work an hour a day Monday through Friday. That at least paid for my five noon meals each week. There was much competition for jobs washing dishes for meals in private boarding houses. Whenever I had thirty cents to spare on Sundays, I'd splurge it for a boarding house dinner. Those sweet ladies would really feed us on Sunday. They usually had a wonderful fruit salad that I loved, along with mashed potatoes and gravy, vegetables, fried chicken, home made rolls and a dessert.

Most of the week I existed on melted cheese sandwiches and a malted milk for a cost of 15 cents a day. One day I saw an electric hot plate for sale at Walgreen's and bought it. I then bought some cheese, a quart of milk and a loaf of bread. I made my own melted cheese sandwiches in my room. (Of course we weren't supposed to cook in the room, but—)

One of the best jobs I landed was delivering flowers for Eldon Powell's flower shop, Easter and Mother's day. I drove their delivery van.

One summer I was hired by the Bureau of Economic Geology, getting to work several hours a day for most of the summer. That summer I also attended summer school and made better grades. I really enjoyed studying a course in Petroleum Production Engineering.

I went to all my classes regularly, although some misty dark winter mornings I would get awfully sleepy. A few times a week between classes I'd practice tennis or shoot basketball goals at the Gym.

I always looked forward to practicing in the Symphony Orchestra each week during the winter semesters. I loved playing in the orchestra more than anything else I did.

It was easier for me when I had my bicycle during the second year at the university. I even carried my cello on the bicycle. The distance from Little Campus Dormitory to the practice hall was eight or ten blocks.

I played tennis on the university team, but each time I made a bad grade I was bounced back to the number twenty position on the team. I would work myself up to the top ten by challenging higher rated players. When I won I would reach the top ten. Then, invariably I'd get a bad grade and be bounced back to number twenty again. I got in some good tennis, though. I think what I really needed was a tutor for my studies. I realize today how much the handicap of my defective hearing affected me.

Faegene Eddleman enrolled in the university in my second year. Her mother came with her and rented a house. I enjoyed some home-cooked meals more often that year. It was nice having Faegene there in Austin. We were able to get around more in her car. We could go to Barton Springs to go swimming a few times in the spring.

Unfortunately for Faegene and me, that summer Mrs. Eddleman had to move out to McCamey. The next year Faegene roomed and boarded in a sorority house. I was able to attend some of their social functions. Somehow I managed to buy a tuxedo for one of their sorority dances.

At mid-term of my fourth year I was about played out, physically and mentally. The effort just didn't seem worth it. I had no money and no jobs and my grades were down. My friend Jayter suggested I move in with him until I decided what I could do. He was renting a room in a private home. I had already reduced my semester hours the past semester to 12 hours, so I still lacked a full year to graduate.

When Pop Eddleman offered me a job in McCamey, Texas, at $10 a week, room and board, I made the decision to take it and save up to return to school the next fall. As I look back on it, that was poor planning, thinking I could save money on $10.00 a week.

- The Dropout Goes to Work in McCamey, Texas

As the bus topped a small rise five miles east of McCamey, the sight of many fires appeared suddenly along the road on both sides. Fires were lighting the area, even scattered up the sides of the five hundred foot mountains.

A familiar odor filled my nostrils, that of Hydrogen sulfide, (H_2S). The odor brought memories of Chemistry Lab. The H_2S could be quite deadly when concentrated, so that explained the burning as a safety measure. That odor sure characterized the oil fields of West Texas. Oil produced from the McCamey field was called Sour Crude because of the Sulphur content.

The next day I began to work for West Texas Distributors, Claude (Pop) Eddleman's auto parts store, and put in 16 hours. I began learning about cars and car parts by straightening up the stock. I was shown how to re-line brake shoes and rebuild fuel pumps. Enjoying this kind of work made the day seem shorter for me...

Sweeping out the sand that the all-night wind piled up was a daily chore. I shoveled it out of the street along the curb, out of the store and wheeled it to the alley for pick-up by the city. The sand also came sliding inside under the front doors covering about 15 feet of the floor. The drought of several years had dried up the weeds and bushes, releasing the sand. The constant strong winds spread it all over the countryside.

Merel, Faegene's older brother, sold Harley Davidson motorcycles, and was gone most of the time. On several occasions Pop and I worked late at night overhauling or repairing the motorcycle trade-ins. Early next morning I rode them out on the highway to break-in the engine a little and check the motorcycle for performance.

What fun that was to ride in the open spaces at sunup, breathing in the pleasant fragrance from the desert plants in the cool early morning air. There must have been some slight moisture evaporating into the cooler air of those early mornings, causing the black brush and creosote brush to release those pleasant odors.

McCamey was a very different town than any I had known. The weather was dry, hot and windy, with virtually no trees in sight. Pop's business was in the west side of the Picture Show Building, and the one tree downtown was the pecan tree on the east side. Also the town had six hotels, six cafes, three large grocery stores, two picture shows, two bakeries, two drug stores, two lumber companies, and several major brand oil field supply stores. There were two machine shops and several welding shops. What a different place this was compared with Sonora. There were also mercantile stores, a Ford and a GM Motor Co. agency and six service stations.

In addition to the above there were major oil companies such as; Shell Oil and Shell Pipe Line Companies; Stanolind Oil Co.; Humble Oil and Humble Pipe Line Companies, to name a few; a Gulf and a Texaco Consignee, and several service companies for oil related needs such as equipment, pipe, roustabouts and drilling units. There were also several other independent businesses.

Unfortunately the price and demand for oil had dropped by 1940. The town was threatening to become another oil boom ghost town. It was still hanging on expecting an economic recovery "right around the corner."

- The Rattlesnake Derby

"The Rattlesnake Derby" was scheduled for my first spring after arriving in McCamey. Brownie had Brownie's Pool Hall on the corner of 5th St. and Burleson and was the instigator of this remarkable event. He kept his collection of rattlesnakes in special boxes under some of his pool tables. He also kept a five-foot flexible rope handy to throw on the floor under any unsuspecting customer, and yell, "Snake." If you had a weak heart it wasn't advisable to enter Brownie's Pool Hall.

The Derby was held on the football field after school year was ended. Brownie and his volunteers stuck a solid ring of croquet hoops in the ground, making a big circle about 60 feet in diameter in the center of the football field. The snakes were confined in boxes and were placed on a large metal plate in the center. Each hoop was numbered and the prize was for the tickets on the hoop through which the first snake went. The tickets sold for a dollar each. You could buy as many chances as you wished on any hoop or hoops.

On the big day several men wearing high-topped boots volunteered to help Brownie dump all the snakes out on the metal plate. A small charge of electricity was turned onto the plates, stirring the rattlesnakes into action. The men kept the snakes moving with their sticks, but not guided. "Esmeralda" was one of the big favorites. The real challenge then came, catching and replacing the rattlesnakes into their boxes before the stands emptied. I don't know what Brownie did with the snakes after the Derby was over.

There were also some TT Motorcycle races held each year on a dirt track just north-east of town, and there was at least one motorcycle hill climb.

The Green Gables Café, owned and operated by Mr. and Mrs. F, C. (Mary) Carter, was open late every night. She had problems with live jackrabbits being turned loose in the Café late at night by the bikers. They had caught the rabbits with their bikes. There were not many quiet times in McCamey in those days.

Sure enough, about fifteen years later McCamey had become pretty much of a ghost town, and by the year 2000 it was "An authentic Oil Field Ghost Town," with no service stations, two cafés, a Dairy Queen, one grocery store, two convenience stores having gas pumps, a newspaper and no hotel or tourist court or package store. They have since added a nice new motel.

There is now a hospital with a nursing home attached, a fine school and a No.1 rated volunteer fire department, an emergency ambulance service and a few other small businesses.

One morning after the Rattlesnake Derby a young man drove up to West Texas Distributors on a good-looking Harley Davidson "65" CC motorcycle, wanting to sell it. I suggested he might be interested in a trade for Merel's Ford car that was for sale. He was interested so I told Pop I'd run the motorcycle out the road and check it. The motorcycle ran like a top and quickly reached 100 miles an hour. I let off on the throttle just as a bug hit my bare arm, and even though I tried my best to prevent a re-action, I still jerked my arm, causing a high-speed shimmy. I didn't know what to do, but instinctively eased in on both front and rear brakes, then quickly released them. The shimmy momentarily stopped, then started again. I again touched the brakes and on the third short application I had full control again. I then tried to stop my body from shimmying.

That was a close call and I was lucky to have avoided a one hundred mph slide down the middle of the highway. Somehow I've continued to avoid bad injuries and death during my lifetime. We all need some luck or miracles in our lives, don't we? God has a plan for each of us.

Well, we traded the car for the motorcycle. Merel later bragged that it was the best deal he'd ever made. That really was a neat trick as he was nowhere around when Pop and I made that deal. Pop and I had a laugh over that.

A Plane-Tabling (surveying) crew moved into town, and needed a helper. I applied for the job and was hired, partly because I had studied Geology and knew a little about surveying and math.

Pop was glad for me to take the job. They received orders, though, after a month, to move for a three-year contract in Venezuela. They begged me to go with them. I wanted to but I had other plans, mostly about Faegene. I just didn't want to be gone to South America for three years.

- I Was My Own Boss, Until I Got Married

In the early fall of 1940 I decided to buy out Jimmie Taylor's radio repair business. I was still too short of money to go to school, so I took this opportunity to open my own business of repairing radios. I borrowed the $80 Jim wanted for his equipment, and he joined the Navy and was put into the submarines corps, much to his disgust.

Although I knew little about repairing radios, I had to study a book on electronics. I also received some help from talking to local amateur radio operators. I had decided to "take the bull by the horns" and "get my feet wet," so to speak. In a short time I was making a little more than I'd been making while working for Pop, and proposed to Faegene. She said yes. I had made the right decision not to go to South America.

We had a nice well-attended Methodist Church wedding, with a ring bearer and everything. Little Eddy Boy Halmichek was our ring bearer. A good friend, Darden McCollum, acted as one of the ushers and also candle lighter. Trouble was, he forgot where he was and proceeded to strike the match on the seat of his pants. Marie Watkins, my former piano teacher, sang "I Love You Truly." Faegene's Uncle Otho showed up with a wheelbarrow to "drive" Faegene down the street for an old fashioned "cheve-al-ree". Don't remember if he talked her into taking that ride or not. After the wedding our friends met us at Rankin at a little nightclub for dancing and a get together. Faegene and I danced for a few minutes, then slipped out and drove on to San Angelo, 120 miles east of McCamey.

We didn't arrive at San Angelo until nearly one a.m., as there was a thick fog. Wouldn't you know it. We barely got there in time to get a hamburger and a glass of milk from a drive-in. I accidentally spilled my glass of milk on Faegene's new "going away" suit. Was I mortified. So was she. We checked in the Cactus Hotel, and I arranged for the suit to be cleaned and pressed by the time we planned to leave next morning.

There was rice in all our clothes, and we were careful to hide it to keep anyone from knowing we were newlyweds. I think we were only fooling ourselves. We were tired but up and ready to leave by 8:00 AM. Faegene's suit was cleaned and we were ready to go.

We spent the next three days of our honeymoon in Ft. Worth and took time to visit my old friend Ted Gilmore. The three days were over too quickly, and we had to start home as we only had Pop Eddleman's Humble Oil credit card and no money left. We came into Stephenville, Texas, low on gas and looking for a Humble Service Station. There wasn't one. I don't remember how we managed to get gas, but somehow we must have as we arrived home late that night.

We had already rented a house, even on our tight budget. From time to time we moved to a nicer home as we could find them. McCamey was an oil boomtown and full of shacks. The best shacks usually stayed rented until the occupants left the area looking for work elsewhere. The shacks were called "shotgun houses" because they were long and narrow. The turnover of oil field working personnel in McCamey was very high, fluctuating with the price of oil. Depression and drought was still covering Western Texas through 1940.

- I Learn To Fly

Luck was with me when I met Frank Hines, a pilot and flight instructor from Hobbs, New Mexico. He had flown to McCamey to see Faegene's uncle, Otho Eddleman, on business. Frank gave me a flying lesson and signed off my time in a logbook he gave me, showing my first lesson. It was going to cost about four dollars an hour so I bought about 30 minutes worth each time he flew in. Today it costs about $60.00 an hour.

About two months later Merel made a contract with the Porterfield Airplane Factory to sell their airplanes in Texas. They were little tandem two-seaters with 65 horsepower.

He promoted a wonderful deal by organizing a club with ten people, each to pay $10.00 down payment, then ten dollars a month plus four dollars an hour for each hour you flew. This would pay all expenses and add a little cash for future expenses. Merel furnished an instructor free of charge until we soloed. I had to sacrifice, but managed to buy in, with Faegene's help. Ours was the first club, and Merel sold at least ten more airplanes in West Texas with his plan. Over a hundred people learned to fly in that plan.

I soloed after only six hours of total instruction, not knowing much more than how to take off and land. Merel brought instructor Monte Lane, of San Angelo, in to McCamey one weekend. He soloed me on a Saturday morning in November. There was an inch of snow on the ground, and Monte took me up first. After a trip around the pattern and landing, I could see the crooked tracks of my take-off. I turned the plane around and taxied back to the take-off end of the runway and he got out. "You take it around and this time and keep it straight on your landing." he said.

I was pointing up the runway and just opened my throttle. Before I knew it, the airplane seemed to "jump" off the ground. With the front seat empty, that airplane really climbed fast. I had 1200 feet on the downwind leg, instead of the 800 feet I was supposed to have. With the throttle closed when turning on base leg I slowed down to the proper gliding speed and turned on the final landing leg. I still had to push forward on the stick to maintain flying speed. That wasn't right, but I knew to keep my gliding speed up. I made a fair landing, keeping it straighter this time. When I taxied back to the instructor I asked him why I had to push forward on the stick all the time. He was surprised I didn't know, but showed me a little wheel behind and below the front seat that controlled the stick pressure. My six hours of instruction had been with several different instructors and I just missed that information.

Early the next morning I was practicing landings and takeoffs until I felt quite comfortable with them. Some of the other members of the club rushed out to tell me I wasn't supposed to be flying solo without supervision. I didn't know that, but it was too late anyway. During 1940 and 1941 I earned my private license and now wanted to qualify for a Commercial License. That required at least 200 hours of flight time. After several months I was still short 10 flight hours and didn't have enough money to pay for them.

The World War had already become a fact for us, now that Japan had attacked Pearl Harbor. The draft was threatening to put me into the walking army. I wanted to fly, not walk. There was a rumor around that one might get a job instructing cadets at various Primary Army Flight Schools springing up around the country, and be exempt from being drafted.

I would have to get my Commercial License and Instructors' rating to be eligible to be hired as an instructor. Faegene's aunt was living close by, and we knew she usually carried extra money. Faegene suggested her aunt might loan me some, so I approached the aunt and explained the situation to her, telling her that fifty dollars would help me get enough flying time required for the Commercial tests. She said she could afford that much for me, and I promised I'd pay her back within the next few months. She was a mighty nice aunt to have. I paid her back in two months.

In a short time I completed my needed hours. When notice came that the FAA inspector was to be in Lubbock, 200 miles due north, I decided to go. In few days I took off in our Porterfield airplane for Lubbock. I re-fueled at the Big Spring airfield, which was under major construction, and then continued on to Lubbock. However, before I reached the next town, Lamesa, the head wind had picked up and I realized I had too little fuel to reach Lubbock. There were no other landing fields available, so I reluctantly returned to Big Springs. The strong wind had already reached Big Spring, so I needed to make a wheel landing, my first ever. The only runway was short due to the construction, but it was into the wind. One pilot on the field congratulated me later on a fine wheel landing. That compliment was a pleasant surprise to me as I wasn't sure I had done it correctly. The wind was so strong I couldn't taxi to the hanger without help, so some students came running out from the hanger to assist me.

Early the next morning I arrived in Lubbock to find the FAA examiner getting ready to fly on to Hobbs, New Mexico. He said he'd fly with me there, so I gassed up and flew on to Hobbs. Before the inspector would fly with me, I had to take the five-part written test for the Commercial license. I finished that and was quite nervous about the flight test.

Finally the examiner said: "Let's get it over with." By that time I was really nervous. This examiner was a big German and had the reputation of being difficult to please. We began the flight and quickly realized I didn't know much of anything about the required maneuvers. I had read some about those maneuvers but had no instruction in them at all. How I passed the flight test is beyond me. He had me do maneuvers I was not at all familiar with, and he would have to explain them to me first. After we landed he started walking away, so I asked him, weakly, how I did. He said I passed. I couldn't believe my ears. What a relief. I flew back to McCamey that afternoon, dazed but happy.

The next week I heard there were plans to build a new Army Primary Training Field in Ft. Stockton, Texas, 46 miles west of McCamey. The next day I borrowed Pop's car and went to Fort Stockton, found the personnel in charge of hiring instructors, and I was hired, just like that. Thurman Yates, from New Mexico, was also there. He and I were the first to be hired. We became close friends that lasted his lifetime. We worked together the entire time at Fort Stockton. I was really thrilled to be hired.

They had told me not to worry about the instructors' rating, as they would help me get it. I went home and went right to the Selective Board chairman and showed him my papers for re-assignment of my Selective Service rating from 1-A to a rating of essential wartime work. What a relief. Now I'd get to fly. I'd swear the Selective Board Chairman looked unhappy about it.

About 10 days later I was notified to report for work. Faegene drove me to Fort Stockton, and we found me a room to share with a young man named Delbert. My salary would be only $60 a month until we started instructing cadets, at which time we would be earning $350.00. That was a lot of money to me at that time.

- Preparing To Instruct Army Air Corp Cadets

Rex Chenault was in charge of the instructor's school. Seven instructors had left the Army Primary Flight School at Stamford, Texas to form a nucleus of command for the school at Fort Stockton. They would instruct us, and then, later, be the Asst. Flight Commanders, Flight Commanders, Squadron Commanders and the Chief Flight Instructor. My instructor, Johnny Smith, became the Director of Flying.

We began the ground school studies right away, and when five Kinner Fleet biplanes with Warner radial engines were flown in, our flight instruction began. These were older model airplanes with tailskids instead of tail wheels, but fully rated for acrobatics, which we would have to learn. The regular Army Air Force PT-17 trainers would arrive later.

Johnny Smith started me on basic maneuvers, and then progressed to all the ones I would be teaching. I had developed a bad habit during my earlier years of unsupervised flying of *fighting the controls* in rough air. Johnny had to work hard to eliminate that bad habit of mine. "Fighting" the controls only made the flying jerky. That was a bad habit and, if not corrected, would become tiring and make a rougher flight. Rough air was quite normal in the hot West Texas.

Because these were all open cockpit airplanes we wore cloth helmets and goggles. Our flight training had begun in May and we tanned rapidly in the hot wind, making us look rather *owlish*. By the time we knocked off work in the afternoons we were quite hot, tired, and thirsty. Thurman Yates and I started going to town together after work, to find some cool place to eat.

Next door to a good cafe there was a pool hall with a small bar petitioned off from the pool tables by a green swinging door. I was almost a teetotaler myself but drank a glass of ice-cold draught beer there one day. Later I suggested to Thurman we each have a beer before supper. I think he was just hot and dry enough that it appealed to him, and we began a ritual that went on for about thirty days. It was fifty years later I found out he was indeed a teetotaler and never drank beer or whisky.

We thoroughly enjoyed that relaxation and the chance to discuss our day. That cold beer was *just what the doctor ordered*. That period of my life was the only daily beer drinking I ever indulged in and seldom drank it.

Finally five Stearman PT-17 bi-planes were flown in for our use. We immediately began flying them. They had a stearable tail wheel, and were "top heavy," causing difficulty in keeping the plane rolling straight after landing. The Stearmans also had more power and the controls were more sensitive than in the older Kenner Fleets.

We had been flying the Stearmans less than a week when a thunderstorm came roaring in one hot afternoon. We stood in the open end of the hanger, but there was no room for the planes inside. We watched hail the size of baseballs pounding down through the wings of the airplanes and bouncing off the ground, which was still dry. Some of the hailstones bounced higher than the twenty-five foot hanger roof.

When the storm was over the mechanics immediately started to work on the damaged airplanes. We were lucky the damages turned out to be relatively minor, although a good many of the wing ribs needed to be re-built and the linen patching was quickly done. Three days later all planes were flying again.

Rex Chenault was a large man who was motivated to teach. He took over the instructors' instruction school. He had a loud voice and used it effectively. All instructors but Rex spoke to his student through a small funnel inserted into a rubber hose that reached back and hooked into the students' helmet. This was a one-way sound system. When Rex was in an airplane instructing landings though, we could hear him talking to his student all the way around the rectangular traffic pattern. One word he always mispronounced was "doing." It sounded like "derring". He was a character with a big smile, and likeable. He worked hard and expected all of us to do the same.

After we understood most of the low altitude maneuvers such as rectangle courses and S-turns across a road, we started on acrobatics. The first acrobatics Johnny showed me was inverted flight. Talk about exciting. Inverted I would try to hold myself in the seat. It took some "guts" for me to completely depend on the seat belt to hold me in the airplane. I had to be real sure that belt was latched properly, for if not fastened, you'd go sailing out. Although we wore parachutes, we preferred to stay in the plane. Flying upside down required more skill as the engine would quit, the propeller only wind-milling (rotating by passing through the air). The first time upside down was really scary. You could look up and see the ground, but it didn't take long to get used to it. I was taught acrobatics such as slow rolls, snap rolls, Immelman turns, and much more.

When I was qualified as an instructor, I began teaching other prospective instructors. I remember one instructor named Rudicill, who had trouble doing a maneuver called an Immelman. In the hot weather there was an area of hot air rising just south of the town of Fort Stockton, and I used this rising air for additional lift, and began demonstrating a true Immelman, which is a 180 degree turn while gaining altitude at the same time. It was like a loop where you roll out on top. With the added lift from the hot air we were even able to gain altitude, using proper technique.

Well, Rudy did fine until he reached the vertical. Then, instead of pulling the nose on over and rolling out, he just stopped moving the controls leaving the nose sticking straight up. We would run out of flying speed quickly, and down we'd go, sliding backwards on the tail. The nose quickly reversed places with the tail. The pilot was helpless until the weight of the nose pulled the airplane down and the gravity gave us increasing speed to regain flight control. That was exciting—too exciting.

We were flying above 2000 feet, high enough so there was no danger if we lost control momentarily, but one did wonder if the tail might pop off. Fortunately, that airplane was strong and well-built, so there was no danger of that happening, but it sure made me feel funny to suddenly start sliding backward with the prop turning against the wind. It also sounded wrong.

Rudy never did a really good Immelman for me, but with time and experience I'm sure he improved. We all enjoyed doing acrobatics, and learned to do just about any kind of acrobatics the airplane was capable of doing. I even did an outside loop one time. Once was enough. The engine, of course, quits running when flying upside down, so I was gliding upside down. In the outside loop, instead of "blacking out" (too little blood to the eyes) you would "Red Out" (blinded by excess blood to the eyes).

- Western Hospitality

The wonderful people of Fort Stockton showed their love and cooperation by accepting Aviation cadets with open arms. They did all they could to make the cadets and instructors feel at home. The women, especially, recognized the need to support those lonely young men we called U.S. Army Aviation Cadets. They had come from all parts of the United States, and found themselves in a strange land with few trees, hot winds, and Texas people. These Fort Stockton women arranged to have a meeting place in the Comanche Springs Park for the cadets when they were allowed to come to town. These women brought homemade cookies, drinks, music and their daughters for dances, fun and companionship.

Of course, the cadets didn't get off the Post often, but when they did, at least they had some place to go and hang out. My first student, Cadet Dick Alves, told me when I visited him in 1997, how nice they were treated in Fort Stockton. He said that period of time was the finest time of his life. He described how the country looked to him when the cadets got off the train, seeing only open land, few trees and the lowly creosote and black brush. It didn't look like home to them, but the people of Fort Stockton made up for the scenery, and made them feel appreciated.

Army Flight Instructor/Flight Commander—1942 - 1944
Gibbs Field, Fort Stockton, Texas

Flight Officer—1946

Chapter 7

I Begin My Career as Flight Instructor: Teaching Army Cadets

Before the first contingent of Aviation cadets arrived, we instructors were quite busy preparing. Then the big day finally arrived in July, 1942. Our first cadets reported for flight training and I was given four students for my first class. How great it felt to begin teaching cadets. My first student was Dick Alves, fresh out of college with a degree in Aeronautical Engineering. One of the other young men assigned to me was from New York and had been a lineman (climbed electric high line poles). The other two were two-year college students. All four were eager to finally begin their flight training after having gone through their basic training. Because of his older age, Dick barely made it under the cut-off age for cadets. The others were eager nineteen-year olds.

The student who was a lineman from New York was quite tense in thought and actions, and, combined with his powerful legs, became a difficult man to teach. He'd never driven a car, either, and I felt that fact might have influenced his confidence and ability to coordinate. I did my best, but just couldn't get through to him. After teaching him for about eight hours I finally had to send him up for an elimination ride with the Army captain.

I warned the captain to be "on his toes" when the student was attempting to land, as this boy would push a rudder and no one knows which he would push. I also warned him the student had strong legs. Sure enough, on the landing roll, the plane started off to the right, and the captain pushed so hard on the other rudder he pushed himself high up in his seat. The boy was "washed" out of flight training.

We always regretted the necessity to *wash out* one of these cadets. They were so ambitious and eager, but we only had a limited time to work with each one. We sometimes felt we may have failed, but time was always a consideration. The other three of my students passed and completed their Primary Training in the six weeks given, and were sent on to Basic Training in Pecos, Texas.

In landing these top-heavy Stearmans, ground looping was a danger. Ground looping was losing control and spinning around on the ground. We had to teach the student how to kick the rudder rather than holding it. Holding the rudder quickly over-controls and leads to a ground loop. Also if you apply both brakes together you might nose down, hitting the ground with your propeller. This can cause injury to the engine and can even break a wing spar (heavy wood support for the wing structure). Today's airplanes generally sit level on three wheels, like a tri-cycle, and directional control is by turning the nose-wheel with the rudders. These systems are much simpler than the conventional tail-wheel control on the Stearmans. Most of these young men learned fast, though, putting the pressure on the instructors to teach the cadets in a manner they would understand.

These young men would face life and death situations in combat; the better they learned the basics and perfected the maneuvers the better their chance of survival in combat. During my fifty years of instructing, I have strongly felt my responsibility to teach safety and good judgment as well as flying skills to all my students.

It was not difficult to teach cadets, as they were so eager to learn and tried hard. We impressed upon each student the importance of looking before all turns, and to scan the entire area for other airplanes. We had hundreds of airplanes in the skies at all times, and used exact flight patterns on each of the two auxiliary landing fields as well as the home field.

- Settling Down To Home Life in Fort Stockton

I was now financially able to rent a nice old house so we moved in. It was located a block away from the icehouse where a cold drinking fountain was on the front. The local water was quite "gippi", containing gypsum and only tasted better when ice-cold. On many nights I would walk the short distance to the icehouse for a drink of ice-cold water. That would sometimes help me go to sleep.

The added burden of housing due to the influx of several hundred-flight instructors brought in some FHA housing. My wife and I bought one of the first of these houses. We instructors had been offered first choice. Life was much better for me having Faegene with me.

My neighbor, another flight Instructor, found where he could obtain some natural fertilizer from the "City Pond." I came home one night and his whole front yard was covered with about two inches of *fertilizer* – sewage. He had the water sprinkler running full blast, and that just seemed to release all the smell.

After about ten days of suffering with the odor, the plot began turning green with what looked like grass or weeds. Before I went down to get some of the fertilizer for our yard, I took another look at the greenery and what do you know. The lawn was covered solid with tomato plants. When they ripened there were alligator tomatoes, small reds, big reds, yellows, all sizes and many varieties I'd never seen before. My neighbor and his family started selling the plants, and later sold many ripe tomatoes. This was the only tomato plant lawn I ever saw.

After graduating two classes of cadets someone told me of an older pilot called Swede, who, I was told, was a fine pilot. I looked him up and asked if he would fly with me. We checked out a Stearman and went flying, doing a few maneuvers and, of course, a few acrobatics. I was amazed at the smoothness of Swede's flying. I tried to emulate his smoothness. He suggested a better way for me to instruct. I tried that, and it worked quite well.

Probably as a result of my improved methods of teaching learned from Swede, I was promoted to Assistant Flight Commander. My class of five students had been so outstanding in the next class that I was able to even teach them most of the acrobatics maneuvers. One boy, having some previous time, learned to perform some of the acrobatics as well as I could... This new system of instructing really worked well for me.

As assistant Flight Commander to Thurman Yates, we would take the few "overflow" students until there were openings for them to be assigned to other instructors. One of my temporary students was Air Cadet Murphy, from Garland, Texas. On his first flight he became airsick shortly after leaving the departure pattern, so I re-entered the pattern and landed. Well, this happened the next time also, so I thought that if I kept him busy enough he might get over that airsickness. Being a Fight Commander, I had extra time at the beginning of the class, allowing me to take him on several short flights each day. I kept him busy by having him do all the flying: start the airplane, taxi out, take off, fly the pattern around the pattern and land, instructing him all the way. This plan was working, a little slow, but working. He was learning to fly and was not getting so sick. He now could usually fly about thirty minutes before getting sick.

But one morning he walked up to me and announced he was going to quit. He said he was a burden to me and to the Air Force, and felt it would be better for everyone if he just quit. Well, some fifty years later at the first re-union held at Gibbs Field, he told me how I'd explained to him how the Army Air Force was depending on him, how much money they had spent on him and how much he was needed.

After that talk he agreed to stay in. Well, he also began to progress faster, and I assigned him to another instructor. He graduated from Primary Flight School, continued through basic and advanced training to become a Flight Officer. At the time I had no way of knowing if he had made it all the way, but when I ran across him a year later in an airfield at Chengkung, China, it gave me a good feeling that he had become an Army Air Force Pilot. He had conquered his airsickness.

Sixty years later I had an occasion to visit him in his home at Garland, Texas. He couldn't say enough in his gratitude that I had kept him flying. By continuing his training, his life had taken on a new meaning, having experiences that he would have never had, otherwise. This gave me a satisfying feeling that I had been successful with him.

After nearly a year the army replaced our Stearmans with the low-winged Fairchild aircraft, which had less power and an in-line engine instead of a radial. The Fairchilds were a newer model airplane, not as strongly built as the Stearmans and had only one wing. Bi-planes were out. We instructors, of course, needed to familiarize ourselves with the feel of the Fairchilds and began practice flying them after working hours. The first two instructors to fly these Fairchilds began a maneuver and dived to gain some speed when one wing broke in two. Wearing parachutes, both instructors quickly bailed out. They landed unharmed but were, of course, quite nervous. Inspection located a faulty repair of a previously broken spar on the Fairchild. It took some more time before our confidence in these ships was restored.

A tragedy occurred that killed an instructor and a cadet pilot. While flying in the traffic pattern the student had carelessly dropped below traffic altitude in the traffic pattern, and either the instructor or the student pulled the ship up abruptly hitting the bottom of a trainer being flown by a solo student. Of course the solo student was unable to see the ship below him. Although the student and instructor were killed, the solo student in the other plane was able to land safely.

With the war going on there were no new cars for sale and few used ones. Faegene and I managed to buy an Ambassador Eight Nash owned by an Upton County Commissioner. He had illegally purchased tires for use on his car. Tire and gasoline rationing had become strict, and the Commissioner had no choice but to jack up his car and return all his new tires. I heard about it and called him, offering to purchase his car. He quickly agreed on a price, so we then owned a car with no tires. As I was in an essential job I had no trouble in getting a permit to buy new tires.

President Roosevelt, following the example of several European nations, mandated gasoline rationing in the U. S. as part of the country's wartime effort. This was just one of the many measures taken during those years as the entire nation was transformed into a unified war machine. Women took to the factories, households tried to conserve energy and automobile manufacturers shifted to producing tanks and planes.

Faegene had been going to her doctor in McCamey as well as one in Fort Stockton and was sure she was pregnant. Both her doctors assured her she wasn't. Well, as you have probably guessed, she was right, and Faegene wanted her doctor in McCamey to deliver our first baby.

She was visiting her parents in McCamey when she went into labor about four a.m. the thirtieth of January, 1943. I had been quite busy working every day at Gibbs Field. That morning about four o'clock when my phone rang, I wasn't too surprised when my father-in-law, Pop, called to tell me I'd better come "a-runnin." Ten minutes later I was in the car wondering if I had enough gasoline in the tank to make it to McCamey, some forty-six miles. I had kept plenty of gasoline day to day, but as it always seems to happen when the time comes, I was short. I did make it to McCamey all right, but I "sweated it out" all the way. There were no cars on the highway at five AM. I could "see" myself running twenty miles or so to get to the hospital in time.

Well, I did get there in time, even before the doctor. The nurses had gone twice to his home across the street from the hospital to get him, but he still hadn't come, so Pop Eddleman said, "I'll get him," and he did. In the meantime, Faegene was in labor and in considerable pain. I could see the top of my daughter's head before they made me get out. In another three minutes the doctor would have missed the birth. It was only about two minutes later when I heard Sherry announcing her arrival in loud cries.

I was worried about Faegene because of so much pain, but she was finally given some pain medication after she gave birth. My thoughts: "We have a baby! I am a father." I would have to go find some cigars to give out, as was the custom. There was a war going on and all I would find would be cheap cigars.

When they finally got Sherry cleaned and wrapped in a baby blanket, she was put in the nursery where we could see her. My Baby. I realized just like other fathers probably do, "I'm a father."

After a week or so with her parents in McCamey, I brought Faegene and Sherry home to Fort Stockton. We hired Consuela, a young Latin girl, to help Faegene. She was a lifesaver for Faegene, as she knew how to help with our baby daughter, as well as the house keeping. I was able to pitch in a little at night, and it was nice we were in our new home. We had found no washing machine to buy, though, other than a tiny electric washer. There were no disposal diapers in those days, so diapers had to be washed in the bathtub by hand. It was difficult for Faegene during this time, even with the help we had.

- The Inevitable Happens

When we were in training to be instructors, it was pointed out how easy it was to accidentally loosen the seat belt. Sooner or later an instructor would fall out of his airplane, we were told. Well, it finally happened as predicted. An instructor fell out of his airplane while demonstrating a slow roll. The student flew the ship back to the field, landed, and reported he'd lost his instructor. I could imagine how the instructor must have felt when suddenly, he found himself floating in the air with no wings. His parachute worked fine, and he gladly carried it back to the parachute rigger, Wilkie (Wilkinson,) and took him out to dinner in appreciation for Wilkie having repacked and aired those chutes properly. That instructor received plenty of teasing, but you can be sure the rest of us kept a closer check on our own seat belt.

Merel (my brother-in-law) had been awarded a pre-glider school from the Army Air Corps, at McCamey. He trained about twenty-five Army Air Force glider pilots both in ground school as well as flying. They stayed in a local hotel, which also fed them. He graduated them then sent them on to an advanced glider school in Lamesa, Texas. Merel's school was closed down when the Army had all the glider pilots they needed, so he came over to Fort Stockton to teach in Gibbs Field at Fort Stockton.

After Merel taught his second group of cadets, however, they did not progress enough to keep up with our schedule and had to be eliminated. Merel was an excellent flight instructor, but he hadn't been able to adjust to the accelerated program of the Army Air Corps.

He then found a job in Arizona teaching Basic Training and did quite well with the more advanced class.

Later on he was accepted into the Air Transport Command and sent to the St. Joseph, Missouri Instrument Training School to learn instrument flying, flying out of St. Joseph Army Air Base. When he completed that training he was then sent to the Reno Training School to prepare him for flying the Hump in the CBI (China-Burma-India War Theater). This was extra preparation needed for flying in the terrible weather and high mountains of the Himalayas.

I was promoted to Flight Commander while still serving under my good friend Thurman Yates, who was now a Squadron Commander. I had already spent two weeks working as Flight Commander under Squadron Commander Wes Long. When the next class came in I was put back under Thurman Yates as a Flight Commander.

Quite often the judgment of the Army Check Pilot on the twenty-hour check ride kept a student in the program when the instructor and Flight Commander both knew the student couldn't make it through the forty-hour check ride. Then, as we expected, on the forty-hour check the Army Check Pilot would usually "wash out" (or eliminate the student from flight training).

I thought it would be more humane not to encourage the student, but to wash him out earlier on the twenty-hour check ride. The disappointment might be less for the student than to go ahead and wash him out on the forty-hour check ride. It was a "catch-all plan" and a student might or might not be washed out in the forty-hour follow-up army flight check, but generally was. I was out of sorts about this one day when the Army Check Pilot, after overriding my twenty-five hour recommendation earlier to wash him out, eliminated a student officer on his forty-hour check ride, as I had anticipated. That hit me wrong, and I went to the commanding officer and explained this to the colonel, citing slowness of learning being the student's main problem. The colonel smiled and asked if I thought the student could catch up if held over in the next class? I answered, "Yes Sir."

"Then that's what we'll do," he said.

Would you believe, about a year later I was in active duty, stationed in Luliang, China and was called for flight one morning. Who was the first pilot? You guessed it, that same student pilot. This cadet had no idea that I had gone to bat for him and still doesn't, as far as I know, but I was happy he'd made it through. We flew to Peiyshi with me as his co-pilot. On his approach it looked as if he'd bounce our loaded airplane. He did. I said: "Lieutenant, you still can't land the darn airplane, can you." We just laughed.

- An Unusual Weather Phenomenon

One morning in Fort Stockton, Texas, there was a weather phenomenon I have never seen before or since. I was flying with a student in the first period that morning, at about a thousand feet, and noticed solid low clouds all the way across the horizon in the north. I kept watching that solid bank of clouds moving toward our flight. I instructed my student to get between the distant cloud and the airfield.

I soon realized this cloud was moving toward us rapidly. As it came closer I could see the cloud reached from 3,000 feet all the way to the ground. It was a solid wall of fog approaching our area, where more than two hundred airplanes were in the air, many of them being flown by solo students.

I began signaling to all the others planes to land. Other Instructors joined me in getting the attention of solo students to get them safely on the ground. There was one auxiliary landing field farther south, but this fog was moving fast. I stayed in the air until it nearly caught us. The fog blanketed me while I was still rolling on my landing. It was so thick that even taxiing was difficult. When we finally got parked on the ramp I saw the Director of Flying taking off in the fog. I knew he was going up to check for pilots that were still above the fog. Fortunately, Johnny had located a plane having basic blind flying instruments. There was no way we could safely land in this fog with or without radio equipment for blind landing.

The Director of Flying was successful in rounding up the rest of the students, about five, caught above the clouds, and led them safely to an airport fifty miles to the southwest, and nearly 2,000 feet higher in elevation, at Alpine, Texas.

We were extremely fortunate to have averted a great tragedy that morning. About two hours later the fog dissipated, and we were able to resume our training flights.

Chapter 8

Army Air Force Career Begins

The Army Primary training program had become so successful the Army began curtailing the program by closing down several Primary Flight Schools, ours being one of them. My job would be gone and the war was still going on, so I decided to volunteer for the Ferry Command rather than being drafted. The Ferry Command had offered the instructors the opportunity to join the Army Air Force as a commissioned officer and that appealed to most of us. I hoped I could then be stationed in Dallas and have my family with me. Things did not turn out as I hoped they would. The Air Force just put us where they wanted us.

I passed the I.Q. test successfully with a score of 162, and was then sent to Goodfellow Air Base in San Angelo, Texas, for the required Army Flight physical. Then they shot me. I found that the Army would "shoot" us, injecting us for immunity every time we turned around. I don't know what all the shots were for, but I was beginning to feel like a pincushion. One private had the job of drawing out some of my blood. After trying unsuccessfully for about thirty minutes, I was getting light headed. He finally went for help and brought a nurse who did the job quickly and efficiently, in about ten seconds.

This was on Feb. 12, 1944, and I was to report to Dallas, Texas, in a week, some 425 miles northeast of McCamey. Once the Army gets you in their ranks, you usually have to wait and wait and wait some more, but I wasn't even in yet. We waited in Dallas a couple of days more until they sent us to Randolph Field, San Antonio, Texas, for special flight training.

When reporting to the 5th Ferry Command at Love Field, Dallas, Texas, I ran into a friend, Florene Miller, from Odessa, Texas. She had been a flight instructor just before Pearl Harbor and was now flying for the Air Transport Command (Ferry Command) out of Dallas. There were very few girls with her experience at that time. I watched her making some practice landings in an A-24 Dive Bomber.

We received orders to be flown to Randolph Field at San Antonio, Texas. I was lucky to catch a ride in an old B-18 bomber, where two of us crawled down into the front plexiglas nose space used by the Bombardier. We had a birds-eye view of the country from Dallas to San Antonio. About ten more of us were riding wherever they could find space throughout the body of the plane.

There were 285 of us former flight instructors in the group sent to Randolph for Twin Engine checkout and Instrument ratings. We were required to have at least 1,000 hours of flying experience before being accepted by the Army Air Force. Consequently, all we needed was to check out in multi-engine type aircraft and learn to fly on instruments.

My instructor was Lieutenant Alford, an instrument instructor in the recently closed Instrument School at Bryan, Texas. I had experience flying a Link Trainer at the field in Fort Stockton. A link Trainer is a closed-in cockpit, which an operator outside was able to submit simulated blind flying instrument practice for the pilot. We had also been teaching a few of the cadets at Fort Stockton instrument flying in some Stearman having a portable cover over the student's cockpit. Because of that previous experience I was able to breeze through Lieutenant Alford's instruction and was sent up for my flight instrument test during the first two weeks of training at Randolph Field.

In those days there was only the aural range, in which the pilot was guided by listening to radio signals sent in directional beams. On the morning of my flight test there was a 400-

foot ceiling. The Examiner had me close the cockpit of the BT-13 and take off on instruments. When we were about 600 feet up he had me open the cockpit cover, which allowed me to see we were on solid instrument conditions. I followed all his instructions and after the instrument flight test I made my let down by instruments for landing. We broke out of the clouds at 400 feet right over Randolph Field, on a collision course with some AT-9s. The examiner pulled us abruptly back up into the clouds and said, "OK, climb up and do it again." I did and again came in right over Randolph Field. This time we were clear to land.

We were to be at Randolph Field six weeks, but I had completed the required training in less than two weeks. Lieutenant Alford suggested that I continue *honing* my instrument flying by using the link trainer, which I was glad to do. The aural radio range blind flying landing system is no longer used today. It was well that I was proficient at flying instruments, though, as in less than a year I was flying in some of the worst instrument weather in the world — the China-Burma-India (CBI) Theater of War.

At Randolph Field the Link Trainer available to us was located in a hanger on the flight line about three quarters of a mile from our barracks. One day, after flying simulated instruments for two hours in the Link Trainer, I was walking back to the barracks. I was wearing my flight coveralls with no insignia when I noticed a command car with several little yellow flags on it, driving slowly up the aircraft parking-ramp. I paid no more attention to it. After it passed by I heard someone call "Mister." I looked around and didn't see anyone. Then I heard it again. I spotted an officer standing in a control tower. He ordered me to come up. I wondered what he wanted. As I came into his presence I came to attention, although I was not in uniform or even in the Army. "What is your name, rank, and serial number, mister?" he asked.

He looked a little shocked when I answered, "My name is Kenneth Babcock, I have no rank, and I have no serial number."

He then asked, "What the hell are you doing here, then?" I explained the situation to him. He then said, "Do you realize you just snubbed the Commanding General of the United States Army Air Force, General Hap Arnold?"

"No Sir," I answered. He then explained that the five yellow flags meant a 5-star general was in the vehicle. Wow!

Well, the more I thought of my boo-boo the more nervous I became. I located Colonel Roy Ward, whom I knew from my hometown, and who was based on the field. I walked over to his quarters and told him what I'd done. He just laughed and explained there would probably be no trouble as the general was a very understanding person. He said that if I heard anything more about the matter just let him know. I felt relieved. Colonel Ward was friendly and I was glad I'd come to see him. As a boy I had seen Colonel Ward flying to Sonora several times in an Army Air Force plane from Randolph Field to visit his parents. One time I even saw him do a spin above his parents' ranch house, which was only a half-mile west of Sonora.

One day three of us were picked to fly a cross-country flight. I never knew why this was done, but we were glad of the diversion. We flew some BT 13 type aircraft to Waco, Texas, and then to Enid, Oklahoma where we spent the night. My good friend Gordon Wendell had forgotten to bring his razor, so I loaned him mine: a straight razor. This was Gordon's first time to shave with a straight razor. He did a good job of it, though, I must admit. Gordon and his wife Betty and I have since had many a laugh at that memory.

Upon leaving Enid we flew directly to Lubbock Air Force Base, where we again had to spend the night. Next morning we left for a direct flight to Randolph Field.

I was homesick for Faegene, and called her long distance. She decided to drive the 325 miles to San Antonio from McCamey for a visit. I was only waiting for the next step the Air Force planned for us pilots, so we were able to be together the three days she was there. That was wonderful for our moral. We were looking forward to being together when I was assigned to a post, hopefully Love Field, Dallas.

It was announced to us one day we were to leave for a special six weeks Officer's Training School set up at Berry Field, Nashville, Tennessee. We were to be qualified as officers and learn some advanced navigation methods. So off we went, by train, to Nashville, Tennessee.

From the time we arrived at Berry Field until we left, we marched and sang in cadence every step we took on the field. We marched all over the training field, learned close order drill and all the necessary marching steps. We drilled every day and attended classes about army structure all the way up to the President. We studied the navigation methods thoroughly. We were even sent on a fourteen-mile hike carrying full pack including a gas mask. Some of us were unable to march that far as we were fatter than we should have been, including my good friend Lonnie Glasscock from Corpus Christi, Texas. His feet were just unable to carry him that far. We were fliers, not foot soldiers, or so we thought. They had a truck for those unable to complete the hike, and Lonnie rode the last seven miles.

Later we were given a few passes to go to town during one or two weekends. We took a bus to town where we could visit a nice restaurant, movie or nightclub. You could take a taxi to attend a nightclub at the edge of town and see some fairly good shows. All they had in the way of drinks were cokes and sloe gin, which weren't very appetizing drinks. We did enjoy getting out and being on our own time for a change.

Just before payday I wanted to call Faegene, but only had about fifty cents. We had a slot machine for dimes in the Officer's mess, and I put my last dimes in it. Would you believe, I hit the Jackpot for the first and only time in my life. I now had five dollars and was able to call home.

When we finally completed this training after six weeks, we were looking forward to becoming Commissioned Officers. Much to our disgust, we were told the day before graduation that instead of being commissioned we would be appointed as Flight Officers. I think a couple of us just quit at that notice, but most of us went ahead although disgusted, and marched on parade that last Saturday as a graduating class. We had been trained to be officers by an Officers Training Group that was sent in to give us special training. It made no sense to us to be appointed instead of being commissioned. I had observed for some time that the regular Army Air Force looked down upon civilian pilots, but the joke was really on them. We civilians had been teaching cadets to be commissioned officer pilots in the Army Air Force for several years.

Later on when we were overseas, things looked better for us. Being F/O (Flight Officers), we were paid a twenty percent increase in flight pay for overseas service instead of the ten per cent paid to regular commissioned officers. We were considered officers but were also better accepted by the enlisted personnel. The real joke was that we were not supposed to be in combat. I had nearly 600 hours of combat time in the CBI (China-Burma-India) Theater of War.

- Assigned To Air Transport Command, Ferry Command

We flight officers were assigned to the various Ferry Command bases all over the United States. I was sent to Wilmington, Delaware, New Castle Army Air Base, along with five others including my friend Lonnie Glasscock. Although it was early May, the weather was quite chilly. He and I had to share an upper bunk on the train that night. I out maneuvered Lonnie so that he was on the outside edge of the bunk, next to the cold outside wall. He hollered from time to time when he got against that cold metal. There wasn't too much room for two large men in an upper bunk.

The train arrived at Wilmington, Delaware at 6:00 A.M. We were met by an army truck, which carried us to the base some fifteen miles from Wilmington, Delaware. We were assigned to BOQ (Bachelor Officer's Quarters) and being Sunday, we just slept some and walked around to look over the base. The next day we were assigned to a squadron and went through the usual procedures of checking in to the Quartermaster stores to be issued the necessary items such as a parachute, A-2 bag, an Army suitcase (A-4), and a .45- caliber pistol. I carried that pistol on my belt holster. I was also happy to have that parachute, too, but never had to use it except to sit on, thank God.

The job of the Ferrying Division of the Air Transport Command was to move aircraft to wherever and whenever they were needed. Most new aircraft were flown to airfields where they received special installations and modifications, then sent into combat. We also flew the modified aircraft to specified places, either in the U. S., England, Australia or the CBI (China Burma India Theater). While I was stationed at New Castle Army Air Base, we were generally busy flying B-26 Martin Marauders (Medium Bombers) to: Savannah, Georgia, Nashville, Tennessee, the Bahamas Islands, England and North Africa or wherever else they were needed.

When we took off in an airplane from the factory, this completed the sale of that plane to the Army Air Force. We were trained to check the airplane thoroughly before taking off, which was for our own safety as well as protecting the property for the Army Air Force. The Martin plant at Baltimore, where we picked up the new B-26's, was always cooperative and thorough. Any complaint we had was promptly taken care of.

- Ferrying the Martin B-26 Bomber and Other Planes

Sometimes we ferried used planes, or combat weary planes. One day two of us first pilots were flown to Rome, New York, to ferry a war weary early model B-26 to the Aberdeen, Maryland proving ground. The name on the B 26 bomber we were picking up had painted on its nose: "THE COUGHING COFFIN." This was not an encouraging name. The Martin B-26 bombers were already nicknamed "The Widow Makers."

During 1941, cadets assigned to fly this early model of the B-26 bombers were too inexperienced to be flying that airplane, and crashed as many as ten planes in one week, most of them fatal. Some of the cadets then refused to fly them, offering to give up their flying status instead. The Air Corps called in General Doolittle, a highly experienced pilot. He recommended more instruction for both the pilots and the mechanics. The Martin Plant also added three feet to the wing for added stability. These actions improved the situation but the Martin B-26 continued having a bad reputation until combat exonerated the airplane by proving they could take a lot of punishment from the flack and German fighters. This protected the men and got them home. The B-26 also earned an excellent record of accuracy in bombing.

The day the two of us first pilots were sent to ferry a war weary B 26 to Aberdeen, Maryland, we made a thorough inspection of this war weary clipped wing B-26. We noted some leaking hydraulics and some loose fastenings, but nothing too apparent to keep us from making a safe flight. We were confident in determining the plane's safety.

We took off, everything fine, until we broke ground at about 120 MPH. The small escape door directly above the other pilot came unhooked and flew open. I quickly pushed the wheel forward to hold it in place with my knees and then grabbed the belt of the other pilot while he unbuckled his seat belt to rise up and pull the door down and lock it. With full power and no time to trim there was a lot of pressure on my knees but the suction of the open door might have pulled my buddy out the hatch. The length of time it took to close the hatch was about half the time it takes to write this, but it seemed much longer. Together we then trimmed the elevators nose down and reduced the power to normal climb. Whew! It was a wonder my partner was able to get the latch to close after pulling the door down into place. The suction of the 140 MPH wind and strong propeller blast was hard to overcome. He managed it though.

When we got everything under control it was much quieter, and we relaxed a little. We re-checked instruments and looked around. We decided we could safely continue to ferry it on down to Aberdeen, Maryland, our destination. As this was one of the early model B-26s, it had to be handled differently on takeoff than the later models we had been flying. Because of the different technique we used a little more speed on takeoff.

A few weeks later two of us were sent on another ferry job, which again required two first pilots. We were to pick up a retired Boeing Canadian airliner that was being used in some experimental instrument landings by Sperry Instruments at New York's LaGuardia airport. We took the train to New York and checked into the Astor Hotel. Our appointment was to pick up the airplane at LaGuardia airport early the next day.

When we walked across the street from Hotel Astor, we saw an ice skating rink down on a lower level. That was the first ice rink I'd seen. We were lucky to also get to see the Radio City Rockets perform in the theater close by the ice skating rink. When the curtain of the theater opened, there, on the stage, were about 20 large beautiful cups and saucers. Then when the music started the cups and saucers began to change shape into a fantastic moving review of the Rockets. Their electrifying show was perfect and very beautiful. After the Rockets performed there was an outstanding movie, but all I remember is that Irene Dunn was the heroine.

Later that night we found a nightclub located in the hotel. The orchestra was Harry James and his band. I wanted to dance to the live music of Harry James. There were few people there and no one for me to dance with. In looking around I noticed a girl sitting with her parents. I went over, introduced myself, and received permission to dance with their daughter. What a thrill to dance to the music of Harry James in person. I remember he was a shorter man than I had expected. I hoped his wife, Betty Grable, would come on stage and sing, but she didn't.

Next morning we took the subway out to LaGuardia field. We had to get checked out in this airplane, as we'd never even seen one like it. This was one of the first modern airliners used in Canada prior to 1942, built by Boeing. It had no flaps, but had mechanical brakes and retractable landing gear. The landing gear lowered itself by gravity when released, then had to be ratcheted in locked position by the co-pilot. In retracting the gear an electric motor raised it, but the final raising was by the co-pilot using the ratchet handle to lock it in position.

The pilot for Sperry Gyroscopes, Barney Brunch, flew us around the pattern at LaGuardia, first adding some sand bags for weight to the tail for balance. Without the ballast it would have been too nose heavy to handle. Incidentally, Barney told us he had flown that very plane in Canada for thousands of hours on Canadian airways.

We left later that morning after the practice landings at LaGuardia Field. Our first re-fueling stop was Olmstead Field, Harrisburg, Pennsylvania.

With no flaps to help slow us, our landing speed seemed fast, and keeping directional control with those mechanical brakes was a challenge.

After refueling, we filed an instrument flight plan for Wright Patterson airfield, as the clouds had closed in. The radios were quite ancient but operated well. After take-off we were in solid clouds. We turned on course, "riding" the steady hum of the radio beam (Aural Range). We could hear the "key clicks," which you only heard when exactly on course. Suddenly we only heard clear "dit-dahs." The other pilot said "What the hell?" On an aural range of that day this meant we had suddenly found ourselves way off course into the "A" quadrant. I burst out laughing. The other pilot wanted to know what was so "d—" funny. I then explained that I had flown this course many times in a Link Trainer instrument simulator, and it was a unique bent radio beam, known only at Olmstead Field. I then told him the signal would soon return back to the solid hum, which it did. This confirmed we were still right on course.

We arrived at Wright Patterson that afternoon, and turned the airplane over to the proper authorities. We caught a commercial airliner back to Washington International Airport, took a limousine to the Train Station and returned to Wilmington, Delaware, arriving at six o'clock a.m. About every airline return I made to Wilmington was made with this same routine.

One thing that facilitated our travel was the "T. R." book (A book of Transport Receipts) issued to Ferry Pilots. We just wrote our own tickets for any commercial form of travel, as we needed to move as fast as possible to ferry as many airplanes as we could. Those planes we flew were needed in combat. Our job was so essential that we had top priority to travel, except for the president of the United States and his Cabinet. Although the transportation facilities were always filled to capacity during wartime, all we ferry pilots had to do was write out the T.R. Receipt and we were guaranteed a seat, *bumping* someone if necessary to make room for us.

One time I ferried a C-47 to Louisville, KY, and learned that a B-24 was to be ferried to Montreal, Canada the next morning. I left with that plane and went to Montreal, getting there in the late afternoon. We then caught an airliner for New York, making a quick stop at Burlington, Vermont, then on to what is now Kennedy Airport in New York City. We had to take a limousine all the way to LaGuardia Airport through Brooklyn, Queens, and I don't know where else. We caught a C-54 MAT (Military Air Transport) at LaGuardia, flying back to our New Castle Army Air Base at Wilmington.

I ferried the Martin B-26 Marauder more than any other type of airplane. It was called the "Widow Maker," because of its high record of fatal accidents, and many of the pilots were quite nervous about flying it. In my opinion it was a very fine airplane to fly, and safer than some, if you were well trained in certain procedures. Proper landing and single engine failure techniques on take-off varied according to the model being flown. On any of the models, losing an engine on takeoff, immediate reduction of power on the good engine was imperative to prevent a fatal snap roll when close to the ground on take-off. Full power on one engine was too much power for the vertical tail and rudder to control. The gasoline valve to the dead engine was then quickly turned off and the propeller feathered (to reduce drag), and power further adjusted on the good engine as needed. Of course quickness was vital with an engine failure, especially on take-offs. After single engine procedure was set up the B-26 could then climb 200 feet per minute on a single engine, according to the book.

During my check out as first pilot in the B-26, I was given simulated instrument (blind flying), and engine failures in all anticipated situations, particularly on take-offs. The empty B-26 performed perfectly. All of us Flight Instructors who had joined the Army Air Force had 1000 hours or more of flying experience and had little trouble flying the B-26. Regular army pilots going into combat during World War Two had some difficulty flying this airplane because of their lack of experience in flying. I loved flying the Martin B-26s and felt that they landed beautifully. Landing speed was around 110 MPH, but many pilots landed it at 120 to 130, then using the entire runway because of the extra speed.

One time we ferried five B-26s to Nashville from the Martin Plant in Baltimore. The flight leader ordered us all to land because of approaching darkness. We landed at a field close to Atlanta, Georgia. I was first to land, and explained and demonstrated to my co-pilot my method for landing the B-26, landing close to the beginning edge of the runway. The runway was a little shorter than most airports but I had no trouble turning off the runway before the reaching the end. I parked the plane on the ramp, and we watched the other four make their landings. Each one landed long and had to ride the brakes mercilessly, barely stopping before the end of the runway; smoke was streaming behind the tires as they sped down the runway. I then showed the co-pilot the tires on the other planes, which had flat places from the excessive braking.

One pilot I rode with at New Castle Army Air Base became my good friend. He always let me fly some, and I played gin rummy with him. He always beat me. Maybe that was why we were good friends. Ha. Ha. He let me do some practice stalls in the B-26 so I could get the feel of a stall in the B-26, and I did some coordination exercises to learn how the ship responded to the controls. As an experienced instructor I only needed to compare the handling of a heavy, faster airplane with those I'd been flying before joining the Army Air Corps. The principal of flying is the same on all airplanes, but the *feel* is different, and some airplanes reacted differently in a stall. Stalling a B-26 can be dangerous as you could lose control and go into a spin. Recovering from a spin is difficult in that ship, I was told.

This is, in my opinion, what happened when this friend was killed when he spun in on a flight to Nashville, Tennessee. He probably let the inexperienced Sergeant Pilot, who was his co-pilot, do some stalls and they lost control, resulting in a spin. It needs to be noted that parachuting out of this aircraft is quite difficult, as you have to lower the landing gear first. You then struggle down a ladder through the nose landing gear compartment with your parachute on your back, then jump off the ladder.

One Sunday I had nothing to do, and decided to check out the little UC-78 trainer twin engine we had on the field, and fly up to Boston for a Maine Lobster dinner. We were encouraged to increase our flight experience by using this little ship. A navigator, sitting in Operations, was looking for a possible flight to Buffalo, New York, to see his folks. He said he'd not seen them for two years, so I let him talk me into taking him to buffalo. He said he would take me to see Niagara Falls.

This little plane had a speed of only 150 mph, but we arrived in time to see the famous Niagara Falls in daylight. How impressive. We were able to walk down into the dam about 50 feet. That much water tumbling all around you was noisy and rather frightening. The word "crashing" seemed to apply to the sounds surrounding us.

Drinking some Vintner's Ginger Beer was the "in-thing" to do in the little town of Niagara, I discovered. The navigator and his family were with me and showed me around the Falls and the little town of Niagara.

Flying over the beautiful scenery across New York State such as the Finger-Lakes and a battlefield from our Revolution of 1776 was rather unexpected but quite interesting to me. This was my first trip across New York State, and my passenger told me much about this area.

We took off from Niagara at one thirty a.m. for the return trip and would refuel in Philadelphia. We had been enjoying the clear moonless night and the steady drone of the engines, when suddenly light reflections from the wing lights indicated we had flown into clouds. We continued on instruments and reported our location by radio when we passed over New York City. They cleared us direct to Philadelphia, Pennsylvania. At Philadelphia I was cautioned of a shallow layer of fog lying about ten feet above the runway. As I approached my landing the runway was hiding below that thin layer of fog, reflecting the light so that I could no longer see the runway. I continued my let down approach through the small layer of fog and saw the runway "pop" into view an instant before I landed.

We re-fueled and took off for the short flight to New Castle Air Base, landing at six a.m. Monday morning. I checked out at operations and walked over to my ready-room to wait for it to open. I sat down on the ground, leaned against a big tree and went to sleep. An hour later I was awakened by voices and went into the ready room. I had just lain down on the couch when my name was called. I was to take my checkout ride in the B-26. After flying all night? I can do it, I told myself.

The check pilot and I were flown to the Martin Plant at Baltimore and checked the new B-26 thoroughly. As the plane left the ground the check pilot had me lower my seat to the lowest setting, and put a hood on my head so I couldn't see out. The Check Pilot then instructed me to do all the flying by instruments. I also had to do the navigation and all radio check reports. We made several practice blind landing approaches and takeoffs at the Raleigh-Durham airport, about half way to Savannah. Simulated engine failures were called, testing my ability and reaction time, which were critical in this type of aircraft. This Check Pilot really "put me through", so to speak.

By the time we arrived in Savannah he was satisfied I could fly this airplane and I was exhausted and very sleepy. We couldn't board the only return airline out of Savannah until eleven o'clock p.m., so we spent some time that afternoon in the Base Picture Show, where I promptly went to sleep.

When we finally were shuttled out to the airline terminal to catch the plane for Washington National Airport, I recognized a former fellow-instructor I knew, sprawled in a chair sound asleep. I kicked his feet to awaken and surprise him. He opened his eyes, saw me, and yelled: "Babcock, I thought you were dead." He told me there had been a report of a Flight Officer Babcock flying a B-26 across Africa, being killed in a crash. I assured him it wasn't me.

It was rather odd, but the next time I saw him was in Kunming, China, a year later, at which time he told me how he'd found himself hanging on the parachute straps in the air above Kunming after a mid-air collision. Apparently he was knocked out of his C-87 with his parachute on. He had no memory of how he got out of the C-87. Was that luck, or fate? Maybe a little of both.

When I got back to New Castle Air Base I called Faegene. Through a radio broadcast she and her family had heard about a Babcock being killed in a B-26 in Africa. They were relieved when I called. War is sure hell for the families of servicemen.

I had become good friends with my Check Pilot, and he looked me up to share a breathtaking experience. He told about flying a B-26 from Nashville to the Bahamas, and having both engines quit while over the Atlantic Ocean. A quick check located no reason for the engines to stop. With no inflatable raft or emergency provisions, he thought they were "goners." Just above the water the engines suddenly came roaring back on. He was in the Bermuda Triangle area. There must be something about that area. What caused both engines to quit, and then re-start? I had flown that exact route and I had no problem, thanks be to God.

While still flying as a co-pilot in a B-26, we arrived at Hunter Field, Savannah, Georgia on a ferry flight. A light wind was drifting dense smoke from a nearby paper factory, covering our base leg pattern so thickly we had to go on instruments on the base leg and final approach to the runway. The first pilot didn't lower our altitude until he could see the runway, and was too high to land. He cut the throttle anyway and dropped the nose down in preparation for landing. We landed half way down the runway. The pilot hit the brakes, but we went so far down the runway we ran off the end. Thank goodness the land had been hardened beyond the end, so no harm was done. I started breathing again. The pilot appeared embarrassed, Years later I saw the evaluation he gave me as co-pilot on that flight: "A weak pilot. Needs more time before checkout." You know, I thought he was flying that plane, not me. I don't think I even touched the controls on that entire flight, or said a word except, maybe, "whee." I do know had I been flying I could have done better, but I didn't say that to him.

- Army Air Force Shenanigans

In August, I was trying to get a short leave to bring my family to Wilmington, Delaware. I hadn't earned any leave time yet, so when a possible transfer to Palm Springs, California, came up, I asked for the transfer. With a transfer to Palm Springs I'd be able to stop at McCamey and pick up my family. Ideal situation. The leave I'd applied for earlier, though, came through first, so I went to the same authority to cancel my application for transfer.

I then caught a ride on a C-47 being ferried to California. I wanted off at Amarillo, Texas, some 300 miles north of McCamey, so I got off when we arrived at English Field, east of Amarillo. I caught a bus for McCamey. I really enjoyed the clear skies and seeing the horizon clearly in the distance. Just smell that wonderful clean air. Wonderful West Texas.

It was sure great being with my family again, but time was short. We three loaded up and left right away, going by way of St. Joseph, Mo. to visit Faegene's brother Merel. He had been transferred there for some actual instrument flight training and experience.

Going through Oklahoma I looked on the map and found a short cut. What a short cut it was: one mile north, one mile west, one mile north, one mile east, etc. Take my advice: don't take any short cuts in Oklahoma. The newer highway, when I found it, was much straighter. The speed limit during the war, to save much needed rubber and gasoline, was 45 miles per hour, so it was slow traveling.

Arriving in St. Joseph, Missouri, we visited Merel, and I called my command to get a two-day delay en route due to some car trouble. The request was approved and was told, "Get back as quickly as possible! You have been granted that transfer to Palm Springs you wanted." Well, damn! I was learning about the *blankety-blank* army. They must have failed to cancel that transfer.

We turned the trip into a mini vacation and stopped at Hannibal, Mo. to see Tom Sawyer's town, then Springfield to see Lincoln's house, then to the log cabin in the country where he grew up.

When we reached the Pennsylvania Turnpike we were allowed to drive up to sixty miles per hour. This first super highway in the United States had no posted speed limit. What a pleasure to be driving on it. There were no sharp turns, no stop signs and no regular place to turn on or off this highway except at both ends. This was the forerunner of our modern highways. There were no traffic lights, stop signs or towns for the entire distance of the Turnpike.

At New Castle Air Base I quickly cleared the base and we left for Palm Springs with a mattress on top of other bags and boxes on the back seat. This Nash was a big car. We used the mattress as a bed so we could alternate driving day and night. We did stop to see the Capitol Building in Washington, D.C., taking a picture of Faegene holding baby Sherry. She can prove by that picture she'd seen the Capitol and the Lincoln Memorial. We also visited Mount Vernon.

We next visited the Natural Bridge of Virginia, which was right on our way, and reached Chattanooga, Tennessee about 2:00 a.m. Faegene was driving and stopped to buy a hamburger at a small roadside café. (I was asleep on the mattress). She woke me up to show me ground glass on the hamburger. That was scary.

As we pulled away from the small café there was a police car tailing us. Why? We decided we'd keep going unless stopped. The police car pulled off when we reached the city limits. What was going on? Faegene said, "I just want to get away from here." We were glad to be away from Chattanooga. I'm still a little nervous whenever I visit Chattanooga even today.

We went on to Shreveport, Louisiana, where we visited my sister Gertrude and her husband, Edward Tipton. Ed had returned from England after flying 64 missions in B-26 Martin Marauder medium bombers, and was spending the rest of the war teaching bomber pilots in the Martin B 26 bomber school at the Shreveport Army Field. Doing that was about as dangerous as flying combat. Before Pearl Harbor Ed had been a Canadian flight instructor in Toronto, Canada. He had been an inch too tall, six feet two, to be accepted in the Army Air Force. After Pearl Harbor, though, he was accepted into the U.S. Army Air Force as a pilot, and left Toronto. He was assigned to fly in the smallest cockpit of all combat planes, the P-39. As he was so uncomfortable flying in the small cockpit, he was lucky to be sick in the hospital when his P-39 Squadron was sent overseas. He was then assigned to a B-26 Squadron. There was plenty of cockpit room for him in the B-26s.

After a short visit we traveled on to McCamey to unpack and overhaul our eight-cylinder Nash Ambassador. Lige McCullough, a good mechanic, and I did the actual overhaul.

Before leaving we bought a small evaporator air conditioner for our car window, to help keep Sherry (and us) cool while crossing the Arizona desert. The little air conditioner held some ice or water in a pan so that the air was cooled as it was forced over the water or ice and through the damp straw as we drove.

The weather was like Heaven in Palm Springs that fall. At last we could settle down together as a family. We found a nice small apartment and I started getting some training flying a B-25 from the right seat. This was preparatory to being checked out in the A-20, a smaller, faster, light twin-engine bomber. You didn't have a co-pilot in this plane.

The sixth day in Palm Springs I was sitting on the flight line waiting for an A-20 to be brought in for my first solo flight, when a corporal came rushing up to me and asked if I was Babcock. I admitted I was. He said I was to check in at our squadron office at once. "Oh. Oh." I thought, "This is not good."

I was right. The squadron lieutenant informed me I was to leave the post at once for an overseas assignment, by way of Nashville, Tennessee. We had only been there six days. The orders specified that I was not to take my family with me. Isn't the Army great? So considerate and caring. I was allowed barely enough time to get to Nashville. Army politics had just reared its ugly head. I realized the transfer was made to meet a quota for Palm Springs Air Base so they would not have to send any of their personnel overseas. I was transferred all the way across the continent to take his place.

Faegene and I had been looking forward for nine months to finally being able to enjoy some time together with our little daughter. How I hated to tell Faegene. It just wasn't right. Yes, she was very disappointed. There was just no other choice for us. Of course it was not the absolute worst thing that could happen, but….

We were forced to accept it again and packed up and left. We planned to go through Reno where Merel was now in training. I had been in the Army for eight months and Faegene and I had not been together quite three weeks. She had been staying with her parents all this time, and our stay in a "paradise" was over in six days. Of course this was wartime, but what a way to run an Army.

We only had time to spend one night in Reno visiting Merel. We continued the next day, crossing the barren state of Nevada. Have you ever driven across Nevada at forty-five miles an hour? If not, then, I advise you not to, as it is a long, lonely, dry and boring trip. We finally reached Las Vegas and then continued across part of Utah and Arizona to Texas. We quickly unpacked the car and Faegene and I caught the train in Odessa for Nashville, Tennessee, leaving Sherry with her grandparents, Mommy and Pop Eddleman.

Sherry had surprised me several times while we were returning from California, by turning to her mother and saying: "Mommy, take your baby." She sounded so poignant, and I was so proud of her, already talking at less than two years old. I talked, too, at about that age, I was told. Mother said that Daddy heard me say something like "Huttup" and he was so proud of me. Mother didn't have the heart to tell him I was actually saying "Shut up."

I took Faegene with me to Nashville against the Army's orders. My train tickets called for a transfer to Nashville at St Louis, and guess what: when changing trains at St. Louis I accidentally left my briefcase filled with all my orders on that train, which continued to N.Y., N. Y.

Well, here I was back at Berry Field, Nashville, Tennessee, again. "Where are my orders? Oh, heavens! They must be on the train going to New York." That was all I could say. I was then told I'd be notified when my orders were returned to Nashville. I was supposed to turn in my I.D. card, but I had already maneuvered to keep it. With this card I could pass in and out of the gate of the Field. I had been on orders to be shipped out the next day, but now I couldn't be, without those orders and papers.

For the next thirty days Faegene and I enjoyed eating out at the Cross Keys and the Andrew Jackson restaurants, visiting the sights of Nashville including the Parthenon, a duplicate of the original, built on a hill in Nashville. We also did some shopping, buying Faegene a full-length fur coat and myself an overcoat. Nashville is pretty cold in the winter.

We were enjoying a second honeymoon, but even having a month it ended all too quickly for us. I felt we had needed that time together.

I had been reporting to the field every day, and then, one morning, I was told the orders were in and my plane would be leaving the next day. I met the lieutenant who would be deadheading with me, Lieutenant Horace Pietsch, from Cleveland, Ohio. He shared with me that his wife had just had a baby girl the day before in Cleveland, Ohio, but he wasn't allowed off the base. He never got to see his baby girl, as in three months he was killed in an airplane crash at Jorhat, India.

I went back to the hotel and told Faegene I had to leave the next day. It was agony again for both of us. We had been going through these good-byes ever since I'd volunteered, and it was becoming harder each time. There was a definite possibility this could be our last good-bye. There is nothing fair about war. The only important thing was the war and the Army Air Force, not the individual. I can still see in my mind and feel in my heart the pain and the terrible sinking feeling we both had. But, as I said, that was war, and many millions of us had to go through the trauma of saying good-bye. Too many of them were final ones.

Chapter 9

Leaving the United States

I left Faegene at the hotel room door early the next morning, tears in our eyes, lumps in our throats, unable to say more than "I love you." My thoughts flashed through my head, picturing her on the train, physically ill, (she had a cold) and fending for herself on the overloaded train. She'd have to change trains, too. I couldn't help but feel I had let her down.

Piestsch and I left Nashville that morning as passengers in a C-47, flying to Homestead Field, Miami, Florida, for two days of modifications on the airplane.

I spent some time walking around Miami Beach by myself, absorbing as much of the good old U. S. as I could. I walked on the sandy beach, seeing the people enjoying their vacation time on Miami Beach, oblivious to men like me on the way to foreign countries to protect their freedom. I just wanted to cram into my memories as much of the U.S. I could.

I found a pay phone and called Faegene, hoping she would be home by then. She was. She answered the phone. Yes, she'd been sick with a cold but was home with her parents. She told me she had to stand up part of the way home and sit on her suitcases the rest of the time. I told her where I was and told her good-bye one more time. I had been worried about her so much and felt relieved knowing she was safely at home. I planned to send letters when I could, but knew that receiving my mail would be delayed until I was assigned a station.

Well, we took off that night, and were commanded not to open our orders for several hours. On finally opening our orders we found that Pietsch and I were to report to Casablanca, French Morocco, Africa, for re-assignment. What were we thinking? Que sera sera. (What will be will be).

- Puerto Rico

We arrived over the island of Puerto Rico just after daylight. When I looked down I exclaimed: "Hey Pietsch, look at the mountains under us."

"Yeah, and look at that dense vegetation on them," was his reply. So, this must be the San Juan Hill, Teddy Roosevelt, the former president of the United States and his "Rough Riders" fought for years ago. This was where he said, "Walk softly but carry a big stick." Thick, green vegetation covered all the mountains. In a short time we reached Berinquin Field, Puerto Rico, our destination. The field was located on the level land on the southeast part of the Island, not far from the city of San Juan.

There was a million dollar officer's club on the airfield, hanging over the Caribbean Sea on a one hundred foot bluff. In record time Pietsch and I were sitting by a huge picture window overlooking a beach and the Caribbean Sea, sipping frozen daiquiris. Those were the best frozen-daiquiris I'd tasted (probably my first), and it made me feel like a millionaire. The bartender told us he'd been a New York bartender before he joined the Army Air Corps. Nothing is too good for the good old Army Air Corps.

After the daiquiris and a dinner, Pietsch and I went over to the PX and bought some souvenirs. I sent Faegene a woman's purse made entirely of a small baby alligator hide, including its head. I purchased about six bottles of Puerto Rican rum and a box of cigars to take along for myself. Pietsch also sent home some souvenirs.

We asked about a golf course and were soon playing golf. We were warned it would shower, which it did, at two thirty as predicted. I wondered how one could get assigned to this field? Probably by knowing the President of the United States.

The weather was pleasant even though it was late October and we enjoyed the golf. What an idyllic setting for a golf course, tall date palms, banana trees, a cool breeze from the nearby Mediterranean and plenty of sunshine. We thought of the cold weather back in Nashville. What a wonderful place this would be to spend the winter.

The next morning we took off for British Guyana, flying close by Trinidad, looking down at the town on the coast of this mountainous Island. We continued our flight over water to the airport near Georgetown, British Guiana, South America. In the airport there was a live Ant Eater on a leash, the first we'd ever seen. After supper I joined a poker game and won about seventy-five dollars. I wasn't a good poker player, just lucky that time. I quit while I was ahead in spite of some complaints.

- On To Belem, Brazil, and Across the Amazon Jungle

The next morning we flew across the Orinoco River jungle, and finally, that afternoon we began to cross the mouth of the great Amazon River. At the point where we crossed it was some 120 miles wide. Island after island we crossed. Some larger ones were pasturing cattle. Where the Amazons waters reached into the ocean, there was a sharp line separating the lighter weight muddy Amazon water from clear Atlantic Ocean. As we approached Belen, the jungles appeared quite thick with under-brush. I wondered how hard it had been to clear the runway out of that thick jungle.

The airport at Belem, Brazil, was just across the Amazon River. Jungle surrounded the airfield on the three other sides. After landing we looked up at the trees, which seemed to be of two heights in the jungle, some nearly twice as tall as the others. The tallest trees must have been nearly 200 feet high. What a thrill to be right beside the Amazon River we'd heard and read about so much. I could now believe the stories I'd read about adventures on the Amazon and the Amazon Jungle.

After supper we put our tired bodies to bed. Early breakfast was memorable as we were served fresh, sweet pineapple with our eggs. For "dessert" I received three mosquito bites while walking to the airplane. At least one was an anopheles, carrying Malaria, I found out about ten days later, when I became sick with Malaria.

I took another good look at the Amazon Jungle around us and wondered how it would be to explore that awesome jungle and river.

After getting into the airplane to leave, two soldiers came aboard, closed the door, and sprayed DDT inside the plane and on us. Any mosquitoes we carried away with us were dead!

We were then flying over more Amazon jungles for many, many miles, just solid jungle under us except for an occasional tiny clearing about the size of a football field or even smaller. We could usually see some water in those tiny clearings. From time to time there would be a huge tree reaching above the jungle canopy, covered with bright red bougainvillea. How beautiful they were, their brightly colored blooms standing out above the level of the jungle some twenty five to thirty feet.

Flying farther south, the jungle was gradually shrinking in appearance, becoming more like the desert of West Texas I had left nearly a year ago. We were approaching the equator and the sun seemed to be getting brighter, or was it our imagination? The temperature was rising just like it does in West Texas as the day progresses.

As is normal over hot dry country, the air became rough. I was used to flying in hot rough air but one of us wasn't: 2nd Lieutenant Cotler, from Brooklyn, New York. Like Pietsch and me, he was just one of the three passengers, and he was becoming nauseated. He undoubtedly had never experienced flying in rough air. He actually thought the pilot was causing the bouncing effect. He went to the cockpit and complained to the pilot flying the ship and made such a fuss about it the pilot ordered him to stay out of the cockpit.

After we arrived in Natal, Brazil, Pietsch and I heard Cottler complaining to the operations officer, wanting to court marshal our pilot. Pietsch and I winked at the operations officer and took Lieutenant Cotler under both his arms and carried him outside. We sat him down and talked to him, explaining the rough air to him. Can you believe that guy? He was inexperienced and loud, as well as out of place. When he accumulated a little experience I'm sure he would realize his mistake. Later on he was flying the Hump in the CBI. He found some really rough air there.

There was a wait of three days at Natal for favorable winds, as the distance to our next stop at Ascension Island in the Atlantic Ocean was quite a long trip.

Several of the waiting airmen went swimming in the ocean nearby. Remember, this is barely south of the Equator. They were cautioned about sunburn, but most paid no mind. Every day, for two or three days, they spent time on the beach. Several days later some of these men had to be hospitalized when they reached Marrakech, French Morocco. I talked to one of those men years later. He said they had been badly burned by that hot sun, had run fever and were quite sick from that overexposure.

- Ascension Island

Natal was our jumping off place for overseas. Ascension Island was only one mile wide and three miles long, some 600 miles west of Africa in the Atlantic Ocean. The best time to take off for Ascension Island was at night, so that we would have the added visibility of daylight to see the Island when arriving. The south end of the island was a mountain nearly 3000 feet high, virtually always covered by clouds, which helped us to spot the island in daylight. Of course, there was also a radio beacon for our Direction Finder to pick up when in range. With our navigator on board he took fixes from the stars, so we had no trouble finding Ascension Island. We were right on target and landed on the one-mile long runway, which reached ocean to ocean. Had we overshot the runway we would have ended up in it.

Instead of going to bed in daylight, I walked down the 100 foot drop off, to the edge of the water, and became fascinated watching the black sea water piranha washing up onto the beach, then riding and sliding with waves back into the ocean. These black salt-water Piranhas were shaped like overgrown perch. Before seeing them I had thought about going swimming in that beautiful ocean water. They changed my mind.

I found a few seashells, but mostly I just enjoyed walking and looking. After about an hour I wandered back to the mess hall for some dinner, a large steak of fresh Tuna fish.

Pietsch came in while I was eating and suggested we play some golf. "What, out here? Where?" I asked.

"There's a golf course here, believe it or not," he answered.

That part of the Island was very dry and covered with small scrub brush and no grass, but Pietsch insisted. We checked out some clubs and started playing golf on the island in the middle of the Atlantic Ocean. Well, the golf course was called a golf course, but that really was stretching the imagination a bit. When a sergeant drove up in a jeep and started talking with us, we became interested in what he had to say. It seems his job was to furnish fish for the mess hall there as well as for Natal, Brazil, and at Roberts's field in Africa. He asked if we'd like to go fishing. "Sure" we answered. We were glad to abandon our attempt at golfing, and went with him. He had a fishing boat and the works. He baited two bamboo-fishing poles and we shortly found ourselves trolling at a fast clip on the ocean. Each of us caught a fish the sergeant called Del Valles. Mine weighed about twenty-five pounds, and really put up a lot of fight. Pietsch's fish was at least fifteen pounds, and he also had a real "thrill" reeling it in.

We really enjoyed this little trip out on the deep water in the middle of the Atlantic Ocean. The sergeant told us he caught large tuna by fishing deep, and had no trouble furnishing the three mess halls, Robert's Field in Africa, Natal in Brazil and Ascension Island, with all the tuna they wanted.

He told us about the mountain on the other end of the island, on top of which he obtained his Bamboo fishing poles. We had about forgotten about the mountain because it was mostly covered with clouds and out of sight, although only about two miles away.

This Island had been a British possession since about 1600 A.D. There was no fresh water on the Island at all, so the British had cemented a floor on the western slope of the high ridge, to catch the rain for a large cistern. It took about fifty years of slave labor to dig the tunnel eight feet high and about ten feet wide through the ridge to the east side. On a small level area on the east side of the mountain in the cooler air of about 3,000 feet, two lovely homes complete with gorgeous gardens and grass lawns had been built. These were the homes for the caretakers of the Island. The water for the two families was gravity fed through the tunnel from the underground water storage of the rainwater caught on the west side of the mountain. I read in his book, "Charles Darwin," about his visiting this Island and taking samples of the rocks. He stated there were people living in a home with a garden and a grass lawn.

There was a narrow road, difficult even for a jeep, going up the mountain to the houses. We had to back up to get around some of the curves.

A black man with a cute monkey sitting on his shoulder materialized from the side of the road just below the houses, so we stopped and talked with him. He told us he was a descendant of the slaves who had spent fifty years building the tunnel, from 1620 to 1670. His pronunciation was very British, and coming from a black man, it was intriguing to us.

The monkey suddenly jumped upon my shoulder and began fishing in my shirt pocket where he quickly found some chewing gum. He helped himself, and hopped off carrying the chewing gum. The monkey surprised us and gave us a good laugh.

How interesting this island was, all by itself in the Atlantic Ocean, wholly dependent upon ships from England for their food and supplies. What a welcome sight it must have been for the sailing ships of past times to sight this land. Of course, with the runway built many airplanes will now land and can supply the two families that live on the Mountain.

The sergeant said, "Let's walk through the tunnel and I'll show you the other side." Sure enough, the tunnel was roomy enough to walk through. How ingenious of the English back in 1620 to establish their supply of fresh water. On the west side of the mountain the area had pavement or concrete to catch the rainwater and it was directed into a large cistern. There were some pipes lying in a ditch along the side in the tunnel. We wondered what was the real advantage of owning this small Island, which had only a shallow port and not much other value we could see? Had it been worth their trouble and expense? Now we go on to Africa and Casablanca.

That night we flew to Freetown, Sierra Leone, in the Equatorial Jungles of Africa, and went right to bed. All we saw there was jungle and tropical vegetation. Next morning after breakfast, we took off for the few hours' flight to the next stop, Dakar, Senegal, Africa.

Although this trip was enjoyable, we were constantly concerned and worried about our loved ones back home. If only they could have been sharing with us the wonders we were seeing. Pietsch and I were able to share with each other, which made it better for each of us. We did not know the future, but we did know we were to do our part in this terrible world war. Pietsch and I both had a young daughter at home. He had not even seen his or even a picture of her.

Dakar was a poor town on the edge of a large desert, close enough to the Equator to be hot even in November. We again had to wait for a favorable wind as the next hop was quite long again. During our wait for the wind change we took the time to go swimming in the Atlantic Ocean, and what fun it turned out to be.

The beach was all sand but became as hard as rock when wet. When dry that sand was extremely loose. The waves came in much higher than our heads, so we dove through them as they came rolling in. This was a new experience for me. What fun it was in diving into those ten-foot waves. We hollered back and forth, but when one of us missed the wave, it wasn't very funny. Helpless, we were rolled and skidded back up on the beach by the wave. Many times the memory of those waves rolling in too high to see past comes flashing back into my mind. How very much we had enjoyed that intermission in our lives. Horace Pietsch at least had some fun in the last few months of his life.

On the beach was a native boy with a grown camel, which kept trying to bite whoever came close. Pietsch suggested I take a ride. I answered, "If you think it would be so much fun why don't you do it?"

He answered, "His breath's too bad, and beside that, he keeps trying to bite me." I agreed with him. The camel's breath was really bad. His teeth looked bad, too, but maybe all camels have bad teeth.

After a three-day wait, we took off for our next stop, Marrakech, French Morocco, Africa. Our flight took us over more desert and few villages. We were flying nearly parallel to the coast, going north up the west coast of Africa. We saw few signs of roads or people.

When about halfway to Marrakech, our radio operator told us he intercepted a message sent from an A-26, flying near our location. He reported to Marrakech he'd lost an engine and was continuing to Marrakech. We looked and looked, but didn't see him. Arriving in Marrakech we found the A-26 already there. Single engine performance like that was quite impressive. It had flown on one engine faster than the C-47 had on two engines, for about 500 miles.

After going to Marakech for supper that night, a group of us were returning from the town in a covered six-by-six army truck, with some young inexperienced fighter pilots. They, like us, had just arrived, and they were arguing that the flying ability of a fighter pilot was better than other pilots. I hadn't opened my mouth during the entire ride to the field but just as we turned in to the field I made the mistake of saying something in an attempt to appease the argument. One drunken fighter pilot took offence and said to me, "I'll knock your block off when we get out." I was at the back and just eased down out of the back off the truck when it stopped. I stood there as the young fighter pilot came clambering out of the truck. He caught his foot on the tailgate and fell flat on his face, which was quite a fall. He struggled up and cried out to me, "Don't hit me again, Lieutenant, don't hit me again." I answered, "Okay," and walked off.

Next day Pietsch and I caught an airplane for Casablanca, as the C-47 we had been flying in all this way, flew on to be delivered to England.

We were assigned to cots in the Italian Consulate building in Casablanca, which was being used for us transients. We shared a large room with other transients, and there we were stuck for a month waiting for orders. O.K., there was a Red Cross building downtown, and it became our headquarters.

We could buy a few candy bars and some food, thank goodness. Chairs, tables and stationery were available for our use. Other soldiers were there with whom we could play cards and talk. One night there was a native dance performed by an Arab girl dancing barefooted and in native dress. The Red Cross was cooperative and helpful to all us service men.

Pietsch and I wandered around the town looking at the few stores that were open. We went a short way into the Old Medina, quickly getting the impression we were out of place. Streets were about fifteen feet wide and lowest in the middle, so that everything swept out of the houses would wash on out of the Medina down the middle of the paved street. There were shops just outside the Old Medina selling handmade items such as billfolds made from camel leather.

There were more Arabs on the streets of Casablanca than any other nationalities, although there were many refugees in the City from the war zone on the continent. Two Polish refugees operated a small shop selling firs. Casablanca was pretty far south and on the western Atlantic Ocean, so we wondered at the idea of selling furs in such a warm climate. These two men spoke only German and French. I spoke to them in my limited German and they told me they were from Poland. They had left ahead of the German invasion. All they had to sell were the furs they had escaped with. We gave them a chocolate bar and they were thrilled. Many French and Spanish people had also escaped the possible German occupation of their country, and were living in Casablanca.

After we had been in Casablanca for several days, I became sick with a high fever. We had stopped taking the Atabrine tablets protecting us from Malaria, and were still staying in the Italian Consulate. I asked Pietsch to go to the field and arrange to get me out to the base hospital.

He came back and said they told him I would have to get up and go there. I didn't think I could physically do so, and I asked Pietsch to find me some Atabrine tablets if he could. He found some somewhere, and I started recovering within less than 24 hours of taking a few tablets. I heard years later Atabrine wasn't a cure for Malaria, but it sure worked for me.

I don't remember how we met this army captain, but he was stationed at Casablanca and had an office at the airfield. He showed Pietsch and me around Casablanca in his Jeep. He even fed us a meal at a mess hall in the city that was under his supervision. ("Mess" was soldier talk for an army dining room.) The captain, as it turned out, was in charge of all the Army mess halls in and around Casablanca.

One day the captain took us for a ride in his Jeep with his beautiful French secretary. He drove us all over town while she kept up a running conversation in French. The captain also spoke French fluently, but neither Pietsch nor I could. She was a lovely vivacious lady who spoke French rapidly with such enthusiasm. She included us all in her exuberance as if we could understand her. What a beautiful language French is, especially when spoken by a beautiful French lady. She was also married, and owned a small sidewalk café where we stopped for a glass of wine, courtesy of the establishment.

While touring the countryside we saw an Arab plowing a field with a camel, hitched alongside a small donkey. The captain explained that the donkey was guiding the camel, which was doing all the work. How strange it looked, that little bit of a donkey and that huge camel harnessed together and plodding up and down the field.

Another time the captain took us to a mansion where our general was living. This was a privately owned mansion that our armed forces had apparently confiscated for the duration. The floors were all of marble, statues in evidence everywhere, and banana trees growing in the courtyard. There was also a swimming pool. In the courtyard was a large meeting room with cushioned pillow-covered benches extending all the way around the room. The light fixtures in the ceiling were carved into the wooden ceiling itself, in beautiful hand-made designs. We didn't get to go up the marble stairs to the upper floor, but I'm sure the upstairs was every bit as luxurious as well. I understood the owner had brought in Persian artisans to do the beautiful designs in the ceilings.

We were in contact occasionally with refugees who spoke English. One of these was in a conversation with me and casually asked if the Republic of Texas was near the United States. I answered, "Yes. As a matter of fact, it is located between the United States and Mexico."

Of course, being from Texas, I am modest, but I heard another Texan say one day, "When I die, don't send me to heaven, just send me back to Texas."

- Temporary Assignment to Casablanca Airfield

I was ordered to move out to the airfield and was put on flying status as co-pilot on a C-46 Curtis Commando transport. I felt right at home in the C-46, as the engines and electric propellers were the same type used in the B- 26 s I'd been flying in the States.

On my first flight from Casablanca we carried passengers. We landed at Tripoli where another crew took over our plane, flying on to Cairo. We rested while waiting our turn to fly another plane on to Cairo. We would then have a one-day layover in Cairo, so when our name appeared for flight we would fly the next plane to Cairo. This rotation was repeated in reverse as we returned to Tripoli from Cairo, then on to Casablanca. This arrangement gave me a chance while in Egypt to visit the Egyptian pyramids.

On my first flight we were carrying a plane full of armed forces personnel and flew at 10,000 feet to stay above a sand storm on the Sahara Desert. I was walking down the aisle when I recognized one of our passengers: Colonel Dietrich. "Colonel Dietrich, What are you doing over here in Africa?" "I could ask you the same thing, Babcock." We had known each other for nearly two years while he was the Commanding Officer of the Flight School at Fort Stockton, Texas. We had a happy re-union. The colonel was likable, and we enjoyed our unexpected visit. The Army Air Corp was indeed "shrinking" the world.

The hangers at Tripoli showed the effects from our bombing, large holes and ripped tin. We must have been fighting Rommel in that part of Africa. After dark we continued our trip from Tripoli by way of Benghazi, turning a few degrees to the right toward Cairo. We flew directly over the battlefield near Benghazi where the Allies had recently won the battle for Africa. Because the Germans had installed a powerful radio station on an island, it bent our radio beam so we used the shoreline for our navigation. Had we followed that beam on past the bend in the coastline, we would likely have ended up close to German fortifications on the sea. Looking down at the desert we could see, even at night, the damaged tanks and equipment left in the sand near Benghazi.

- Cairo, Egypt

In Cairo I checked into the Sheppard Hotel, the famous old hotel I'd read about. Shortly after the war the Sheppard Hotel would catch fire and burn to the ground. What a shame.

The next night I attended a performance at a nightclub there in the hotel. I was quite impressed. The first part of the show was the usual beautiful barefoot dancing girls with flowing, exotic clothing, not much different from the dancing girls in the U.S. After the dancing, however, the curtain rose, exposing a man painted completely in gold color, posing as the statue of the "Discus Thrower." He then slowly changed his position smoothly into "The Thinker," then into other postures of famous Greek statues. He would change his pose slowly and hold each for about two minutes. If only I could have shared such a show with my family.

Next morning I caught a bus to the pyramids. There were shoeshine boys at the bus stop, who wouldn't let me get past them until I let one of them shine my shoes. They even deliberately stepped on my shoes. I quickly hired one so the others would let me board the bus.

I viewed the teeming city from the bus as we passed through the town and crossed the river bridge to the pyramids on the other side of the Nile River. Seeing this exotic city was a thrill, and I tried to remember all I saw, but only retained some memory of Egyptian architecture and the crowded streets. Across the river was a desert of sand, no farms.

I walked around and through the Sphinx, full of wonder at this odd statue. After a few minutes I spent observing the Sphinx, I walked over to the nearby pyramid.

The Sahara Desert seems to extend west from the Nile River almost to Casablanca. The white sand glistened in the sunlight all around the pyramids. On the north side of the pyramid was a little sandwich stand with a concrete platform and a few sightseers, with the usual young boy selling rides on his camel.

I ordered a sandwich and some ginger beer, before a guide led us up the side of the pyramid to a large crack. This crack revealed a hallway, which, in turn, led to a square room well inside, containing an empty rock coffin. I was simply amazed at the huge rectangular blocks of rock fitting so perfectly. They were cut approximately four by eight feet. We asked ourselves, "How did they do it?" Even with today's equipment it would be a big challenge to put them in place as the Egyptians did. The mystery of the building of the pyramids was more of a mystery to me after having been there. Just think, this area was only a tiny example of their works.

There was much farming on the east bank along the Nile River reflecting the richness of the delta. I could see the farmers and the animals working these rich fields and walking on the trails between the farms. All farming was on the east side of the River Nile there at Cairo.

Well, time came to report back to the airfield, so another bus ride through the uniquely designed architecture of the city, going through hordes of Egyptians still crowding the streets of Cairo.

Our assigned airplane was loaded and ready to fly, so away we went for our return trip to Casablanca by way of Tripoli, fully loaded with Coca Cola. Coca Cola? Yes, that was a surprise. There must have been a Coca Cola bottling company in Cairo.

I caught a slight cold on the return trip, as the heaters weren't working and the cold air was blowing like an air-conditioner, the cold air hitting the top of my head. When we began our descent from 13,000 feet I could feel the pressure building up in my ears. To protect my ears we slowed our descent to ease the pressure on my eardrums. One ear bled a little, but there was nothing else we could do. The next day I went to the flight surgeon, but there was nothing he could do for me but ground me for a week.

We arrived back in Casablanca for Christmas. Pietsch and I enjoyed ours at the Red Cross Center in town, where we were served a big turkey dinner. It helped ease the thoughts of home and family. I did get a letter, though, and that helped my Christmas spirit considerably. I pictured in my mind the Christmas in McCamey and Sonora and my heart ached for my loved ones.

December 1944—Casablanca, French Morocca, North Africa

Kenneth and Pietsch

An Arab vendor selling his potatoes

Pietsch still hadn't received orders for reassignment. The day after Christmas while we were walking down the main street of Casablanca, a well-dressed young Arab man spoke to us in excellent English. He handed us his business card and invited us to come to a New Year's party in his apartment to celebrate. His name was Abdul, Abdul the Third. We gratefully accepted the invitation, and were anxious to see how these people lived and would celebrate the New Year.

During wartime sugar was a rare commodity, so the cookies and cakes for the party were not very sweet but still rather tasty. The excellent Muscatel Wine made up for any lack of sugar in the cookies, and there were at least a couple of cases of this excellent wine. Pietsch and I enjoyed sipping a little of this wine while rubbing elbows with the well-dressed crowd in this fourth floor apartment, right in the center of downtown Casablanca. The host was gracious and this was a party for us to remember. Although few of the attending people spoke English the party was much like being home in the U.S. We looked down at the nice apartment on the third floor of the building, and looked out on the small balcony so common in Casablanca.

On the streets of Casablanca - December 1944

Baby carried on the back of small child

Main street of Casablanca

Pietsch and Kenneth
Still awating orders
December 1944

Three months after these pictures were taken, Lt. Horace
Pietsch crashed and died at Jorhat, India

Curtiss C-46D "Commando" — Built for the Hump

A few minutes before midnight a well-dressed lady joined the party, and at exactly midnight the lights were turned off and this lady, apparently an opera singer, sang "Ave Maria" a cappella. How beautiful and impressive it was to Pietsch and me.

Here we were in the heart of a foreign city, thousands of miles from home, attending a New Year's party, listening to a beautiful soprano singing Ave Maria. This experience put our picture of the Arab people in a different light. For the first time I realized that all Arabs were not necessarily Moslem but could be of any religion, and some of the Arabs were well mannered and educated. Most native Arabs we had seen on the streets wore white cloth, sometimes several layers at a time. It was said the materials were not replaced, just added to when they got dirty or ragged. We had observed a few of the men squatting on the sidewalks in the middle of the city, and noticed urine running out from under their sheets. I understand, of course, that there are many different tribes of Arabs who have various customs, beliefs and living conditions in Africa. I'm glad that we met Abdul Abdul the Third and the class of better-educated people than others we had seen.

On the streets the native women wore white material and covered their hair and faces. Their eyes were dark and seemed to us to be a little flirtatious. Most of the youth dressed more like the rest of the world—that is, the boys did. I don't remember seeing many young girls on the streets. The ladies and gentlemen at the New Years party had been dressed just as we do in the States. Although we couldn't speak their language, they made us feel welcome.

Several times during the day we would hear the prayers called out by the Moslems. They would always kneel down and face the east. Also in the mornings on the streets there were venders carrying large basket of fresh loafs of French bread in a basket, loudly calling out their wares. Their voices were clearly heard, as there was little other noise in the streets.

- Pietsch Re-assigned

Only a few days into the New Year Pietsch received orders to depart for India and just like that, he was gone. Boy, did I miss him. Our companionship had helped each other adapt to our situation and I will always have memory of him in my heart.

The day after Pietsch left, I went to a local theater showing an American film with the Arabian language dubbed in. I don't remember the show, but I remember it was hot and close in the theatre building. A damp cloth was passed around, and everyone in turn wiped his face, except me. Attending the picture show once was enough for me.

Another experience that could have had a much different ending occurred late in the day. While walking down an empty street I noticed some Arabs blocking the end of the street. I looked back and there were three young men closing in on me from behind. I quickly unfastened my holster and pulled out my loaded "45" automatic pistol. I raised it up ready to use it. All the young men disappeared as if they had melted. I heaved a sigh of relief, but I would certainly have used the gun had any more action developed. Hearing some of the Military Police talking about some of their problems, I knew to protect myself with that pistol, if necessary. I had seen one French lady walking down the street wearing a nice warm jacket, and saw some young men try to yank it off of her shoulder. As I approached, the men quickly ran off.

In the second week of the New Year, my transfer orders came for me to report to Karachi, India for re-assignment. I would have liked to remain in Casablanca, but the army way prevailed. I was a little surprised at the length of time I had already been there. I knew I would really miss those Champagne Cocktails at the downtown Officers' Club. Talk about good. They were so good I had to force myself to stop drinking them after only two.

Within twenty-four hours I'd cleared the post and climbed into a waiting C-46 as a passenger. Some fifty of us sat on metal bench seats along the side of the C-46, facing the center, where our luggage was piled high. We all had parachutes and all our belongings. We were fully loaded. Our destination was Karachi, India, by way of Tripoli, Cairo, and Abadan, Iran.

After re-fueling we left Cairo and climbed up above the Suez Canal with the Red Sea to our right, disappearing into the distance. It was easy to picture in my mind the Red Sea below us opening a channel for Moses. We could even see some of the Holy Land to the north.

Then the Dead Sea came into view. What a strange sight to see a lake 1500 feet below sea level. The washed out ravines led down to the Dead Sea from all directions. There were little, if any, signs of life visible from our distance and altitude. The Bible told about the Essenes living in caves scattered in that rugged terrain, writing scrolls of history before and during the time of Jesus. I could easily see the possibility of many caves being throughout that rugged area.

In another two hours we were above Iraq. The Tigress and Euphrates Rivers could be clearly seen. Wasn't this where the Garden of Eden was thought to be?

We landed late afternoon at Abadan, Iran and boy, was it hot. After re-fuelling the temperature was too hot for us to take off. Heat affects the lifting ability of the air. It was after 2200 hours (ten o'clock at night) before we could safely take off with our load, so I had time to purchase a few souvenirs including a native doll for Sherry.

I worried about our take-off as we sped down the runway, but that C-46 airplane climbed right on up into a cooler stratum of air. It was a dark night and as tired as we were, I think we slept until letting down at Karachi, India several hours later.

A medic crew was waiting for us to give us more shots, although it was only 3:30 in the morning. We followed into the huge dirigible hanger now being used by the Army Air Corps, and were shot and vaccinated. It mattered not that we had been "shot" and vaccinated before we left the States. We were "shot" again. I was standing in line to be shot when I remembered the four bottles of rum in my A-2 bag. I left the line in a run back to our airplane in time to see the crew pitch my A-2 bag down onto the truck. I heard the glass break. Only two bottles were saved.

For several days I smelled like rum as most of my clothes in the A-2 bag were saturated with fine Puerto Rican rum.

During the three days of waiting for orders, we went to town to Karachi. Of interest to us was a small raised platform in the middle of the intersections downtown, with a uniformed policeman on it, directing traffic. His arms waved, controlling that traffic better than our red and green lights back home. The traffic consisted of a few cars and trucks plus horse-drawn carts and many pedestrians.

For a few annas (about six cents) a little boy, who spoke some English, offered to guide us to the zoo. We stopped on the way to watch a cobra and Mongoose demonstration right on the street. We paid a few annas to see the Mongoose and the Cobra battle. The snake was too slow, and had no chance. The snake charmer had to struggle to separate them before the snake was killed. I wondered if the Cobras were more expensive to replace than the mongoose.

We continued our walk to the zoo where we saw the usual animals. The turtles, though, caught our attention. They were the largest I had ever seen. They were giants. Our young guide crawled over the low fence and stood on top of one turtle, who paid no attention to the boy standing on his back, even when the turtle decided to walk around.

After seeing the zoo we wandered around town a little, but there wasn't much else to see in town, so we went back to the army camp early enough to get our supper.

The next day we were interviewed and were asked to volunteer to be stationed in China. No one volunteered. We had already heard enough rumors about China, such as flying behind enemy lines, flying over the high Himalayan Mountains and flying in terrible weather.

Well, they assigned me to Lalminar Hat, Bengal, India. (called Lal Hat, for short). Two of us were assigned to deliver a C-46 there, so we left early in the morning for Agra where we would refuel. Shortly after leaving Karachi the topography turned to rugged and desert-like country. I learned later a cloud of ash from an ancient volcano had hung above this area for about three years. This allowed no rain and little sunlight, leaving a desert across this part of Pakistan. We saw on the top of mountains cities that had been built and completely abandoned. Faint trails went up and down to the abandoned cities, leading to and from the gates in the walls.

By the time we reached the Taj Mahal, there were farms and lots of people to be seen. We flew lower in order to see it better as we circled it. What a magnificent sight. A river flowing behind it was crowded with people doing their laundry and bathing. Fort Agra seen up river a thousand yards or so, was built of red rock, in contrast with the white marble of the Taj Mahal. I understand there were many beautiful gardens at Fort Agra. The landscaping around the Taj Mahal was quite attractively done with shallow pools of water.

- Lalminar Hat, Bengal, India, My New Assignment

Not having the time to see it on foot, we just gassed up our C-46 and took off for Lalminar Hat. Gradually the countryside was appearing greener with a few forests and farms covering the plains. "Lal Hat" was in the south end of the Assam Valley and the north end of the state of Bengal. In the upper reaches of this valley in Assam were our airfields supporting the air supply line to China. Lal Hat was more than 200 miles south of those bases.

Although we arrived in the middle of winter, the temperature was hot and quite humid. Native Indian males only wore loincloths and the women a sara, a kind of loose wrapping or draping, covering most of their body.

Our supper at our newly assigned base was a little disappointing, "Bully Beef" and raisin bread, without the raisins. (The cooked weevils slightly resembled raisins.). Bully Beef was British canned beef, tough and dry. Our food had become worse since leaving Casablanca, and unfortunately would continue to downgrade in China. Spam was served mostly for breakfast, but never served to me in China. The shipping of gasoline across the Hump into China was the highest priority for China; gasoline and war materials were top priority. No food was supposed to be carried over the Hump. Cost of flying gasoline to china was eighty-eight dollars a gallon.

I made one flight from Lal Hat to Mitkiyina, Burma. Mitkiyina is pronounced "Mishenaw." The names are becoming foreign sounding to the English speaking nations, and I read that when the Allies conquered Mandalay later on, Winston Churchill remarked: "Well, thank goodness we've finally captured a town whose name we can pronounce."

The Japanese had just been pushed out of Mitkyina and across the Irrawaddi River, but the tower advised us to put our base leg over the north half of the river to avoid sniper fire from the jungle. After landing we had to walk along flagged pathways to avoid possibly stepping on a land mine. There was one wrecked C-47 aircraft on the field, badly shot-up, so I felt we were close to combat.

Next day, several of us visited the small town of Laminar Hat, a short distance from our field. A railroad stop was all it was. The only substantial building was a red brick schoolhouse used to teach the Indians through the sixth grade only. The British prohibited the vast majority of school children from progressing past the sixth grade.

The rest of the town consisted of open-air markets sitting on the ground, some with a temporary thatched top above with no sides. The appearance of this scene could have been occurring a hundred years ago: a barber shop where the customer sits on the ground while getting a hair cut with shears, food passed out in coconut shells to be eaten with fingers scooping the food into their mouths. Other venders had baskets of fruit being offered for sale, and there were no chairs visible anywhere. Natives just folded their legs and sat on the ground.

There were three longhaired hill people at the barbershop, their hair tangled and dirty. The Indians gathered around and made fun of these hill people, pointing at them and laughing. The Indians themselves were pretty clean as they bathed often in the rivers. I heard that taking a bath was a religious ritual to them. The hill people seemed to accept this attention with good humor. They looked more civilized after getting their long hair trimmed.

A universal habit of all the Indians was that of chewing Betel Nut leaves, containing some white powder (lime) rolled up in them. This concoction turned the interior of their mouths bright red, and their spittle was also bright red. I heard that this was a weak drug. Nearly all men and women, including children, chewed Betel Nut.

I saw only one beggar in the tiny town, a girl about thirteen years old sitting on the ground. It was obvious to all she had a bad infection. No one was paying any attention to her. Beggars were a common sight in India. I have read of professional beggars with twisted members of their bodies, which were self-inflicted, giving them a better chance for "Bockshee" (gifts). All beggars lived at the mercy of their fellow Indians; most were sick and starving, grateful to receive even a few annas (pennies). It was said that in Calcutta each morning wagons were sent through the streets to pick up the bodies of those who died during the night, mostly from starvation.

I took pictures of all the street venders and barbershop, but my camera was stolen two days later with the film still in it. That really made me sick. That film was irreplaceable. I had just purchased the camera in Casablanca for $75.00. The camera with film was taken from my luggage.

That first night in Lal Hat I saw a former flight instructor from Ft. Stockton, so I got together with George Bradford who was stationed in Lal Hat. When I mentioned I had some rum he insisted on having some, so I opened a bottle. We visited and sipped rum until George decided to go to bed. I stayed up. We had emptied the rum bottle, and in a few minutes I began to "feel" it, so I finally turned in also.

Chapter 10

China, the End of the Road

Like it or not, I was transferred to Chanyi, China. The Army Air Corps probably planned all along to send me to China. Why did they even bother to ask me?

I was sent to Chabua to await transport to China. The only way to get to China was by air, and we had to wait a few days on the weather, as personnel at that time were only flown over the Hump, preferably in good weather. I arrived in Chanyi, China late one afternoon, after a beautiful afternoon flight over the Hump. That flight over was the only time I ever really saw the Hump, as in the future it was night and/or solid instruments when I flew across. Yes, it looked quite rugged but beautiful under the late afternoon sun.

Field elevation at Chanyi was 6100 feet and colder than at the 200-foot elevation of the Assam Valley. After all, this was the middle of winter. I was wearing my summer uniform and only my leather flight jacket to keep me warm. I checked in at the BQ (Bachelor's Quarters) office and was assigned to a tent for the night. I was issued two army blankets. I found my tent as darkness was settling in, and there was no light within. The tent was vacant except for 10 empty cots, no heat and no other bedding. At least it had a wooden floor. "Welcome to China, Ken." A friend in Chabua had suggested I bring an extra blanket along and I was sure glad I did.

I crawled onto my cot with my three blankets while still in my clothes. I spent a cold, dark night alone, hearing the drone of the airplanes in the instrument holding patterns directly above my tent, back and forth, back and forth, the engines seemed to roar all night long. I was just plain cold and I was thinking, "Here I am in exotic China. Ha." I slept little and was too cold to be nervous.

A bad winter storm had moved into China that same night. I never met my Commanding Officer since he was flying Chinese soldiers that night and crashed due to heavy icing conditions. Ice causes loss of communication and added weight and caused loss of lift. The pilots could not all bail out, as we didn't furnish parachutes for the Chinese troops. He and his co-pilot were killed while the engineer and radio operator managed to escape out the door.

The next day I was reassigned to a barracks where there were charcoal burning stoves, which kept us warm but emitted a gas that gave everyone a headache after a few hours.

I was called out for flight duty the third night in Chanyi, about 21:30 (9:30 at night) to be co-pilot with a pilot I'd formerly flown with out of New Castle Army Air Base, Delaware. He was a fine pilot and I was happy to be his co-pilot for my first flight in China. He told me to file our flight plan, so I went into the weather room for briefing.

I was given a wind of 125 miles per hour from the NW. I began plotting our course with my E-6B computer, but it couldn't compute that much wind. I had to ask the pilot about it. He laughed and said, "Just divide the wind speed by two, figure the course, and then multiply it all back by two. Simple." I ended up with a 45-degree wind drift correction angle in the C-47 on the first leg and an even larger angle on the second leg. Ceiling was about 500 feet at destination so the flight would be all on instruments. I had never dreamed of such a large wind drift angle.

I am sure it will require some imagination and understanding for pilots not in our theater, to put themselves into the cockpit during flights in the CBI (China-Burma- India) Theater, World War II, and even more so for non-pilots. Our flying was often in turbulent weather, possible with icing conditions and few radio navigational aids. It was a real challenge to our flying knowledge and ability. For myself, I dreaded severe icing conditions more than turbulence. Ice was not only heavy but changed the shape of the airfoil of the wings, reducing the lift and was hard to remove. Having a 45-degree drift correction angle that night was so extreme it was almost unbelievable. As far as I know there is no other place on Earth with any worse flying conditions than those encountered in the CBI. What an education this assignment to China was going to be.

Our flight continued as planned. It was important that co-pilots gain such experience as I was getting that night, in order to be qualified as first pilot in this Theater. We would need all the experience we could get before taking over as first pilot.

The first pilot told me, as we approached the fighter base in north east China, that at this location we make all turns to the west in our instrument let down, as there was a line of mountains to the east. We had been flying at about 14,000 feet, and were letting down to the field elevation of 3500 feet, using instrument letdown approach. In breaking out of the clouds there was only a dim light visible in the darkness dead ahead. That was the runway marker. The light being so dim helped keep Japanese pilots from seeing the runway easily at night.

As we approached the runway dim runway lights became visible, facilitating our landing. We landed and were led to our parking spot by a dimly lighted jeep.

An unloading crew drove up and started rolling out our cargo of bombs, bouncing them on each other as they dropped out the door. I was already nervous, so this action caused me to tell the unloading crew of Chinese, emphatically with hand signals, to wait until we were clear.

When walking toward the flight operations shack in complete darkness, we were suddenly accosted by a guttural voice in a strange language. The pilot quickly answered, "Maygua, Joe, Maygua. Ding How, Joe, Ding How." This interpreted to: "American, Joe, American. All is well, Joe, all is O.K." Then this big Chinese stepped forward, gun in hand, and said, "Ding How," and allowed us to continue. Upon our inquiry about the guard, the operations told us the Japanese had been sneaking onto the field at night and slicing the tires of the B-25 bombers stationed there.

In planning our flight back to our home field we were told the field was closed to flight traffic due to low cloud cover, so we planned our flight to Kunming. It was 100 miles from our base but was open with a 400-foot ceiling. The first pilot explained that being on the edge of a large lake, surrounded by mountains, the ceiling at Kunming was usually high enough for instrument landings and sometimes completely clear when every other field in the area was closed. I wondered what else would happen on my first flight in China.

We took off for Kunming, climbing up into the darkness and clouds, planning to fly at 16,000 feet as assigned by traffic control. We settled down to climbing steadily on course, everything fine, instruments glowing from the black light focused directly on the instrument panel, engines running smoothly. Then silence. Both engines had quit. Immediately the pilot checked over the panel while I checked the carburetor heat and gas gages. He pumped the throttles a little and adjusted the mixture controls. The engines began to sputter, then smoothed out with increasing RPMs (prop revolutions per minute) up to normal climbing power. The crew chief then announced that the wings were icing up. We aimed our flashlights on the leading edge to gauge the amount of ice forming. It was quite visible.

Fortunately we had one of the few C-47 aircraft with good de-icing boots. We turned them on and off alternately inflating and deflating to break some ice off the leading edge. We used them intermittently, as leaving them on too long at a time caused the ice to form over the open places, and be no longer effective. After a little while we re-applied the deicer, again breaking more ice off the leading edge of the wings. A loud noise like someone hitting the outside of the fuselage with a sledgehammer startled me, and I realized the pilot had revved up the engines, slinging ice off the props. He had also turned on the deicing fluid (alcohol) onto the windshields and the propellers to help loosen the ice. Whenever the engines began to run rough again we could rev up the props and sling off more of the ice, which in turn pounded the fuselage with ice chunks. The pilot said we would try to climb higher to get above the icing level. I kept watch on the carburetor intake temperature and instruments.

Fortunately, we were not loaded, so we were able to climb higher, reaching 21,000 feet and above the icing level. The ice began melting. Just behind the cockpit the fuselage would show on the outside many indentations, and possibly holes as the result of the ice bombardment slung off the props.

The ice had melted by the time we reached the Kunming area. There was a huge opening in the clouds above the lake. We were directed to land across the lake from Kunming at a fighter base called Chengkung. We again entered instrument conditions and again I was told to make these turns to the west, as there was a range of mountains to the east here also.

After landing we checked in with Operations. Our base was still closed, so we went to bed. Our plane was flown, with a local crew, back across the Hump to pick up another load of gasoline.

When I awakened a few hours later, I went to the base mess hall and had hotcakes with syrup. I decided things weren't so bad if we could have hotcakes with syrup. There was a little bit of grittiness, but that was no big problem. Would you believe, this was the only time I saw or had any pancakes in my entire stay in China? This being a fighter base, it seems they had better food than the Air Transport Command Bases where I was stationed.

Having most of the day to spend waiting on the weather, I looked around and saw P-38s in their protective compounds along the runway, partly protected in case of air attack.

One empty compound was badly smoked up, and an airdrome officer standing close by told me a loaded P-38 crashed into it on take-off, loaded with bombs.

I looked at the airdrome officer, and realized I was looking at F/O Murphy, the student I'd had a year ago in Gibbs Field, Fort Stockton, Texas. He was the flight cadet who had the sickness problem. Here was a pilot that would not have been there except for my encouragement. We had quite a reunion, telling each other how strange that we both ended up in China. F/O Murphy had just arrived in China, as had I, and he assured me he no longer had any problems with airsickness.

Later that afternoon we were able to return to our home base and a few days later I was on a night flight to Mitkiyina, Burma. The weather was clear; air was smooth, and my stomach empty. Our food had been rice and scrambled eggs, period. There was no real salt or pepper or any other condiments, so I was looking forward to some good old Spam and army food. In China the Chinese Government had the contract to furnish the food for all the A T C (Air Transport Command) personnel in China and their food so far was extremely limited in quality. There seemed to be plenty of rice, though.

In Mitkiyina, Burma, I ate my fill of Spam and drank plenty of canned juice such as grapefruit. It really tasted good. We were taking off from Mitkiyina in our loaded airplane when all of a sudden I became sick to my stomach. My stomach apparently couldn't handle that much Spam, I figured. However, after arriving back at our base I continued to feel rather sick, and went to the Base infirmary, where the Flight Surgeon checked me. He swabbed out my throat with silver nitrate as well as my ears, which were infected by a fungus called "Dobie Itch". The "Dobie Itch" was picked up at Lal Hat by the laundry marks.

My throat had been a little sore, but I thought it only temporary. As the week progressed my throat hurt more and I was feeling sicker, possibly with fever. I told the flight surgeons but they only continued to swab out my throat and my ears with Silver Nitrate.

Being grounded for my illness I was sitting in the sun watching the Chinese coming through our camp, many loaded down with charcoal sticks they had produced up in the mountains. Along came one lady, stooped with age and carrying a load of newly made charcoal on her back. She was walking as if on short stilts. I realized that I was seeing the last of the ancient custom of feet binding of the women. The bottoms of her feet were only about ¾ of an inch wide and ¾ inch long.

At night I started going up to the OSS (Office of Strategic Services) Hospital nearby, getting a nurse to swab my throat with Argyrol, which gave me temporary relief.

The feeling of being sick while on the other side of the world so far from home made me feel quite nervous. I felt the doctors weren't helping, as I was feeling worse each day. This really came home to me while sitting around with a sore throat and fever, feeling worse day after day.

On the third night I visited the OSS (Office of Strategic Services) Hospital. An RN checked me, called her doctor, and came back with orders to put me to bed. There's no way to tell how relieved I felt. At last I'd get proper care. Our ATC only operated one Air Force hospital in China, and it was a hundred miles away, in Kunming. Without orders from my flight surgeon I'd not be sent there for treatment.

I told the RN to be sure and notify my commanding officer or flight surgeon that I was in the OSS Hospital. As it turned out, no one seemed to have been notified. They began treatment on me for strep throat, using Sulfa drugs and canned fruit juice. My infection began clearing up in three days. I sure felt better when I was released. Of course I reported to my doctor on the base. He wanted to know where I'd been, and I was pleased to tell him.

I had been surprised when I realized the hospital was strictly operated by the OSS and had no connection with the Army Air Force. The OSS was gathering strategic intelligence in China from the Japanese activity and was also organizing insurgent resistance against the Japanese. I don't think I was supposed to have been in the OSS Hospital, but I was more than happy to have received the care I needed. I also appreciated the well-trained Chinese nurses working in this hospital.

After my next flight, the weather really turned bad, with rain, then ice and snow. During the next two weeks we were grounded by fog and snowstorms, which left thirteen inches of snow on the ground and runway. That weather lasted for two weeks and so did the thirteen inches of snow.

Too much time staying in the barracks gave us headaches from the stove gases escaping from the stovepipes and our food supply was reduced. We were served scrambled eggs and rice, a few bean sprouts, but more eggs, some more "overripe than usual." Practically all the men in my barracks were sick with bellyaches, diarrhea and vomiting, me included. Facilities were limited, and we were a bunch of unhappy young men. We prayed for a letup in the weather. A gallon can of British lemon drops showed up from somewhere, and they were a Godsend. We ate enough to pucker our lips but they seemed to sooth our stomachs somewhat.

One day I just had to get some fresh air and anyway I wanted to look around in the mountains behind our camp. I put on my winter (fleece lined) flying boots, pants, jacket and a scarf, my 45-automatic also in its holster and walked off behind our camp, following a trail in the snow going up the bottom of the valley between the mountains.

I was crossing a little rivulet of ice water when I became aware of a young Chinese boy behind me. I turned off the trail when I noticed he had no shoes or coat and his feet were bleeding. I could tell that he was afraid of me, so when I turned off the trail he hurried on past me.

I continued on the trail until I came to an enclosed courtyard with twenty-foot high thick walls, built in a rectangular shape, only a short distance from the trail. The large wooden gate was partly open so I inched slowly inside, carefully feeling my pistol.

On my right in the north wall the upper story held hay and feed for the livestock penned directly underneath. Facing me was a thirty-foot wall of mud brick. I turned to the left and saw the living quarters inside or against the east wall. I could see inside just enough to spot a small cooking fire built on top of a mud brick table against the inside wall. A roofing tile mounted through the wall above the stove at an upward angle carried out some of the smoke. There was a stool or two and a low bed made of mud bricks, with some kind of cover on it. A few people were inside. That was all I could see. I moved quickly on to the south wall.

Inside the south wall of the compound there was a large room containing statues of all kinds. I recognized a fertility god, a statue of a large woman with many little statues of children gathered around her, several fierce looking statues, a large Buddha, and many, many other statues of different sizes and odd faces. I felt these must represent every spirit of the Chinese people, good and bad. There were some open windows, letting in light so I was able to see clearly in the room.

I was feeling more than a little spooked. I had a strong feeling I was someplace I had no business being. Was this their church? Or what? After a few minutes looking at those strange figures my nervousness was increasing so I decided to get out. I turned and walked out the gate, watching all around me. No one had come out.

I left that compound and went back to my Army Camp. I wondered about what I had seen but never learned anything more about it. It was evident in China that the Chinese farmers must have made their living quarters together for safety. In the past, the towns had built twenty-to thirty-foot high walls about thirty feet thick, completely surrounding their cities. There were always several narrow gates, just large enough for their ox-carts to pass through.

The Chinese in town did have running water for their bathrooms. Rock-lined ditches covered with flat rocks carried the water in ditches through the bathrooms, uncovered and back out to the covered street ditches. The ditches continued the journey along the street to the river. Even today in the big modern cities in China, you can see the evidence of these ditches in the older sections of town. In some outlying towns these ditches are still in use.

Back at our barracks I shook off the feelings I'd had, but still wondered more about the religious life of these people. Their beliefs seemed rather primitive to me. Yet they had managed to exist for thousands of years. I feel and hope that their future will improve their living and give them much happiness.

One of my friends took off from Chanyi for India one afternoon. After several hours without picking up any radio signal in solid instrument conditions, he climbed to 27,000 feet but was still unsuccessful in getting clear of clouds. They had left Chanyi seven hours earlier in their C-47 and were quite low in fuel and completely lost. They lowered their altitude to 16,000 feet and bailed out, expecting to land somewhere in India. Instead, they were still in China.

We later determined they must have had a head wind of about 140 miles an hour. They were fortunate. Had they bailed out above the Himalayas Mountains or even India, they would have been fortunate indeed to be found dead or alive. As it was, they landed in China and were able to walk out. No one was badly injured.

One cold morning, I put on my overcoat, which had no insignia on it, and crossed a small bridge in our camp, when heading to the latrine. I met the new Commanding Officer and another officer. I was immediately called down for not saluting. The C.O. asked me my name and from that time on knew me on sight. I thought that being out of uniform I wasn't required to salute. I found out I was wrong. However, when we were in forward airfields close to the fighting we sure didn't salute, as the snipers would then identify an officer, their preferred target. In forward areas it was safer not to wear insignia, either. Same reason. Having a brand new C.O. right out of the Inspector General's command in "Uncle Sugar" (United States) the *spit and polish* he demanded seemed out of place under the circumstances in this area. After he spent some time in China I understand he lightened up on the men and became a fine C.O.

In one forward airfield, Chihkiang, there were snipers in the mountains around the base. I frequently flew into this base during a siege by the Japanese, and was alerted not to wear insignia of an officer and not to salute. There was a Japanese spy caught working in the mess hall during this time. This was, indeed, a forward fighter base, only a few miles from combat.

A special operation to bring in trained Chinese army personnel to clean out those snipers was begun, called "The Rooster Movement." This operation moved experienced Chinese Troops from Burma to Chanyi. Then Chanyi and Luliang pilots and planes carried those trained personnel and their equipment on to the Chihkiang Airbase.

On our first take-off at Chanyi, we rolled down the runway fully loaded with these troops and their equipment; and quickly realized we wouldn't have enough speed to clear the runway. We were over-loaded with those Special Forces and equipment. We aborted our takeoff and taxied back to the starting pad. This time we opened the throttle early, gaining speed as we rolled onto the runway. With that early start, we were just able to take off, clearing the 50-foot dike at the end of the runway by only a few feet. Within 24 hours of our arrival at Chihkiang, these experienced Chinese troops had cleared out the snipers.

- Transfer To Luliang

I found out the Luliang Air Base used C-46 Curtis Commando Transport Planes like I had flown in Africa. The C-46 used the same engines and propellers as in the B-26's. I was quite familiar with those engines and propellers, and liked them a lot.

I liked that increased power, their large size, and the flight characteristics of the C-46 over the C-47s, which was still a great airplane. When I asked the C.O. for a transfer, he seemed only too happy to oblige. The very next day my orders came through, and I caught a plane to my new base at Luliang, China.

This base was only about 90 miles from Chanyi, and about 90 miles from Kunming. The airfield had been designed as a B-29 bomber refueling base for planes en route to bomb the Island of Kyushu, Japan. Even refueling the B-29s at Luliang, the distance was still too far to Kyushu, Japan, with return to Luliang, to be safe. This operation was discontinued also due to our inability to supply enough gasoline for those B-29s. The B-29s used a longer runway than other planes, and Luliang had built the longest runway in China—over 12,000 feet—for the B-29s.

There were closer bombing targets such as Hong Kong, ships in the China Sea, Eastern China, Manchuria and Korea so the B-29 operation moved to Chentu, in central China, closer to the targets of Manchuria and Korea. A few B 29s occasionally came through Luliang. Due to having a sick co-pilot, one of our men took his place on a bombing raid. The rest of us felt that pilot was lucky to get a trip to Japan and back. Of course there was a chance of being shot down over Japan or the ocean, though. It seems foolish to have been jealous of him but I guess we were pretty young and eager.

When I arrived in Luliang I learned an old friend from Fort Stockton days was stationed there. It was assistant chief pilot, Captain George Shoemaker. He had me assigned to the 2nd

Air Transport Squadron attached to the twentieth Bomb Command. I had been in the ATC (Air Transport command) since becoming a Flight Officer, but now I was a member of the 2nd Air Transport Command, Twentieth Air Force. Luliang Air Field was a designated Air Transport Command Base also, so ATC pilots were stationed there as well. We all did the same flying, but in case of an emergency move, the 2nd ATS was unique in that it was organized to fly intact in one group flight, all personnel, supplies and equipment and was able to establish full operations at a new location within twenty-four hours. Later, in July of 1945, we were alerted to do just that, a move to Manila, Philippines. Those plans got changed at the last minute, and I'm sure knowledge of the Atomic Bomb completion caused the change in plans.

There was a squadron of General Chennault's 14th Air Force fighters, and one group of B-24 bombers located on the far side of our field, along with a Squadron of Combat Cargo.

I was first put into a tent with two other men. The tent was located between the barracks buildings, and within easy walking distance to the airfield.

George Yost in Luliang - In front of barracks and tent
(Pictures from daughter Rose Fairchok)

I had only been on the base three days when my friend George Shoemaker took me to join Major Sylvester, the C.O., and some other officers, for a supper at Wong's café, in the town of Luliang. The town was eight miles from the airfield. Our jeep scraped both sides going through the gate in the huge 40-foot wall surrounding the city. Wong was a refugee from Kweilen when the Japanese overran that Air Field. He served a miraculous five-course dinner to us, by far the best I ever had in China.

Rice wine was served, which I only sipped, while the others imbibed more freely, especially the major. When he insisted that George sing "Ole Man River," I was surprised and pleased that George had such a fine voice.

However, as more Jing Bow (Air Raid) juice was downed, the major started asking Wong if he was a Communist, speaking a little too loud. In this part of China being known as a Communist was a death sentence. We tried to hush the major, but to no avail. Drunken majors don't listen very well. The next day the café had been completely abandoned. We never saw or heard of Wong again. There were no other cafes or eating-places for us, then, except at our mess hall.

Major Sylvester was rotated home within the next month, and Colonel Stelling, former chief pilot of Eastern Airlines, replaced him. Major Sylvester had operated "Sylvester's Flying Circus" in the States and some of our C-46s had that name painted on the noses. Major Sylvester had been Commanding Officer of the Second Air Transport when it left the U.S. The Squadron had a fine record.

Our new C.O. was more formal in his decisions, such as his extreme caution about sanitation. Our food was limited to scrambled eggs and steamed rice, period. Well, once in a while we would have a few slices of water chestnut but it had no flavor, just a little crispness.

One of my tent mates wanted to get out of China any way he could. I don't know what his problems were, but I finally agreed one evening to go with him to a place about four miles from the base that sold rice wine. This drink was served in bottles looking much like beer bottles. Perhaps this lulled us into thinking we could drink it like beer.

We were the only customers in the room, which was large enough for dancing. There were a few tables scattered here and there. When we came in, we were shown to a table and the waiter unscrewed a cap off an oilcan sitting on the table; at least it looked like an oilcan. He poured in a little water and lighted the gas (carbide) that started coming out of the small opening at the top of the spout. When it lighted a bright white flame about two inches high lit up our immediate area, and put out an odor similar to garlic.

We were served the bottles of rice wine, the only drink available. He talked about how unhappy he was and how he could manage to get sent back to the U.S.A. I noticed that every thirty minutes or so an M.P. looked in on us from the door, asking if we were ready for a ride back to the field. After a couple of bottles each we began to feel some effect of the rice wine, so we accepted the MP's offer.

The MP left us at the steps to some barracks, and I handed him a dollar asking him to bring another bottle. I then sat down on the long porch with my feet hanging off. It turned out I was directly in front of the Commanding Officer's room. My drinking partner went from room to room, probably irritating the sober officers. After what seemed like a short time the M.P. brought me the bottle I had ordered, which I promptly accidentally knocked over. It broke and spilled "Jing Bow juice" in front of the CO's door. I just left it all there.

When my drinking partner came staggering back, I got up and we both staggered down the steps, both falling onto the gravel. Brother, were we drunk. When the Jing Bow juice hits it does so with a *wallop*." We couldn't even stand up by ourselves, but had to put our shoulders against each other and push with our feet and legs. In that position we managed to stagger the fifty feet or so to our tent, lying down on our backs on our cots and holding on with both hands while everything else whirled around. Not falling off my cot took a real effort.

Needless to say I avoided that Jing Bow stuff after that. I can honestly say that I never again allowed myself to get that drunk. Never.

This airman continued trying to be returned to the U. S. and one way he may have tried was under Section Eight, which means mental instability. This would also probably mean dismissal from the service. My other roommate and I wondered if he was trying to get out under that provision when we begun noticing a bad odor. In looking around in the tent beside this guy's cot, we found a mess kit he was using as a chamber pot. When he returned we saw to it he emptied that little pot right then. I never did find out what happened to him, but he was soon gone.

By the time I had arrived in Luliang, there was a temporary glut of former civilian Army Air Force flight instructors. They had arrived in the CBI area the same time as I had. We were experienced pilots and were needed badly to be first pilots, but we had to learn about the routes, airfields and instrument procedure. Some of us lacked experience in the type of airplanes, especially the emergency procedures.

This Theater was known as having some of the worst weather under the most difficult flying conditions in the world. There was virtually no weather information or navigational aids available in most of this area in which we were flying and there was always the possibility of Japanese fighter plane intervention. The Japanese shot down two of our Second Air Transport planes while I was stationed there.

The Japanese had invaded Eastern China, Korea and Mongolia in 1935 with virtually no resistance. Before 1935 the Communists had started a campaign in northern China to take over the Chinese government. Chiang Kai Shek returned from army training in Japan and eventually became the head of China's Nationalist party of South China. He was fighting the Communists in the north as well as the well-trained and well-equipped Japanese armies occupying Shanghai and Beijing and other cities of central and Northern China. Chiang Kai Shek was squeezed in several ways, one of which was his necessity of dealing with the Chinese Warlords, who had their own armies. He needed their help to protect China.

Japan kept the Communists and the Chinese army occupied, but conversely the Japanese were also kept tied down in China. Chiang was really trying to fight two wars at one time with poorly equipped soldiers and virtually no Air Force until General Chennault and the 14th Air Force was formed. Chiang didn't want to lose any of his soldiers fighting the Japanese, so he fought a stalling war, saving his soldiers as much as he could to fight the Communists after the United States defeated Japan.

Chiang Kai Shek was also reluctant to participate with Stillwell in Burma, fearing loss of men. Chiang Kai Shek tried to avoid risking his men in Burma where Stillwell was counting on their help. China could not be depended on to support Stillwell, which put Stillwell in an intolerable position. He had to retreat his armies in Burma. According to information in General Stillwell's biography, the Peanut, as he called Chiang, thought nothing of lying to suit his own plans.

The first six months of 1942 Claire Chennault, who had been hired by Chiang Kai Shek in 1937 to direct the badly outdated Chinese Air Force, obtained some volunteer pilots and mechanics from America with the support of President Roosevelt. These volunteers were to maintain and fly some P-40 fighter planes sent to China from the U. S. in late 1941, and were called the "Flying Tiger's," named from the Tiger Shark Teeth painted on the noses of the P-40s.

These men were successful in fighting the Japanese Air Force under General Chennault's expert and innovative instructions. For several months these "Flying Tigers" defeated the air offensive of the advancing Japanese forces in Burma. Not having enough airplanes, pilots, and material to maintain his successes, Chennault was forced to return to Kunming. From there his pilots managed to keep the Japanese out of western China with repeated air strikes at the Japanese army at a bridge on the Salween River. Decimation of the Japanese air force by the Flying Tigers complicated the plans of the Japanese. The Japanese finally pulled out much of their air force as they were losing so many planes in China.

Mao, head of the Communist Army in Northern China, and Chiang Ka Shek in the South, both turned to fighting the Japanese instead of each other, by temporarily postponing their own conflict. When the twentieth Air Force (B 29s) was sent to the CBI Theater, General Curtis Lemay sent word to Mao in Hsian, offering him needed supplies if they would in return aid in rescuing our men who were forced to bail out, or crashed in the northern areas of China and

Mongolia. General Lemay and Mao agreed, and lived up to their agreement. This explains the very capable help our downed airmen in the north received during the rest of the war with Japan.

One of our Second ATS planes from my base was shot down in northern China. The pilot had accidentally flown into enemy territory in inclement weather and was attacked at once, resulting in a quick bailout of all four crewmen.

Mao's communist army rushed in a rescue team quickly, moving the American flyers farther behind the front lines to escape the Japanese soldiers. Had the Americans been captured, the Japanese most likely would have killed the pilots.

I personally talked to one of these airmen. He told me one man had broken his leg parachuting into a Chinese graveyard. There were some temporary hiding spots behind the tombstones, but Communists quickly rushed them farther behind the lines of battle. The airman told me they blended in as peasant farmers when the rescuers obtained Chinese peasant clothes.

An ox-cart was obtained for the injured man and he was laid in the cart and covered with straw. The rest of the airmen changed into native clothes and successfully traveled farther from the battlefield. They were led by the Communist patrol, slowly working their way, village to village, taking a month to reach Hsian, where we had B-25 bombers stationed at our airfield.

Sometimes they would spend several days in a village. The Patrol seemed to be circling to the northwest.

After a month the airmen happily recognized they were entering Hsian.

Mao, head of the Communist army, held a "Gambay" celebration for the rescued airmen. What is a Gambay Party? My confidant told me rice wine was served to all, and when the man doing the toasting offered up his cup and said "Gambay", the receiver of the "Gambay" was expected to lift his glass of rice wine and down it. The rest of the men only sipped theirs. Evidently, Gambay means "Bottoms Up". By the time the airmen caught on they were all drunk but quite happy to have been rescued.

I have read about the communist army rescuing our bailed out airmen or men who crashed landed. Most of these were crews of B-29 bombers returning after bombing runs to Korea and Mongolia. The OSS rescued many airmen also, farther to the South.

Wyatt Cox, my friend and fellow pilot in the Second Air Transport Squadron, now living in Dallas, Texas, was shot down and injured in the Burma area. Somehow, the crew all got out. He doesn't remember anything past the bailout. He found himself in a hospital in India and was sent to the States for further treatment. He couldn't remember any more about the bailout. He and his crew were lucky.

- Life of the Chinese

In 1945 only a few larger cities of western China had electric lights. The people living only a short way from those cities had no electricity, no water piped in, few roads, no telephones and no money. This was much like our own pioneers in the U. S. A. during the seventeenth and eighteenth centuries.

Many of the people in China only knew how to work the fields and how to do some menial tasks. They were superstitious and lived hand to mouth. There were no schools that I know of, and yet their engineering of irrigation and water management was expert.

The Chinese personality was a ready smile and a sense of humor that belied their menial existence. These people were ingenious and capable. Although poor and overworked, they kept their sense of humor and quickly returned our smiles.

- Unusual Stories of Flying In China

One day a fellow pilot was flying a load of newly recruited Chinese soldiers on their first airplane ride, at about 14,000 feet. It was a hot day and some of the soldiers were airsick, a common occurrence. The crew chief came into the cockpit for a few minutes to avoid the bad odors.

One Chinese soldier went over to an open escape hatch in the side of the airplane and vomited out the window. Another soldier, apparently as a joke, went over and kicked the sick soldier in the seat of his pants; others joined in the fun and kicked the poor guy completely out of the airplane. They apparently thought that was funny as they were all laughing. The poor soldier that was kicked out of the airplane probably didn't think it very funny while sailing through the air without a parachute. He must have had a birds-eye view on the way down, though. (O.K., my sense of humor is a little weird, too, at times). Life was cheap in China with life expectancy of only thirty-five to forty years at that time.

One of the unusual rules the Chinese lived by was that by saving a person's life you were responsible for that persons welfare the rest of his or her life. An example: If you threw a rope out to a drowning person and pulled him in, saving his life, you were then responsible for him and had to feed and take care of him the rest of his life. Presumably the spirits of the Chinese were always waiting to do harm or make one's life miserable. This explains why the Chinese ran closely in front of our airplane's propellers when we were landing, to chop up their evil spirits. I wondered about the good spirits? Did they have any? Often this action actually resulted in a cut-off arm, or a chopped-up Chinese.

Another interesting item about these Chinese peasant farmers, men, women and children, was their reaction to our smiles and the question "Ding Hao"? (Thumb up), "everything's OK," and "Boo Hao" (thumb down), "everything's terrible." They would answer with a great big grin, sticking their thumbs up or down, repeating "Ding Hao" or "Boo Hao". Even today in China that is often the response.

We respected these people and their genial nature, and it was indeed unfortunate we could not supply the soldiers with parachutes when we flew them in our airplanes.

One of the stories told as gospel truth came about one stormy night with a load of Chinese soldiers on board. The airplane was icing up and, as usual, was lost. The Chinese soldiers, having no parachutes, knew that someone would have to remain at the controls.

The radioman said, "Hey, I've got an idea. Let me, with my parachute on, demonstrate to these soldiers how to gather the four corners of their army blanket and hold it above them when they bail out. This will resemble a parachute. Then I'll jump out holding the blanket above my head."

The engineer caught on and helped every one of the Chinese out the open door while each held their blanket above their head. All the crew was saved as they could now bail out using their parachutes before the ship crashed. Better to save our crew than to lose all. It was sad but true; life for Chinese soldiers was sometimes rather short.

- An All-Day Walk-Across the Valley

One day my roommate Richard Bloomer, a geologist, joined me on an exploring walk across the valley our airfield was on. We could see a rock formation on the other side that interested me. At daybreak we were walking through the irrigated farming section seeing the farmers and their families transplanting rice in the flooded fields. Other Chinese were lined up walking from town to their farm, oldest in front, youngest in the rear. All except the smallest children would be working.

This area had been farmed so long the cart trails were worn down as much as six or eight feet below the plots of rice. We noticed the families all carried their "honey pots" along to fertilize their fields.

Late in the afternoon we were returning through these farms and saw the Chinese returning to their homes in Luliang, the oldest of the family again in front, followed by younger members in order of age.

It was farther across the valley than we had realized, so we had to rush to get back without getting to see the rock formation I was interested in. It was well after dark before we reached the airfield. We enjoyed this opportunity to observe the hard working life of the Chinese.

- More Flying

Most of our flying was nighttime, with daytime saved for maintenance and repairs. There were no hangers or lighting sufficient for nighttime maintenance and loading followed maintenance at our field. The flight crews were generally called out late at night or very early in the morning, as the planes were made ready to fly. Orderlies were sent after each member of the crew when a plane was loaded and ready to go. In only a few minutes we would be dressed and in the air.

I was called out for a flight one dark cloudy night at three o'clock in the morning. I was driven directly to the flight line. The first pilot seemed in a hurry to take off, unhappy that the engineer wasn't there yet. The rest of the crew was on board awaiting the crew chief. The pilot did a short inspection of the airplane. Finally the engineer came running out in the darkness and stood ready with the fire extinguisher for the pilot to start the left engine. When the engines were running the engineer climbed the ladder into the airplane, and the pilot immediately commenced taxiing.

With a quick take-off check the pilot opened both engines to take-off power and off we went into the dark oblivion of solid nighttime instrument flying. Suddenly the engineer came into the cockpit and said, "Sir, the gas caps are all off and the gasoline is streaming out behind the wings." Wow. I thought we should have taken another five minutes to check the airplane.

We had to climb up to minimum altitude of 11,000 feet to be above the mountains. I helped the crew roll four drums of gasoline out the doors over the estimated position of Luliang Lake, thereby reducing gross weight for a safer landing. We then had to be admitted back into the instrument pattern procedure and land.

The crew chief quickly put the tank caps firmly in place. This time after takeoff we were able to continue on course. I made a mental resolution that when I was checked out as first pilot, I'd always check my airplane thoroughly before taxiing. The rest of the flight was normal, but I had some reservations about the pilot whose name I no longer remember.

My next flight as co-pilot was in daylight. When I met my pilot I recognized him at once: he was the cadet I had instructed and kept the Army from eliminating at Gibbs Field, Ft. Stockton, Texas. He was the slow learner, and I had talked to the Commanding Officer, who agreed to hold him to graduate in the next class.

He was a first pilot in this largest of cargo planes, the C-46, and flying in some of the roughest and worst flying conditions in the world. I was his co-pilot instead of his flight commander. What a turnaround. I felt happy that he had graduated from flight school, and that he became a capable pilot. I don't think he ever knew about my part in his becoming a pilot, though.

He did a pretty good job of flying, but bounced the loaded airplane upon landing on the short landing strip at Peyishi. I said "My gosh, Lieutenant, you still can't land the *dern* airplane." We had a good laugh.

We were required to have a minimum of 650 hours of flying in the CBI Theater before being rotated back to the States, so we were eager to fly as much as we could.

Mail arrival was erratic, and although my wife wrote often mail delivery time was undependable. Sometimes several letters would arrive at one time. I was always hungry for news of my wife and daughter. Perhaps I should have written more, but we were not allowed to write about where we were, where we went or what we were doing, so it was difficult for us to write interesting letters.

One time she wrote me that one of my letters had been censored (cut-up) so badly she couldn't make any sense out of it. We were not even allowed to write about the weather. What then could we say in our letters? As I have said, we ate nothing but eggs and rice, and even that odd statement may have been censored. I told her we only had some pulverized salt that didn't taste like salt and pepper made from the bark of some kind of tree, and no other seasoning. Too bad she couldn't tune in to "Tokyo Rose." She could probably have found out all she wanted to know about all that was going on in our theater of war.

The cooks tried to make bread from the rice flour, but with no yeast or baking powder the bread was so soggy all we could eat was what we could gnaw off the burned edges. During my time in China I lost 45 pounds. The cooks tried cooking some water buffalo for us, but I'm quite certain it must have been a tough old water buffalo. We'd chew 'till we got tired and then just spit it out. None of what I have written is exaggerated. It is true as written.

In this part of China the farmers were very poor, and sanitation was not practiced. They either knew nothing about sanitation, or were unable to do better. Every drop of water we drank was thoroughly boiled, and left residue on the drinking glasses. There was little sickness among us, though. Our commanding officer was quite concerned about sanitation, and was negative about us being served vegetables grown using human fertilizer. So we ate only eggs and rice. I often wondered: "How did they fertilize the rice? And "Were the chicken roosts clean?"

- St. Elmo's Fire

One cold, cloudy night we flew up north to Liangshan, and flew right into an electrically charged storm causing St. Elmo's fire to break out all over the front of the airplane. The windshield wiper seemed to drag this purplish "fire" back and forth across the windshield and fireballs came rolling in from the ends of the wing, striking the fuselage, sometimes softly and sometimes with a thump. Every drop of water left a spot or streak of purple on the windshield. There was the scent of ozone in the cockpit. Fire seemed to be dancing all over the airplane, making a crackling sound. Every time I encountered St. Elmo's fire there was an uneasy feeling inside me. I must say, though, that it was beautiful and always intriguing.

- Check Out By Pilot Bill Miegel

In the early spring of 1945, I finally was assigned to a check-pilot, Bill Miegle. He had to be sure I was knowledgeable of routes and procedures in our war theater. Being familiar with different airports and letdown procedures was required. I felt I was ready to get checked out as first pilot and was eager to do the flying.

My first ride with Bill was a beautiful moonlight flight to Mitkyina, Burma. The ride back was so smooth I remember getting quite sleepy. There was another flight to Chihkiang, China, late on a rainy night. While dropping rapidly the thousand feet or so along the slope of the mountains to the runway, the windshields fogged over. Not being able to see out I turned to Bill: "What do we do now?" He answered, "Land the damn thing." So I did. That field had only one runway, with fifty-foot drops off both ends, and mountains close to both ends of the relatively short runway. Fortunately the windshield "cleared" enough in time for us to land.

On another trip on instruments, we were still on instruments when we returned to Luliang. We waited in the traffic pattern flying back and forth for three and a half hours. There was a C-109 tanker aircraft sitting on the field with a collapsed landing gear. This wasn't too unusual as the loaded C-109s and C-87s were a little too heavy for their landing gear. It took time to clear the runway, so Bill told me I could demonstrate my instrument flying ability while staying in the holding pattern. I guess it was good practice for me.

My next and last check flight occurred with a delivery of heavy equipment to a new paved fighter landing strip. A heavy rain had left the field quite muddy everywhere except on the runway and paved taxi strips. Bill, sitting on the right side of the cockpit, said he'd better take over the taxiing and proceeded to accidentally taxi off the left side of the taxi strip. The left wheel went right down into the soft mud. I knew Bill was mortified.

I thought, "We'll have to hook up some ground equipment to pull this C-46 out of that mud, after it's unloaded."

By the time we climbed out and reached the bottom of our ladder onto the mud, we were quickly surrounded by hundreds of curious Chinese who seemed to come from nowhere. As we were looking the situation over, I pulled out my pipe and lighted it with my Zippo lighter. This caused the Chinese to murmur in wonder. I flicked the lighter again, making the Chinese laugh each time the fire jumped out of the little "box". Undoubtedly they were seeing their first cigarette lighter. They must have thought there was fire contained inside the lighter. The miracle to me was that the lighter ignited each time I flipped it. My lighter fluid was the 100-octane gasoline used in the airplane engines.

After about two hours the ground crews finally got us unloaded and pulled out of the mud and we were able to leave for home. Bill said: "Okay, Ken. You're checked out." At last I was a first pilot.

Glory be. I was finally moved out of the tent into an end room of the barracks, to join four other pilots, Martin Hurd, Ed (Barlow) Wimmer, Earl Roloff, and Richard Bloomer. Richard was a geologist from Virginia, with a Master's degree from the University of Texas. I had also studied Geology at the University of Texas at the same time, but didn't remember him. He was working as an assistant instructor while I was an underclassman. After the war Richard went back to school and earned his Ph.D. in Geology. Martin was from Iowa, Ed from Salt Lake City and Earl was from Chicago. They had been instructing on B-25 medium bombers at La Junta, Colorado. Tired of instructing, they volunteered for foreign duty—and they sure got it!

There was an empty upper bunk for me above Ed. The mattress was nearly an inch thick and needed for our comfort (ah, sweet comfort) when lying on the loosely woven rope "springs." We were issued a bed sheet, an army blanket and mosquito netting.

Coming in after a mission, usually in the middle of the day, we would be too tense to sleep. Each crewmember was given a permit good for a shot of whiskey (combat ration) from the Infirmary. Although I didn't care for whisky, the effect helped my body to "unwind" and ease me into sleep. Usually one of the crew didn't want his shots, so I would help him out and take his also. Two shots of whisky seemed to be just right for me.

Mosquito netting was quite handy in keeping mice and rats out of our beds as well as mosquitoes. One time I left my mosquito netting off and woke up feeling soft little feet walking on my nose. That was one big rat. From then on I used my mosquito netting.

I was lying in my bunk reading one afternoon when I noticed Martin, who was lying on his bunk, begin easing his 45-caliber pistol out of his holster. He aimed and fired at a huge rat standing in the middle of our room. The bullet missed and ricocheted, striking the bedpost (a 4 by 4) just inches from Earl's head. He was asleep but woke up quite suddenly. That was a close call. We abandoned that type of rat control. What a mess we would have had if Martin had hit what he aimed at. In a few weeks we located some screen wire and lined a drawer with it to protect our pantry.

None of us in our room was a good gambler and had little money to gamble with anyway, so we began playing bridge instead of poker. The game caught on. We enjoyed playing Rubber Bridge for small stakes. Ed and I teamed up and weren't doing too badly. However, one night about 2300 hours (eleven p.m.) we were playing bridge when an orderly came to get Ed for a flight. Unfortunately, that was to be the last time we saw him. A few minutes after he took off he lost an engine on climb-out and crashed into the mountain, only about ten miles from the field. The crashed plane was so hard to see from the air, it wasn't spotted for several days. We were flying right over it in our departure pattern. All four of the crew had died instantly. The accident investigators announced that Ed had a single engine failure and had done all anyone could have done. He just didn't have a chance. That engine had quit on climb-out. My thought at the time were, had I been flying that airplane I would have been killed just as Ed was.

I caught a ride over to Kunming to attend the burial ceremony on a hill overlooking the Kunming airfield. I'll never forget standing there hearing the bugler playing Taps. Even today my eyes tear up when hearing taps being played.

Horace Pietsch, my companion for two months in Morocco, flying from Chentu, China, crashed at his home base of Jorhat when his four engines quit, out of fuel. He had returned from a flight hauling gasoline in his C-109 airplane to Chentu, China. He had arrived back to the Jorhat instrument flight pattern during the intense monsoon weather and had no choice but to wait his turn for let-down. When he returned to Jorhat, due to the Monsoon, there wasn't enough fuel left after holding so long in the instrument pattern, to be let down for his landing. His engines quit on the final radio checkpoint on final approach, about one minute short of the field. He remained at the controls to hold up the nose as long as possible, giving the crew a chance to bail out. Only two of the crew bailed out safely. Pietsch and his co-pilot died in the crash. They could have bailed out over the jungles in that black night but that would have been quite dangerous also. Had Pietsch not stayed to hold the nose up those few extra seconds, it was highly doubtful anyone would have survived. As far as I know his wife never received any posthumous award for his sacrifice of his life for others.

I had learned of Pietsch's death only a few days before Ed was killed, so I was already feeling low. I had written a letter to Barbara Pietsch, Horace's widow in Cleveland. I felt badly that Pietsch had not even seen his daughter that was born the day before he left for overseas. I wrote Ed Wimmer's widow and sent his things to her. I finally got to meet her some forty-three years later. Ed also had a daughter he'd hardly known, who was now married and living in California. Mrs. Wimmer told me she had been notified of Ed's death by a telegram one morning while she was working in her flower garden in her front yard. A delivery boy on a bicycle came up, handed her the telegram and left.

- Playing Bridge

Martin Hurd and I teamed up as bridge partners and did quite well, even picking up a few dollars. We devised our own system of bidding, although neither of us were experts. Another pilot, Dudley Hodgkins, had teamed up with a former professional bridge player. Martin and I had never played with them until a duplicate bridge tournament was held on our airbase not long before the end of the war. The four of us got acquainted in the first games of the tournament, competing against each other.

At the beginning of the tournament an explanation was given of the rules that none of us knew much about, and by the end of the first day we were slightly ahead of Dudley and his partner. The next day, however, Dudley and his partner out-scored us, winning the tournament. It was a lot of fun, and we appreciated getting the opportunity to compete, especially against such knowledgeable players.

A few nights later Martin and I challenged Dudley and his partner to come to our room for a friendly bridge game. Well, as it turned out, Martin and I had more than we could handle, and the final game was something for the books, so to speak. When Dudley bid seven no trump, I doubled and he redoubled. Dudley's partner didn't say a word. Dudley fooled us all, playing superb bridge. He set up the final play finessing me to take the next to last trick with the seven of hearts. It was a game to be remembered, and I thought of it many times through the years, trying to remember Dudley's last name, and hoping to run across him at a reunion.

As this game was played near the end of the war in China, I didn't see Dudley again until the 1987 Hump Pilot Reunion in Arizona, forty-two years later. I spotted him sitting at a table with several of our buddies and his lovely wife. When I spoke to him he came unwound. I mentioned that bridge game. He practically hollered, "Yes and I made it, doubled and re-doubled! By finessing your six of hearts! I've been telling everybody about that game for the past forty years. Thank goodness you're here and can affirm it." What a nice feeling to see him after all those years, and to meet Marcia, his wife. Dudley Hodgkins died a few years later, and I felt the loss of another buddy. I have kept in touch with his wife.

- First Pilot At Last

As First Pilot, I began to get more trips and this gave me a feeling of satisfaction. Stacking up more time put me in the position of reaching the required flight hours to qualify for a return to "Uncle Sugar" (United States). One problem, however, was that a new First Pilot was required to have at least a year of overseas duty. You can count on the Army Air Corps; it made rules you didn't like. If they counted the time I left the States that wouldn't hurt me, though, but if they only counted the time in China I would still have three more months to go. We needed something else to worry about, I guess.

I was flying into the airfields close to the active battles: Liangshan, Peyishi, Chihkiang, and a little later, Liuchow, to name a few. The last severe winter storm caught me on one of my first flights as first pilot. It was always so surprising how rapidly the ice would build up on all leading edges of the airplane, including windshields and wings. In a short time we lost all radio reception because of the ice-covered antennas.

We applied de-icing alcohol to the propellers and windshields, helping the windshield wipers to clear the ice and loosening the ice on the propellers. We had no deicers on these C-46 airplanes. The radio operator had several radios to work with, one with the wire antenna he could extend about 200 feet behind us. This was considerable help for him to receive and send when the other radios wouldn't work, but it, also, would finally ice up.

I asked the radio operator to get us a "fix", that is, to find our exact location by triangulations from ground stations. That particular time we were fortunate and got it, so we were able to continue safely to our home base. Because we were carrying no cargo we were able to carry more ice safely. We were quite tense, though, as there is a limit to how much extra weight of ice we could carry. It was a constant strain to keep the windshield clear and the propeller ice spun off. Fortunately most of the ice was melted before reaching our home base of Luliang.

The jet aircraft in use today can climb rapidly through icing conditions before too much ice attaches to the fuselage. In severe weather conditions, however, there is still a limit of ice that even they can handle.

I was being sent to Chihkiang airfield quite often and became familiar with the complicated instrument letdown procedure there. A take-off from Chihkiang required an immediate turn in order to avoid the mountains. On one hot summer day I was ready for takeoff behind two P-51 fighters carrying bombs beneath each wing. The Japanese were attempting to take the Chihkiang airbase at that time and were only a few miles away. The P-51 fighter planes would take off, make a quick run, dropping personnel bombs and strafing the trenches with their machine guns. Then they would land for more bombs and to re-load their guns.

The heat of that day reduced the lifting ability of an airplane. I was waiting to take off after the two P-51s. The first one opened his throttle and started down the gravel runway. Halfway down the runway the pilot apparently realized he couldn't get off safely, closed his throttle and ground-looped off the runway to the left, bouncing over the rough terrain and low bushes until he came to a stop. I was sweating out the possibility of the bombs jarring off the wing and exploding. Then the second P-51 rolled out on the runway, opened his throttle, and did the same as the first, but ground looped off to the right, also bouncing over the rough terrain. I took off and "got out of there" feeling safer away from those bombs.

Next day we returned to Chihkiang with another load of gasoline, but the weather had closed in so that we couldn't land. This field had a minimum ceiling of 800 feet. The proximity of the mountains made it dangerous in case of a missed approach, as the surrounding mountains were close.

We reported to operations and a "round robin" series of flights, at intervals, had begun, in order to get gasoline supply for the fighter base as the weather lifted. All ground vehicles in Chihkiang also needed gasoline to supply the front lines.

Flying again to Chihkiang, I found the ceiling was still below minimum. In discussing the situation with my crew, they told me to do what I thought best, so I radioed the tower and asked the present ceiling and how badly they needed the gas. They replied that the ceiling was 400 feet and they were desperate for gasoline, expecting to lose the field to the Japanese within the next few days if they didn't get some. I asked for special permission to land. The answer was a quick "Affirmative," with another caution about the low ceiling.

I knew my co-pilot was "sharp" at flying instruments so we decided to attempt the landing. My co-pilot could double-check my flying as we made our procedure letdown. Remember, during a war, we took chances when we considered it vital.

The visibility was reported clear below the 400 feet, so we started our procedure. We had to fly straight at 180 degrees from the station for one minute, then make a one needle-width turn of 135 degrees to the left, then fly straight for one more minute, then another one needle-width turn of 135 degrees to the left. Then, with gear and full flaps, throttle pulled back, we set up an immediate 2000-feet-per-minute descent. When we broke out of the clouds at about 400 feet, there was the runway, thank God, dead ahead. I only had to ease the wheel back and land. Before we were fully parked a truck was backing up to the door of the airplane. We may have saved the base from being captured, as it was several more days before anyone else was able to land.

- Three Strikes and You're Out

Several days later I was called out for a daylight flight and a missionary was seeking a ride to Laohwangping Air Base, only a short distance from Chihkiang. In our pre-flight check of the airplane, the radio was found to be inoperative. We returned to operations for assignment to another airplane. On the next airplane I found oil on the outside of the cowling of the left engine. The engineer hurriedly checked the engine and found a broken cylinder.

For the third time we went back to Operations. I thought of the rule that with three airplanes turned down for flight we could postpone our flight. Too much stress.

This airplane checked out good. However, I noticed in the form 1 (a tablet containing a special page for pilots and crew chiefs to record problems that need attention) that the last pilot reported a problem with one of the propellers. A mechanic has to sign it off when he fixes the problem. The mechanic had cleared the form.

We started the engines, went through our printed checklist thoroughly, and taxied to the take-off pad. We again checked everything. All instruments and propellers checked O.K. I looked back at the passenger, and noted he was buckled in and reading the Bible. I thought: "That's good."

Our take-off was normal until we were about 50 feet above the runway, when that propeller began running away, increasing RPMs out of control. I immediately switched the manual propeller toggle switch and reduced the RPMs to normal. The cockpit then began filling with smoke, so we began turning off electric switches rapidly. When I reached above me to the ceiling panel and turned off the fuel booster pumps used on takeoff, the smoke began to clear out a little.

When the smoke continued to thin out we turned the radios back on and notified the tower. The tower affirmed a return to the runway. I happened to look back at our passenger and he was sure reading that bible. I was glad to have the missionary aboard; we could always use some help on these flights.

Being assigned the third airplane we had to turn down, I talked to Bill Crawford, the operation officer, and cancelled out. Bill approved and scheduled me for another flight in about eight hours. I was called out at five o'clock the next morning for a beautiful daylight flight to Chihkiang.

- The Missionary Gets to His Mission

Arriving in Chihkiang next day, there stood our missionary, looking for a flight to Laohwangping. I told him I'd take him when my airplane was unloaded, unless he caught another ride first. Laohwangping was not a regular stop for us.

That was the first time for me to land at Laohwangping, and I was delighted at the long, paved runway. Years later I read that this base was built for B-29 s, but the operation was closed down. A captain came running up to our airplane when I stopped to let our passenger off and asked for a ride. I told him O. K. if he hurried. Travel in China was difficult unless you could fly. There were few roads, vehicles and bridges so there was little road traffic.

It took about fifteen minutes for him to get back and our engines had to idle at 1200 RPMs. I disliked idling these engines so long but I waited.

As the weather was beautiful, we flew on at about a thousand feet above the terrain to enjoy a good view of rivers, farms, cart trails and communities.

I crossed one large river flowing down a gorge that was about two hundred feet deep. One third of the way up the east cliff was a large cave opening, half filled with water shooting out and cascading down into the river. I would say it was undoubtedly the largest spring I had ever seen. What an awesome sight.

In China there were many unusual natural wonders to see. I would like to have been able to explore China by air, but then, I guess I had been doing that. If only more flights could be made in the daylight.

- My Friend, Gordon Wendell, and Crew Bail Out

Back in Randolph Field in 1944, Gordon Wendell and I were two of the four who were assigned to make a cross-country flight in BT 13s to Waco, Texas, Enid, Oklahoma, Lubbock, Texas and return. Now in India, he was flying out of Sookerating.

One day in January he took off, loaded for a flight to Kunming, China, and flew into an ice storm over the Hump. With all his de-icer equipment turned on the ice was still building up and they were losing altitude. Then his engines began cutting out. He and his crew quickly bailed out.

Fortunately for them they were just about to the border of Burma in China when they bailed out. They landed on the mountains north of the Burma Road. Had they bailed out 10 minutes earlier they would have landed in the jungles of Burma or in the high Himalayan Mountains. I thought about how rough it was just to bail out and wondered if I'd have had enough guts to do so. Gordon told me they had jumped quickly, and all but one managed to join together shortly when on the ground. They knew they were somewhere pretty close to the Burma Road. It was several days before the fourth member of the crew joined the others. They had some adventure filled times, but finally reached the Burma Road and eventually managed a ride to Yunanyi, China. It all sounds simple to hear it, but in reality, what a trauma it must have been.

There were many airmen that bailed out both over the Jungles or over the Himalayan Mountains. Many of them lived to tell their stories and experiences in our four published Hump Pilot books. Many of them died there.

- A Special Mission

A special daylight mission sent a flight of five airplanes to North China. We landed on a grass runway. I've long wondered what we carried. I think it might have been radio equipment. We had flown so far north that we were beyond any radio contact. We spent several hours waiting to get unloaded and refueled from barrels of gasoline carried by one of the planes. The small city nearby must have been quite ancient and must have been a special place as the floors of the building we waited in were marble. No one was around except the few Chinese who unloaded us.

When ready to return to our home base, there was a solid overcast. Being out of radio range, we took off at five-minute intervals for separation and agreed to climb until above the overcast. We then would fly according to VFR rules (Visual Flight Rules-see and be seen).

I leveled off at 21,000 feet just above a solid floor of clouds. I set my autopilot at cruising speed. Those large multi-engine airplanes kept pilot and co-pilot busy for a few minutes, doing the myriad adjustments necessary for establishing cruising speed. The high altitude and load affected flight characteristics and needed some fine adjustments. These were automatic for pilot and co-pilot, such as adjustments of oxygen supply for auto-mix oxygen for breathing, re-setting gyro compass to correct processing, putting cowl flaps on trail or closed, mixture control on auto-lean, power setting (manifold pressure), reviewing panel instruments, and finally making the minute adjustments setting of synchronizing the propellers. We were then able to lean back in our seats and relax.

I turned to my co-pilot to say something and just sat there with my mouth open staring through his window at a mountain that stuck up out of the tops of the clouds so high I had to lean over to see its top. I knew it wasn't Mount Everest, but it looked about that tall. I never learned for sure what mountain it was, but will never forget how awestruck we were. Imagine being at 21,000 feet and seeing a mountain coming up out of the clouds to at least six or seven thousand feet higher. The Himalayan Mountains are spectacular. There were many peaks above 25,000 feet, and this one was certainly one of them.

- Sergeant Buys A Chinese Wife

One of my previous flights to Nanning Air Base near Indo-China was while I was still a co-pilot. This was shortly after we recaptured it from the Japanese and we landed on the grass beside the field to avoid any bombs the Japs may have planted on the runway area.

A rumor started circulating back at Luliang in a few days that an enlisted man (EM) on the flight had smuggled on board a "wife" purchased in Nanning. When word of this reached our commanding officer you know what hit the fan. The honeymoon ended and the girl was flown back to Nanning. In those days in China, buying a wife was apparently easy and inexpensive, but certainly not allowed by the Armed Forces of the United States. The Chinese people needed their children's help in their fields, and girls were not strong enough to be as useful as a boy, so the girls were a liability to the family. To sell the girl or arrange an early marriage relieved the family of that liability.

I never heard what punishment was meted out to the "husband" by our C.O. The "husband" was an EM (Enlisted Man), so I would assume he became a lowly private.

There was only one woman on our base at Luliang—a Red Cross girl who maintained a small library and a small recreation room used by the enlisted men. We had a "number one" boy who cleaned our rooms and washrooms. One day he announced he was getting married. We judged him to be no older than sixteen years old himself. His bride to be had been committed to marry him when she reached twelve years of age, all arranged by the parents. Sure enough, one day our No. one boy moved her into his tiny room in our barracks. We seldom saw her, but now there were two ladies on base.

The building used to show pictures in was also used as our church, where the Chaplain, a Catholic, conducted all denominational services. The picture show operated only when and if some film arrived. After showing a film a few times, it would then be sent to another base for showing. I never saw a USO show while in the Army.

We had to find our own morale lifters and about all we could find was playing cards of some kind. What gambling we did was usually low limit poker. There was virtually nothing to spend money on. We were promised we could buy a bottle of whiskey, six cigars, or a carton of cigarettes each month from the commissary, but seldom, if at all, did this happen. I can remember two times during the entire time while I was on the base that anything of that nature reached the Commissary. There was usually toothpaste and toothbrushes on hand for sale. I remember some whiskey being sold only one time and I traded mine for some cigars.

When my wife could find pipe tobacco or candy back home in McCamey she would mail me some. One time she managed to send a full box of Baby Ruth candy bars and wrapped some bars of soap in the box with them. What a thrill it was to receive this, as soap was in short supply, not to mention the candy. Although the Baby Ruth bars tasted just like soap that turned out well for me as no one else wanted any. I ate every piece myself.

There came a light knock on the barracks door while I was lying in my bunk one summer afternoon. I glanced up and I saw a young Chinese boy at the door holding some roasted peanuts. They looked delicious. He had wrapped them in some rice paper tied at four corners. I paid the boy more than he asked for them, hoping he would bring more. As far as I know he never came back. Those peanuts were a lifesaver for me. I'll never forget how good they tasted. I thought, "Why couldn't the base commander have peanuts for us to eat, if this kid could come up with them?" Since our diet was only rice and scrambled eggs, with no bread, no butter, no pepper that tasted like pepper, and some powdered salt and no real coffee (ground bark of some tree), those peanuts would have been a good food for us. I saved that rice paper and fifty years later it was still in perfect condition. That makes one think, "How do they make paper that lasts so long?"

One dark night we were all reading in our room about 2200 when a gunshot rang out, then a man's voice yelled "Help me, help me, I've been shot." We rushed out of the barracks, and ran toward the sounds coming from the mess hall. It seems that one large enlisted man had been bullying a smaller sized enlisted man. They both had been drinking rice wine off the base and an argument developed involving a Chinese girl. This disagreement was continuing when they returned to the base and mess hall. The smaller man went to his tent, got his rifle, came back to the mess hall and then the ruckus ended with the smaller man shooting the larger one. The injured man was flown to the hospital in Kunming. I heard later he had died.

One can visualize a situation like this developing in China, when mixing that potent rice wine with the extreme shortage of women and considering the morale of the men after two or three years of working, day after day, living in tents with little food to eat. All flights from our field carried two enlisted men, a radio operator and an aircraft engineer. The flying, at times, was so rough and dangerous I'm sure those men may have been scared and so were the pilots. There was no choice. Orders were orders. Their safety was largely dependent upon the skill and judgment of the pilots and co-pilots. Stress could build up for them in time.

There were few activities to divert the minds of the E.M. when not working. The work was monotonous and the worries of loved ones at home were constant, not knowing when they would get to go home, if ever. Being nervous about flying didn't help the situation. Of course these situations were everywhere with the world at war. Many soldiers had it much rougher than others, of course, but war is war and all suffer, not just the soldiers, the people at home also. One sergeant received a letter from home informing him his wife was divorcing him and marrying his father. In desperation he applied to the Red Cross and the Chaplain for an emergency leave to go home to straighten things out and was refused. He had already been in the China Theater over two years. He solved the problem by committing suicide.

- Single Engine

Late one afternoon on a flight to Chihkiang, the engines were running perfectly in the smoothness of the late evening air. About an hour before reaching our destination the crew chief reported oil appearing on one engine cowling. Quickly checking it out I decided to "kill" the engine and "feather" the prop on the bad engine, (feathering the four bladed propeller blades meant lining up the blades into the wind for least resistance). With one engine dead it was necessary to re-trim the airplane and add more power to the good engine. Everything went well as our minimum altitude in that area was about 4,500 feet, low enough that the "good" engine didn't overheat. When we arrived at Chihkiang, I "brought in" the damaged engine at the last minute, in case of emergency. This was a tight field to get in or out of because of the closeness of the mountains. I was careful not to overshoot my approach. After parking, the crew chief found a bad cylinder. A new one would arrive in the morning. We then checked in with BOQ (Bachelor Officers' Quarters) for that night.

After supper the Co-Pilot and I wanted to take this opportunity to see the town, so we asked some local GIs what there was to see. We were informed the place to go to was the Mission. We both thought they were referring to a sort of nightclub, as they said it was the most popular place in town to visit.

Instructions were given us, and we were nervous as we went down this dark street to a closed gate in a tall adobe wall. We opened the gate and entered a dark yard, nervously easing our way toward a faint light. We came to another adobe wall, with a door partly open. We eased through that door and found ourselves in a well-lighted courtyard containing tables and benches. GIs were sitting around the tables drinking glasses of water. What a surprise. This was a Catholic Mission.

Serving the water was a Priest and two Sisters, none of whom spoke English. They spoke German and probably Polish. When we came up, the Sisters pulled a large ten-gallon glass jug up from 60 feet deep in a covered water well, and poured us fresh, cold water. Perhaps you're wondering, "What's the big deal?" This was the first cold water I'd had since leaving the United States over a year ago. I spoke our thanks to them with the limited German I knew. They generously offered cold water to all who came. We sat around about an hour, drinking the cold water, talking and eating cookies (there was little sugar in them, of course, but they were edible). How unusual and nice this was for us.

Since being in the Army Air Corps I have continuously been amazed at the ability of the aviation mechanics to keep our airplanes repaired. I was not disappointed in our crew chief (mechanic) as he "borrowed" some helpers and had the new cylinder installed and tested, all ready to leave for Luliang well before noon the next day.

My next flight from Luliang was in daylight and not far, to a new paved landing strip right by the great Yangtze River near Loping, China. I walked the short distance down to the river, thinking that maybe I could sail a rock across it. Alas, I found I was no George Washington. The river must have been at least a half-mile wide at that point. Looking across it I noticed the water was higher in the center than its edges. The water appeared to be rushing by in desperation to reach the ocean as fast as possible. It was obvious to me that this was one powerful river to be reckoned with.

The thought went through my mind that boats coming up-river would need to stay close to the sides to avoid the strong current in the center. The water-polished rocks covered the banks for about 150 feet out from the water on both sides. The name "Yangtze" implied to me it would mean something like "Snarling Tiger." But no. It only means "Blue River."

- Crashes and Accidents

Most major crashes that occurred in the CBI were generally caused by situations beyond the pilots' control. Of course there were pilot errors that resulted in fatal accidents, such as the fighter pilot returning from combat in the China Sea 300 miles away, flying all the way back to Luliang in his P-38 fighter on one engine. On the final approach to our 12,000-foot runway he approached too short and had to add power, too much power. Well, with gear and flaps down, a P-38 on single engine would immediately do a fatal snap roll when too much power is applied, and dive into the earth. The pilot was killed instantly. Just think, after "sweating it out" for three hundred miles, he undershot the longest runway in China, if not in the world. Considering the stress he had been under, I would think undershooting a runway would be the last thing he'd do.

Another pilot error occurring one dark night was fatal to all on board a C-54 four-engine transport carrying barrels of gasoline, while attempting to land at Luliang. A second radio beacon had been added west of the field, supplementing the other one located east of the field.

When the C-54 entered our instrument holding pattern, and when cleared for the final leg into the field, they made their final turn west instead of east, flying into the ground, killing them all. I was told there were two colonels and two majors, along with their crew, carrying a load of gasoline in the 4-engine C-54. I understand they were flying to make the required minimum hours to earn their monthly flight pay.

The majority of the accidents in the CBI occurred from engine failures, ice and getting lost over the Hump at high altitude. There were few radio checkpoints on the Hump. There were also unknown high wind conditions that contributed to the problem of navigation.

Running out of gasoline was another cause of accidents. The valley planes flying the Hump had limited gasoline for the return trip from China. In order to get a few more net gallons of gasoline across the Hump, gasoline was drained out of the wing tanks of the 4-engine transports to 1200 gallons maximum before being allowed to leave China for their home base in India. This was sometimes not enough fuel when monsoon weather or engine problems caused more gas to be used than planned, leading to a bail out or the plane to crash. As previously mentioned, it wasn't enough gasoline for my buddy Horace Pietsch, who was killed as he ran out of gasoline about one minute short of landing. All his engines quit due to fuel starvation. He only needed about ten more gallons.

That was not a pilot's error; it was a general's error. A statement made by General Tunner, head of Hump Operations, "All consideration of orders emphasize safety for the pilots involved in the Hump Operation." My answer to that statement is: "Why weren't the airplanes allowed more gasoline for emergencies when leaving China, especially during known monsoon activity?"

Although many crashes on the Hump were caused by severe icing and engine failure, there were other unknown factors as well. Maydays (SOS)'s were often heard and attempts then made to locate those probable bailouts areas later, when the plane was reported missing. There was an organization in India called "Search and Rescue" that was on duty day and night. They could immediately be dispatched from their field in the Assam valley at a moments notice. They proved to be an efficient organization, locating downed crews and dropping special items needed for survival such as salt and dope—yes, dope—for the natives. These mountain people used dope daily. They would work for dope before they would work for money, which was about worthless in the Mountains.

However, the area was so large and rough it was difficult to locate crashes or bailouts. When a bailed-out crew was located, supplies were dropped for them. One of the mountain men in a small village high in the Himalayas pointed east and said "China." Then he pointed west and said "India". Then he pointed straight up and said "USA."

No matter what happens, life goes on. We had a job to do and we did it. Now there were only four of us left in our room and what fine men these roommates were. When one received some goodies, we all shared. Richard Bloomer, being an instructor pilot, quite often flew the Hump, and traded eggs with the cooks in the mess halls in India for Spam, canned juice and once even a pie made from a can of fruit cocktail.

In China our Army Base never received any Army food rations from America. The top priority was getting the gasoline, oil and war supplies to China. In late Spring Earl Roloff received some summer sausage from home. That was really great. Richard Bloomer had just brought in a small brass stove from India and we were able to heat food or make some hot chocolate. Where did the chocolate come from? Richard Bloomer. He traded eggs for a can of chocolate from a Chabua mess sergeant. Martin Hurd came up with some cookies from home from time to time.

Eating our supper of rice and eggs one night, there was an Admiral, an older man, eating with us at our table. He was passing through our base by airplane. I had recently found out the Navy had operations in China behind the enemy lines, keeping track of Japanese ships passing through the China Sea, therefore I was no longer surprised to find a Navy man at our mess hall, but for him to be an Admiral. Wow. When we griped as usual about the food, the Admiral called us down. He told us he'd had a tour in the far north in Alaska one time, and had to eat raw meat. After having frozen it on top of their igloo it turned green and then it was edible. He said we had it good here. Well, maybe we did at that. We all knew it couldn't be much worse, though. That raw frozen meat sounded good to us. At least it was meat.

Once I was sent for a load of gasoline at Paoshan, China, on the Burma Road. This was the first town in China after leaving Burma. The aviation gasoline had come by pipeline from Calcutta, India. That was the first I knew about this pipeline being completed across the terrible jungles and 10,000-foot Mountains of Burma, not to mention the monsoons dumping hundreds of inches of rain on them.

What an accomplishment. My hats are off to the pipeline builders and others that completed a nearly impossible task. Gasoline would be pumped into Kunming before long. I hadn't even known the Burma Road was open or that the pipeline had been completed that far. My flight was a daylight flight and being able to get our load of gasoline in Paoshan would save us some of the dangerous trips over the Hump. An item about Paoshan: on take-off a quick turn to the left was necessary after breaking ground, in order to avoid a steeple due to the short runway.

- Setting a Record of Cargo over the Hump

The Hump flights remained in operation as our air supply line had been carrying many times more than the trucks on the Burma Road, but the need was greater than ever. Our combat operation in China had become a major operation since the victory in Europe.

General Tunner, Commander of the Air Traffic Command set aside one day in July for the ATC (Air Transport Command) to go all out and carry as many tons of cargo from India over the Hump to China in one 24-hour period as possible. China pilots were instructed to leave their home fields and not come back until after the 24-hour period was over. Orders were to avoid landing in the three airfields designated as receiving stations—Luliang, Kunming and Chanyi—during the designated period.

I left Luliang the night before the big push, carrying a load to Chihkiang. I then flew north and over-flew Liangshan and turned to Chengtu. In Chengtu I asked for a load to Hsian. The Operations officer was stubborn and insisted I carry a load to Chanyi first. Chanyi was a receiving station during this "push" and I was under orders to stay out of there until the designated 24-hour period was over. I could not convince the Chengtu Operations Officer of that. He told me he had some mail to send to Hsian provided I flew the load of rice to Chanyi first. I finally agreed.

Sure enough Chanyi was swamped with airplanes waiting to be unloaded. As luck would have it, the first person I saw after landing at Chanyi was the Commanding Officer. "Babcock, what are you doing here today"? "Sir, I was ordered by Chengtu Operations to bring this rice here, in spite of my efforts to convince him otherwise. I reluctantly agreed to bring it," I told him. Although the C.O. was upset I was finally unloaded and left, returning to Chengtu. We hurriedly gassed up at Chengtu and left for Hsian with the mail.

We landed in Hsian late that afternoon. We had been gone from our home base a full day and a half without sleep and as usual, very little food. The climate and terrain in Hsian was similar to Texas, not as hot, though. I had heard about a café in downtown Hsian that served steak, so my co-pilot and I hired a couple of bare-foot coolies to take us downtown by rickshaw and they ran the whole way, about seven miles. We really enjoyed the steaks, as they were quite edible. Our coolies were waiting, and away they went, running all the way back without stopping. I paid them a small bonus. They sure earned it.

There were some small shops close to the airfield, so we did some shopping. I was shown a beautiful thick table covering made of pure silk, having beautiful pictures of Chinese royalty woven into it. What a beautiful, thick silk table cover with many bright colors. I only had twenty-four dollars and managed to get his price down to twenty-five dollars with much haggling. His bottom price was one dollar more than we had with us. No one had any money to loan me, so I didn't get to buy it. In my inexperienced eyes I thought the value in the United States would be at least a thousand dollars, but I wasn't buying it to sell. I wanted it as a gift for my wife. "That's the way the ball bounces," I thought. I was getting so sleepy my eyes were beginning to film over, so we all went to bed. I had been awake about fifty hours by this time.

The next morning I did buy fifteen large watermelons to take back to Luliang. These were the first large watermelons I'd seen in China. All of a sudden I became a popular guy back at Luliang and we gorged ourselves with watermelon. They tasted as good as any I had eaten in the United States. I will mention, however, that I gave one to Colonel Stelling, the Commanding Officer. He thanked me. He must have felt it would have been unhealthy to eat, though, as I found out he gave it away.

I had saved the biggest and most hollow-sounding melon for last. Several of us were standing around, mouths watering, waiting to eat our fill. When I stuck in my knife it went in quite easily. The melon was completely hollow. What a disappointment.

After the big "push" to set a record of "Tons over the Hump" the record for the largest number of tons of cargo carried by air over the Hump had been set for the 24-hour airlift. I don't remember how many tons it was, but it was quite a lot.

A couple of days later I flew to Kunming for a load for Liuzhou, which we had just re-captured from the Japanese.

As the loading of our airplane would take some time, I checked in with BOQ to get a room for some rest, and had just lain down when someone knocked on my screen door, and I heard "Hey Kenneth." It was my brother-in-law, Merel, from McCamey, Texas. He had just arrived in India and was flying out of Chabua, Assam, India. He had brought a load of gasoline to Kunming, and checked the operations just in case he'd know anyone listed on the records.

He saw my name and came right to the room. How nice it was to see someone so close to me show up on the other side of the world. We had a nice visit and he promised to bring me some beer (they had beer in India) his next flight to Luliang. Neither of us cared much for beer but I assured him I would be glad to get it. The beer would be cool after being carried over the Hump.

After Merel left I slept a couple of hours, then checked with operations. The airplane was nearly loaded. A colonel walked up to me, introduced himself, and asked if I was the pilot flying to Liuzhou. I answered "Yes Sir." He then asked if he could ride with me. I told him I'd be happy to have him along. Then he asked if I had room to carry a refrigerator. A refrigerator? It had been over a year since I'd even seen a refrigerator. Where did he get it? The "Thieves Market," he answered. I'd heard of that. I was told it really was a thieves' market, and now I believed it.

I was glad to oblige the colonel and we took off for Liuzhou. Our song we sang now was "Four o'clock in the morning, now we're on the way…"

I don't know how many times I saw the sun come up from my cockpit. The sunrises in China were never particularly beautiful and I still wonder why.

Approaching Liuzhou the topography was unique: sharp pointed peaks about five hundred feet high, sticking up all around the area, with rice farms in between. This topography extended east at least a hundred miles to Kweilin and Canton. Liuchou was a fighter base we had lost to the Japanese in November or December of 1944, after also losing Kweilin. One mountain peak was close to the east edge of the airfield, and a large navigable river separated the mountain and airfield from the town of Liuzhou. We saw a bomb go off at one end of the remains of the large bridge that had spanned the river. I guessed the bomb squad must have set it off. Another bomb was exploded on the airfield after we landed: an anti-personnel bomb. I had already seen one bomb tripped on purpose at Mitkiyina, Burma, back at the first of the year. Sometimes it was easier to set them off than to dig them up, I suppose.

We were used to eating at any time of day or night at the flight line mess halls, which were open twenty-four hours a day at all our China and India airfields. This one had not had time to set up facilities as yet. My crew and I were quite hungry. I asked about food, it being two thirty in the afternoon. The sergeant in the kitchen told me they only served meals for breakfast, noon, and supper. I was" fit to be tied." I started for Operations to contact my Commanding Officer, as I knew it would be nearly five more hours before getting back to Luliang.

The colonel then approached me and invited us to join him for dinner at his base location. "When my transportation arrives," he added. Well, although I was still mad I wasn't ready to "cut off my nose to spite my face," so I gratefully accepted the invitation. It turned out I made a good decision, as the colonel loaded us on his jeep and took us to the other side of the field. He was in command of a communication company, and told the cook to fix us some good grub, and boy, did he. Fried Chicken and French Fried Potatoes, with salt and pepper. My crew and I felt like royalty. I had done the colonel a favor, all right, and he more than re-paid us. We flew home with full stomachs for the first time in a long while, contented and happy. We flew low over the sampans traveling slowly up and down the river there at Liuzhou. We watched the crews excitedly jumping around. They were expecting me to fly low enough for my prop-blast to blow them over. After a few miles we climbed above the mountain spires to cruising altitude and flew on back to Luliang.

In July I heard of plans to move the second Air Transport Squadron, which was attached to the Twentieth Air Force, in one move to the Philippines. The Squadron had been organized and trained in the USA to carry all of the Squadron's records, personnel and all items needed for changing our operating base, this time to Manila, Philippines. I wasn't too happy about it, as it would mean most or all of our flying operations would probably be over the ocean, and I wasn't too good a swimmer. We were given special training on Loran Navigation System for flying over water. A short time later, however, this plan for moving to Manila was cancelled and I think the whole squadron was transferred to the Air Transport Command. We had heard some scuttlebutt that something big was coming up, which probably caused the change in plans. We just continued doing as we were doing, hoping the war would end soon.

To provide insight to our flying, as previously mentioned, on each airplane was kept a record of repairs and mechanical problems or complaints of that particular airplane, called a *Form-1*. One of the crew chiefs would check the form after each flight for any complaints from the pilot or crew chief. One example of using the Form-1 involved a "sister" aircraft, with the call numbers 053, which flew like a "Lead balloon" and the other, 035, flew like a "Dream." I flew those two airplanes often and one day I was to fly 053 I decided to try something. As 053 flew "tail heavy" in flight, I told the crew chief to move a barrel of gasoline from the back to the front of the load, thereby shifting the balance of the load quite a bit.

I could see an improvement on take-off, and in level flight our cruising speed had gained about ten miles per hour at normal cruising power. I then wrote this up in the Form-1 of .053. The future loads should be loaded for best flight efficiency. We didn't find why this airplane was tail heavy, but this action sure "cured" the problem.

- Theft Of A Gun

An interesting problem arose when another friend of mine, named Ernster, from Cuero, Texas, stationed in Chabua, hung his 45 automatic pistol and holster in the cockpit. He closed the door to the cockpit and walked to the operations office. When the ship was unloaded Ernster returned to find his gun and holster missing.

In those days it was a death penalty in China for any unauthorized Chinese to have in his possession any kind of gun. There were communist bandits and others that wanted guns badly and were offering large sums to buy them. Although these small towns in China had no jail, the mayor of the town had the power of life and death over the people, and the Chinese Army was also so empowered, apparently.

My friend reported his gun missing then left for his station in India. The Provost Marshal contacted the small contingent of Chinese soldiers stationed in Luliang Air Field. Our MPs and the Chinese soldiers drove to the Shipping and Handling office where they found that one man of the unloading crew was missing.

They then drove the eight miles into town and spotted the missing Chinese coolie, who tried to run. A Chinese soldier shot him in the leg. The coolie had the missing gun and holster on him. The coolie was laid across the hood of the jeep and carried back to the field. They reported to the Provost Marshals' office on the field, filled out the required forms and then drove to the unloading area. They threw the wounded man on the ground, and shot him dead. He was left on the ground a couple of days where the loading and unloading crews walked right by him. This was a warning to the rest of the coolies. Cruel? Yes, but very effective.

- More about the Local Chinese

We were stationed in one of the poorest areas of China, a part of China that had been only an agricultural area. These people in the small villages still had no running water, other than the sewage and they made charcoal for fuel from sticks taken from bushes growing on the sides of the mountain. Their charcoal-making fires were seen dotting the hillsides in the wintertime. The women generally did this job and carried the bundles of charcoal home on their heads or backs. The larger trees in this area had long ago been chopped down—probably for cooking and heating—leaving only brush and small trees on the mountains.

There was a dirt road passing by the town of Luliang, an extension to the Burma Road. All plowing of the nearby fields was done by water buffalo. The families did the planting and harvesting. Few family necessities were available in the town and no luxuries were to be found. Clothes worn in the winter were all quilted pants and coats, for men, women and children. There were no facilities for bathing or washing clothes that I ever found, other than the river nearby. In the spring, bathing in the river lightened their skin considerably. Light summer clothes replaced the quilted pants and coats worn in the winter. The summer clothes were lightweight and sometimes ragged and skimpy. In summer most men were bare legged.

In spite of the difficult life the Chinese were living, most of them were still friendly and smiled at us when we approached them, especially when we raised a thumb and said, "Ding How." They accepted their need to work hard with only meager earnings.

- An Extremely Rare Phenomenon

One night my crew and I saw a fantastic display of nature. We were flying in another beautiful moonlit night in central China, cruising altitude about 12,000 feet, and our direction of flight was to the east. I had "George" (automatic pilot) flying the airplane and in the distance I could see the outline of a thunderstorm, perhaps fifty miles away. Suddenly I was shocked to see a lightening bolt shoot straight up about twenty miles from the top of that thunderstorm. Then another. I called my crew to see this and we watched together while bolt after bolt shot straight upward, each bolt looking like a huge rocket each time, fire dropping off the sides. I didn't count them but it couldn't have lasted more than about 20 seconds. We were absolutely astounded. There was silence for a few seconds. We just didn't know what to say. That phenomenon defied description.

When I told others about this later I could see the doubt and unbelief on the faces of the listeners. Perhaps the concept was too strange to imagine. I could see they thought I had exaggerated the story, so I finally decided to just be quiet about it.

Some forty years later two scientists reported seeing and taking pictures of a comparative phenomenon. They explained that only a few pilots had ever seen this and virtually no one from ground observation. Their description was exactly as we saw it in China. One of my good Hump Pilot friends, Milo Walters, had also sent me a copy of his story about a similar observation. His description didn't quite match what we saw, but was also quite unusual.

Here is the write-up published in the San Angelo Standard
Times, San Angelo, Texas, in the early 1980s, titled:

- Researcher Photographs Rare Form of Lightning

Quote: *Minneapolis-Physicists announced recently that they have photographed a rare form of lightning that shoots upward in miles-wide plumes from the top of a thunderstorm. The larger of two plumes photographed was twelve miles tall and about three miles wide.*

This twin plume had a fountain-like appearance that is totally unlike the bolts of lightning normally seen in a thunderstorm.

Conventional lightning goes from one cloud to another, or between a cloud and the ground, rather than from the top of a cloud upward as the plumes do.

The photographs, believed to be the first ever made of this phenomenon, may help scientists better understand storms and the upper atmosphere. The University of Minnesota researchers' report is in the latest issue of the journal "Science". "The photographs were taken last summer. (Early 1980s)

Robert Nemzek said there have been only occasional reports from airline pilots and a few Earth-based observers of this type of lightning rising from cloud tops toward space.

It's all conjecture about what effect this might have on an aircraft if it tried to fly through this type of lightning," said John Winckler, a university physicist and co-author of the reports.

This article amazed me when I saw it in the paper. That phenomenon being so rare I am happy to be able to share what we saw that night in China in the summer of 1945. That picture was still so impressive it was burned into my memory.

- End of WW II in Sight

In August, 1945, the first atomic bomb was dropped and M-1 Rifles were quickly issued to all officers on air bases in China anticipating attacks by Communist forces. The war between the Communist and the Nationalist Chinese Government had already begun to flare up again. Both Communists and Chiang Kai Shek Nationalists wanted all our war materials, including airplanes and were ready to fight for them. The war wasn't officially over but it might as well be as far as the Communists and Nationalists were concerned.

I had served as Organization and Operations Officer of the field for a couple of months, in addition to my flying duties. I was familiar with locations of strategic supplies and how they were or were not protected. I had reported lack of protection and needed defense of the airfield with several suggestions. It was apparent we were unable to set up a competent defense for our strategic materials. I finally withdrew from this job, realizing how little defense capabilities would be initiated. Had we been attacked in force we would have had no effective defense. In only a few weeks or so the war ending was official.

I flew an airplane to Kunming one night to pick up cargo. On my final approach for landing, I happened to look down and saw little spots of light on the ground. It dawned on me that we were being shot at. I quickly pulled up into a climbing turn and called Kunming Air Field informing them of the situation. They told me to circle a few minutes. I did and in only a few minutes more they radioed me "all clear." I approached again for landing and there were no more pinpoints of light below. I was told by Operations there were bandits (probably Communist) and the Chinese soldiers chased them away.

A week later I was called out to fly a load to Shanghai and enjoyed a long daylight flight of about 1200 miles non-stop from Kunming to Shanghai. We saw a lot of China on that flight, with the final miles over flat land intertwined with canals through farms and small towns. The big city of Shanghai came into view and we spotted the large airport with many parked aircraft. We landed with no tower communication, as we still did not have U. S. Army Air Force communication equipment in place. We could see C-46s parked on the north side of the field, so we taxied all the way across the field, about three miles, in a thirty-mile per hour crosswind. The C-46 was the largest airplane of World War II, except for the B-29 bomber, and our large tail caught the wind causing difficulty in holding the rudder when taxing in such a crosswind at sea level. The co-pilot helped me with the rudder during the taxiing. By the time we reached our parking area both our left legs were shaking from exhaustion.

Our operations told us to check back in three days to see if our plane had been unloaded, as they were so busy. There were many airplanes already on the field waiting to be unloaded and our crews were re-organizing the field operations. Our radiomen were busy replacing Japanese equipment and several crews of coolies were busy unloading airplanes.

One pilot told us he was walking by some coolies unloading his airplane and one of them said to him, "I say, old chap, how are things in Merry Old England?" The startled soldier told him England had been hard hit during the war, but would survive. It turned out the "coolie" was an Oxford graduate that was caught in Shanghai in the early stages of the war.

Well, we had three days to spend in Shanghai. It was no problem finding a hotel room. There were crowds of people in the streets, just seeming to be walking around in circles. The hotels were not very busy. We checked into one, cleaned up a little and then looked for a place to eat. We found an upstairs restaurant where I ordered shrimp. My mouth just watered. I asked about changing my fifty-dollar Gold bill. Almost before I knew it a waiter grabbed it and indicated he'd be right back. I "sweated it out" until he came back shortly with a million dollars Japanese occupation money. I was a little surprised that the restaurant accepted Japanese money. Well, we sure lived high for a little bit, paying our bill of $20,000 dollars. The shrimp were small and boiled in oil, but much better than scrambled eggs and rice.

The Japanese were nearly all gone from Shanghai, or at least I didn't see any. The downtown Shanghai store shelves were nearly vacant. I felt that the Chinese merchants would bring out more merchandise shortly. I did manage to find a Japanese Kimono, a silk lace blouse, and not much else to take home with me. I looked in several stores, to no avail. The long war and occupation had taken its toll on quality merchandise there and likely the merchants had hidden their finest goods from the Japanese.

The next night I went out alone, taking a bicycle rickshaw. I told the coolie "White Russian Sector," and he took off. I wanted to see what White Russians looked like. When I arrived at the Sector I almost felt as if I was back home. I saw people who looked the same as the folks in the USA—many blondes and white-skinned. There were White Russian girls there that stirred memories of the girls at home. I knew no Russian words and they knew no English. The White Russians seemed happy to see us, though. After so long under Japanese control, I would certainly think so.

There were some fellow Army Air Force personnel in the bar who told me the White Russians had escaped Russian persecutions years ago by moving to Shanghai.

I just sat there just enjoying watching other white people. I did try dancing with some of the girls and they were good dancers. The Russian vodka went down smoothly, so I made a mental note not to drink too much. I had done little drinking previous to going in the Service and drank little while in the Service, partly because I couldn't get it. This was certainly no place to "let myself go," although I felt pretty safe and respected while around these people. Nevertheless I was happy to have my 45 automatic handy just in case.

I left the Russian Sector fairly early that night and found another bicycle Rickshaw. I remember this ride back to my hotel as being a long distance in the dark. We passed through some business and housing districts and the streets were nearly vacant. My hotel was located in the busiest part of town.

It had been only a few weeks that the Japanese were occupying this city and had occupied it for nine years. These people now released from living under Japanese rule must have had some strong feelings about being free. Not knowing their language we could not really communicate. I would have like to have known their personal feelings about the end of the nine years of Japanese occupation.

The next day my co-pilot and I decided to try out a Chinese bathhouse and massage. (Our hotel had no bath.) It was a true bathhouse. We left there quite clean and relaxed, feeling pampered. At least it was a new experience for us to remember.

I decided we'd better go out to the field and check in, and there was our commanding officer, Colonel Stelling, seeming happy to see me. "Babcock" he said, "I'm glad to see you. Your plane is the only one unloaded, so I want you to take a message back to Luliang." After receiving the message I gathered up my crew, and I was a little surprised my crew was all there and ready to go. Our airplane was already full of gas and after a thorough inspection we took off for Luliang.

What a beautiful daylight flight it was. It was pleasurable sitting in the cockpit "zipping right along" at cruising power airspeed at 200 MPH, watching China passing under us. It was interesting to note that our airspeed was ten MPH slower than when coming to Shanghai loaded. That was the opposite of what I had expected.

We got another good look at the villages, farms, streams and people working on the farms. I was seeing China back at work after long years at war.

What a shock was waiting for me when I checked in at Luliang. Another roommate and best buddy was missing, Martin Hurd. I had a hard time believing this. The war was over and we had been thinking about post war plans together. He had been on a nighttime flight to Kunming, only a ninety-mile flight, when he disappeared

It was four days more before the wreckage of his plane was found, a little over halfway between Luliang and Kunming, smashed by flying directly into the side of a mountain. A CNAC (China National Airways) pilot reported spotting the wreckage while flying their regular route to Kunming from India. He was flying rather low and in daylight or he might not have spotted it.

Martin had contacted Kunming approach control by radio for landing instructions ten minutes earlier than his flight plan. He was quite experienced and I can only guess that he must have been letting a newly arrived co-pilot fly. Martin must not have been as attentive as he should have been, but as the war was over, perhaps he wasn't. It's hard for me to believe that but we'll never know.

This was the third close friend of mine to be killed since I left the United States. Each of these was a special friend.

I went to Kunming for Martin's funeral. This was my second trip to this little hill to bury a close friend. Standing there overlooking Kunming airfield again and listening to Taps being played, I could feel the tears rolling down my face and thought of all three of my close friends who were gone from this earth, leaving their relatives and friends to handle their grief. War is no respecter of human tragedy. That moment on the hill will remain in my heart always.

I went to the flight surgeon and asked to be relieved from flight duty for a few days, to let me cope with my feelings. I did not feel it would be fair to my crew for me to risk their lives flying before my nerves were quite settled. The doctor was understanding, offering to send me to a little rest camp, which happened to be located on a lake close to where Martin had been killed. I declined his offer, thanked him, and told him I didn't want to miss getting my mail from home even for a week. My two other roommates were out on flights, so I was quite alone.

After three days I was ready to return to flying. I needed to be busy, and had to convince the flight surgeon that I felt in full control. I had already written Martin's parents a letter, and returned his personal effects to them.

After a few days I again felt confident to be flying again. I needed that confidence early one morning when returning from a flight on solid instruments. Luliang Airbase only had a 200-foot ceiling and a half-mile of visibility, our minimum. Having only the directional radio compass (we called it a "Bird Dog") for my approach, I dropped a few feet below minimum and was right over the runway too far down to land. I flew on to the end of the runway, did a low-altitude turn-around procedure at 200 feet, arriving back over the far end of the runway. I again spotted the runway right under me and cut my engines and landed. I'd had full confidence in those maneuvers and was quite relaxed even flying so close to the ground. I knew exactly what I was doing. That comes from practice. It was a tricky and demanding maneuver. I decided my nerves were quite settled now.

The war was officially over. When I was called out for a flight about 3:00 a.m., another solid instrument condition, I checked the weather first thing, noting how low the ceiling was. I had the crew with me as I climbed the Control Tower. The ceiling was oscillating between 175 and 200 feet and visibility was a half-mile. This is less than minimum altitude. In the Control Tower I looked at the ceiling and talked with the tower operator. I again checked with operations and found the ceiling at destination was just under minimum but expected to lift by the time we would arrive. The alternate field, several hundred miles away, was open at the moment. There was a possibility the weather there would deteriorate. This made it questionable as an alternate. I explained this to my crew, then to the Operations Officer, Bill Crawford. I told him I was canceling out, suggesting he consider shutting down the field for an hour or two for loaded aircraft take-offs. I don't believe he did, however.

A young pilot heard me when he was filing his flight plan, turned to me and said, "What's the matter, lieutenant, scared?" I thought how ignorant he was and resisted the urge to clobber him. I pointed out patiently that the war was over, why take unnecessary chances. I then turned on my heels and went back to my barracks room and turned in. I was called out later for a nice daylight flight.

A couple of days later I woke up one morning and both roommates were out on flights. As usual my thoughts were about home and I wondered when we would be shipped back to the good old U. S. The war had been over a month. I got dressed and went over to the Mess hall for the usual breakfast of scrambled eggs and rice, same as I'd had for every breakfast, except one, since arriving in China some ten months ago.

- Going Home

The scuttlebutt about leaving was going around. No one seemed to know anything definite. I went over to the Executive Officer to see what I could find out. He said the wheels are turning and we'd be leaving any day. He told me I had enough points to be among the next to leave. I was feeling low after Martin's crash and just couldn't get those three roommates I'd lost out of my mind. Even knowing the war was over I still couldn't quite realize that we'd be heading home.

There was no one to talk to and I didn't feel like reading. There just was nothing to do but wait. I was getting more and more nervous and anxious.

I knew that my life-style was going to change drastically and wondered if I could handle that change. I had been living under stress and responsibilities and felt somewhat nervous about going home to family living and different responsibilities. This was going to be another major change in my life. I couldn't help wondering how successful I would be returning to family life. Maybe I had lost some of my confidence.

I was inactive and by myself for two more days and then, thank God, I received orders to leave the field the next day to Kunming. I had everything packed and ready to go. Arriving in Kunming I was told to turn in all government items (Gun and holster, parachute and I don't remember what else). I was then assigned to a tent in a bivouac area (temporary camp) awaiting transportation back over the Hump to India. I thought of how, not long ago, I'd had the feeling I'd never get home. Now I was on the way.

The thought of going home was becoming more real to me, especially when "Sentimental Journey" and other great music was being played over the loudspeaker system.

After two days of waiting in the rain and mud, my name was called. I was in a C-54 (4-engine transport) with seats in it, taking off for Calcutta. I hung around the cockpit talking to the pilots. It was interesting to me that this C-54 had been diverted from Australia to help evacuate personnel from China.

Getting all personnel out of China had become a high priority as the Communists were taking over all material they could and becoming more threatening. They had already resumed their fight against the Nationalists. More than likely the dropping of the Atomic Bomb had saved my life, just as it saved thousands of others. Now we wouldn't have to fight our way into Japan. I glanced out the windows at the Himalayan Mountains all around that I'd been avoiding so long. They seemed less threatening now as I looked out the windows of the C-54. I thought of my three friends that would never see home again. I thanked God for my life and for the family I was returning to. I thanked God for the comradeship I'd had with all three of these wonderful men, as well as my other roommates. My life is better for having known them, and I'll be a better person because of knowing them.

We landed at Dum Dum (Calcutta airport), India and were carried in the usual 6X6 truck the thirty miles or so to Camp Kanchrapara, north of Calcutta. There we would wait for a steam-ship to arrive in Calcutta to take us home. This camp was apparently a staging area for most of the troops returning to the "States" from India and China. I had always thought we'd fly home or ride the MAT (Military Air Transport) back to the USA. That just wasn't to be. We heard that ships were already on the way to pick us up. We had to leave most of our China based airplanes for the Chinese so now we had to go home by water.

That first night in India about ten of us slept in a tent on an open grass covered field. It was dark by the time I set my bags on the foot of the cot and crawled on. There was one bright electric light in the tent. We could see to get to bed. Or should I say *to cot*?

I had been in India enough to be aware of monsoon rain, so I had taken the precaution to put my bags on the foot of my cot. My precaution paid off. About midnight I was awakened by my fellow tent-mates cursing and hollering. Someone had turned on the electric light and I saw about six inches of water flowing under our cots. I just had to laugh at the poor soldiers who had their things on the ground. Didn't they know they were in India in monsoon season?

The next night I was assigned to the middle cot in a three-place tent. About midnight I woke up to the sound of jackals howling in the distance. I lay there listening and heard their howls getting louder. All of a sudden they became silent. Oh. Oh. This disturbed me for good reason, as here they came, one trotting rapidly into and out of our tent, apparently looking for food. He came so close I could have easily touched him. I'm glad they didn't eat people. However, there were some man-eating tigers around, some weighing as much as 600 pounds. I hoped to see none of them.

The next day I was moved to a barracks for the remainder of my three-week stay. The weather was typical of monsoon season as we would be soaking wet with perspiration from the heat, then a hard rain shower would hit and we wouldn't be any wetter.

In the meantime there was little for us to do. I did go into Calcutta one day, via a 6x6 truck, of course. We passed another 6x6 truck stopped on the road with an angry crowd of Indians around it. It had killed a cow that was lying in the middle of the road. Indian law gives the cattle right of way everywhere. All cows are considered sacred in India. We went on around the scene, not stopping.

Calcutta is Calcutta. As far as I could see it was a unique city with a high number of under-nourished and impoverished homeless people, including children. There were thousands of beggars everywhere. A few annas a day were the difference between life and death. We shared what we could with these poor people, but there was no end to the giving.

The beautiful Jain Temple was one of the sights to see in Calcutta. This is a sharp contrast with the actual life of the area. We really needed more time to see the sights in such a large city. The Great Eastern Hotel in downtown Calcutta was a modern hotel where wealthy Englishmen came and went. I was drinking tea in a balcony dining area in the afternoon when some Englishmen and their ladies entered for their afternoon tea. The women were dressed in fancy clothes. I tried to restrain myself from laughing out loud at the bony knees and fancy clothes worn by the men. Lah de dah. We were at least polite enough to turn our heads when we laughed.

Next day at camp Katchrapara my new friend, Lieutenant Dan Drommerhousen, and I walked over to the EM recreation room to watch a high-stakes poker game. The players and table were isolated about six to eight feet from spectators, and the usual white, low priced chip was valued at twenty-five dollars, the yellow at fifty dollars and the red one at a hundred dollars. I saw pots as high as $5,000.00. The men had apparently been successful playing poker and those winners were now "having it out" between themselves. It was quite interesting to watch.

The next day I wanted to play some tennis and looked up a man I had known back in Luliang who had been a professional tennis coach before the war. He had coached a champion USA ladies tennis player and wanted to improve my playing. Well, we checked out some equipment from the P.X. and started playing. He gave me some good instructions but quit after two days because he said I was making him work harder than he wanted to. I never really got to use those pointers, though, as there weren't enough tennis players around McCamey.

I even got in a few rubbers of bridge, teaming up with F/O Sheard whom I'd played against at Luliang. He wasn't an expert, but neither was I. Later, aboard the ship while going home, we teamed up again.

- Next Stop: New York, New York, USA.

On the eighth of November 1945, my name came up along with 3500 others (including some 50 nurses and Red Cross women) to board a U. S. Marine ship, the U.S.S General Adolphus Washington Greely, destination New York. We were marched to five-high hammocks, down in Number Five hold. It was hot, clammy, stuffy and confined. We didn't care. We were on the way home.

We could feel the engines running and moving us down the river toward the sea. About twenty minutes later we slowed to a stop. The tide had gone out and we were sitting on the mud bottom of the river. When the tide came in hours later, we floated free from the mud. When we woke up that morning we were moving down the river on our journey home. After breakfast I went on deck. I looked out excitedly on the Bay of Bengal. We were really and truly on the way to the USA now. About noon the ship anchored in sight of a large Island, Sri Lanka, formally called "Ceylon." We needed to take on more fresh water, which took hours.

"Water, water all around and not a drop to drink," or bathe in. When underway, we found fresh water was only available in the showers a short time each day. I think I only had a fresh-water bath two or three times the entire 29 days. I never seemed to get there at the right time. Ever bathe in salt water? We had salt-water soap, which was more like a bar of sand, no foam at all. Try taking a bath or washing your clothes with salt water and saltwater soap sometime. What a letdown. The best way to wash your pants would be tying them to a rope and trailing them behind the huge ship. Shaving was an adventure. Which made a good excuse for growing the mustache I now sported.

We were on the Indian Ocean where the flying fishes came shooting from one large wave to another. Rudyard Kipling's writing of the flying fishes was so romantic. It was fun to watch them. I didn't feel particularly romantic by watching them, though. But the dolphins were intriguing to watch, swimming effortlessly while keeping up with our ship all day long.

The weather was clear and hot so many of us stayed on deck day and night, garbed only in cut-offs and worn-out shoes. We sure caught up with any deficiency of vitamin D by sunbathing all day every day. Some of the higher-grade officers complained that EM (enlisted men) were coming to the top deck. Only officers should be allowed on top deck, they said. These guys were what were known as "regular army". I admit we were out of uniform, so we just pinned our officer's insignia on our shorts so they could see we were officers. We wore no shirts while on top deck.

Just seeing water day to day, roasting us in the sun, I was cheered to hear an announcement over the loudspeakers there would be a duplicate Bridge Tournament. I turned to F/O Sheard and said: "Let's play in the tournament." He eagerly agreed. The games started the next day as we entered the smooth waters of the Red Sea.

The following is a quote from the newspaper distributed aboard the U.S.S. Gen Greely the fifteenth November, 1945: "Second Bridge Tournament Results: Cpl. Keval and M/Sgt Walkev were high point scorers in the first section of the weekly duplicate bridge tournament that was held last night in the Troop Officers' Mess. The Keval-Walkev team ran up a total of 130 points from the East-West position to outscore seventeen other pairs."

"F/O Babcock and F/O Sheard were the top pair playing the North-South hands with a point score of 117."

In the run-off we were defeated. I thought we did quite well, though.

Sailing up the Red Sea we could see the desert and mountains on both sides of us and steamed right by Mount Ararat. When Port Said came into sight there were several ships and boats at anchor. Several were already waiting their turn to go through the Suez Canal. We anchored our ship to wait our turn.

I watched the fishing boats moving away from port, bobbing up and down like corks. Anyone on those boats not acclimated to the constant bobbing would probably be sick shortly. I appreciated being on the large steam ship we were on, as ours was sitting in the water solid as a rock. I commented to myself, "Babcock, just wait 'till you're in the North Atlantic!"

We could see in the distance tops of other ships crossing in the Canal. They looked as if they were floating on the desert. At night we located the Southern Cross and enjoyed sleeping under the stars, even on the metal deck.

The empty gun turret in the front of the top deck was my preferred place to sleep. Top deck was always cooler than in the holds (decks) where the EM slept. When moving, the ship would swing rhythmically down a wave, do a little twist, and then swing up with another twist at the top, rocking us to sleep. This was much cooler than in the stuffy hold called Five Charlie, to which we were assigned.

Most of the men had entered a mustache contest. Who could grow the biggest? I believe a Red Cross lady initiated this contest and hundreds entered. Although I grew one, I didn't have a ghost of a chance. The winner had a handlebar neatly waxed and almost wide enough to reach his ears. Who wanted to shave in cold seawater anyway?

This Red Cross lady had gained so much weight she was about to pop out all over and had no clothes that fit properly. The captain (from Fort Worth, Texas) was somewhat portly, so he loaned her some of his clothes. She looked better in pants. She initiated diversions for us, such as the mustache contest, putting on the bridge tournament and other programs for entertainment, mostly for the EM.

Finally our turn came to cross to the Mediterranean through the Suez Canal for an unforgettable trip through the desert. We were close to the Biblical land where Jesus had lived. What a thrill to see the area we'd read so much about in the Bible. Most of the scenery we could see from the ship was desert.

Upon reaching the Mediterranean Sea, our ship slipped through the smooth water almost effortless. I didn't see any land while passing through the Mediterranean Sea until passing through the straits along the Rock of Gibraltar. The Sea blended in with the Atlantic Ocean waves as we passed by "The Rock," and the colder air suddenly took our breath away. That night was the last night I spent on top deck. Cold water was splashing on me making it just too "dern" cold. It was now December. What a change this was from the tropics.

As we sailed toward the North Sea, the waves became higher and higher. The propeller would go *flop-flop* as it came out of the water in its rotation, making the whole ship shudder, while the nose dropped down into the trough. Up and down went the nose, the stern following, on and on, up and down. The winter storm of the North Atlantic was rapidly getting worse. The ship's loudspeaker warned everyone to be cautious when walking. Within a day or two it was announced over the ship's public address system: "Now hear this. Now hear this. One soldier has received a broken leg while walking to mess. Keep your hand on the handrails."

The next night I gladly went below and crawled meekly onto my hammock. It was easy to sleep in as it just rocked side to side and, it was warm. The ship continued wallowing through the winter storm, making walking to the mess difficult and cold, as we had to walk in the open air. It was announced the ship had come within one degree of capsizing. All persons I've talked to that came home across the North Sea agreed that there was a bad winter storm when they crossed. One ship farther south of us lost her propeller and sent out an SOS. We thought for a time we would try to rescue the stricken ship but a closer ship had already gone to their aid. After feeling the shudders through our huge ship when the propeller came out of the water, I now could understand better how a propeller could break off.

Incidentally, when we heard the loudspeaker squawk, "Now hear this, now hear this, all officers from C-Charlie line up on the starboard side of the ship ready for chow," we hurried into that line. That loud speaker would be coming on and off all day and half the night, it seemed. It always began with: "SQUAWK, Now Hear This, Now Hear This."

Suez Canal—1945—On ship coming home from the war

Captain from Fort Worth, TX

When we came into radio range of New York the radio was turned into the Loud Speaker system of the ship, and said: SQUAWK "Now hear this." Advertising ditties came in on the live broadcasts from New York City, causing everyone on board to convulse in laughter. We'd paid no attention to them before we went overseas, but now they really "caught our attention". How silly they sounded. After being overseas two or three years, these little ditties sounded so ridiculously, i.e. (in a small voice) "Dentine Chewing Gum, Dentine Chewing Gum ...etc." "Super Suds, Super Suds... etc." We absolutely laughed until our sides ached.

It was still another night before reaching the waters of the United States. When finally we approached New York Harbor, we stood on top deck trying to see the Statue of Liberty through the morning mist and fog. Finally she began to come into view. The feeling when seeing her is difficult to describe. This meant the war was really over and we were HOME. Liberty we had fought for, the Pursuit of Happiness also, but the greatest of these is FREEDOM. Going through our minds at the moment were thoughts of the millions of soldiers who had died for that "freedom for all." There were many damp eyes. That great lady was the finest sight I'd ever seen—not just a statue, she representing freedom itself. This was the first time I really appreciated that grand old lady.

As I gazed upon the Statue of Liberty, my mind went back to the little known fierce battle fought in Kohima, India. This is the battle that turned back the Japanese from invading India. The Japanese had fought an intense and desperate battle, causing many casualties on both sides. They were successfully resisted by the combined efforts of the British, Indian, Australian and American armed forces. One tombstone at Kohima says it like this, "We gave up our tomorrows for your todays." How true. Few Americans know or even heard of that desperate battle, one of the most intense and important battles of the war in the CBI.

We finally docked in the harbor of New York. All 3500 of us departed the ship onto a large open warehouse. The Red Cross was there, shoving milk cartons into our hands as fast as they could. Yes, milk. This was the nutritional item I missed most while overseas.

The twenty-nine days at sea were over at last. This was the first taste of milk for me in a year and a half. It wasn't long until there were about 3000 men and 300 women looking for a restroom and not a one to be found.

A couple of long hours later we were loaded on a ferryboat to cross over the bay to Camp Kilmer, New Jersey, an Army Base. There were some restrooms on the Ferry taking us to New Jersey, but not enough. Many of the men stood close to the rail doing what we had to do.

Several phones were available at Camp Kilmer and were all busy for some time. What a thrill it was to hear my wife's voice again and tell her, "I love you and I'm on the way." I was thinking that after almost two years my three-year-old daughter wouldn't even know me, but we would be together.

We were all issued a "Steak Card" at Fort Kilmer, N. J. which, when presented to the mess hall, was good for a free steak with all the trimmings, including ice cream and cake, etc. All we could eat at no cost to us. Each of us piled on much more food than we could then have eaten in a week. I felt ashamed I could not even eat half the T-bone steak, much less all the other food, including pie and ice cream. What a waste. In China I would have gladly paid fifty dollars for such a meal, and could have dined on it for several days. All of us were now in the same fix, wanting to stuff it all in, yet unable to eat more than a few bites.

Being this close but having to wait for transportation made the two days seem like weeks. It was already December 8, 1945 and Christmas was "Right around the corner." Yet there was nothing to do but wait. One night some of the men had slipped out of camp and enjoyed some nightlife in New York City. I didn't dare leave for fear I'd miss my ride.

Some day-coaches were finally brought in for those of us going to Texas, and we all got aboard. When we felt the bump of the train engine hooking on to our coaches, we knew most of the 13,000-mile trip home, started seven weeks ago, was behind us now.

When one soldier started a game of "Black Jack" Poker, I thought to myself I was so broke I might as well risk the few dollars I had left. This game helped to pass the time. Lady Luck smiled on me; I quit playing when I had won ninety dollars.

Going home! This thought kept sweeping through my head: going home. It made me feel a little shaky. The good old United States countryside was a thrill to see as we went clickity-clacking along.

What a change from living in a combat zone, flying in storms over unbelievable terrain and now sitting in a train rolling along in the good old US of A. Almost before I knew it, we were entering the Saint Louis Railroad Terminal where they switched our coaches to the Katy Railroad Line. The last leg of railroad would take us to the great state of Texas. "We're nearly there," I thought: "Maybe tonight?"

Arriving at the Dallas Terminal after dark, I searched the crowd almost desperately for my wife. She wasn't there. Then I saw her father waving at me. Tears came to my eyes and again I thanked God for my being alive and home. Pop looked like a million dollars to me and he just handed me the keys to my Ambassador Nash sedan and told me Faegene was waiting for me at such and such a motel. He was catching the train to return to West Texas. My homecoming had taken a long time and that waiting was about over at last. I thought how such a short time ago I felt I'd never live to get home. I hadn't driven a car for about sixteen months. I somehow managed the Dallas traffic.

I realize that my explanation of the feelings and thoughts in my mind are beyond my ability to fully express, my readers. It is sufficient to say, I felt as if my life was beginning again.

Faegene was waiting for me in bed.

We pilots had to check in to Love Field for arrangements for being relieved from active duty. It took them three days to give me a 19-day delay in route to Randolph Field, San Antonio, Texas for separation from the Army Air Corps.

Due to that nineteen-day delay in route, we had time to have Christmas with our families in both McCamey and Sonora. What a switch from last year in the Red Cross Building in Casablanca, French Morocco, Africa. It now seemed like at least two years ago. So much had happened in that long fifteen months overseas.

At Randolph Field a quickly arranged medical examination was given us by non-professional personnel, then issued papers and orders that culminated in my being separated from the service, effective the seventeenth of February, 1946.

It was easier to get out of the Army Air Corps than it had been to get in, by golly! I was now as good as out. I could make my own mistakes and decisions again. Some of the men, smarter than me, signed up for another two years in order to receive their forty-five day vacation with pay offered upon ending our overseas tour.

Upon reporting back after forty-five days, they simply told the Army Air Force they changed their minds and wanted out. They were then released from the Army Air Corps, after enjoying their forty-five day vacation. Good old Army. I was just glad to be getting out so I could resume living my family life again.

My brother-in-law Merel also made it home before Christmas, so the whole family was able to celebrate together. The bad dream we had been living was now over. How strange it seemed, yet how great it was.

Bob and Opal Parham were both working for Pop Eddleman in the airplane re-building business. Pop had been buying Army Liaison planes the Army no longer wanted. Bob was a licensed airplane mechanic, flight instructor and had his commercial license. Opal worked with the fabric wing covering and whatever was needed. When Pop couldn't find any more planes to rebuild, Bob and Opal took their son Bill Turnbull and moved to Monahans, where Bob set up an aviation business at the local airport. He had also passed his instruments flight rating. One night he made a night Charter flight and got caught in a storm late that night when arriving back at the Wink airport. He crashed in the terrible weather trying to make an instrument approach to land there.

Opal took over the flying business and moved to Pecos. Somehow she made her living and her son Bill became a pilot for her. She began a cotton-dusting air service with her airplane.

Home at last!

1947 - Kenneth, Faegene and Sherry

1948 - Kenneth, Faegene and Sherry

Chapter 11

A Civilian Again and In Business

I had been used to making my own decisions when flying and living my military life during the past three and a half years. Now I failed to realize my wife had plans and hopes, too. I found out later that her hopes were to join me in preparing our store for our appliance and radio business. We failed to communicate. She had rented a vacant store building for our new business and I automatically thought of all the things I'd have to do, excluding her from doing any work. Although I'm sure she tried to "reach" me, I did not realize she was looking forward to helping.

I borrowed an air compressor and paint gun, bought the color paint I wanted for the twelve-foot ceiling, walls and floor, and proceeded to paint the whole sixty-foot by thirty five foot building to suit myself.

I then made an evaporative air conditioner out of wood, metal, and chicken wire, and installed an old circular electric fan inside the cooler box. The squirrel-cage type fans were not yet available. I rigged up some copper tubing with dripping holes cut into the bottom of the tubing and installed directly above the wood shavings held between the walls of chicken wire. I could turn the water on and off with a valve I installed inside the store. That rigging made it definitely cooler inside the building.

I built a divider wall to separate the repair bench in the back from the office, which was behind a counter stretching almost across the room. I also built a desk. Now all I needed was merchandise and I'd be in business. Did you notice I said: "I'd" be in business? Faegene didn't say anything, but I know now how I was hurting her by my blindness to her feelings. She never was one to express her feelings.

Today as I look back to 1946, I wonder how other returning servicemen were handling their plans and their lives after the long interval spent in wartime under years of stress. We married men, especially those of us who had children, had been under more stress, I believe, than most of the single men. The worry of loved ones at home created a constant stress problem for us. Playing bridge or poker helped relieve some of that stress. Our wives wanted to receive letters often, but due to the 15,000 mile mail delivery it wasn't too regular. Some of our letters undoubtedly ended up scattered on the mountainsides of the Himalayan Mountains. Now that I'm home, I didn't have to worry any more, right? Well, not exactly. Communication is a must in a marriage.

Returning to the life we had left was difficult. Much time had gone by and situations had changed. Returning home needed more understanding for families. While life overseas went on for us, life also continued on for those at home. We returning men and women had to recognize and catch up with the progress of about three years. To resume the role of husband and father I needed to adjust my thinking. My daughter was four years old with no memories of me.

Life goes on, adjustments came, sometimes slowly. Our life was returning to normal little by little. "Am I the kind of father I should be?" I wondered to myself. Was I putting too much emphasis on work rather than family? As there were no houses for rent or sale, we were still staying with my in-laws. That was not good for our family relationship either.

I was able to hire J.E Alexander under the G I Bill to work as a radio repairman. One day a salesman came through with some small radios in wooden cases in the back seat of his car. I bought them, and had little trouble selling them. But where were all the appliances and larger radios I had ordered? I drove to El Paso, taking two other merchants with me. We all were trying to buy merchandise to sell. I brought back some promises, but couldn't sell a one. There was no market for promises.

- Back to Flight Instructor Again

In 1947 my brother-in-law, Merel Eddleman, established a flight school for veterans, under the GI Bill. He needed me to instruct and I needed a job. Another young man, Bill Williams, had returned from the war as a pilot and joined Merel and me as an instructor.

To help create more interest in flying, we offered a free instructional ride to eligible Veterans, quickly signing up about twelve men. We offered to take their wives up to acquaint them with the safety of flying. I took my new students' wives for an airplane ride, all but one. I asked her husband why she had not come out. He said: "Do you really want to take her up?" I answered "Sure." "Well, O.K., I'll go get her."

By the time she arrived the West Texas sun had climbed higher, the hot air lowering the "lift" in these little two-place sixty-five HP airplanes. When I saw my students' wife I guessed her weight as at least two hundred and fifty pounds. I figured my plane in this heat would be strained to carry both of us. We taxied to the longest runway, opened the throttle wide open, released the brakes and started rolling, faster and faster, until we finally eased off the ground, heading toward the electric high wires at the end of the runway. It had always puzzled me that airports seemed to always have high lines around it.

Little by little we climbed until we cleared the wires. I almost had to go under them. I managed to inch the plane up to about 150 feet. We made a big circle of the town and went right back to the airport. She really enjoyed her first airplane ride. I didn't let her know how happy I was to get us back on the ground.

One of my first students was having trouble learning how to make a simple turn. I would explain, demonstrate, and have him try it. Next day he would do it wrong again. When this happened the third time I asked him why he couldn't do it correctly. He answered: "Because you are teaching me wrong."

I asked what he meant. He answered: "The 1941 Encyclopedia Britannica tells the right way. You are teaching me wrong." He brought the book to me, and sure enough, it told how to make a turn, "Push the rudder in the direction you wish to go." That was completely incorrect. Even dangerous. It was difficult to convince my student the need to coordinate the rudder with the aileron and then apply some backpressure on the elevator, which actually turns the airplane. The written word is usually expected to be correct, especially in an encyclopedia. It isn't always. I was able to finally prove to him I was right and the book was wrong, but it was a struggle.

Another time we were taking a group of students, some dual and some solo, on a cross-country trip together. When we started flying under some broken clouds not far above us, one of my solo students suddenly turned around, dropped his nose a little, and flew back toward an airport, with throttle wide open, and landed. I wondered what in the world was wrong, engine trouble, sickness?

I followed him to the airport to ask him what was wrong. He said: "Didn't you see those clouds coming at us? I had to get on the ground before they caught me." It took some tall talking to convince him they were not only above us, we were approaching them, and they weren't approaching us. He just knew we couldn't fly in clouds even if we had the instruments, and was really frightened that the clouds would engulf him. He had to think about it a little while before it finally dawned on him about the clouds. He only had about five solo hours. He continued taking lessons and earned a commercial pilots' license. He proved himself as a pilot once; while practicing spins solo, his engine quit. He made a safe forced landing in the greasewood. We were proud of him.

One of my students, Ed Hall, a fellow member of the United Methodist Church, was one of those men who was able to promote jobs I would never think about, such as building a concrete tennis court behind the church. One Saturday morning I found myself shoveling sand and gravel into one of two cement mixers and pouring concrete, along with five other Methodist men. It took us most of the day with Ed working right along with us.

When he decided to learn to fly he "tore" into that with his usual passion and enthusiasm, becoming a good student and a fine pilot. His enthusiasm through life has continued with the cooperation of his wife, Mary, as they raised three fine children. Their son Leslie even learned to fly and graduated from college as a Methodist minister of the Gospel.

- Post-War Housing Problems

So many soldiers returning from WW II badly needed housing, as evidenced by my own difficulties. The smaller towns like McCamey were apparently low-priority to Government housing promotion.

After living with Faegene's family for about a year, we finally found a small house to rent and immediately moved into it. Then during the next three months we moved twice more. The last move left us next door to a schoolteacher and his family. The house was a nice three-bedroom house much larger than ours. When they later moved out of town, we quickly rented it. It seemed like a palace compared to the small cottages we had lived in. We were much happier in our new home.

One night my wife heard a noise outside, and woke me up. I hurriedly reached in the closet for my shotgun. It wasn't there. Faegene had put it in the top of the closet behind some boxes. I didn't know that, however, and had to rush outside without it. Someone was at the back door and apparently heard me going out the front, started running and hit our clothesline in the back yard. I was too late to catch him. Running into a clothesline would deter most people. In the days to follow I watched around town for a man with a bruised neck. I never did find him. I did convince Faegene not to hide the gun again, though.

A month later I was at our store working late when someone again tried to get in the back door of the house. Faegene called the police. "Shorty" Belcher, constable, came out to investigate. He came to the front door, and sent Faegene around on the dark side of the house while he took the lighted side. Again the prowler escaped, thank goodness. Faegene might have been hurt.

- Flying in West Texas Weather

Since it was required in our G I flying school curriculum that our students fly ten hours at night, Merel paid me to ride with them as a safety precaution in case of unexpected bad weather. Even an experienced student might have difficulty handling some of the bad weather we quite often had. The weather was quite unpredictable in that part of Texas; strong winds could and did hit without warning.

My accompanying the students at night paid off all right. One night a student, Bob McKinney, and I had been flying for several hours. In the meantime I became aware the wind had come up, but Bob hadn't noticed it. When he returned to the airport to land he was unable to get lined up with the runway. A forty or fifty mile an hour crosswind had come up. I waited until he had tried several times. He just couldn't get it to stay lined up in order to land, not fully realizing what the problem was. At night a lighted runway just seems to float around if you have a crosswind, particularly when you're not used to night flying. Bob finally said: "Kenneth, you take it, I can't handle this."

Had an experienced pilot not been with Bob, he would have been in big trouble. I believe he or almost any other inexperienced pilot would have been completely unable to handle such a situation safely. He would have probably damaged the airplane and possibly himself. I took over and made a wheel landing at an air speed of about fifty miles per hour, into the wind and across the lighted runway instead of down it. The wind direction had changed considerably. We rolled only about fifty or seventy-five feet at a slow ground speed, about the width of the runway before coming to a stop.

In addition to requiring nighttime flying, some of the students were ready for larger airplane flying. Merel had a low-wing 150 mile per hour Bellanca, which had flaps and retractable landing gear. He would carry three students at a time with him in the Bellanca and give them cross-country experience as well as familiarization with flaps and landing gear retracting.

Sooner or later most pilots who fly aircraft with retractable landing gear will forget to lower the landing gear prior to landing. We used an acronym to help us avoid forgetting to lower the gear, "GUMP" (Gas on fullest tank, Undercarriage down, Mixture full rich, and Propeller in high pitch). I have used this acronym every landing I made in a retractable-geared aircraft. Today, now that I've retired from flying, I can brag about it. No landings have I made without letting the gear down.

Merel had several thousand hours of flying, including many airplanes with retractable gears. He had some students on an instructional cross-country flight one day and kept talking to his students while landing at the Big Springs airfield. The tower was telling him by radio over and over that his gear was up. Merel couldn't hear them, because the "gear up" warning horn in the cockpit was so loud. He was an unhappy pilot when he realized just seconds before he landed that his wheels were still retracted. The plane was suddenly skidding on its belly.

Later I had to razz him some as I had also been flying many retractable landing gear planes. I also razzed Merel for talking too much when he should have been listening. Fortunately the damages were minor on the Bellanca and he had it flying again in a couple of days. He never again forgot to lower the gear.

On student "Chick" Comstock's long cross-country flight we flew to El Paso. He was working toward his commercial flight license and needed more cross-country time. We flew a Porterfield two-place tandem sixty-five horsepower airplane that cruised about ninety-six MPH. We flew the two hundred and thirty miles non-stop to El Paso, re-fueled and took off for home. A thunderstorm formed rapidly ahead of us, causing us to divert from our course a few miles to avoid it. Approaching Salt Flats about ninety-five miles from El Paso, the clouds began closing together just ahead of us on Guadeloupe pass. We landed at Salt Flat emergency airport and were soaked with rain while re-fueling. Without instruments and an appropriate aircraft, we could not go over the pass in that storm. We needed a place to spend the night, but where?

We went over to the one building, a service station located on the highway, where I paid for the gas and asked about lodging. We were told there was no lodging to be had there and they would be closing down after the El Paso Bus stopped by on its way to Carlsbad, N.M.

No place to stay, and the rain was still falling hard. We found out that the bus would come back through Salt Flats early the next morning, so we bought round-trip tickets to Carlsbad and slept the 100 miles into Carlsbad.

We called home to let our wives know where we were then walked around Carlsbad a little while, went to a picture show and then back to the bus station. We were able to wait in the bus and woke up back at Salt Flats early that morning. We had slept on the bus all the way back to Salt Flats.

It was about an hour later before we could takeoff for home, and we climbed over the pass on course for McCamey, some 175 miles away. We passed close to the tallest mountain in Texas, Guadalupe Peak. The clouds had all disappeared and we had a beautiful early morning trip over the pass and on over the town of Pecos and home.

Several of our G.I. flying school graduates continued flying after finishing the government program, some even buying airplanes of their own. Although the school only lasted about a year, there were about thirty students that completed the course. Most of them earned their Private License with three or four received their Commercial License. I was glad that these men took advantage of the G.I. Bill to learn to fly because soon the government support for our school was discontinued and I was again without a job other than my store.

I turned all my attention to making my store pay off. J.E. Alexander had found himself a better job and left, so I was back to repairing radios myself and selling what little merchandise I could obtain. I was barely holding my own, financially, and was getting a bit pessimistic, when things suddenly changed, for the worse.

One Friday afternoon in March, 1948, my stomach began hurting, so after a little while I closed up my store and went to my doctor. He said: "Get up on the table. Before I give you medicine I want to check you for appendicitis. "Well," he decided, "You don't have appendicitis." He then gave me a laxative.

I still had the stomachache all night Friday and Saturday. On Saturday night I literally walked the floor all night with pain, so about five o'clock a.m. Sunday morning I tried to wake up my doctor by banging on his door, but no luck. After having walked the floor all night from the pain, I was getting desperate. I went to another doctor's house about 6:00 A.M., managing to awaken his wife. She called the doctor out of bed and I could tell he was just barely awake. He didn't check me, just telephoned instructions to the hospital to give me a laxative (I think) and some pain pills. I went directly to the hospital for the pills.

This laxative or the pain pills gave me relief, and I stayed home and slept most of Sunday and Sunday night. Monday morning I also continued to sleep, getting up about dinnertime. Then, Monday afternoon about five o'clock, the second doctor's older brother, Dr. James Cooper, called me to come to the hospital so he could check me. I told him I was feeling pretty good, but he insisted. I went on down to the hospital, and he found I had a painful spot on my stomach. He shocked me by telling me we had to operate at once. When I proposed going a hundred and twenty miles to San Angelo where there was a larger hospital, he said, "No, there isn't time. You have to have an operation now." So I called Faegene to come down, and told her what Doctor Cooper had said. We told him to go ahead. He was ready to operate. It was six p.m.

As it turned out, my appendix had ruptured, even adhering to the liver, causing much infection in that area. They tell me I died twice on the operating table. The doctor told Faegene on one occasion that it didn't look good at all. He didn't think I would make it. She had been praying, and with absolute confidence assured him I would. There was a group of our Sunday school class over in the church across the street praying, also.

A search went out for a blood donor, and fortunately they found a match. At this time, to find a blood donor, one headed to town where people congregated (usually the cafe), opened the door and hollered, "Does anyone have type __ blood?"

Faegene called my parents about eleven o'clock Monday night (living in Sonora, Texas, a hundred and twenty miles away) and told my partially deaf father I was very sick and might die. He thanked her for calling and said, "Well, if he gets any worse let us know." He surely didn't hear what she told him. I was rolled to my room at four o'clock the next morning. I felt fine and surprised the nurses by crawling on my hands and knees onto my bed and flopping onto my back. I felt no pain.

This was the beginning of twenty long days in the hospital, getting hourly shots of Penicillin. In those days Penicillin was new and could only be given in small quantities. Daily shots of Vitamin B-12 were added and what else I didn't know. On Saturday, six days after the operation, I had a reaction to a blood transfusion and the RN from Fort Stockton, a friend Faegene had hired to be the night RN for me, immediately stopped the transfusion and sent another nurse for the doctor. Dr. James Cooper was attending a party in his honor and had instructed his brother (Dr. Hal Cooper) not to leave the hospital until the party was over. He left anyway to check on his oil business out in the country and was delayed on his return by a flat tire.

Dr. James, as we called him, arrived shortly and took care of the problem. He was sure upset at his brother. That was another close call for me—and probably for his brother, too.

The following Monday the wound opened and the infection started draining. That scared me. Dr. Cooper heard me call out, rushed to my room and looked in and then said with a big smile on his face, "That's what I've been hoping to see happen. You'll make it now." Heck, I'd never doubted that.

We were now in the hot season in West Texas and I complained a lot about being too hot. I begged for a little air conditioning. I was ignored and kept on complaining and griping until Pop installed an evaporative cooler in the window. The fan was blowing away from me and there wasn't any water on it, not cooling me at all. I later found out Doctor James wanted the room hot. Now why didn't he tell me that in the first place?

During the first days in the hospital I had no appetite. Sybil, Merel's sister-in-law, brought me some homemade chicken soup and fed it to me. It tasted good and made me feel better. I sure appreciated her thoughtfulness. Next day I was given a slice of tomato and was surprised that I'd forgotten what tomatoes tasted like.

As I began to feel better I began reading Readers Digest. I read about a doctor who went to Africa to practice and while there developed a successful hernia operation, using camel leather. I don't know why I remembered that.

Near the end of my twenty-day stay I also had a reaction to the B-12 shot I'd been getting daily. I can still taste the strong liver-flavor of that B-12 shot.

I was released from the hospital on the twenty-first day, and happy to go home and sit on the front porch during the day while Faegene was at our store. We had a young man, Ernest "Abey" Lindsey, working for us at the store. He was able to keep the store open and clean while I was sick. I was back to work in about another week and became busy repairing the radios that were waiting to be fixed. I gave thanks to the Almighty that he had again spared me from death.

About three months later I was still struggling to break even financially when Army Armstrong and Mel Reeves from Odessa walked into my store. Army was a friend who owned a Music store in Odessa, and Mel was now his partner. They had extra pianos to sell and needed another outlet. "How about selling some pianos out of your store, Ken? We can put some on your floor." I was thrilled. I would make a small commission on each piano sold. This would work out well for all of us. Being a pianist I could demonstrate them.

Almost before I knew it we had seven pianos on the floor. We sold several, some to the churches and to individuals. To be able to demonstrate the pianos I spent some time practicing. I also hired a fine young lady piano teacher to work in our store during the summer. She was a big help in demonstrating and selling pianos. She helped out also as a clerk. Both of us played piano and sometimes gave a little concert for those who came by to listen. One piece we played was a Mozart Concerto written for piano and Orchestra. She played the score for orchestra on a second piano, while I played the Concerto. Can you picture such a thing occurring in a small oil field town far out in the desert of West Texas, creosote and black brush all around, many miles away from big city Music Halls?

One of our first piano sales was to Darrel Warren, a farmer living in the new farming area six miles south of McCamey, as the crow flies. The only road to that new area was a heavily traveled ranch road with alkali dusts about ten inches deep. The Pecos River made it necessary to detour across a bridge so that six miles as the crow flies became twenty miles, twelve on the highway. A friend took me through six miles of alkali dust to visit the prospective customer and I sold a piano to Darrel's wife Barbara for their twin daughters. Hers was also the first new home built in the new farming area. When we returned to town after selling the piano, I had my friend's car washed. I've never seen a dustier car, inside and out.

All good things come to an end, it seems, as the Piano Company partnership broke up less than a year later. Army had to return his pianos to Odessa. My business was still not doing well. The depression and drought of the 1950s was beginning and the price of oil had dropped. I was repairing a few car radios now, with Abbey taking them out and re-installing them for me. When my health improved I was able to slide in under the steering wheel, with my feet hanging over the back of the front seat to work on the radio while upside down. I was a mite younger than I am now.

By 1950 most of my income was coming from radio repairs and I was making a few house calls. One afternoon I started on a call a mile east of town. I noticed the wind was a little higher than usual, but didn't think much about it, as the wind was nearly always blowing in West Texas. As I reached the edge of town I saw a sign near the road topple over. I was driving into the wind and realized the wind was really increasing. Then a large sign on the other side of the road blew over. I then realized that I had better go back and check on Faegene and Sherry in that ramshackle building we were living in by the airport.

The wind had become a steady high wind right out of the east. Arriving at the airport, I saw the big hanger doors hanging straight out by the top runners. There were two planes already blown out of the hanger, their noses pointing east and their tails up in the air, rolling backward. Another plane came rolling out, the wind holding its tail up also. A couple of them flopped over on their backs. WOW. I started to go try to stop the planes from rolling and quickly thought better of doing that. Our house was shaking with that wind.

When the wind finally subsided we found the planes inside the hanger had become wedged by the wind. Fortunately the planes that were blown out sustained little damage. We were just lucky. This was the only time I've ever seen such a strong, steady high wind that just kept blowing for over an hour. I have no idea what weather phenomenon caused it. We decided it was a cyclone.

At that time Trans-Texas airlines had an office on the airport with weather recording. The wind registered a steady eighty miles an hour.

In 1949 I began stocking phonograph records. I was already selling record players and combination radio-record players. At the time the 78-rpm phonograph records was all there was but in a few short months Columbia Records came out with some 33 1/3 rpm 7-inch records and some 10 and 12 inch long-play 33 1/3 speed records. In a few months RCA then put the large-hole seven inch 45 RPMs on the market. What a mess this was. RCA flooded the market with special big-hole record players in order to push their new size records. Other manufactures of players were faced with having to make automatic record changer for all three speeds and three sizes. Just think, three speeds and three sizes, with two different hole-sizes to "boot". This caused new designs in record players and gave all repairmen headaches.

I handled Western music, which sold best out in that section of the country and some popular and classical music as well in albums. I had to handle records and record players for all three speeds and sizes.

When Elvis Presley became a star some two years later, sales of records really boomed. Christmas I sold many of his albums and record players on which to play them. I sold other paraphernalia featuring Elvis also: guitars, accessories and Christmas music books. This made my best Christmas ever.

Mr. Seals came in from the town of Rankin with his two sons, buying violin and guitar supplies. Many times he would play a guitar for us. He was a professional artist on the guitar or violin and taught his two sons to play those instruments. Both became well known artists, particularly Dan Seals (England Dan), who made many recordings. Jimmy was the younger of the two and could play anything he picked up.

As we travel through life the people we meet influence us, or we sometimes influence others. Putting in the music line and records attracted some younger customers, including one young high school boy, Bob Thompson. I encouraged him to join the recently founded Symphony Orchestra of Midland and Odessa as he played a bassoon quite well in the school orchestra at McCamey. I also encouraged Bob to come in and listen to classical music records of which I had many. He was enthralled. My experience of playing in the Austin and University of Texas Symphony Orchestras were so fulfilling to me I wanted to encourage others to get that opportunity.

Bob began playing in the Odessa-Midland Orchestra with full cooperation from his mom and dad. When Bob graduated from high school his parents were able to send him to study in some outstanding musical schools where he majored in playing the bassoon.

Professor Thompson taught graduate ensemble music in the graduate school of the University of Wisconsin, in Milwaukee. He played concerts from time to time, usually with the London Symphony Orchestra in London, as bassoon soloist. Thompson, recently retired, is acclaimed as one of the leading solo bassoonists in the world today and I am proud that I gave a little encouragement at the right time to help him get his opportunity.

On July 4, 1948, we took our first real family vacation. We drove to Cloudcroft, New Mexico, a small tourist town located on top of a 9,000-foot mountain.

The next day I rented a gentle old horse for Sherry Gene (age five) to ride and the old horse followed along behind my horse, walking slowly of course. I looked back often and happened to be looking back just in time to see Sherry being dragged off her horse by a clothesline I hadn't seen. I yelled for her to "duck". She didn't understand. Her horse had walked right under it. Sherry just fell off in slow motion. There was nothing I could do. The old horse obediently stopped when she fell off. That was quite a tumble for a five year old. She wasn't hurt, just had the breath knocked out of her and when I put her back on the horse she was still happy to continue the ride. I kept a sharper lookout for clotheslines. She remembers that fall to this day. It didn't dampen her love for horses though.

We drove over to Mescalera to see the Mescalera (Apache) Indians. They expected to be paid to pose for pictures, so we took few pictures. It was interesting to us to see these Indians, as only sixty or seventy years earlier they had been making raids across West Texas and all the way into Old Mexico, bringing slaves and horses back to their New Mexico camps.

Ken in his Radio-Television Shop

Chapter 12

Thirty Years of Crop-dusting

Seeing the land being cleared for farming only six miles away across the Pecos River gave me an idea. I called my friend Opal Parham, who was operating a crop-dusting operation 100 miles west in Pecos, Texas. I needed more income and called her about the prospect of crop-dusting in the new farming community south of McCamey. She told me she would send her pilot, Glenn Carlsguard, down to talk to me.

I made a deal with her after he came down and looked over the prospects. She offered to furnish me a plane to fly on a commission of a cent a pound, and I would pay the expenses out of the other two cents, sending her the difference. I thought to myself that maybe I might be able to pay on my hospital bill. I appreciated her confidence. She knew and trusted me and I certainly trusted her.

I had never done any crop-dusting, but felt that with my flight experience I could quickly learn. Glenn and Bob Gilmore, a pilot-mechanic working for Opal, flew down in two planes to help me get started on our first job.

Crop-dusting—the most dangerous flying job known. What a reputation crop-duster pilots have earned. They operate from short dirt runways or roads, fly under electric and phone lines, carry heavy loads, make short turnarounds at each end of the farm and fly inches above the crops. Standpipes, posts, wires and equipment all have to be dodged. Every second requires alertness to the dangers. These pilots are often thought of as being crazy, over-confident, etc. In retrospect, I think perhaps it does help if you are a little crazy.

I will never forget my first attempt at crop-dusting. Glenn explained how it was done, then had me follow behind him in the other loaded airplane. It was a J-3 Piper Cub with a 2600 RPM propeller (normally 2300 RPMs). The extra RPMs gave the cub a little more power.

Glenn dived down over the highline leveling off just above the short cotton plants, with me following a swath-width up-wind to his left. I remembered to open my hopper to let the cotton dust start coming out, looking back quickly time to time to guess how much dust I was putting out. I hadn't trimmed the airplane and the nose kept dipping down a little, once allowing my wheels to bump the top of a border of soft dirt. I quickly adjusted the nose trim and again checked the flow of dust, still guessing how much to open the gate. I was very busy. Flying on the return run downwind I almost waited too long to pull up, barely clearing the high lines at the edge of the field. The tailwind increased the ground speed, which, along with the load weight, caused my slight misjudgment in timing of my pull-up. I quickly learned how much and when to open or close the dust hopper door. Also learning, on the first round trip across the field, when to start my downwind pull-up.

When I ran out of dust I flew back and landed on the little road for another load and to check the landing gear. Bob checked the landing gear and straightened it up again. Him being a pilot, I could understand his being a little disgusted.

After we finished that job, we drove Bob Gilmore back to Pecos. We kept both planes in McCamey so that Glen could work with me another day or two.

One morning a few days later, Glenn and I finished our dusting and went down to the drug store and sat at the bar drinking a pineapple milkshake. We had not cleaned up since working, and I admit we carried a strong distinctive odor from the mixture of Sulphur, DDT, and BHC dust we had used. We overheard a couple sitting at a table not far from where we were sitting, complaining about that strange smell. After a few minutes we told them what caused the smell and got a good laugh out of everyone. From then on we tried to clean up before going to town after dusting. We loaded the hopper ourselves, lifting the sacks up and dumping the dust into the hopper behind the pilot's seat, with the propeller blast blowing the dust and sacks behind the airplane and in our faces. We did wear goggles, which protected our eyes from that powder.

Glenn stayed with me a couple of days and then left me to operate by myself on a commission basis. This worked out well financially for Opal and myself. I did quite a bit of crop-dusting that first year. Part of my job was the inspecting of the crops for the various insects and their eggs to checking the results of my dusting. I found that you could only be effective when the wind was fairly calm and the temperature was comparatively cool. Otherwise the dust just flew up and away. Humidity also affected our work.

I learned about what kind of insects laid their eggs and what the eggs looked like. Some were "good" insects so I had to decide whether or not there were enough "good" insects to eat up the worm eggs. Being a crop-duster required special knowledge and ability. It takes time to accumulate the needed experience.

I learned that most operators would likely not hire a crop-duster pilot until he had already completed two seasons. Statistics showed most crop-duster accidents occurred within their first two years. I could certainly appreciate that.

On one occasion in my second year of dusting I needed some help to keep up. Glenn came over and brought up a second duster pilot, Jimmy , with airplanes from the Rio Grande Valley. With three of us operating off one little dirt strip, it was necessary to time our flying just right. Jimmy Mauldin was "pound hungry", as we called it, and kept pushing us in our turns, wanting to carry more loads and cut corners. Finally he and Glenn had an argument about it and when Glenn told him to take it easy, Jimmy started swinging. This became really comical as Glenn was a foot taller than Jimmy, and just held him off by putting his hand on Jimmy's head, while Jimmy just kept swinging away. Of course Jimmy never touched him, so Glenn calmly cooled Jimmy by talking to him.

The reason for telling this story is to show Jimmy's uncontrolled thinking. He had once landed his airplane on top of a car while working off a road in the Rio Grande Valley. He was fired when he did it the second time. He was a good pilot though his attitude was poor. He just rushed too much and didn't think ahead. A year later I heard that Jimmy was killed while working in California, by flying into some high lines. We were sad but felt that Jimmy just did not have the emotional control needed for crop-dusting and that had possibly contributed to his death.

- I Buy My First Crop-dusting Airplane

The next Spring Glenn told me Piper Aircraft had designed an airplane with twice the horsepower of our J-3 Cubs. Neither of us had enough money to buy one, so we approached some farmers, sold them some insecticide in advance, making some profit. With their cooperation we made enough money for a down payment. I financed the rest with my bank, and we were each then able to buy a new airplane.

We purchased these aircraft through Frank Hines of Hobbs, New Mexico, the pilot who had given me my first flight instruction in 1940. Frank had a four-place piper pacer to fly us, along with a student of his, to Lockhaven, Pennsylvania, to pick up our airplanes. We flew from Hobbs, New Mexico, across Oklahoma, where the drought had devastated the farmlands, on to St. Louis for refueling. Next stop was Zanesville, Ohio. We checked into a hotel and found a café. This was only a short time before we starved to death.

That night I heard of a "Y" bridge and took a cab to see what a "Y" bridge was. I had never heard of one before. The bridge simply splits in mid-stream, making a "Y." Yes, it was unusual and well worth seeing.

Early the next morning we flew on to the factory at Lockhaven, Pennsylvania, and picked up our new PA-18 Piper aircraft. Boy, what performance those planes had compared to the J-3 Piper Cubs. We also had a gasoline tank in both wings, giving us extra gasoline. We could take off in only ninety feet and climb rapidly to our cruising altitude. It was fun flying this new airplane and I remember zooming down across an abandoned airfield in Pennsylvania at about fifty feet and scaring two deer.

After spending that night in Zanesville we left early the next morning for Oklahoma in our new planes. We would spend the night with Glenn's parents in Oklahoma. What a nice day it was.

The morning dawned clear and cool and the view below was just beautiful as we flew over the farms and forests. Our average speed was over a hundred miles an hour. Flying relatively low, we enjoyed seeing the changing country as we flew a thousand miles, arriving before dark.

The next morning I left Glenn with his parents and flew non-stop to McCamey. I had a wonderful feeling when flying across the country, seeing so much of life going on below me. This kind of flying is like no other. It's as if you are floating effortlessly above the earth with no troubles to bother you. All is well. You do feel sorry for the people on the ground who cannot see the beauty pilots see from the air. I have always enjoyed sharing this feeling of elation and peace with others when taking them up for a flight.

Arriving at the airport at McCamey, I was proud to show off my new airplane. I took some of my friends and family up for short rides. The next day I flew to Frank Hines Flying Service at Hobbs, New Mexico, to have him replace the rear seat with a dust hopper, and attach a dust spreader. It took about three days including installing a mirror to make it easier to see the dust coming out the spreader. I had remembered my first dusting flight when I had to look back and bounced off that dirt border. That mirror would make things safer while dusting. Although I found that the spreader slowed me some, I still could work at about 100 mile per hour.

Naturally I couldn't wait to show my new equipment to my customers, flying low over the farms. I contacted some potential customers and when the season began I was quite pleased with the performance of my new airplane and the installation. My speed had increased about 40 MPH over those 65 horsepower models. I more than doubled my previous production. Another big plus was my being able to keep the three cents a pound of dust I charged to dust the crops. It wasn't long until I had all my bills paid except the balance on the airplane. I paid that off in the fall.

- Strange Air Currents

Most of my dusting in the McCamey area took place downwind from a 700-foot hill. I used a newly paved road as a runway. Most of the fields were farther away from the hill, away from the air sweeping down the slopes. There were often strong air currents that hit me at take-off and landings, but the fields farther away from the hills were usually free of those air currents.

Early one morning I was loaded and began my take-off on the paved road, going east. I hadn't reached enough flying speed for my tail to lift when I suddenly found myself straddling the fence 60 feet to the left. I was all the way across the barrow ditch and above the fence. Before I could say "Jack Robinson" I was right back on the center of the road with my tail wheel rolling solidly on the pavement again. I still didn't have enough speed for my tail to be off the road. I just sat there continuing the rest of my take-off. I was really dumbfounded at what had happened. As I continued my take-off run, the tail had come up normally; my acceleration then lifted me off the ground as usual. I couldn't explain it and was rather dazed. It had happened so quickly.

Another time early in the morning, I was taking off with a full load on this same road, the tail wheel still running firmly on the pavement, when suddenly I found myself flying above the road about six or eight feet. Within three or four seconds I was back on the pavement without flying speed. I just continued my takeoff run until the tail lifted and I was able to take off normally. I can't explain that incident either. It had to be caused by some kind of horizontal whirlwind or some type of powerful circular wind gust, with the lifting power of at least a 40-mile per hour wind. The average wind at that time was not more than 15 mph.

My passion becomes Reality...

1946 — Our first airplane

Left to right: Father-in-law, Pop Eddleman; daughter, Sherry Babcock; wife, Faegene Babcock; pilot, Ken Babcock

Pop Eddleman and Ken

...And my family shares my dream!

- Preparing For Dispensing Liquid Pesticides

During the spring of 1952 I bought a used Piper PA 18 from Frank Hines and had him equip it for spraying only, with pump, pump fan and booms, complete with nozzles. Now I began spraying liquid, which could be dispensed in winds up to 20 mph., often the wind velocity in my area of operation.

I also bought a portable 1½-inch gasoline pump with hoses to load water into the mixing tank built on the flat bed of the one and a half ton Ford truck. I had already explained to Aaron Cranford, my young truck driver and mixer as much about safety as I could think of, as well as how to mix the chemicals.

We began the spraying applications, using a 4-gallon per acre mixture, until we learned we could do as well if not better with two gallons total liquid per acre. Lowering the volume speeded up our application time and still did a good job. A few years later I changed my rigging again, this time by installing three spinners on each side booms instead of the nozzles, and applied one pint up to one quart of straight chemical per acre, no water. This was also quite effective, particularly when using Methyl Parathion, the so-called "Nerve Gas." When I had first begun spraying we used a 4-gallon mixture of DDT and Toxaphene per acre. This mixture was effective in controlling the bollworms in cotton. Now, with DDT and Toxaphene banned, we had tried switching to Seven dust, with poor results with the budworms. We switched to Methyl Parathion, the nerve gas, applied at the rate of l to 2 pints per acre. This chemical was quite dangerous to humans, whereas the DDT was not, and we had to take precautions. It was also effective on young worms, however, killing them instantly.

While still spraying the four-gallon mixture including Methyl Parathion, Aaron was doing the mixing and loading and was furnished with special rubberized gloves for handling the toxic chemicals. A special charcoal filter mask was also used. When he went to work for me I think he was only 16 years old, or possibly younger. When I had an extra boy working I had him help Aaron. Over the years I worked many young boys and enjoyed them very much. There were too many to mention each one, but they were a special group of young men to me.

My business was growing and I needed a more efficient set up for spraying, especially for Mesquite spraying. Before the next year I found some used equipment at the Midland Airport, a gasoline delivery truck with a two-compartment tank, one compartment for 1,000 gallons of aviation fuel and the other for 500 gallons of truck gasoline. I also bought an old 2-ton truck with a 2,000 gallon tank to carry water when spraying mesquite or defoliating cotton. There was a gear pump installed on each truck, and a 30-foot 1 ½-inch plastic hose to the pump.

I needed a mixing and loader truck, so I made one out of a used fresh-water delivery truck I had purchased. There was a two-compartment tank already installed, and with a little plumbing I was ready for efficient mixing and loading. I cut a 5-foot length of 1 ½ inch metal pipe with a quick connect fitting for 1 ½ inch hose and filed marks for each gallon for the fifty five and the thirty-gallon barrels. Now we could slide that pipe into a fifty or thirty-gallon barrel and suck the exact amount of chemical needed right out of the barrel and into the mixing tank. It was really a neat set up and much faster and safer.

Now those handling chemicals need not make direct contact with the chemicals. I plumbed in a 2-inch rubber flexible hose 24 inches long so that if the valves were closed and the pump was engaged, the flexible hose would blow out, saving the pump and the equipment. The pump was turned on and off by moving a metal bar, installed upright in the floor of the truck. Forward was push, pulling it back was to suck the mixture to the tank. This was ideal for mixing and then loading my spray plane.

The Korean War had begun, and I could use another pilot. I knew Chick Comstock was a good pilot and on reserve status with the Air Force. I suggested to him I could use him as a pilot if he was interested, and he was, as the "handwriting on the wall for him" was to be recalled for the Korean War. I told him I was in an essential industry and working for me would probably excuse him from service. With that in mind, he made the decision to become a crop-duster. When the season began he came to work for me.

- Tractor Application Of Fertilizer

I also put myself into the fertilizing business of treating the cotton with liquid Nitrogen and liquid Phosphoric Acid. I side-dressed the chemicals into the dirt beside the cotton plants by using a WD 45 model Allis Chalmers tractor rigged for applying four rows of the chemicals at a time. By piping both chemicals with separate hoses we dropped it into the grooves of dirt made by knives installed on the tool bar. This effectively gave the young cotton plants a quick boost in growth of about 10 inches in a week.

I was able to start most of the fertilizing two months before the spraying season, so there was little conflict with my crop-dusting. I enjoyed the work although I was often driving the tractor from before daylight until dark. One day a hose came loose and began spraying me on my torso with the anhydrous ammonia, which was extremely cold. I immediately jumped off the tractor and headed for water trying to get some air into my lungs. The nearest water was an irrigation ditch and I jumped right in. I spent several days in the hospital recovering from the ammonia burns. Seemed everything I tried to do involved danger.

Some stiff competition in the fertilizing business entered our farming area the next year — a man named Billy Sol Estes. That guy was a *wheeler-dealer* operator, and managed to buy large quantities of Anhydrous Ammonia (Nitrogen) on credit until the fall. He would then sell it for cash slightly less than his cost, operating his vast farming interests on the income. This was much cheaper for him than paying interest on borrowed money and prevented him from having to borrow large sums of money for his operation. The interest cost amounted to about two percent. This action just cut me out of the fertilizer business, as he was selling Anhydrous Ammonia at less than my cost. It wasn't long until a couple of Pecos Texas businessmen were able to gather enough evidence of fraud on Billy's part to get him convicted and sent to prison for several years.

A former customer of mine, Pete Looney, moved back to our farming area and told me he wanted me to fertilize his cotton and take care of all insect control. He followed all my advice. I was quite pleased, and so was he, when he harvested his cotton with an average of a little over three bales to the acre of clean, top quality long-staple cotton, and was able to pick it all by machine. Unfortunately for me he left the area with his grubstake. He was now able to finance some heavy machinery contracts with better profit than farming. His crop had set a production record for the area.

When I had my first forced landing I had already logged five-thousand hours of total flight time. My crew had gassed up my airplane by pumping it from a 55-gallon barrel after I finished a defoliating cotton job near Denver City, Texas.

I left for home by taking off on the road to the west, climbing quickly and turning to wave farewell to Albert White. The engine quit cold. I just continued my turn and glided back over the fence, landing in New Mexico. My gasoline-settling bowl was full of water. I drained it and took off again, climbing quickly. When I again turned the plane to wave, the engine quit a second time. Five thousand hours before my first forced landing, then five minutes before my second one. Same problem. This time we used an Allen wrench and drained both wing tanks from a plug under each wing. By mistake, water had been pumped into the tanks along with the gasoline. We had almost a gallon of water in those tanks. In McCamey the next morning we installed quick-drain connections under both wings. Once more I had learned the hard way.

- Lloyd McKinney, Now Foreman

I had talked my good friend Lloyd McKinney into working for me as "swamper" (foreman) one summer. He had just retired from the City of McCamey as bookkeeper and city manager. He wanted to get out into the open air. I guaranteed him to be outside and have plenty of open air.

Lloyd took over the job of running the mixing truck and the ground crew. I was sure happy to have him and he did a great job. We also enjoyed each other's company.

We would start the spraying year early by spraying Mesquite to control tree growth using herbicides. The herbicide would temporarily stop the growth of mesquite by killing the leaves for several years. This released more water for the grass and allowed more sunlight, which improved the quality and quantity of grass for the livestock.

During the fifteen years we sprayed brush in Sutton County (Sonora, Texas), we would first move the equipment to Sonora, and work out of there for about six weeks. We would then return to McCamey in time to begin spraying cotton. Each year when we were preparing to go to work, Lloyd would forget which way to move the pump handle in the truck. When we began to work he invariably pushed the pump control handle when he should have pulled. This would blow out the safety hose, spraying whoever was opening the valves, usually me. After the first "blow-out," he remembered how to do it until the next season. They always got a good laugh at that, all except me.

Kenneth with friends, Freddie and Lloyd McKinney

- Cashes Taylor

Cashes Taylor

When in Sonora I stayed with my parents. I would do some weeding and mowing around our home when there was a break in my spraying. There was always something to do when I had the time.

I worked closely with the ASCS government office. Cashes Taylor, their Field Agent, helped the ranchers and myself in locating and measuring the blocks of mesquite infestation to be sprayed. Cashes and I had known each other ever since I was a small boy when he was Deputy Sheriff of Sonora, Sutton County in the early 1930s. He and his wife, Nancy, had lived in the Jail House with his wife and two children.

Due to the hilly terrain and fenced land, some of my work in Sutton County was difficult to measure. Cashes and I would get in his pick-up with the aerial maps and locate the perimeters, then mark and measure them on the aerial map. Cashes took me on some wild rides through the brush and trees and up over the hills, not speeding, just crawling over rocks and ledges using his "Grandma" gear. Cashes was an expert at that.

While we were often together Cashes would talk to me about how God was letting us be the caretaker of His land. Cashes always came up with excellent ideas and suggestions about life. He also told me about his daughter whom I'd only known as a small child. She had graduated from the University of Texas at Austin and worked for the Railroad Commission to help pay her way. He was proud of his daughter. She had married her childhood sweetheart before graduating from the University and was then living in Wichita Falls, Texas. Cashes expressed the wish that I could meet her some day when we both were in Sonora. I enjoyed the times we spent together in the West Texas pastures of Sutton County, also learning of his early cowboy days on his dad's ranch in the mountains of New Mexico.

- A Close Call, Forced Landing at the Airport.

One morning I was ready to spray mesquite on the Meckel ranch six miles north of town. As usual we were up about 4:30 AM for breakfast. I always bought breakfast for the crew and myself at the Big Tree Restaurant early each morning.

I sent the boys on out to get in position to begin flagging when the sun allowed me to begin to work all day, so I insisted they all eat breakfast. If the weather permitted we would work all day long and skip dinner.

This day, I miscalculated the time and was too anxious to take off. After taking off I realized it was still too early, so I decided to circle the airport before heading toward the Meckel ranch. As I circled the field I began thinking of the solid growth of larger mesquite trees, the phone lines, high lines and fences I would be flying over that I could not see in the dark. I thought to myself there would be no possible safe place to land for six miles out to my landing strip.

The engine was running smoothly until I had nearly finished the first circle of the airport and then it quit cold. I dropped the nose, turned onto a short base leg, turned to the runway and landed. The momentum of landing carried me to the parking area, with just enough momentum to swing my tail around into a perfect parking attitude exactly by the tie-down ropes. This space was also right beside a pay phone booth there on the airport. I sat there a minute in the seat, thinking what a close call that had been. God must have known I needed help. Had I not circled the airport that dark morning that could have been the end of my airplane and probably me.

I had a mechanic's name and phone number in my pocket notebook so I called Midland and woke him up. He told me he could grab some tools, rent an 182 Cessna and be in Sonora in about an hour and a half. I told him to get with it. I'm glad I carried his phone number and arranged for this possibility ahead of time.

Sure enough, in a little over an hour he was landing his plane. He went right to work, and found the problem in the carburetor. A half round piece of solder was sitting right on the carburetor opening feeding gasoline to the engine. This plane had been having some minor engine problems that I thought had been repaired. Well, it was fixed now. The next morning I was back to work flying on the job.

- DDT and Toxaphene Removed From Insect Control.
  Now We Had To Use Dangerous Chemicals.

Back in the middle of August, about 1955, the environmentalists in Washington condemned the use of DDT and a little later, Toxaphene. I had never heard of any ill effects on any person or warm-blooded animal from DDT. The politics must have been powerful to eliminate the most effective chemical to control mosquitoes throughout the world. This was a terrible blow to agriculture worldwide, not to mention the loss of Malaria control everywhere. The monetary losses, just in the small area of cotton growers where I worked, were many thousands of dollars. We naturally expected the facts put out through Government channels to be absolutely true. However, when the government banned DDT the truth was NOT told. There actually was no danger to man or Eagles. The propaganda was so effective the public took it for granted and still believe it today. My father had been one of the scientists to test the toxicity of DDT before it was released to the public back in 1940 and had approved its use on humans prior to our entry into WW II. He worked for the U. S. Agriculture Department as an entomologist in West Texas. DDT saved untold thousands of lives by eliminating mosquitoes where sprayed or dusted, as well as killing all body lice on service men. All air transport aircraft traveling through the tropics was thoroughly sprayed with DDT, including passengers.

How did this condemnation happen? Politics. It is recorded in the 1960s by the Environmental Protection Agency examiner in a 9,000 page report of their research," DDT IS NOT A CARCINOGENIC HAZARD TO MAN." It also emphasized that it doesn't harm fish, birds or other wildlife. Dr. William Hazeltine has found that small amounts of DDT ACTUALLIY LOWERED THE RISK OF LEUKEMIA AND BREAST CANCER IN LAB ANIMALS.

EPA head William Ruckleshous went ahead and banned DDT. Aides later said he never read even one page of the studies conducted on the DDT. He had helped to hatch the DDT scare and couldn't bring himself to admit he was wrong.

That DDT ban caused us to turn to the nerve gas Methyl Parathion. Now that is a real poison. Three drops in the mouth would be irreversible death for a human. That is what took the place of the safe chemical DDT. It was about eighteen years before Methyl Parathion was removed from use on farms. It was only effective on the small worms, not on the grown ones. We who worked with it always used the masks and protective gloves, as it was so extremely poisonous.

We had tried mixing the Parathion with water that first year after the DDT ban, then switched to six spinners the next year to use the Parathion undiluted. This was more effective and economical. The heat in the summer in West Texas caused the Methyl Parathion to evaporate within three or four hours. That was a safety factor. I usually sprayed four to eight ounces of Parathion per acre, using my wind-driven pump to push the chemical through my system.

Isn't it an odd quirk that we replaced a safe chemical, DDT, with an extremely dangerous one? Parathion can be absorbed through the skin, by inhalation, or gestation. I instructed my workers thoroughly in the need to use the masks and gloves. We also had to replace the carbon filters often in our masks.

DDT was used all over the world during WW II, killing the Anopheles mosquitoes, controlling the spread of Malaria and thereby saving millions of lives. Not one proven incident of poisoning of humans with DDT have I found, and it couldn't be toxic as much as we crop-dusters handled it without incident. We had it all over us every day. We got sold a bill of goods, folks. Some other countries have continued using the DDT against Mosquitoes.

Two of my fellow sprayer pilots were killed because of contact with the Parathion. Another walked into a turning prop after inhaling some of it. He was lucky, as he only had to have a plate put in his head.

I always carried a small bottle of antidote tablets, in case of an accident while using Parathion. I never had to use them, although not long after we started using Parathion my truck-driver operator, Aaron and the boys decided to enjoy some of the fresh cantaloupe from the area. That would have been okay, but Aaron peeled his and held it in his unwashed hands to eat it. It wasn't long before he was deathly ill from the methyl parathion. He spent several days in the hospital before being able to return home and gradually go back to work. There were no after effects noted for the next forty-five years. He's still quite healthy.

At the beginning of my second spraying season, Chick Comstock started flying for me. This speeded up our spraying time. His first flying was spraying mesquite near Big Lake, Texas, and he seemed to catch on quickly. This was good experience for him.

Most of our spraying of crops was done in the average winds of West Texas, up to twenty miles per hour. Mesquite spraying was limited to a maximum of ten miles per hour. Temperature was usually about 100 degrees when spraying cotton, with the maximum of 113 degrees. Chick was flying in that day the temperature was 113 degrees and wind about five mph, and I was filling in as flagger. Somehow Chick was able to withstand the heat but I had a problem. I had driven the pick-up to where I began flagging. When I went back to get the pickup I had to push it off by myself, as the battery was dead. Talk about hot.

Higher wind speed causes extra planning in turns, especially in the higher heat. The downwind turns are longer and slower than the up-wind turns and the timing of the approach when flying back to the cotton has to be quick, exacting and with near-perfect timing. When one does this fifteen hours every day four months of the year, it poses no major problem. I was making from eighteen to twenty-six second turns of 180 degrees at each ends of the cotton fields most of the day.

To emphasize the need of perfect timing and planning, there was a crop-duster spraying a field one morning only a few miles from where I noticed the wind forty feet above the ground was from one direction, while below forty feet the wind was blowing from the opposite direction. This variance was a little unusual and can cause problems to a low flying crop-duster.

The report came to me that this pilot missed his first and second approaches to begin his first spraying run. Because of the different wind directions, his maneuvering in position was causing him difficulties in getting lined up. Maneuvering with a full load is sometimes quite difficult, so in his third attempt he must have tried to force the loaded airplane onto his planned swath line-up, stalling the plane, diving into the ground, killing himself. When I heard about it I realized that the different wind directions were a contributing cause. I'd done some quick adjusting myself that morning. My years of experience paid off for me. You can see how the wind enters into one's planning and timing while spraying or dusting. Experience can and often does save your life.

- Some Aspects Of Crop-dusting

One rancher had developed several hundred acres of ranch land into a farm. Marshal Nevill, the oldest brother, did the farming while his brother called "Ironhead" (Harrell) operated the rest as a ranch. Ironhead liked to drive his cars like a race-driver.

I had a close call early one morning when Ironhead came "shooting" around the curve approaching me just as I was taking off south on that paved road, fully loaded. "Ironhead" went off the road and didn't slow up, giving me room. The dust covered the road and I was nearly at take-off speed. I continued my takeoff into the dust and met a car. All I could do was try to lift my left wing enough to clear the car. At the last second I applied right aileron and had just enough "lift" to lift the left wing barely clearing the car. I continued my takeoff safely in the dust. That was the closest "call" I had in the thirty years using those roads as runways.

When applying pesticides I made it a practice to plan my entire flight path ahead, when possible and stay with it. An example, "Will I go over the high lines at the end of my run or shall I go under them?" I learned not to change my mind once I decided. Of course I had to know ahead of time if there would be clearance to go under the lines. My friend, Chick Comstock, was flying my duster and I tried to impress this practice upon him.

He was to do some dusting that morning. Before he began I drove him around the field to show him where phone lines were being installed under the high line wires we usually flew under. I pointed out that the 'phone line workers would be pulling up about a quarter of a mile of wire at a time with their truck so you couldn't see when they would be pulled up. I suggested that he plan to go over the high lines each time.

I returned to my spraying and when finishing my first load I was returning for another. I flew directly above the field Chick was dusting and saw him flying on a run toward the lines I'd warned him about. I sensed he was going to fly under the high lines. He must have forgotten and realized too late the phone line had just been pulled up. He tried to "squeeze" between the telephone lines and the fence. Well, he managed to do so, but caught the top of the vertical tail (vertical stabilizer) in the two phone lines. I saw that one phone line had broken loose from one direction, while the other broke loose from the other direction. The wires were sliding both directions across the vertical stabilizer tail, finally sliding off, releasing the airplane just in time to prevent it from hitting the ground. In the meantime a wire had wrapped around the high lines and was bouncing on the ground, kicking up fire. Olin Smith and Leland Haren had been welding on the ground level below the lines. They started jumping around avoiding that live wire. I'd swear I saw Olin jump up and stay in the air. Neither man was hurt but as I think of it again I still have to laugh at that sight.

Chick had control of the airplane and with throttle wide open made a big long turn, landing at our little dirt strip a half-mile away. Chick was pretty "shook-up" but the airplane wasn't damaged too badly. I let him fly the airplane to town after the mechanic came out and checked it for safety and made temporary repairs. Next morning we had it working again.

I've always wondered why Chick went under the lines after I showed it to him. He must have been daydreaming, either when I was showing him the field or after he was working. The human brain works in odd ways at times. He was learning though and became a good crop-duster, learning a lot from that incidence.

At the beginning of the next season I was busy dusting and Chick came flying out in the high wing spray plane, forgetting about the booms mounted below the struts. When he landed on the same road I was using as my runway, his spray booms caught in the sunflowers and jerked him to the left over a ditch. My duster plane had no spray booms, so they cleared the sunflowers.

Only the left boom on the sprayer was damaged. It took all of us to get the airplane back over the ditch, though. These things are examples of how a crop-duster has to be alert at all times. One can see how the two years experience is a valuable necessity. I had to train myself to "shove" all problems completely out of my mind while working. I also trained myself to keep my eyes open while sneezing, because, invariably, I would have to sneeze at crucial times. Try it. It took some effort, but it can be done.

Sometimes I had severe hay fever, causing lots of sneezing and tears in my eyes. There were times I flew with a wet handkerchief alternating from one eye to the other when I was affected by hay fever. Traveling along just off the ground, at 90 to 100 miles an hour, dodging obstructions, you'd better have at least one eye open. You need all your senses and at times I felt I had so little sense I needed to use every bit of what I had. Pun intended.

Being out in the sun, working all day long, becomes monotonous for the flaggers in the field. Their job was to keep me lined up on my swaths with their flags. One day I put on an old straw hat my young mixer-loader was wearing. I was flying quite low, as usual, about twelve inches above the cotton. The flaggers all did a double take as I dusted by them wearing that old hat. It looked to them as if the "mixer" was flying. On the next load I was shocked as one of the flaggers was standing in the middle of the field stark naked, waving his flag. A sense of humor is a valuable thing to have, but I hope he didn't get sunburned.

I also flew a hundred mile oil pipeline twice a week, checking for oil leaks. As it was located close to my spraying area, I was sometimes able to fly it while the boys were moving the equipment. It was a nice break for me as I often saw many flag tail and mule deer near the pipeline, which went up and around the many hills in the area. It always thrills me to see those beautiful, graceful animals. During the late fall I would spot several Golden Eagles, which only showed up after the buzzards had flown south for the winter.

When the air contained extra moisture the purple sage would come into full blossom on the hillsides, turning bushes into a solid purple color. This turned the poorest soil on the hills into a fabulous ring of color. The purple sage seemed to prefer that poorer soil. At a certain time of the spring, weather favorable, the large white blossoms of the dagger plants would bloom, literally turning the sides of the hills to an almost solid white. These were more visible from the air than from the ground. Keep in mind that I was usually flying lower than the tops of the hills even when not spraying or dusting, so I had unobstructed close-up views.

One day late in the afternoon I had finished spraying and was flying toward town just inches above the scattered black brush. I jumped a fox, which started running full speed directly away from and in front of me. When he dived into his hole without slowing up his rear end and tail continued with his momentum and flopped on over the hole. It then slowly followed his body into his hole. I was glad my seat belt was fastened or I might have laughed myself right out of the airplane. I bet that poor fox needed to visit a chiropractor next day.

We constantly had to plan our work in order to complete it all within our daily schedules. Being a day late might allow a big increase in damaging insects, and a severe loss of cotton production. One of the cotton growing area I worked on was located around Imperial, Texas, forty miles west of McCamey, while another farm area I took care of was halfway between Imperial and McCamey. The largest farm area began only six miles south of McCamey and extended about fifteen miles farther south. Moving our ground equipment had to be coordinated to save time, and my schedule was tight.

On several occasions in the fall, Faegene would drive to where I was working on Friday afternoons and pick me up to go to a football game to watch Sherry playing in the band and see the game. On those occasions Chick would fly my airplane home for me.

The big tanker was so slow I didn't use it much when spraying farm crops. I used it more when spraying mesquite brush.

A Result of the Severe Drought in the 1950s in West Texas

EARTH CRACKS—Kenneth Babcock, McCamey flyer, inspects earth fissure near McCamey, which he spotted along with others while flying over the Lockland Ranch northwest of McCamey. The unexplained cracks range up to half a mile in length, ten feet in depth and five feet across. Seven of these cracks are on the ranch, in addition to many smaller ones. The one in the picture cuts across a ranch road. They were first noticed this fall and seem to have occurred in a period of a few days. There has been no explanation of the reason for their occurrence.

I worked high school boys as much as possible, keeping them busy and out of trouble. They enjoyed the outdoors and the proximity to the flying. Because of early football practice they had to quit working in the peak of my season. In college the students could work most of the summer. They always did a great job for me.

...And then it flooded!

Pecos River 1954 Spring Flood

Devestation of the 1954 Pecos River flood

Deer walking among the debris after the flood

All that's left of the Highway 290 bridge over Pecos River—view from Ken's airplane
(Note airplane strut in right side of picture)

- A Hurricane and Cold Front Collide. Cause Heaviest Rains, a Record in Texas

In the spring of 1954, not long before spraying season, we unexpectedly had flooding rains up to thirty inches in twenty-four hours, south and southeast of McCamey about thirty-five miles wide. I was called upon to fly Charlie Shepard, production foreman for West Texas Utilities, out to check on damages to the high lines. We did not yet know how much it had rained or flooded. All Charlie had known was that some of the West Texas Utilities' big standards (high line poles on the main electric supply lines) along the highway south of McCamey some fifty miles were apparently washed out a few miles east of Sheffield, Texas.

We took off in my airplane just before daylight, arriving at the Pecos River crossing east of Sheffield at first light of day. We found the Live Oak Creek concrete highway bridge completely under water. Some of it was actually washed out, and the junction of the creek and the Pecos River was about a mile wide. Seven big standards were down, and water was covering most of the valley. Charlie said we'd better check the rest of the line, and on we went another twenty miles, flying over Hoover Draw, which was normally dry. It was now a half mile wide. Another fifteen miles we came around the north end of the hill just west of Ozona.

We were shocked. There was water from hill to hill. Houses in the town of Ozona were nearly all sitting in five to ten feet of water. One house was on fire while sitting in about six feet of water. People were waving at us, sitting stranded on top of truck trailers on the main highway, waiting to be rescued. It was now 6:00 A.M. We wondered how long they'd been waiting. We flew low over them, waving our wings to let them know they were seen then flew straight back to McCamey. Charlie said he would call San Angelo to inform the Red Cross they could only reach flooded Ozona from the north.

I gassed up and was on my way to carrying a rancher to check on his ranch 100 miles south of McCamey. We flew down the Pecos River, seeing more water roaring down the canyon than I believed possible. His ranch was west of Pandale and all was O.K. After returning to McCamey I was asked to check on some local men that had gone fishing on the lower Pecos River. With a photographer along I flew back down the Pecos looking for signs of the men. Chandler's fishing camp, 70 miles south of McCamey, had been covered over with water from the Pecos, oak trees and all. About thirty miles on down the river I found some of the McCamey men on top of a hill above the Pecos River where they had been fishing. Their pick-ups were not in sight. They had driven the pickups to safety, I later learned. We spotted an Army Helicopter from Del Rio with A.C. Ashenhurst, one of the fishermen and a flight student of mine, standing in the door waving to us as we flew by.

The lower Pecos River was now about eighty feet deep. Normally it would be about eight feet deep. The Pecos River Canyon was deep with high bluffs on each side. The big highway bridge above the lower Pecos River canyon, a couple of miles from the junction with the Rio Grande, was completely covered with water. (It had been completely washed out.) We landed on the main highway. Would you believe it? We landed on a flat tire. There we were, 160 miles from home, no help available. We had no way to repair our tire. The highway was closed so there was no through traffic. But wait. There was a jeep coming down the road.

"Yeah, we have a pump and some patches." How lucky can you get? These boys in the jeep jumped out and had that balloon tire repaired in nothing "flat." They even had a tire pump. Thank goodness they were prepared.

We returned to McCamey flying up Howard draw late in the afternoon. The water had now run down quite a bit. Although nearly dark we could see the heavily washed out channel, rocks and gravel beds about three times as wide as before. The road was washed out in many places along Howard Draw.

A large area of about eighty five by two hundred miles had suffered floods and heavily damaging the town of Ozona, Texas.

Three major bridges and several minor ones were washed out. Livestock was killed, several cars washed off the road at Ozona and several people washed away and never found. Nothing was found of several cars and pick-ups in Howard draw, and there was one passenger car caught in Howard draw filled with rocks instead of people. These men were from Odessa. I don't know what happened to them, but I think they survived.

There aren't enough superlative words in my vocabulary to describe all that I saw when I carried two men all the way down to Eagle Pass, Texas, on the Rio Grande, some 240 miles. The Rio Grande River was on flood stage as far as Laredo, about 100 miles south of Del Rio. South of Ozona for forty miles down the Devils River, there were refrigerators, lumber, barrels, odds and ends lying in the shallow valley among the mesquite. One automobile was carried or rolled a couple of miles down river from Ozona. The Ozona draw empties into the Devils River, which empties into new Amistad Lake on the Rio Grande just above Del Rio. This flood nearly filled the lake years ahead of the expected time.

The Pecos and Devils River had filled Amistad Lake, which overflowed into the lower Rio Grande causing flooding.

- Another New Airplane

Ken's last airplane—A Call-aire Crop Duster

I purchased another new plane, this one built in Afton, Wyoming. It was a low winged airplane originally designed by Barlow Call for high altitude flying. I felt it would be able to carry a good load safely at my lower altitude of 2400 feet. I rode Continental Airline to Denver, then DC-8 to Jackson Hole, Wyoming, where Carl Peterson, the airplane salesman, met me. I was quite impressed by the Jackson Hole Country and the mountains. We took time to ride the ski lift just above the town of Jackson, Wyoming. What a beautiful sight, looking down on the town of Jackson, with the Teton Mountains standing right across the valley.

After the beautiful twenty-eight mile drive through the mountains to Afton, I spent three or four days in Afton waiting for a few small changes to be made on the airplane.

They told me that in the wintertime the snow was so deep in the town that hungry elk would come down out of the mountains and walk over the fences on the frozen snow to eat any flowers or plants growing next to the houses.

Most of the little town of Afton was located in Wyoming, but the valley was called the Star Valley of Idaho. The altitude there was over 7,000 feet.

I joined Mr. Peterson to attend a kid's rodeo one night. Being raised in Texas, I was quite familiar with rodeos. This was a great rodeo for junior high and high school boys and girls. Seeing these young cowboys and cowgirls perform, I realized Texas was not the only place that had cowboys and cowgirls. Those young people put on a great rodeo.

My new airplane was called an A-5 Callaire, named after the designer, Barlow Call. It was not very fast, about 80 miles as hour, but had lots of "lift" and when I put it to work I found that it did a wonderful job of spraying. In flying it home there was one problem: it needed more gasoline capacity. I had to "sweat it out" a couple of times between refueling stops. When I was flying toward Lubbock from Amarillo, about 100 miles of straight road, I looked down at the highway and saw cars and trucks passing me. A twenty or thirty mile an hour head wind from the south had slowed my ground speed to about fifty miles an hour.

Well, when we finally put the A-5 to work that spring I was proud of its application. Then, after a few weeks the engine quit for a few seconds, and then ran rough, then smoothed out. Then a little later, it quit and I had to land. I contacted the factory and they sent a specialist down. He checked it out but did not find the problem. A week later Chick was flying it on some small cotton, when the engine again quit cold. When your engine quits in an airplane, it gets all your attention. A split second decision has to be made, and it better be the right one. This time the decision was simple, as the cotton was short. All he needed to do was to make two left turns, and land up the rows of cotton. Chick was nervous and angry at having the engine quit. The airplane had rolled right up to the flagger in the field and stopped. This was the boy's first time as a flagger and he thought Chick landed to correct him about something. The nervous flagger jumped on the wing and said to Chick: "What's the matter, sir, did I foul up?" Things came into focus for Chick and he just had to laugh at the boy.

We had Leon Locker, our aviation mechanic, come out and work on the plane in the field of new cotton. He found the trouble rather quickly and we took off right up the cotton rows and continued working.

Ken spent thirty years crop dusting

When I returned to Sonora for mesquite spraying the next year, 1962, Cashes Taylor was working as ASCS field man in Sonora. How well I had known the Taylor family. I remembered how they all would put forth efforts to succeed in whatever they did. Cashes' youngest sister Cora Belle was in my class in school and two of his young brothers were Jimmie and Basil, only a few grades behind.

The boys were competitive in athletics such as track, basketball and football. I ran track with them all the spring season. Jimmie had played basketball with me and was a Boy Scout, so I knew him quite well. I noticed Basil wouldn't give up on anything and tried extra hard to compensate for his age and size. Jimmie, two years older, was the same way.

I helped Cashes when he measured the mesquite I had sprayed, and he talked to me about his daughter and also told more about his early days as a cowboy in New Mexico. He expressed the wish for me to meet Blanche. He told me she was married, with three children, was a graduate of the University of Texas, and living in Beaumont, Texas. I did get to meet her, some twenty-three years later.

The rest of that story will come later. I will say this, though: no one knows the future.

- Another Summer Spraying Crops

From 1949 until 1980 I was busy spraying crops each summer. During the winter months I operated my Television and Appliance Sales and Repair Shop. Business was always poor in this area of the state of Texas. In order to stay busy I worked on any and all brands and models of TVs, nearly an impossible task as the circuits and parts were practically all different. I did well to make a living during the winter. Being in the desert, there were no homes or people living near the town, unlike more populated areas.

Obtaining necessary T.V. parts was a major problem for me. On three pages of paper, 8 ½ by 11, were addresses and phone numbers of the different supply houses from which I could order parts. Competent help for repairing electronics was also a major problem. This was especially true in a small isolated town like McCamey.

The town was dependent upon the oil business, which fluctuated with the price of oil. When the price of oil was up the population went up, and when the price dropped so did the population. I heard it said that if a man worked in the oil field, sooner or later he worked in McCamey.

What we needed was more work available to the people. Of course there were also a few oil field supply houses, several churches, one bank, and one large grocery store. The nearest large town was Odessa, Texas, fifty-two miles away.

At the end of each dusting season I converted my PA 18 airplane back to a two-seater. Sometimes on Sunday, when the Braceros (cotton pickers from Mexico) were not working, I would fly out to the farms and land close to their camp. I would take them for rides at two dollars each. I could carry them two at a time and take them on a five-minute ride. Some of them were not Mexicans but Indians, and they couldn't speak Spanish, much less English. They sure enjoyed these rides, though, and I enjoyed taking them.

About noon one day in late September, I drove the crew the twenty-two miles west of town to prepare a mixture of defoliant to kill the leaves on the cotton. I left Chick in town with instructions to fly out in about two hours, weather permitting. The weather was clear and warm and we saw only one small cloud too far away to worry about.

I parked the pick-up alongside the tanker, facing back toward the farm road and we began mixing the water and defoliant in the truck tank. We were on top of the big truck and were quite busy. I happened to look up just as we finished the mixing and was shocked to see nothing but storm clouds. I yelled "Hey, let's get out of here." We slammed down the lids and clambered down off the truck into the pickup.

I had noticed it was already raining on the field we were to spray. Clouds had built up unbelievably fast and storms were threatening the entire area. As I was starting the pickup we were enclosed in dust and gravel that was going straight up. It had to be a tornado. I gunned the pickup and shot through the wall of dust onto the road. Wow. Another close call.

We could see the tornado when we turned left on the road. It was traveling parallel to us and very close. I wanted to continue to the highway, but it was so close it looked as if it would intercept us. We parked cross-wise in the road so we could go either way and watched the tornado engulf a house and rotate it a few feet, then sit it back down. When the tornado moved on it became engulfed in heavy rain and hail. We hoped it had gone up into the clouds, but we couldn't tell in the heavy rain and hail. After about five more minutes we drove onto the highway and were in hard rain and hail every one of the twenty miles to town.

We had been in a tornado and lived through it. This was another episode where I was in danger and came out alive and uninjured. The tornado apparently dropped down on us as we had jumped into our pickup. Was it just luck I had the pickup pointed into open ground? How were we able to drive out of it before doing us any damage? Only God knows the answers.

Because of the lack of weather information in the area, about anyone can predict weather as well as the weather bureau. "Warmer and windy with some afternoon clouds" will cover it nine out of ten times. One thing you can be sure of, it isn't likely to snow in the summer. That reminds me of this joke: Some men, tired of fighting snow every winter in the North, came to West Texas looking for a better climate with intent to move. They asked the service station attendant if it snowed out there. The attendant said: "I don't know, I've only lived here a couple of years. You might ask that young man sitting over there. He's lived here all his life." When asked about the snow, the boy said: "Ain't seen any snow, mister, but I 'member it rained onct."

There were so many Oil Field tales that I can't remember them. I should have made recordings of tales told by the old timers sitting at the round table, while drinking coffee and telling tales. One afternoon I joined the coffee drinkers and heard about a trick old Al Warner pulled on the Bluebonnet Café owner, Robbie Robinson.

Robbie had a habit of helping the waitress carry out the dirty dishes whenever he wasn't busy, usually at night when business was slow. One night Robbie had just hired a new girl and Al came in for supper. There weren't many customers and Al caught the eye of the new waitress so he slipped a five-dollar bill under the dinner plate. Just before he left, when she wasn't looking, Al slipped that bill back into his pocket. You guessed it. Robbie carried the dirty dishes into the back and the waitress came up to him and said, "Where's my five dollars, Mr. Robinson?" Of course Robbie didn't know what she was talking about. Al was sitting outside in his car, and watched the new waitress grab her coat and angrily walk out.

- God Working Overtime To Keep Me Alive

Early one spring I took an acquaintance named Blackstock for a hundred mile ride down the Pecos River Valley in my airplane. I liked to see the scenery and how many fishermen were on the Pecos River. We were flying a hundred miles down the river at about 200 feet above the river when we passed some men fishing at the Pandale crossing. I slowed our speed to about eighty miles an hour, with a notch of flaps down for extra stability. We were both looking down at the Pandale River crossing, when "Wham." The windshield broke. I thought for an instant I'd hit a buzzard. I quickly realized a buzzard couldn't knock out my windshield. I looked around and noticed my left strut was bent, almost a kink. Then I knew I'd hit a high voltage high-line. I felt how the airplane had slowed. There had to have been two lines stretched about a half-mile or more across the canyon, from hill to hill, that I didn't see. High line wires were almost invisible to us when flying. You don't expect them at 200 feet above the ground, either. Usually you can see the poles, but these were too far apart. I never did see them and there were no balls on the wires, which would have made the wires more visible to us.

I would have given myself about one chance in a thousand to still be flying after hitting those two large reinforced high tension lines, a span over half a mile long. To be alive at that point had to mean I was living a charmed life. Could this also be an act of God? If so, why did I hit the wires in the first place? Well, we were still alive, so I give God full credit. Perhaps he had something planned for me to do later.

I flew back up the road with the wind beating us in our faces at 70 miles an hour. I watched the left strut and it seemed quite steady. I was thinking "Do I want to fly all the way back to McCamey like this? It would take about 1½ hours. Or do I want to land on the road below?" My passenger decided for me. He said, "Can you land this thing? I'm awfully nervous." "Okay," I said, "I'll land right here." I had to carry power to flatten out the approach with wind drag with no windshield to be diverting the air and landed easily on the dirt road. We tied the airplane just off the road. Here came a salesman in his car. In only another hour and a half we were in McCamey.

Years later I heard that my passenger had never taken another ride in an airplane. He told a friend emphatically that he'd never fly again. I must have made a poor impression on him. I don't say I blame him.

My mechanic and I drove down to the airplane and installed another windshield and strut. I flew the airplane back home without any trouble.

Bob McKinney in front of Ken's Aeronica
Son Bobby in front of a Continental Airlines airplane

- More About Flight Instructing

I was pretty busy spending my off-time instructing flying. I was teaching both men and women how to fly and enjoyed the challenge to teach. My students were all eager, making my job relatively easy.

I had an Aeronica tandem 65 HP Continental engine and a 125 HP Piper Tri-Pacer to teach in. I made it a point to teach as much about flying and flight safety as I had taught the Army cadets. When I finished teaching, my students knew the theory of flight quite well. They had learned how to turn the airplane properly and smoothly, and to trust and understand the magnetic compass. I emphasized the value of planning ahead for emergency landings. I used some open roads with little traffic to make simulated emergency landings, and then I'd have the student actually land on the road. I taught that when an engine failed on take-off, just land in the best area ahead of the airplane, not worrying about the airplane. I demonstrated that there was no way you could glide back to the airport safely.

I taught instrument flying on the basic needle ball airspeed, altitude system. They learned how to make a one needle-width bank and a 180 degree turn under simulated instrument flying, also to be able to fly out of a cloud if inadvertently caught in one.

I have long been concerned that flight students might not be getting the kind of training to assure their safety. Aircraft salesmen tend to emphasize the ease of landing and taking off, neglecting some important emergencies that need emphasis. Those who are pilots understand how the elevator is the one control that actually turns the airplane. The aileron and rudder are used together to put the aircraft smoothly into the desired bank, adding elevator as needed to keep the nose up (to keep it from losing altitude).

Better instrument instruction is needed for emergencies. Much emphasis should be put on the importance of avoiding flying into thunderstorms. I could add much more instruction to this need. I taught students to trust and use the magnetic compass by letting the student get lost on his dual cross-country flight. After getting lost one time, a student will learn the true value of using his magnetic compass, and will use it for all his cross-country flying in the future.

Bobby McKinney is one of our students who followed aviation as a career. When Trans-Pecos Airlines hired him he came home to tell us flying those DC 3s was fun, and he felt he should be paying them for letting him fly them.

Bobby continued flying airlines, retiring from Continental Airlines at age sixty.

Twoie Darby was another excellent student we had, who went to work as a tower operator in San Angelo while attending college. After school he went to work full time in Traffic Control for the Federal Aviation Authority.

There were others who reaped various benefits from their flying, such as piloting their own airplanes. It seems being able to fly an airplane increases ones confidence and gives an improved outlook on life.

- Vacation above Ruidoso, New Mexico

Faegene and I decided we should take Sherry on a nice vacation before my summer spraying began. We arranged to rent two saddle horses with saddles and bridle from a friend ranching in the mountains the other side of Ruidosa, N. M. Faegene didn't wish to ride.

We rented a cabin in Riudosa and drove to the ranch some fifteen miles farther west. At the ranch Sherry and I saddled our horses and rode the six or seven miles to Merel's cabin he and Pop had built a few years earlier. That was a good warm up for future horseback riding. Faegene drove the car and picked us up.

During the week that followed Sherry and I rode over the mountains and through the forest on the trails made for fire fighting. We rode high up on Mt. Blanco until we chickened out. The trail was narrow and steep, and above timberline. The switchback trail above the timber was steep with tight turns. I decided I'd rather be walking. We found a place to turn around and worked our way back down into the forest below.

We had to clear out some of the trails through the forest in order to get through, and found one small pond that had been formed by a beaver dam. We could see some trees freshly cut by some beavers.

Although we knew there were black bears in the mountains, we didn't wish to see any. We stirred up some wild turkeys, however.

Sherry and I rode horseback in the mountains every day for that week, visiting a mine and a valley just over the ridge from the cabin. We saw no sign of civilization in that isolated valley and enjoyed the solitude together.

When we returned to McCamey, I resumed my flight instructing. One of my lady students, Rosemary, surprised me when I was giving her a lesson preparatory to her first flight. Walking up to the front of the airplane, I pointed out, as I did to all my students, that the most dangerous thing about flying was the propeller and to keep everyone clear of the propeller when it was turning.

Then I began explaining the way the lift is developed by the shape of the wing she said, "Oh, you mean Bernoulli's effect?" That's when I found out she had a degree in Geophysics.

Rosemary became a fine pilot and had an interesting experience on her first solo cross country flight. I had given her dual instruction on the same course she would fly on her solo cross country, except we flew in the opposite direction. On her solo flight she flew higher than she was used to, and did not recognize her ground references such as a highway, railroad, or the Rio Grande River. She went flying right across the border into Old Mexico. We know that Old Mexico does not like unexpected airplanes flying over their country.

She realized shortly she was over strange territory. When she spotted a dirt strip she landed on it. A man came out to the airplane and she asked where Del Rio was. "*No comprenda, Senorita.*" Translation: (I do not understand, miss.) She repeated the words "Del Rio" and he pointed, so off she flew in that direction and was relieved to see what she thought was Del Rio in the distance. She landed and was taxiing toward the hangers when some men came running out in dark uniforms. Mexican soldiers. She whirled the airplane around, opened her throttle wide open and took off. She flew across the Rio Grande River and landed on the Del Rio Airport this time. She parked the plane, left an order for re-fueling, rented a car and drove off.

When I had finished my spraying job some fifty miles away, I flew over to Del Rio to check on her. When I found out she'd rented a car and left, I rented one also and drove the short distance to Villa Acuna, Mexico. Sure enough, I spotted her walking the streets window-shopping. She was still "shook up" and told me what happened. I calmed her down by treating her to some Mexican food at the famous Ma Crosby's Café. She felt much better after that good food and the conversation. She said she felt like she could continue around the flight plan back to McCamey. Her flight plan called for returning by way of San Angelo and she had no more problems.

Weeks later she passed her Private Pilots written and flight exam. The inspector congratulated both of us on how well she flew the airplane. This made us both feel good.

One spring I was spraying mesquite on the Schultz ranch east of Sonora and at the end of a swath circled some large oak trees just across the fence in the Lee Allison pasture. There was a Fish Crane nest in the top of the tallest oak tree with two baby cranes about two feet tall watching me circling around them in my turn-a-round. The nest looked far too small for them as they watched me turning until they had to reverse their head position in order to see me complete my turn. They looked so clumsy and oversized for the nest I had a big laugh each time I circled them. These were the first Fish Crane babies I'd ever seen in a nest.

Another funny incident happened on the Schultz's ranch. There was a small group of Javelinas. Javelinas look like small pigs, wild and nearly blind and they have sharp tusks. They weigh about 60 pounds) and were running from the sound of my airplane. They ran right at Tony McKinney (Lloyd's young son) who was flagging for me. He quickly climbed a tree as the Javelinas swept by below him. When I looked for my flagger, there he was, up in a tree.

- Another Interlude of Teaching Flying

One Spring I received a call from Rex Henderson, a young man that had worked for me several years earlier while in high school. He had just graduated from college at Corpus Christi and called to make me an offer, "Teach me to fly and I'll work for you all summer."

"It's a deal," I answered. I was confident he would do a good job at running my ground equipment and crew.

He was ready to start and he did a fine job working for me. I flew with him every chance I had, teaching him thoroughly all the way through his Commercial License. That turned out to be a blessing for each of us. He went to work as an air traffic controller in Houston, and continued his training to become an instructor and even a crop-duster. He had made me an excellent hand all summer and into the fall, until I shut down spraying operations for the year.

While he was working for the Federal Air Traffic Control in Houston, the Air Traffic Controllers union went on strike for higher wages. When it happened Rex's father made this remark to his family: "At least that's something Rex would never do, go on strike." A few days later Rex called to tell his family he had been fired along with some other strikers of the ATC controllers. Mr. Henderson said: "I knew it. I knew it." We had a good laugh about that, at least.

Rex managed to pass his instructor's permit and began instructing others to fly. I am proud he went ahead with his flying. He also continued some crop-dusting.

Teaching many people to fly has given me a feeling of satisfaction, especially when I put students through the stages for earning their ratings and licenses. My intent in teaching flying was always to prepare the student to fly as safely as possible, and be prepared for emergencies.

Each student is unique and finding effective methods of teaching is a constant challenge. One of my students had insisted he needed no compass, as he always knew the directions. I managed to let him get lost on a little 30-mile flight. He then began to realize why we needed a compass. He already had logged some time before he came to me and wanted to qualify for a Private License. I prepared him for flight test, adding the required maneuvers for his Private License, along with a few things to make him a safer pilot. He didn't want to fly lower than 500 feet even when I told him he needed the experience. Although he was reluctant I had him fly just above the ground, climbing up to cross above obstacles such as phone lines and high lines. About two months later he earned his Private License and moved away.

A few months later I received a call one night from Kansas. It was that student. He said: "Ken, I just have to call and thank you for saving my life. I was flying in Illinois and the weather closed in. I knew I couldn't fly instruments and could see no airports so I had to fly low until I reached clear weather. I could never have done that without your making me get that experience. Thanks, Ken". What a good feeling that gave me. I was always proud of my students and would go the "extra mile" to be sure they became safe pilots. I was committed to teach them as much as I could, and put the thought ahead of income. I really didn't charge enough to make a decent profit, but there was a satisfaction that I was developing competent and safe pilots.

There were so many students I taught through the fifty years of instruction that I could not begin to mention them all. One student was a registered nurse working at the Crane Hospital twenty miles from McCamey. Faegene had an operation there one summer and Marilyn was her nurse. When Faegene mentioned to her that I was a flight instructor Marilyn got excited: "I want to learn to fly. Can you teach me?" she asked. I answered, "Sure can."

Well, that began a friendship I still treasure. Marilyn was an eager student and remained exuberant the whole time. She became a competent pilot, earning her Private License. She continued to fly every chance she had. Later she moved to El Paso. One weekend I took a charter flight to El Paso and took Faegene with me. We visited Marilyn and she mentioned that she had met a man who owned his own airplane. Well, this later on resulted in marriage. Both being pilots, Marilyn and George hit it off quite well. George told me he was pleased she was such a good pilot and navigator. Later they traded their Cessna 172 on a Twin Engine Comanche, so she also became a multi-engine pilot.

I have to confess that one time before she soloed, I let her talk me into changing a rule of mine, which was: "Don't compromise myself by getting talked into going against my own judgment." We were shooting landings and I let her talk me into making one more trip around the pattern. I knew I was quite low in gasoline. Sure enough, just before we got back to the runway we ran out of gas and had to land in the low black brush. We landed with no damage or trouble, but we did have to push the airplane back to the runway, after lowering the fence. This gave her confidence, realizing you don't always have to have a paved runway to land on. It also taught me not to be talked into something and then going against my own judgment.

Coffee time was always welcome in the winter. At the "round table" in the café where we gathered for coffee and talk, about four o'clock in the afternoon, it became obvious to me there was a desire among oil field workers to play tricks on their friends. Sam Monroe pulled a trick on his breakfast partner one morning. He and Olin Smith had breakfast together nearly every morning and Olin liked to razz Roy Sharp, the owner of Benoit Café, about those little "Bantam" eggs he served. Roy would gripe back at him about the quality of his customers that always had to gripe about something.

This gave Sam an idea. I had noticed one day Sam had a goose living in his fenced back yard. When the goose began laying eggs Sam slipped one to Roy for him to cook the next morning for Olin. When Olin began his usual ranting about those tiny eggs Roy brought in the cooked goose egg and sort of pitched the plate onto the table saying "There. I hope you're satisfied now." The egg completely filled the dish. Olin just sat there and stared at that egg. Finally he turned to Roy and asked meekly, "Would you mind too much to bring me some of those little eggs. I just don't think I can eat this one."

- I Buy Another Spray Plane

I was doing more brush control spraying in the spring of the year, and needed a larger airplane. I traded in my Callair A-5 on a newly designed Callair called an A-9. The A-9 was powered with a 300 horse-power engine, reduced to 260 horsepower in order to use the more available and lower priced 80-octane aviation fuel. This airplane had an adjustable seat in a cabin set higher for good visibility, a larger tail and landing gear.

When the factory notified me it was about ready, I called a man in Big Lake who wanted to fly me to the factory in Afton, Wyoming just to get the experience for his brother in my four-place Piper Tri-pacer. He and his brother took off with me for the long flight to Afton, Wyoming early one morning. We refueled at Dalhart, Texas, then again in Denver, Colorado. From there to Rocksprings, Wyoming, we were flying against a 40-mile an hour headwind. We had barely enough fuel to reach Rocksprings. I needed to rest and settle down after that gas scare. We had plenty of time to cover the last 100 miles before dark.

My friend and his brother left Afton in the Tri-Pacer early the next morning, arriving in McCamey that afternoon. There was a good tailwind, they told me later, and they had no problem getting home in one day in my Tri-Pacer.

I spent a couple of extra days at the factory in Afton having a safety cable installed from the top of the enclosed cockpit to the top of the tail (vertical). I designed and had installed a heavy metal cutting edge to be mounted outside the center of the windshield, to prevent the pilot from being decapitated if he hit a high-line. We also installed two cutting edges on the landing gear. In the years that passed I noticed many other airplanes had adapted those same safety measures. I never did find out if they worked, thank goodness.

The dust-spreader was so large I had to install it to be able to carry it home. The spreader produced more drag than I expected. Leaving Afton I refueled at the flattop mountain airport nearly a thousand feet above Rocksprings, Wyoming. When I took off from Rocksprings I became nervous as the airplane was actually losing altitude with full power. I didn't realize I had taken off on one magneto instead of both. When I checked the cockpit to see what was wrong I spotted the magneto switch was on "left" only. I switched to both and that did it. With both magnetos turned on I now had plenty of power. For safety and efficiency airplanes have dual magnetos and dual spark plugs. My air speed was still only 75 mph, and with that big dust spreader, this slower speed would reduce my gasoline range and require refueling more often.

I refueled again in Laramie, Wyoming, elevation over 7,000 feet. I climbed over the pass into Colorado and arrived at Denver airport after dark. I at least had navigation lights and radio, but the radio had so much static I could not hear the tower. To land I decided to drop down on the end of the runway and turn off at the first high-speed turnoff. I apparently wasn't seen until I was taxing close to the tower after landing. They called asking me where I'd come from. I inferred they'd just cleared me for landing. I really had called them before landing and heard no reply. I was right under the tower when they called. That close to them I could understand them.

I spent the night in the Cosmopolitan Hotel, downtown Denver. Next day there were some thunderstorms that looked threatening. Some of the pilots at the airport said they just looked bad and really weren't. Anyway it would be clear in the direction I was going, and there were some emergency airports located along my course. After wasting nearly half a day because of the storms, I took off, flying on down to Boulder, Colorado, where I spent the night. That dust spreader cut my fuel range by about twenty percent.

Early the next morning I took off for Dalhart, Texas, having to cross over some low mountains and rough country, making me even more nervous about my fuel. I finally made it to a small town in New Mexico but there was no airport. I continued on to Dalhart and by golly, I made it and still had a small amount of gasoline in one tank. Those gauges were accurate, contrary to what I had been told by the factory.

The next stop or fly-by would be Amarillo. I took no chances on gasoline. I gassed up at the little airport on the south edge of town. Flying above the road to Lubbock, just as I had in my previous Callair, the cars and trucks were again passing me. The head winds seemed to be built into my airplanes.

I spent the night at Lubbock, not wanting to fly the last 200 miles at night. I finally arrived in McCamey about one o'clock the next afternoon, circled our house two or three times, waving my wings as a "hello". The controls were so sensitive the wings responded quickly, which I liked. Faegene told me she noted the quickness when I was *rocking* my wings back and forth to her.

The first thing I did the next day was to replace the dust spreader with the spraying attachment. What an improvement in flight performance that made. I was able to take off easily with half power. Later on I converted back to the duster. However, it was so much trouble and so much wind resistance I just converted it permanently back into the spraying configuration. Later on I was able to sell the duster attachment.

I installed six spinner dispensers on the spray booms trailing my wings. This put three spinners on each side. Using this system I was able to spray the concentrate at rates of 4 ounces to two quarts per acre. I was also able to control droplet size. This really worked well on the cotton spraying but I changed them to the regular nozzles for spraying brush. The straight chemical would burn the leaves therefore preventing enough time to absorb the chemical when using straight herbicide.

This was about the time we became grandparents. Sherry had a child she named Shelley, a cutie if there ever was one. We were grandparents at age forty-two.

What a joy to see new life come into our world. I well remembered when Sherry was born and now there was another child to love and cherish. It was 5 years before Sherry had her second girl, Lisa, and five years later came son Chris.

As I look back it seemed to happen so quickly, when actually there were many years passing by while watching these children grow into adults. Now Shelley and Chris have their own families. I regret only seeing them once a year.

As new life comes into the world, some lives leave us. My mother passed away in 1968, and my father died nearly four years later. You never feel that you've expressed your love to them as fully as you wished you had. We also realize at these times how our parents have sacrificed and helped and loved us all their lives. What wonderful memories our parents have left us.

Chapter 13

God Takes Over My Life

I was attending church sporadically, usually only attending the men's Sunday school class. One Sunday in 1969 I was asked to help with a special weekend Church Mission. I agreed and was told I would need my car and to be at the Methodist church Friday after school.

When I reported to the church no one seemed to know what my job was or even what the program would be. Well, I stood around and stood around, waiting and wondering.

Suddenly the front door opened, and a man about six foot three came in, spotted me, gave me a bear hug, saying, "God loves you and I love you." I wondered what I had gotten myself into.

More people were coming in through the front door, doing the same thing. They were being signed in by one of the church ladies, a bank clerk with an artificial smile. She glanced at me with a question in her eyes: "What is this?" she seemed to say. We were completely in the dark.

When the preacher asked me to take an incoming family out to the house of a church member, I understood then it had been prearranged for the visitors to stay in private homes.

When I returned to the church I decided I'd go home, but they talked me into staying for a dinner that was already on the table ready to eat. While eating we heard a Christian witness tell us about his experience with God. Then before I could sneak out, I was maneuvered into a group of eight with a visiting lady-witness as leader, who took us to a pre-selected study in the church.

She sweetly led us through some questions and discussions about our personal religious experiences. She then discussed, for a moment, her own experiences with Jesus, God and religion. We each one gave a short prayer. That was hard for us to do, as we had not been praying any in public. I was home in bed by eleven o'clock but awake at twelve thinking about what we had discussed. I admitted to myself I was interested, although not fully understanding.

Next morning, Saturday, I had breakfast with the men at the café where another witness told of a powerful religious experience. That night was a repeat of the night before, except by a different leader, a Mrs. Campbell, of Big Springs. She guided our discussions and again we shared our thoughts and experiences, encouraged by Mrs. Campbell.

That night I again awoke at twelve o'clock. I meditated and even prayed some.

At the men's Sunday school class next morning another person gave his witness of his experience with God. Then during the church meeting the last witness culminated the weekend by giving a great and powerful message of the power of God. When he gave the altar call we all began singing "Just as I Am." Many people began moving toward the altar, filling the aisle. I felt a strong "pulling" to answer the call. I held back a few moments to sing, then just gave up and started moving to the crowded aisle. Mrs. Campbell was beside me and placed her hand on my head as I knelt in the aisle.

My head under her hand became unbearably hot. How strange. I kind of shook my head and she moved her hand to my shoulder, where I again felt the heat. It was bearable. A person's hand just cannot normally be that hot. I knew it was something special.

I was soon kneeling and praying and then turned my life over to God. My tears flowed. I truly felt my complete release of self and felt God's power filling me with love. A great happiness was in my heart. I did not understand my tears or the heat of her hand. I only understood that God had accepted me as being his.

When I stood up in the aisle I looked around at all the people there, feeling so full of love for my fellow men and women that I felt I couldn't hold any more. I felt as if I could reach up and clutch a great power. My eyes met the eyes of the lady from the bank across from the church and she smiled the most glorious smile. I knew she was smiling from her heart and that she, too, was full of God's love. Later on she testified to the congregation of her former artificial smile. She said now her smiles came from her heart and with love. Her future life proved her sincerity, as she and her husband proved by their actions that they were filled with God's love and Holy Spirit.

Immediately after this meeting was over, all the lay witnesses left for their homes, as planned.

That night the church had a meeting to evaluate the results of the Lay Witness meeting. Many of us testified what this Lay Witness program had meant to us. We realized our church now had our own "Pentecost", just as the disciples had when Christ arose. We had been touched by God and had responded. Praise God.

During the next two days, I was "walking on air" on "Top of the mountain." I felt so full of love I knew I was a changed man. I didn't understand fully but I was happy just to be "On top of the mountain."

That night I woke up at twelve o'clock and prayed and contemplated about it all. Then the most amazing thing happened to me on the third night: a real miracle. At three forty five A.M. I received this direct message from God: "You have been baptized by the Holy Spirit, and there are many denominations but only one Church." That was impressed upon my mind and I knew He was talking to me. There was no doubt. I was, I think, relieved to know I'd been baptized with the Holy Spirit. I felt happy. Yet what did it mean? I then went right to sleep.

For months I had not picked up a Bible. When I awakened at 7:15 that Wednesday morning, the first thing I did was reach for our Bible. I opened it, looked down and read: "I indeed baptize thee with water, but there's one who comes after me, whose shoes I'm not fit to tie, who will baptize thee with the Holy Spirit and with fire." WOW. I knew God had to have directed my hands to open the Bible to that exact page and scripture, and directed my eyes to that exact passage. Matthew 3:11. Talk about a miracle... Just think: I was told I had been baptized with the Holy Spirit, then a few hours later I opened the Bible to the exact page and looked down at the exact words that He had told me. There was absolutely no doubt, it was a real miracle. There was no way I could have opened the Bible to those words on my own, especially being as un-versed as I was at that time in the Bible. I couldn't have done so even if I were a devoted Bible reader.

This became the beginning of a concentrated study and witnessing that had me attending Bible studies every week. Later I began leading Bible studies myself, as I learned the scripture. I wanted to understand exactly what the Holy Spirit was and its purpose. Some weeks I attended as many as three Bible studies a week. This studying and learning continued for the next seven years. During those seven years I studied every moment I could, and as I learned, I taught and witnessed.

I found that the Holy Spirit gave the power to be a witness for God, and the power to change your life to be a better person. The answer, as I found over and over, was: the power of the Holy Spirit gives you the desire to study and learn so that you can become an effective witness for the Truth of God and his Son, Jesus. Since receiving the power of the Holy Spirit

I have witnessed untold numbers of times, never having to find someone to witness to. He just seemed to send people my way to hear my witness.

I found that some of the others receiving the baptism of the Holy Spirit in our Pentecost have become preachers of His "Word," witnesses like myself, and still others became healers. Through the power of the Holy Spirit I have actually seen alcoholics healed instantly, smokers cured and others turn their lives over to God.

My beliefs are simple. Going to church is fine, as it gives you an opportunity to praise God and learn of Him. But what it's all about is the personal relationship between you and Him. An alcoholic, a criminal, an unbeliever, can feel and receive the power of God to change their life just as He changed mine. They can be put on the "road" to Heaven once their heart is opened to Him. It's not special words spoken in special ways that reaches God; it's the honest sincerity coming from your heart that He responds to.

During the next ten or fifteen years, in particular, I spent much of my time witnessing and sharing experiences when opportunities were opened up. I still do His will and witness whenever the opportunity comes. Life and opportunities change, but the love of God is steadfast.

Chapter 14

More Brush Spraying

Early one spring in the late 1970's I went to the Pecos area to spray brush. I sprayed one large area on the Pruit ranch south of Pecos and another on his ranch sixty miles north of Pecos. I moved east of the Pruit ranch and Red Bluff Lake about a mile and sprayed a square mile of mesquite growing in sand dunes.

From the Pruit ranch, I could see White City, New Mexico in the distance. I began my operation by flying right on the Texas-New Mexico line, not over twenty or so miles from White City, New Mexico.

One thing I can say about Pecos Country is that it's hotter than in McCamey, and that's hot. It was 105 degrees the day we made our move to the north some hundred miles for these last jobs. The highest speed for our big truck was about twenty-five to thirty miles per hour.

When we got to where we were going, we found a water supply station a short distance from the road that I planned to use for a runway. We loaded the big truck with water. Then we located positions for starting points for each flagger, and also found a family of coyotes living in a sand dune cave.

We nearly stepped on a sidewinder rattlesnake on that sand. People of West Texas were in the habit of killing poisonous snakes. We found we couldn't kill this one. All we found was a stick as a weapon. When we hit the snake with the stick, the snake would just sink into the sand and keep on going. It didn't seem to faze him.

After we gave up trying to kill him we watched him bury himself in the sand until only his eyes were visible, like an alligator in a swamp pool. We were amazed and it taught us to look more carefully before putting our feet down on that sand.

We were all ready to work next day, so we drove the 50 miles back to Pecos for supper and our motel.

Pecos is an old frontier town at the beginning of nowhere, a few miles west of the Pecos River. For about twenty years the area raised thousands of acres of the famous Pecos cantaloupes and cotton. Farms were irrigated by pumping water out of the ground. Due to higher prices of gas coupled with a lowering water table, the cost of irrigating nearly eliminated the cantaloupe production. A few are still shipped out of the Pecos area, but not like in the early '50s.

My job, however, was to spray the brush before the cantaloupes and cotton were planted.

Pecos also claims to be the home of the first rodeo, at least in Texas. As long as I can remember the Pecos Rodeos were held on the fourth of July, and were rated as the best anywhere. The town built a replica of Judge Roy Bean's bar, next to a rebuilt Pecos Bar famous there in the late 1880's and the early 1900's. We took the time when not spraying to visit those places, as well as stuffing ourselves on the delicious Mexican food available in Pecos. We finally wound up our spraying season in Pecos and returned to McCamey early that summer.

The next year in West Texas was dry and windy the entire spraying season. I only did two jobs, one for weeds and one to control Mesquites. I didn't even break even on expenses. This spraying was some thirty-five miles south of McCamey on a ranch deep in the hills and the wind blew almost constantly, generally too high to spray past about seven o'clock, if that.

I would send the boys out early enough so we could begin spraying when it was light enough for me to see. We could only work a short time each day because of increasing wind. At times we had to fly up and down the slopes of the hills, keeping us alert and challenging.

When we finally finished the job nearly a month later, I flew off to the west to check on a job I planned to do next. Just after I flew over the proposed area I smelled gasoline. I was already headed toward McCamey, twenty-five miles away and was flying over flattop hills. I needed to land as quickly as possible as the danger of fire was imminent. I remembered having seen a landing strip on top of the mountain I was now crossing, a little way to the west. I was flying low with reduced power, ready to crash-land if necessary. Fire in the air is dangerous, as one can imagine. At last I saw the strip and landed post haste. I cut my engine while rolling and rolled up to the house at the end of the strip.

I opened the airplane cowling and found the trouble right away. A neoprene gasoline supply line had split. I took it out and put it in my pocket, then walked around the house, checking for any unlocked door or window. Apparently no one lived there at that time. I turned to a jeep sitting nearby and tried to open the door. Finally I managed to get a window opened. I sure needed that jeep to run. What were the chances the battery would be good? Would there be gasoline? Also I wondered if I could hot-wire it. I've never done so before. Believe it or not, I managed to get that jeep "hot wired" and running. Whew! There seemed to be enough gasoline. And the oil and water seemed okay. I wasn't stranded in this remote area after all. The time was near noon, the temperature 100 degrees. I didn't feel like walking even five—much less twenty-five—miles to McCamey, including going down the 700-foot mountain.

When I drove to the gate I found it chained and locked. That figured. I felt like I was being tested by fate for my ability to handle adversity. I walked down the fence and found some fence staples loose. It only took a few minutes to have that fence lying on the ground with a post holding it down. I was able to drive right over it and then replace the wire.

I felt great driving down the steep crooked trail to the valley. How great it was to have transportation.

It only took a short time in McCamey to find the correct size neoprene hose, gas up the jeep, and drive to my house to let Faegene know what was going on. I called Ben Milam, the foreman of that ranch, long distance. He lived about thirty miles from the landing strip. He was upset, and said he would come check the fence. I assured him it would be stapled in place when he saw it again and the jeep would be gassed up and locked. I think he was disturbed at the fact that someone could manage to get in that jeep and drive it off the ranch if they so desired. If I could do it, he probably reasoned, anyone could.

I had no trouble nailing the fence solidly in place with new staples. I parked, "un-hot wired" the jeep, and re-locked it. In another twenty minutes I had installed the hose and was landing that airplane at the airport in McCamey. I never heard any more from Ben. Many times I have thought of that incident, and thought of how that incident could have ended. Believe me I was still living a charmed life. I'm sure most of us have close calls like I have and wonder that they're still alive

- Flying Stearmans For Gardner Brothers

The next year I'd about decided to quit the spraying business. A new state law was enacted requiring much higher liability insurance and other restrictions difficult to work under. I would need to buy bigger and more expensive equipment, raise more money for the insurance and have to fight a declining industry, at least in my part of the country. As I was wondering what I should do, I thought of Henry Gardner, a friend to whom I owed a big favor. I thought perhaps I could partially repay him by flying for him. I called him, offering to fly one of his Stearmans with him during the brush-spraying season.

Well, we made a deal, so I packed some clothes and drove my pick-up to Victoria near the southeast coast of Texas, where Henry was living. He and his wife made room for me to stay with them the few days before moving the equipment to our first job at Guthrie, in North Texas.

The next day after arriving in Victoria, Texas, I drove the twenty miles back to Cuero where Henry was working in his hanger on his equipment. I looked over Henry's equipment, especially his airplanes, which were hybrid. The basic frames were 1940 Stearmans and the landing gears off of BT-13s. The tail section, engine, propeller and landing gear came also from a BT-13. The wings were Stearman redesigned to "high lift" configuration.

The Stearmans were naturally top-heavy and a little more so with the new configuration. Landing this converted Stearman was a more different experience than landing the Army version. Henry advised me to use brakes to help me guide the landings on those oversize tires, especially on asphalt, in order to keep it straight on the runway.

I climbed into the cockpit and Henry gave me a "Prop". The engine started smoothly. The Tachometer (RPM indicator) didn't work, but I didn't have to have that right then. I taxied around, getting the 'feel' for about twenty minutes. I finally took off, flying around the pattern and landing. Whee. The landing was exciting. I made about five or six more landings, learning how the plane reacted with the uneven pull of those big tires on a paved runway. When I could land with each tire touching at exactly the same instant the pull was even. Doing that, though, was nearly impossible. With one wheel touching down first on a paved runway, the airplane was" jerked" in that direction. A touch of opposite brake compensated for that "jerk." This airplane definitely did not land like the Stearmans of WW II. All this explanation is to impress the reader that we'll be landing on rutted roads, open fields, narrow roads and paved strips, reflecting the need of carefully establishing competence.

In only a few days we were able to leave for Guthrie. Our airplanes carried insufficient gasoline for long flights, so we planned landings in New Braunfels, Brownwood and Abilene. Our landing in New Braunfels was routine, then a little over halfway to Brownwood, Henry suddenly peeled off to the left. As I followed I knew there was a problem, probably short on gas. After landing in Brady, Henry told me his airplane needed gasoline. We both refueled.

We flew low most of the way into Abilene, after refueling again at Brownwood. This land was relatively smooth and gave me the opportunity to get the "feel" of flying this airplane low, as in spraying.

After a couple of days in Abilene, we flew on to the tiny community of Guthrie, a town I'd heard of but never seen. There was only a service station and a couple of houses, as this town was in the middle of the huge Four Sixes Ranch. The ranch had been named after the poker hand that had won it for the present owner, four sixes.

We landed in a small cleared landing strip along the highway where Henry's brother, Lefty, and his ex son-in-law were already spraying with two 600 horse-power Stearmans. Lefty Gardner had converted a big bus, installed bunks, some other conveniences, and brought a cook along. There were tools and supplies in a trailer. We were now about a hundred miles from any large town.

After a short visit we flew over to the adjoining Pitchfork Ranch, another of the huge old cattle ranches of North Texas, where our equipment would be set up shortly. We drove into Dickens, Texas, where we rented rooms, some thirty miles from our operation.

When our ground equipment arrived the next day, we got set up to begin spraying. We carried 200 gallons of Herbicide mixture in each planeload, and with two planes working we covered ground pretty fast. We were able to work most of the daytime, as the wind was seldom above the 10 MPH limit allowed for Mesquite spraying.

We began spraying scrub mesquite on a ridge early one morning, when I "jumped" a mountain lion right in front of my plane. The roar of that 450 horsepower engine must have really scared him. He ran ahead of me, glancing over his shoulder a time or two, and was headed directly at my flagger, who was waving his flag. The lion and the flagger apparently saw each other about the same instant, the lion turning one direction and the flagger the other, dropping his flag. I flew between them, laughing like mad. I wonder what that lion was thinking.

The next day we were finishing up a block of mesquite when we saw a large black cloud of smoke spiraling upward about five miles away where Lefty was working. Henry drove over to check it out, while I finished spraying our block of mesquite.

The black smoke had come from Lefty's airplane. He had been spraying while his partner returned to the strip to re-load. Upon returning his partner fell in beside Lefty, waving like mad indicating the fire under Lefty's plane. Lefty, who had been unaware of the fire, simultaneously closed the throttle, dived to the ground and jumped out when the wheels touched. Only a few seconds later the airplane blew up. Talk about close calls.

Lefty only received second-degree burns on his arm, plus some bruises from jumping out of the rolling airplane at about fifty MPH. A broken or cut gas line had caused the fire. We thought it possible one of the nearby cotton farmers had purposely cut the line. The neighboring farmers were worried that the drift from our herbicide might hit their cotton and damage it. The farmers were naturally quite nervous about our working in proximity to their cotton.

Henry and I completed our spraying on the Pitchfork Ranch, and moved over to the Four-Sixes pasture, operating from an old ranch road on the ranch. We had begun spraying on a section of Mesquite adjoining a root-plowed field beside a ravine. I was flying behind Henry and began to notice some fine oil spray on my windshield.

This began to worry me, but to keep up with Henry I had to maintain my manifold pressure. If too high, it could cause a cylinder to loosen on those older radial engines. I still had about a third of my load in my spray-tank when I pulled up at the end of a swath and was suddenly sprayed with oil. My goggles kept the oil from my eyes, but vision was limited. I increased RPMs looking for a landing spot. Ahead of me was only a rock-strewn ravine, so I turned left not 20 feet above the ground, cutting my engine and landed in seconds on a root-plowed field. I missed all pitfalls in the landing. "Somebody up there" was still looking after me. I was also thankful I was wearing goggles. A special thanks to Henry for he had loaned them to me. I looked at the engine and saw a cylinder was hanging by only the spark plug wire, completely off the engine. Henry completed his turn-a-round, flying right over me, not seeing me. On his next round he spotted me and I saw him do a double-take.

We had to call Abilene to get the mechanic and parts and tools needed for repairs.

I admit I was a little shook-up over this, and when the engine was repaired I nervously flew it out of the root-plowed field, climbing up to a thousand feet with the engine backfiring loudly every few seconds. I hoped the engine would quit backfiring shortly. It didn't. Usually a short caused by water in the magneto would cause this, so I gave it a chance to evaporate, but it didn't. We then had to work on the magneto. Sure enough a little moisture was in the magneto and had created a path for the spark to follow, causing the backfiring. All these difficulties were making me nervous.

While waiting for the airplane to be repaired I placed the flaggers where needed, filling in wherever I could to expedite operations. Jim Waller was the foreman of this Four Sixes ninety-five section pasture (ninety-five square miles.) and hauled me around in the pasture helping me locate future positions for the flaggers. I noticed some huge Bob White Quail.

Jim told me the Bob White and Blue Quail had crossed, making a larger Quail. I had heard they wouldn't crossbreed, but, by golly, they sure had.

Jim told me how he loved to leave the ranch house on his horse and spend several days riding the pasture, personally checking things. I was thinking, "Here are today's real cowboys." The large Pitchfork Ranch kept about twenty-five cowboys that moved from camp to camp, doing their work. Most of them came from the East, wanting to become cowboys.

We finished spraying on the Four-Sixes ranch and moved about thirty miles south, sprayed one day then moved on to Abilene. An interesting sidelight of this last spraying job was that the owner had his own two-place helicopter and flew some of the flaggers to their position, saving us time.

We stopped in Abilene for some light maintenance on the airplanes, then left for San Angelo and refueled. It was only about fifty-five miles farther south to our next job at Ozona, Texas.

We worked a week or so in Ozona, then moved farther southwest about ninety miles, to some higher country for a full day's work. We were in sparsely populated ranch country.

There were several customers back in the Midland area and as we could we moved back and went right to work near Midland. We caught good weather and covered these different blocks of mesquite rather rapidly, all south of Midland. We then moved to Andrews to do our work north and west of Midland. We did some spraying of mesquite beside a nesting area for crows. Henry told me they had caught a young crow there one year and taught it to talk.

There was a one-day job farther north, so we set up operations on a little-used paved road with high-lines and fences on both sides just outside the barrow ditches.

When I started my first take-off run my plane was on the right side of the high centered road and I couldn't get the plane to move back to the center of the road. The posts and poles along the fence on the right were quite close to my wingtip, and the slope kept pulling me to the right. To keep my right wing out of the fence was nip and tuck until I accelerated enough to create some lift in my wings. This lift helped me to inch the wing away from the fence and as the airplane lifted up I was able to fly out safely between the lines.

On my next load I was careful to start my takeoff run directly in the middle of the road, and had no trouble at all from then on.

When we finished up the Midland-Andrews spraying we left for the Panhandle Country near Vega, Texas, west of Amarillo. On the way we were flying along enjoying the scenery over level farmlands east of Seminole, Texas, when all of a sudden Henry started turning and losing altitude. Of course, I followed him. He landed on a farm road between two fields and waved me to land. One cylinder on his plane was coming loose, spraying some oil on his windshield. He could see the cylinder head moving up and down when he changed power settings. I well knew the signs, as I'd already experienced this same thing twice.

I stayed with his airplane while he flew my plane over to Brownfield and rented a pickup. When he came back we pulled the airplane into a farmer's yard for safety, and tied it down.

We drove back to the Brownfield airport where he picked up my plane and flew on to Vega, another 100 miles farther north. I followed later with the crew. We would finish up with only one airplane.

At the ranch on which we would be working, there was an unusual, beautiful and nervous blue-eyed horse in the pens. The ranch manager had received the horse as a gift, and was having to take a lot of time to get the confidence of the horse before he could train him. This horse was a rare breed known only to this original ranch. I don't remember the breed name, but it was a beautiful horse.

We were in old Tascosa Country near a small river running in a sandy canyon. This area had been a "stomping ground" for many cowboys, buffalo hunters and gunslingers in the past. I could easily imagine Billy the Kid riding up to the saloon (I'm sure there must have been a saloon in Old Tascosa) for a glass of red-eye, keeping his eyes on everybody that came in. I wondered how you could tell an Outlaw from a Cowboy, though. This country was, and still is, big, lonesome country, even today.

In the small town of Vega was a real old-time drugstore, with a fountain and metal chairs and tables. One could sit at a table and sip a milkshake or a cherry Coke. This was the kind of drug store I knew when I was growing up in Sonora, Texas in the twenties and early thirties.

I had some time off one day and went jogging around the small old town of Vega. I spotted some large Quonset huts and jogged over to look them over. These were so big there were farm tractors and heavy equipment inside. It was obvious the place had been plowed and a crop grown in it. I would imagine one could raise plenty of vegetables inside in the winter. There were two of these huge Quonset huts. I didn't find out more about them, I'm sorry to say. This is cold country in the winter, though, and some 300 miles farther north than McCamey, where I lived.

All around Vega was prairie, with a few low hills. This land was all a part of the three million acre grant made long ago by the State of Texas to a building company combine. This combine agreed to construct the State Capitol Building at Austin in exchange for the land. They were to use the pink granite quarried near Marble Falls, Texas.

The grant of three million acres was for the flat land in a 300-mile strip bordering New Mexico on the west and commencing at the NW tip of the Texas Panhandle. At the time of the land acquisition there were few watering places. The owners, several of which lived in England, wanted to stock it at once with cattle. A man named Babcock (no kin to me) was put in charge of that impossible task. Without water and fences it was an insurmountable task. They eventually had to sell the land in blocks to get their money, after attempting for several years to raise cattle. To ranch it properly they needed several hundred miles of fencing installed and probably a hundred water wells with tanks and water troughs, etc. There were no trees growing there from which you could make fence posts. There were no neighbors or towns, either. The builders did complete the Capitol building, though.

Looking at those vast plains I cannot imagine an operating ranch controlling 3 million acres. I believe that amounts to 46,875 Sections. (A section is a Square mile).

This was our last Mesquite spraying job of the season, and I hoped the Gardner brothers made a profit in spite of the troubles encountered. We'd had two forced landings and one airplane burned up.

I hope this has provided a better appreciation and understanding of the business of the aerial application of pesticides business. It is hard and dangerous work, but we enjoyed the flying.

- Punching a Time Clock

Working for Henry had been interesting and enjoyable. It had been a little hard on Henry as I had defective hearing. I had misunderstood some of his instructions from time to time. I decided I needed to buy some hearing aids as soon as possible.

I had closed down my appliance business, so I needed a job. The T V Cable manager found out I was unemployed and put me to work helping him part time. We put in new cable, did a good bit of repair, and tuned up the two stations, McCamey and Rankin. We counted and listed each cable hookup, disconnecting several illegal hook-ups in both towns.

One Friday afternoon, we received a call from Rankin that the Dallas T.V. channel was off. This was the night the TV show "Dallas" was going to tell "Who Shot J. R."

Away we went the twenty miles to the head station at Rankin in the truck. I traced the circuit board and found a faulty transistor. Naturally neither of us had the right one in stock, so we piled in his truck and to Midland we drove ("Flew" would be a better word for it) fifty miles to the Midland Electronics Supply, bought the needed transistor, and "flew" back to Rankin.

The phone was ringing in the head station when we walked in. I started replacing the defective transistor. I could hear Fisher talking, trying to be diplomatic and telling the lady "We're working on it." It only took me about ten minutes, but Fisher was still saying, "Yes ma'am, we're working on it, yes ma'am, we'll have it fixed, yes ma'am, yes ma'am, uh, ma'am. ma'am. I say, ma'am. If you'll look on your TV set you'll see "Dallas is on now." I had put it into service the minute the "Dallas" show came on the air. I still don't know who shot J.R., but I believe Fisher could have kissed me that night, heaven forbid. He was an electrical engineer, while I was only a technician. He had the degree and I had the practical experience, so together we made a pretty good team.

A friend told me I might get a flying job in Iraan, thirty miles south of McCamey. I drove down there and sure enough, Bob, a friend of mine, knew I'd been flying for his competitor and wanted me full time. He furnished me a pickup to drive and bought a good, used six-place Piper. I was kept busy flying it, and made several trips to Farmington, New Mexico. One time we spent one whole day and two nights there, and I visited the two neighboring towns in that area, finding some ancient Indian ruins to visit. In the towns I noticed several gardens having some beautiful flowers planted in rows, probably for taking to church or to sell. Both towns I visited had ancient Indian ruins to see, so I enjoyed myself.

Taking off from the Farmington airport we were directly in line with a mountain in the distance called Shiprock. It really did look like a huge ship in the distance. We turned left to a heading for Albuquerque, N.M., destination Iraan, Texas.

Crossing the western New Mexican desert we spotted a few houses in isolated areas, no water to be seen, nothing green. Sometimes a car or an old truck was parked nearby. The occasional mountains, though, had green grass from 7,000 feet up.

We flew at ten thousand feet when passing over Albuquerque, and found ourselves in the middle of military and airlines planes preparing to land. Thank goodness for Traffic Control. They guided us through the traffic safely.

Looking down on Albuquerque you realize the city is located close to the Rio Grande River, yet is surrounded by desert. There were several golf courses that stood out as bright green spots, built a mile or so away from town in the desert.

In about a month Bob traded his Piper airplane for a Bellanca with 300 H.P., flaps and retractable landing gear. It had a cruising speed of 190 MPH. Most of my flights were round trips to Odessa, Texas, (85 miles), to pick up merchandise for oil production. Doing this saved time. We had a car available at the Odessa airfield, so I would land, drive to the various stores in town to pick up our orders, then return to the airport and then be in Iraan in another twenty-five minutes.

One time Bob had me fly him to Illinois to visit his parents. I enjoyed spending the three days in the small town of Sims, Illinois, where I stayed in his parent's house across the road from a railroad. The first night I was sound asleep when a train came by, whistle blowing, bells ringing, and roaring through town at full speed. The whole house seemed to shake. An hour later it happened again. I don't think I ever got used to it. I just endured it.

One day I was out jogging in Sims and was passing by a cherry tree full of ripe red cherries. A lady was picking them, and offered to give me some, so I helped her pick them for a little while. I carried a handful with me when I left. What fun it was, after fifty years, to again be eating red cherries off a tree, just like in Colorado as a small boy. There were also ripe strawberries in some of the many gardens, grown with mostly rainwater.

I saw my first silver leaf maple trees in the distance. How odd it was to see the whole tree turn from green to silver when a puff of wind hit them. When the wind died they turned back to green. How beautiful. One side of the leaves was silver, the other side green.

Flying back to Texas was a pleasure, only landing once for fuel. At 190 miles per hour you cover the ground fast, about three miles a minute.

It was fun flying this ship. We also made an occasional round trip to Houston. One time we brought back fifty dollars worth of fresh shrimp. We had a fine shrimp boil that night, for customers and friends.

Confidence is a good thing, unless it is based on ignorance—ignorance being lack of knowledge. A man I knew who lived in Iraan had learned to fly. He was not taught any blind flying, and took his Private License test from a check pilot not requiring him to demonstrate his ability to fly on instruments. Emergency instrument flying knowledge was actually a mandatory requirement.

When this student purchased a Super Bellanca, I offered to teach him some instrument flying free of charge. He turned me down. A few months after buying this airplane, he took a friend with him for a cross-country flight. Against all advice he went ahead and took off before dawn at Iraan in a very low ceiling. He crashed about four miles from town less than five minutes later, killing them both. It was so foolish, more like suicide. It just made us all sick. To repeat: their deaths were caused by overconfidence and ignorance, leading into bad judgment. His death may have been avoided had he let me help him. This still bothers me.

When my employer sold out his store and his airplane I was again unemployed. I went to Odessa to see about possibilities of a job in electronics existed, Odessa being a much larger city than McCamey.

I spent a day there, with no luck. All I found was one or two assembly line jobs, but no thank you.

A few days later Fisher told me about reading another advertisement in the Odessa Newspaper for an electronic technician. I drove to Odessa, found the location, and talked to the personnel officer who took my qualifications. He told me he would be in touch. Two days later they called, wanting me to come to work the next day, if possible. This was in 1980.

Chapter 15

I Go To Work For Baker, Inc.

Electronics was my line of work, as well as flying, and I enjoyed doing it. I was to repair computer monitors for Totco, a subsidiary of the Baker Co. Totco rented out their computers to be used in deep oil well drilling, and designed and manufactured their computers in their plant in Norman, Oklahoma.

These special computers were used for monitoring several aspects of the actual drilling for oil, with emphasis on monitoring mudflow. Drilling mud is circulated in the well during the drilling operation, to carry out cuttings and provide weight in controlling gas pressure by varying the thickness of the mud. The chance of drilling into a high-pressure pocket of gas is higher in the deep drilling but can be encountered at any depth. The least change in mudflow would indicate higher-pressure gas. The computer readout gives the driller time to add heavier-weight mud into circulation down the well preventing a probable blowout and likely fire.

These computers were rented to rigs drilling deep oil wells, as a rule below 12,000 feet. When the well was bottomed, Totco's clean-up crew would be moved in and recover all the wires, computers, sensors, etc. and return or ship them to the Odessa, Texas store. The computers were then disassembled, cleaned and the computer boards removed, labeled and sent through the electronic section for testing and repairs, if needed. After the repairs the parts were checked in Quality Control then put into "stores" (storage) to be requisitioned when needed.

We received the returned parts from West Texas, Oklahoma, Louisiana and Saudi Arabia.

My primary job was re-assembling the monitors and repairing them. Another job I performed was to modify new monitors to adapt to our equipment. I had to unpack each new monitor from its cardboard box, take the chassis out of the case, make a couple of technical adjustments on it, then re-assemble them and re-pack into their cartons, then send them through quality control. They would then be put into Stores ready to be shipped out. One morning I was brought 625 of the small new monitors for adapting. I worked hard and was able to get them all modified that same day. Another technician asked me why I worked so hard. I told him, "I want to get the job done." After being in business for myself I wanted to put in the effort I was being paid for. I was given three raises in my first year.

I repaired many purge monitors, which are monitors installed in a steel case equipped with Nitrogen gas flowing inside the case, the nitrogen prohibiting any chance of sparks that could ignite any gas present on the drilling floor. There were several smaller monitors used in the "dog house," the trailer houses or wherever the drilling company wanted them. We also had a master recorder that recorded all the readings twenty-four hours a day.

The drilling computers used a "Mother Board" and used thirteen printed circuit boards. We had all parts in "Stores" for repairing these boards: transistors, PCs, resistors, everything. I enjoyed working where they had all the parts I might need to repair even the most technical boards.

I enjoyed my work, although it was sometimes long hours. I had to be at my desk every day at 7:00 A.M., sixty miles from my home in McCamey. I was late only twice in the two years I worked there and that was caused by my waiting for the snow and ice on the highway to be diminished by the truck traffic.

I left McCamey by 5:45 each morning. Often we worked until 6:00 P.M., with a 30-minute dinner break and two fifteen minute coffee breaks. We had our own cafeteria in the building.

One morning before daylight, while driving to work, I was "dive bombed" from the front by a large owl. I couldn't understand him doing this. I saw him a couple of days later lying beside the road, dead. I wonder if he was just blinded by headlights or maybe disgruntled at having to work all night.

One morning on the way to work, I turned west on a short stretch of highway. There, sitting squarely on the pavement, was the big full giant yellow moon. That afternoon when I turned onto the same stretch of highway returning home, there it was sitting right on the other end of the highway. What fantastic sights.

On two or three occasions in the winter I saw a bobcat crossing the road at the same spot on the highway. I also saw quite a few deer and some Javelinas ("J" pronounced as an "H"). These little animals resembled wild pigs (the proper name for them is "Wild Peccaries) that have short, sharp tusks. They have poor eyesight but good hearing, and run in groups of twelve to twenty. Fully-grown male Javelinas can weigh as much as 90 pounds. Like many wild animals, they prefer to hunt or roam at night or early in the mornings. Their main food was a cactus root growing on the hills. They dug them out of the ground and ate the roots.

After working about a year my supervisor called me to his office and told me he had finally found a repairman to help me. They told me he had been working for Montgomery Ward as their field TV repairman. I thought "Oh. Oh." I'd had some experience with those "stop-gap" repairmen as competitors. They usually ended up having to carry the T.V. to someone else for repair. They seldom knew more than how to replace a circuit board. In my work I was repairing the actual printed circuit boards.

When Delbert came to work I found my fears were well founded. He was a fine young man and I liked him but although he had some basic knowledge of TV's, he didn't know how to trace circuitry. With his cooperation I began teaching him how the circuitry worked and how to trace circuitry using the instruments we had, in order to locate the problem. He was willing and worked hard, learning enough to be of help to me. Teaching him also refreshed my memory.

When the price of oil dropped in 1981, so did our business. There were 175 workers in June at Totco and by July most were let out. By August the tenth, twenty-one of us were left, and were assigned to building plywood boxes and packing parts and equipment in them. By the end of September all but seven men were let off. These seven men were moved to the Oklahoma factory. I didn't wish to move, so I was let off.

The company urged us to go on unemployment compensation, so I did, for three months, while looking for a decent job. With the oil price slump there were few jobs available, so I thought about going on Social Security at the age of sixty-four. A thought regarding the receiving of unemployment money was that I had paid into those unemployment funds for over thirty years as an employer, so perhaps I'd get a little of my money back.

You know, it is really odd that during the two years working with Totco I managed to install windows all around my large back porch, including a double sliding glass door. I also installed new shingles on the roof. I put the new shingles on top of the ones already on the house. I was able to do it all by myself, getting plenty of exercise in the process, but I wore the seat of my britches out.

- Some Contract Flying

I was hired by "Gordo" Graciano to fly his six-place Cessna 206, a nice airplane to fly. Later I began flying his twin engine Piper Seneca, which cruised at 200 MPH. It was supercharged and could fly on a single engine at 13,000 feet. That is very good performance. I enjoyed flying this plane very much and made several flights to El Paso and Presidio. We kept it in a hanger there in McCamey, while Gordo lived in Odessa. He could call and I could be the fifty miles to Odessa with a fifteen-minute flight.

Tony Alaniz went along as my interpreter, as Gordo did not speak English. I made one practice 150-mile flight to Abilene from Odessa and had dinner with my ex-China roommate, Richard Bloomer.

When Gordo sold his airplanes that ended my flying, at least for a while. I now checked with the Social Security office and found out how much S.S. would pay me if I retired at age 64. Due to my birth date, I found out my S.S. would be reduced by nearly $100 a month for life, because of what they called the "Notch-Baby". What was the Notch Baby? Why do the WW II veterans have to be penalized for it? Whatever it was it wasn't my fault. The Government has finally acknowledged that it had been a mistake but has done nothing about it. I had been assured that this decision was not a penalty, "just" a thing they needed to do to save Social Security. Seem like they've been trying to save Social Security ever since it was enacted. All persons born in 1917 through 1926 are affected by this penalty. This affects about all the men who fought in WW II. "Welcome home, boys." I have now been on Social Security for twenty-two years, so this involves a reduction to me of some $20,000.00 so far. Are you puzzled about this? Join the "party." One thought: if the gentlemen in Washington would stop using SS for special projects and pay back what they have borrowed, S.S. might not need "saving." I have to admit though, SS has been a big help for me.

I was still giving some flight instruction and flying some charter flights, but not enough to help my finances much. Although I had logged nearly 26,000 hours, I still enjoyed flying, but aviation fuel had reached a dollar eighty eight a gallon and yearly required commercial flight physicals were a hundred dollars and maintenance on the airplanes was much higher in the 1980s. I sold the airplanes I had left, and virtually quit flying. I had been an active pilot and instructor for fifty years.

- Dr. Ernie Sandidge, M.D.

When I returned to McCamey after spraying brush for Henry Gardner in 1980, there was a new doctor in town, Dr. Ernie Sandidge, M. D. I went to him for a physical check-up and a get acquainted visit. I liked his approach to medicine. He looked at my hands and fingernails, looked at my tongue and into my eyes and explained what he derived from that. I told him I was riding bicycles a lot, so was interested in being healthy.

We discussed the resistance of germs to antibiotics, and he told me that exercise kills germs. I asked: "But Doctor, how do you get them to exercise?"

Dr. Ernie also told me he had owned and flown a twin Beechcraft airplane when he was living in Las Vegas, Nevada a few years ago. One thing led to another, and he bought a six-place Piper airplane, hiring me to fly with him. He'd had an illness and wanted to see if he was still able to fly safely.

We enjoyed flying around the country just viewing areas of interest. Dr. Ernie could fly the plane well enough, but his eyesight and poor judgment of altitude prevented my letting him solo.

Target practice with Dr. Ernie with our twenty-two caliber rifles was also a fun thing for both of us. It had been many years since I had even fired my rifle. He was an expert rifleman and had no trouble seeing his target. He was more accurate than I was. He really had a serious hobby of collecting guns. One room of his house was filled with all kinds of rifles and pistols. Later after retirement he planned to sell them.

As a member of the Confederate Air Force, Dr. Sandidge was the emergency doctor at the Confederate Air Force air shows.

I hated it when he sold his airplane, which he didn't really need. Dr. Ernie retired shortly thereafter and moved. We still keep in touch.

- Riding Bicycles

In the late 1970s I bought bicycles for Faegene and myself and we began riding daily. I put in some extra time riding, working up to about fifteen to thirty miles a day. This went on for about ten years. Sometimes I parked the bike and climbed a tall hill and that made it more fun. One time during springtime I surprised a mule deer grazing in the "bar" ditch. He came bouncing right in front of me and ran ahead and jumped over the fence. Another time I was going about twenty-five miles an hour and just as I met a truck I heard a loud "bang." I honestly thought someone had fired a gun at me. My front tire had blown out.

Bicycling was rather rare in that West Texas town of McCamey, and when a stranger came riding in, I was interested. So when Steve Maynard came riding in, I introduced myself to him. He told me he was Steve Maynard, and he was visiting his mother and dad, Dr. B. J. and Mrs. Maynard, in Crane. Steve had come twenty miles to McCamey. That was going to be a forty-mile ride by the time he got home. I found out later on that he often rode fifty to a hundred miles during a day.

During the time he was visiting in Crane we would ride together often, and his encouragement went a long way to help increase my riding. He was quite a bike rider, riding nearly every year in the high mountains of Colorado.

After I came to Fayetteville I began riding ten to fifteen miles a day, five or six days a week, with Carleton Williams, a neighbor. We really enjoyed this bike riding.

Again I had an encounter with a deer. A female deer crossed the road at full speed only a few feet in front of me. I was going over fifteen miles an hour at the time. We didn't tangle, but it was another close call. I was shaking with relief when I realized we had not collided. It would have been a catastrophe for me. Deer and dogs are not friends of bicycle riders.

Later, riding for the first time with the Biking For Life Club, of which we are both charter members, Blanche used her daughter's single-speed 30-year old bike. The ride was only twelve miles long and I had my 18-speed racing bike. It was no problem for me, but Blanche hadn't ridden in years. She kept up, but I knew then she needed a faster and easier riding bike. Guess what. She got a 24-speed cross-country bike for her birthday. We have been riding ever since here in Georgia and also in Texas when we are there for vacations.

Sino-American WW II Vets 2000 Reunion
Kunming, China — 2000

Ken on a Chinese bibycle
Near the WW II home of General Chennault

Thousands of bicycles on the streets of Kunming

Back in Georgia...

At 80, Ken recently added to his life's achievements with a 44-mile bicycle ride from Senoia to Warm Springs, Georgia. This wasn't the longest ride for Ken, a member of Fayetter Biking for Life, but it was the longest since he recently had a hip and both knees replaced.

Below is an excerpt from an article written about Ken Babcock:
by Amber Strong in the Fayette Neighbor Newspaper
Thursday, December 2, 1999
Ken Babcock Can Still Ride With the Best

Ken Babcock of Fayetteville, who turned 81 last month, says he doesn't see any reason his life should slow now.

A retired business owner from Texas, a Hump pilot and former Austin Symphony Orchestra member, Babcock plays the piano, sings in his church choir and makes the most of each day he has.

"God has given me life here on earth and it's the most precious gift any of us can receive. He didn't give it to us to throw away. He gave it to us to live to the fullest, and that's what I'm trying to do," Babcock said.

He flew over the Himalayan peaks, known by the pilots as the "Hump," delivering military supplies to the Chinese army in the 1940s.

"Flying over the 'Hump' was considered the most difficult (flight) in the world at that time. The only way we could get to where we needed to be was by flying over the ice mountains of the world in aircraft not designed to fly that high," Babcock said.

After returning to the U.S., Babcock opened a store and then a crop-dusting business in west Texas, which he ran for 30 years.

Babcock has always been conscious of his health; he attributes his long life to his positive mental attitude and exercise.

Babcock moved to Fayette County in 1999. He became a member of Fayette Biking for Life.

"I ride with people who are much younger than I am, but I keep up," Babcock said.

Babcock and members of the Biking for Life are actively lobbying for bike lanes on Fayette County roads to encourage residents to get out and exercise in a safe atmosphere. Right now, cyclists ride on the edge of the road in flow with the traffic.

The drivers of the cars are polite and considerate of us, but lanes would be a lot safer for everyone concerned," Babcock said.

Chapter 16

My Family

My daughter, Sherry Phillips, became the mayor of McCamey shortly after the recent turn of the century. She had retired from working for the Security State Bank. McCamey is the little old' oil town in West Texas I had lived in for forty-nine years. I've always been proud of Sherry. She's been a good mayor for a town that needed her and she has worked hard in supporting the companies who were building and operating almost a thousand huge wind generators on the mountains in the McCamey area. She was recently sent to Washington by the companies to talk to some of the congressmen in an attempt to get more support for enlarging the field of electrical production. Production of electricity using those huge generators is quite efficient and environmentally clean. McCamey produces the wind these generators need.

With the oil nearly depleted around McCamey, support from the wind generator industry is indeed welcome.

My oldest granddaughter, Shelley Shackelford and husband Cary, live and teach school in Wink, Texas, another old oil field town. Melissa, their oldest daughter, is attending college, and was recently married. Her sister, Lacy, just graduated from Wink High School and Gil, her brother, is in college in New Mexico on a football scholarship. The problem for us today is that I live 1300 miles from their home in Wink.

My grandson, Chris, is happily married and lives near Austin with wife Kristin and my three little great-granddaughters, Mikah 6, Eliya 4, and Gavriella 2 yrs old. My other granddaughter, Lisa, loves living in California. She works full time and is completing her college degree. She is a devoted Christian and has recently spent two weeks in Africa and about the same in India doing missionary work. She also traveled with her church to Mississippi to help restore a church after Hurricane Katrina. She loves her work.

I am proud of them all and feel, as most grandparents and great-grandparents do, that our children are the smartest and most beautiful young people in the world. They do make good grades and excel in whatever they do, just as their mother, Sherry, has always done.

When I married Blanche, January 15, 2000, I added all her children, and as of today we have four daughters, ten granddaughters, three grandsons, six great-granddaughters and one great-grandson, if I have counted them correctly. Since I started writing this book, Blanche's newest editions are Virginia Weatherup, Toni and Cody Phillips, and Cristie Hall and her daughter Savannah. Three of our four daughters are married to men named Phillips, no relation.

Back in 1988 I had decided to improve the looks of my yard in McCamey. I bought a load of cow manure to spread with my little shovel. Shoveling that manure alone was enough good exercise to keep me fit. When springtime came the yard started turning green, and I was delighted until most of the grass turned out to be grass-burrs. You know, the real "stickery" kind. The only way I was able to control "them stickery little rascals," was by pulling them up one by one and carefully disposing of them. It took nearly all summer, but I finally won the battle and had a fine lawn without a single sticker.

One summer we were determined to have flowers by planting them close to the east side of the house, away from the strong dry spring winds from the west. Our house faced west, so we grew some beautiful flowers and shrubs in the back yard and built an arbor for climbing roses. It all grew well with fertilizer and lots of water and T.L.C.

Miss Effie Eagleton, Texas History teacher at McCamey High School, gave me some wild plum trees. I planted them in a little ditch by the alley. They produced real well each year until the dry west spring winds burned up most of the blooms. A few times I harvested a quart or so of excellent wild plums. I was practically raised on wild plum preserves and Algerita berry jelly. There was just too much hot wind for plums in this desert.

Next year I planted a garden and fertilized and prepared the soil. Not a string bean was produced, nor a squash, onion, carrot or even a pod of okra. The garden was just a fertilized, watered, failure. That winter, however, was warm and wet, and in January I discovered hundreds of tiny carrots growing as well as leaf lettuce and new onions all around. That was just unbelievable. It turned out to be a bonanza. I decided I knew nothing about gardening.

Faegene's mother died in 1977. Pop, Faegene's father, lived to be the age of ninety-three. Faegene and I took care of Pop in our home for several years as he was going blind. When he became completely blind, it became too difficult for us. We regretfully put him in the nursing home, and Merel and I took turns feeding and shaving him every day.

When Pop died, some three years later, Merel and Faegene inherited a small amount of oil royalty from Pop. J. Cleo Thompson Oil Company then drilled a new oil well, hitting a good production of oil. They then continued drilling several more holes successfully. Although the price of oil dropped drastically, the production was still enough to help us financially. Had the wells been small producers, we would have received very little. Had we owned all the royalty, we would have been millionaires.

In this discussion of family, I must tell about the wonderful son-in-law I have. My new home in McCamey was next door to Sherry and Jack Phillips, my daughter and son-in-law. Jack has kept my house looking great ever since I moved to Georgia. He even kept the front lawn growing during the drought of the past five years.

Jack also has been watering and taking care of the grass and flowers and trees for the Methodist Church in McCamey. He keeps in shape by walking a few miles daily. He has done this for more than 25 years.

Whenever Blanche and I go to Texas we stay in our own house next door to Sherry and Jack, and even get some fine meals, as our daughter is a wonderful cook.

- Hump Pilot Reunions

In 1985 I found out there was an organization of CBI (Veterans of China, Burma and India) veterans and joined it. Faegene and I then attended the next re-union, held in San Antonio, Texas, in the Hyatt Regency Hotel. It was 11:00 a.m. before we drove into San Antonio, and I got lost in the maze of one-way streets downtown. In desperation I stopped and asked a police officer where the hotel was. He pointed out that it was just around the next corner. Does it ever fail?

When we drove up to the entrance of that hotel, there were several African-Americans standing by the door, wearing tuxedos. Faegene said she would not stay at such a fancy hotel whose bellboys wore tuxedos. She was dead serious. When I checked this out, I learned those men were a part of the wedding party. With that explained, we checked in.

Although we enjoyed the reunion, I only found one man I knew during the war. I was quite disappointed but later found out this organization included all personnel who had been stationed in China, Burma or India, therefore called the CBI Organization.

The other organization open only to personnel who had flown or ridden in an airplane across the ("Hump") Himalayan Mountains into China is called "The CBI Hump Pilots", so when I learned this I promptly joined it. I then received a roster and located several men I knew, including my roommate, Richard Bloomer. I looked forward to seeing these men in the future.

We had a nice visit with our nephew Walter Kokernot in San Antonio. Walter is my sister Edith May's youngest child.

The next year I attended the Hump Pilot reunion at Little Rock, Arkansas, by myself, and found a few of my fellow Luliang buddies were there. What a nice time we had remembering old times and old friends. I also made new friends with Betty and Milo Walters.

Returning from Little Rock, Arkansas, three of us pilots were riding in the back seats of the Southwest Airlines, talking about our flying experiences. During a slight pause in our conversation a little old lady sitting across the aisle, who had been listening to our discussions, leaned over and said seriously, "I'm sure glad you boys are aboard."

The next year I rode Southwest Airlines to attend the Hump Pilot meeting in Scottsdale. I guess my clothes wanted to gamble, as they stayed on the airliner and went on to Las Vegas, Nevada. When I checked on them, there was a message saying they would be in my closet at the motel that evening, and they were.

I played in the Hump Pilot golf tournament at Scottsdale and had a ball. This was a beautiful course and interesting, with cactus everywhere and one hole in the middle of an Island in a small lake.

My good friend Thurmon Yates and his wife, Evelyn arrived in their camper. When they were informed they were not allowed to stay in it on the parking lot, I invited them to share my room. We enjoyed each other's company very much and shared our past camaraderie.

At the Scottsdale meeting I walked into a roomful of pilots and wives just after dinner and spotted Dudley and Marcia Hodgkins. Dudley was the bridge player I played against in China when he made a Grand Slam, doubled and redoubled, against my partner, Hurd and myself.

That sure brought back memories. Yes, I remembered that game quite well. Dudley's partner had been a professional bridge player and was also surprised that Dudley made that grand slam, doubled and re-doubled.

The next reunion Faegene and I attended was in Reno, Nevada. We left a day later than planned and drove to Flagstaff, Arizona to spend the first night. That was about 750 miles. The next day we drove another 750 miles to Reno and checked in at Harrah's Hotel and Casino where the reunion was being held.

I don't remember much about the reunion itself. I think most of the members were gambling most of the time. I know two of my buddies were there, but I never saw them.

We spent one afternoon touring Harrah's beautiful collection of cars. However, we skipped our planned trip to Lake Tahoe because of ice on the road.

I well remember the ride back across Nevada as being a long way and rather boring, with nothing of interest to see. We took the road to Salt Lake City, Utah, hoping we could locate Ed Wimmer's widow and daughter.

Fortunately, Mrs. Wimmer was visiting the area for a family reunion and was able to have dinner with us. She and her husband met us in Salt Lake City. It was good to be able to talk with them. She told me she had been working with her flowers in the front yard of their home when a Western Union boy rode up on his bicycle and handed her the telegram about Ed being killed in action. It shocked me that the Army Air Force had not brought that message to her. I guess there were so many casualties that a telegram was the only way it could be done.

She thanked me again for returning his effects and asked about his knife he carried in a small scabbard. I had to tell her the Chinese who had found and reported the wreckage had stolen it. She thanked me for the letter I had written her, and I was glad to have visited her in person. She also told me they called Ed by the name Barlow. Ed's daughter lived in California.

In 1990 we decided to drive our motor home to Spokane, Washington, for the Hump Pilot Reunion there. We had bought a used motor home, so we loaded it and lived in it for the next five weeks. Having all the clothes and other necessities, including a bed, we were able to travel day and night if we wished. All I had to do was start driving. Being able to keep on "rollin'," we made good time. When Faegene was feeling pretty good, she would come up and sit in the front seat to see the scenery. When she didn't, she went back to bed and watched television.

At the Spokane Reunion there were several men I hadn't seen since leaving China. One was Floyd Smith, with whom I flew as co-pilot a time or two in China. Florence and Floyd became good friends of ours, and we always looked forward to seeing them each year at the reunions. Floyd looked just the same as in 1945 when I first met him.

He and George Shoemaker were chairmen of our reunion in Spokane and were both stationed at Luliang, China with me. George and I had been good friends in Fort Stockton, Texas when we were instructing Army cadets before he left Fort Stockton to join the Army Air Corps.

A film production company came from Seattle to film our reunion, and saw potential for a full-length film on the Hump Pilots. They interviewed many of us, including recording the true stories we told of flying across the Hump. They then decided to film more of "The Unknown War" and eventually made six commercial tapes from our interviews and others they took later. Those tape sets have now been distributed worldwide. I'm sorry to say most of those interviewed are now dead. I knew nearly all of those interviewed in the "Flying the Hump" tape.

Faegene and I stayed in Spokane an extra day to visit with my buddy, George Shoemaker, and his wife. Then we drove on to Seattle.

We had a little problem with our motor home only a few miles before reaching our destination west of Seattle. The alternator quit working and the battery in the motor home was completely run down, causing the engine to quit. We were on a two-lane highway and I had pulled over too close to a guardrail. I couldn't get out. Coasting a short distance backward I was able to maneuver the motor home away from the guardrail. This gave me enough space to open the door.

I determined the problem was the alternator and replaced the motor home battery with the Opals' battery. We were then able to continue on to a nice trailer park about fifteen miles east of Renton, Washington.

There was a town about 1500 feet above our trailer park, so I took out the alternator and drove the little Opal up the mountain to the town. I found a parts store and bought a new alternator. It worked fine. Everything was now "Hunky Dory."

The next day I again drove up to the town. The skies were clear, and as I turned the last corner there was Mount Rainier, right in front and about 14,000 feet above me. What a magnificent sight, so enormous and majestic. All 14,000 feet looked down upon all of us little people below. It was just overpowering. I hadn't even seen this mountain at all until now because of the low visibility. Just imagine, a 14,408-foot mountain virtually in your back yard.

It was a thrill every time we saw that huge mountain, with its snowcap and glaciers. I talked to a local mechanic who worked on our little car, and he told me that he went camping and fishing in the lower slopes nearly every weekend of the summer. Imagine living in such close proximity to such a beautiful place. Back in our hometown of McCamey we had a saying, "We can go 200 miles in any direction and fish." It's hard to imagine a whole mountain virtually in your back yard, with forests and trout streams available to anyone.

Being so close to Seattle we naturally drove into town, saw the *Needle*, ate an excellent fish dinner, and looked over the many wharfs and boats. Right beside the highway on the way out of Seattle was the huge Boeing Aircraft Factory and its full-size airport. It was so nice to see these things we'd only read about.

- Mount St. Helen and Its Devastation

One day we crawled into our little Opal and headed south 200 miles, to see the devastation caused by the 1980 Eruption of Mount St. Helens.

Passing by the city of Tacoma just south of Seattle, we could see some of the mountains in Olympic National Park far to our right. However, there wasn't time on this trip to visit that park. Continuing on, we turned off the main highway about 120 miles farther south of Tacoma. There were overlooks built beside the road we turned on, and we could see Mount St. Helens in the distance. Finally, we turned off that highway onto a Park road taking us through miles of beautiful dense forests of fir trees.

Abruptly, the scenery changed to one of devastation. What a contrast. The road going up the mountain had no standing trees where the forest had been, only knee-deep ash and fallen trees the rest of the way. The road took us several more miles along the higher ridges to the vantage point from which we could clearly see the crater and off to the right, Spirit Lake. Everywhere trees were blown down, denuded and pointing away from the crater. There had been a powerful blast of such high temperature that it had completely driven all moisture from the wood. I picked up a 3-foot log 4 inches thick. It was light as a feather and didn't appear to be burnt. The extreme heat must have instantly evaporated all moisture from the wood without it burning. I stepped on the ash deposit and sank in about a foot.

At the viewing station across the valley from the actual volcano, the trees all around us were laying parallel on the ground pointing away from the volcano. Looking down we saw the former beautiful *Spirit Lake,* which was now a third covered by floating logs. The literature at the viewing spot said that Spirit Lake was about a thousand feet higher in elevation now than before the eruption. There were no green trees anywhere around. All the devastation defied description.

What terrific power it took to blow down forests, destroy life of all kinds in such a large area and send volcanic ashes around the world.

A short time after the volcano erupted, I was flying in the eastern United States in a light rain and landed in Roanoke, Virginia. I discovered wet volcanic ash stuck on the leading edges of the airplane. It had to have come all the way across the nation from St. Helen's eruption.

- Sightseeing and Visiting Relatives on the Road Home

September was a good month for fresh fruits and berries in Washington. All fruit we purchased was ripe and had a richer flavor than those we could buy back in West Texas. I picked some wild blackberries from along the railroad right of way, close to our Motor Home Park. They were incredibly good eating, fat and juicy, and perfect with ice cream. The berries were there for the picking. I found lots of vines along the railroad, just waiting to stab me with their thorns, protecting their fruit. I picked some, very carefully.

- Yellowstone and Teton Mountains

We parked our motor home for the night in West Yellowstone, outside Yellowstone Park. Next morning we drove into the park, going first to Old Faithful Geyser and the Lodge. Not much had changed since my visit of 1935. Old Faithful was only a foot or two short of the 1935 geyser it had been, but was still faithful, shooting its steam up every hour. It was still a marvel to see. For her first time Faegene sat on the benches and watched old Faithful doing its thing.

They no longer fed the bears there. Managing so many hungry bears may have been too difficult and dangerous. There were many bears in 1935.

We visited the Emerald pool, and the "laundry" pool where I had washed my handkerchief in 1935. We visited most of the geysers, including the Norris basin where the Giant Geyser was located. Along the roads tiny jets of steam spewed up in miniature geysers.

We drove all the way to the North Gate to see the Mud Pots of colored mud in wide sheets down from one mud pot to the next.

There were a dozen elk lying around the headquarters building, acting as if they owned it all. Perhaps they did. They were peacefully chewing their cuds. Later that summer the elk made trouble by attacking some tourists. Leave nature alone and it might do the same for you.

I hadn't realized we would have to drive that big motor home over the 10,000-foot pass to continue our circle of the park on the narrow two-lane mountain road. That was a thrill that I could have done without. We made it safely to Yellowstone Lake where we saw dozens of wild buffalo grazing in the rich grass near the lake. Although they seemed to be tame, I was quite nervous watching so many tourists getting out of their cars and taking pictures.

It was only a short way to the beautiful Teton Mountain Peaks, standing all in a line, reaching upwards over 12,000 feet. I'd heard how beautiful they were, and seeing them "live" and up close they are even more beautiful than any pictures. Along the northeastern base of the mountains ran the beautiful Snake River, feeding a picturesque lake reflecting the mountains close above it.

We camped in an RV park on the west side of the town of Jackson, beside a grocery store that featured those giant doughnuts. Wow.

I called my sister Edith and husband Bob, living nearly five hundred feet above the town of Jackson. They drove down their mountain road to get us. Our motor home couldn't go up their winding mountain road.

Bob and Edith really took us on a *grand tour* of the Jackson Hole country. Bob, being a retired geologist, made sure to show us the *Gros Ventre* slide (pronounced *Grow vaunt*) in a canyon draining into the NE portion of the Jackson Hole country. This had been one of the largest slides of shale occurring in the U. S. It had dammed up the small stream in the valley and later caused a severe flood when the water washed out some of the dam. The people and their homes below the dam were washed away in the ensuing flood. This was located close to where the filming of the movie *Flicka* took place.

We took a boat across the Jackson Hole Lake and walked up the path into the mountains. I found ripe raspberries along the trail, so I didn't get much farther along. Bob mentioned he'd met a moose on that trail one day and said he quickly moved off the trail.

We reluctantly left Jackson Hole, to go to Denver by way of Rocksprings and Cheyenne, Wyoming. There was a lot of grass growing on the ranch country along the way. Outside of the cold winters, it would be great to have a ranch there.

After gassing up and driving around the town of Laramie for a quick look-see, we left to drive on to Cheyenne. We came to a pass leading up to a higher plain and just before reaching the top of the climb, we passed a beautiful statue of Abraham Lincoln. It was such an outstanding sight. We'd never heard of it being there and were quite impressed.

Some years later I learned the Lincoln Highway was the first road designated to cover the continent from east to west. This was also the road the first car was driven over from San Francisco to New York.

We were a little disappointed in the town of Cheyenne. It appeared to be an old train and cowboy town. We found an old campground, poorly maintained, in which to park our motor home. Maybe we expected the town to be full of cowboys on their horses riding all around shooting pistols. I watched for the "Cheyenne Social Club" but couldn't find it. I wouldn't have been too surprised to have seen it.

- My Aunt Kathryn Babcock

Grandpa Babcock & Aunt Kathryn Babcock

The following day we cruised down to Denver, where we parked our motor home for five days in the alley behind Aunt Kathryn's home, at 2321 South Saint Paul Street, University Park, Denver, Colorado. Kathryn was my favorite aunt, Daddy's sister.

She had been so nice to us kids when we had visited in the 1920s. I was only about five or six years old when she took Gertrude and me to Eliches Garden Amusement Park in downtown Denver. I think they wore me out on all the rides. Going back to Grandpa's house in a streetcar that night, I saw flashes of light and dozed off and on as we bounced, rattled and rocked. Then, more asleep than awake, I was helped off the streetcar and struggled the two or three blocks to the house, still more asleep than awake.

My aunt was a big fan of the Denver Bronco football team. She and I watched a game on her T.V. How happy it made me to see my aunt so excited about those football games. The Denver Broncos gave her life some *zip*. My being with her made it more fun for both of us. There had been times in Texas when I'd be watching the Denver Broncos playing and call her long distance to discuss some good play the Broncos or Elway made. I knew she'd be watching. She loved that.

Aunt Kathryn was still a lot of fun, and when I asked if she'd like to visit Estes Park, she jumped at the opportunity. She had been there many, many times, but was ready and eager to go again. She directed us every step of the way, going the route she loved to go. The snow that day in Estes Park was one and a half feet deep. I hope she enjoyed that little trip as much as we did. Being from Texas we had never seen so much snow. We visited several nice shops in downtown Estes Park, and drove by the White Hotel where mother had worked in the early 1900s. I think she worked there several summers while going to college.

- Visiting Faegene's Aunt, Mrs. Roy Eddleman

Upon leaving Denver we went through Colorado Springs, and then turned down by the Arkansas River, meeting many trucks loaded to the brim with onions. The road followed the river, along which were many farms and orchards. We went by La Junta, then on to Dodge City, Kansas, the terminal of many cattle trail drives from Texas.

We saw the replica of famous old Dodge City, including the Longbranch Saloon. There was an emporium and other stores, representing the heyday of the cattle drives from Texas. We found an exhibit that sold buffalo burgers, and were they good! Full of buffalo burgers, we drove south into Oklahoma, and followed the crooked roads and open land, seeing few houses and finding Enid, Oklahoma not far from the Kansas border. Following directions in going to Mrs. Eddleman's home we drove carefully, dodging tree limbs because of our tall motor home.

After a couple of days enjoying visiting both Mrs. Roy (Aunt Ted) Eddleman and her daughter Maryann Lovell, we left for Abilene, Texas. We arrived rather late that night, and called my old roommate from China. I drove out to his home, where we spent a short time visiting with him, as it was so late.

Next morning we drove on to Greenwood, as grandson Chris was playing football there that evening. Having traveled about 7,000 miles in the motor home in just a little over a month was quite a trip for us, and naturally, we were glad to be home.

There was a notice in our stack of mail that was awaiting us notifying me that my insurance had been cancelled. It had come due while we were gone and the new insurance man didn't know me. I just took it for granted that it would be renewed as always. I quickly bought more insurance, and got better acquainted with the new owner, Jerry Enman.

Chapter 17

Don't Even Try To Guess What the Future Holds

Cashes Taylor and I had renewed our friendship when I began spraying brush in Sutton County in the spring of 1962. He worked for the ASCS and cooperated with the mesquite spraying program, checking areas to be sprayed and helping us to measure the plots. He was a lot of help, and I appreciated that help and friendship very much.

When we went fishing together at Amistad Lake after my Mesquite spraying season, we spent two days talking, boating and fishing. Several times Cashes had mentioned his daughter Blanche, who was living in another state. She visited Sonora when she could. He was proud of her and her family, and I looked forward to meeting her some day. In my mind I still thought of her as the little girl about three or four years of age, playing with her brother in the big oak tree behind the jailhouse where they lived when I was going to high school. I hadn't seen her since 1936.

About twenty-four years later Cashes was able to introduce Faegene and me to Blanche and her husband, Royce Regeon. We had supper together that afternoon. Yes, something about Blanche brought back memories to me of her uncles, Jimmie, Basil, and Aunt Cora Belle Taylor. Cora Belle was in my class all through high school.

As I had known the Taylor family so well in my youth, I felt as if I knew Blanche already. I guessed that she was probably valedictorian in high school and sure enough, I later learned she had been. I felt comfortable being around her.

In only a few months Blanche's husband Royce died of a continuing heart problem, which had caused his retirement seven years earlier. Then, two years later in 1988, Cashes died, and I went to Sonora for the funeral. I sat with the family beside Cora Bell during the church services. Blanche recognized me after the funeral and invited me to join them at the ranch house, which I did.

I spent about an hour with Blanche at the ranch house, meeting her family and seeing Nancy and other members of the Taylor family. This was when I found out that Royce had died only a few months after I had met him.

I was able to tell Blanche some stories Cashes had told me of his earlier cowboy days, stories she had never heard. She told me years later that she felt if her father liked me enough to make a point for us to meet, then she was sure I was a good man. Of course I was still a married man at that time. I had been impressed with Blanche when we first met. After being with her that hour after Cashes' funeral, I thought to myself what a wonderful wife she would make some lucky man. I also met her three daughters, all attractive young ladies.

Two years later, in 1990, my younger sister called me and told me that she and Bob were going to the Sonora School reunion two days later and wanted me to meet them there. I agreed, but Faegene didn't feel like going. I drove down in my motor home early the morning of the reunion. Bob, Edith and I met and went to the reunion together Saturday morning in the new Sonora High School building. Boy, was that school an improvement from the old one I had attended nearly 60 years ago.

Wandering around the new building I ran across Nancy Taylor and asked about Blanche. She told me Blanche hadn't been able to come. I remember feeling such a distinct letdown that it surprised me. I was walking around seeing who else I knew, when there stood Blanche. I walked up to her and said, "Aren't you Blanche?" She said, "Of course I am, don't you know me?" I answered "Yes, but your mother just told me you weren't here." She laughed and told me her mother had a sister named Blanche West, and it was she who hadn't come. I had forgotten long ago of Nancy's sister, Blanche, a friend of my older sister, Gertrude.

Like me, Blanche Regeon had not planned to be there. Her best friend, Carlene (Peeples) Stacy had called her from Iraan, Texas, just before the reunion, to ask her to meet her there. On the spur of the moment, Blanche caught a plane in Atlanta and flew to San Angelo, where her mother met her.

Well, that night there was a dance under the stars and I danced with Blanche, one of her classmates and her mother, until the band quit playing at one o'clock. It was a fun thing for us. I was surprised at how well they all danced. They kept me on my toes.

The next day, Nancy, Blanche, my sister and Bob, all had a wonderful barbecue together after the church service. We found an empty table there on the courthouse lawn, and we ate that good old West Texas barbeque together. We enjoyed remembering the past years, visiting with each other and were disappointed that Edith and Bob left early. Blanche and her mother were going to the play being put on that afternoon in the top floor of the Court House and invited me to go with them. It was a locally written play by Martha Valliant, a former close neighbor of my parents in Sonora. The story was about the outlaw, Will Carver, who was killed in Sonora about 1900 by lawmen. The play was absolutely the funniest and cleverest play Blanche and I had ever seen. We laughed hard almost every minute of the play.

I had planned to leave after the play was over but waited until Blanche and her mother had supper at a restaurant with Carlene and her family, who had known my parents. In the conversations I found out Nancy was living in her home alone and had no one at all to see about her. I offered to do so each time I came to Sonora. I had my parent's house to look after; therefore, I was in Sonora often to check on it and keep the grass mowed. It wasn't rented at that time. I told Blanche I would make it a point to go by and check on her mother. She appreciated my offer.

The next year in the summer I began re-painting that house in Sonora. Nancy wanted me to stay with her as she had plenty of room and was terribly lonesome. That worked out quite well for me, as I could work a few days, go home often, and come back to Sonora when I could. I realized I would have to spend more time, working a week at a time to get it finished. I had hired a contractor to paint the house. He had put some boys to work, but I was not happy about the job they were doing. I ended up painting or re-painting the rest of the house myself. The contractor repainted the walls inside the house. I also installed new linoleum on the bathroom and the kitchen floors.

I found time to cut Nancy's grass and do minor repairs around her house. I even prepared her evaporative cooler in the early spring and turned it on for her. I always called Blanche to keep her informed of how her mother was getting along and tell her about the bills being paid. I took Nancy for a Mexican supper occasionally, and we ate at the Senior Citizens Center at noon. She appreciated me driving her to see her mother in the Nursing Home in Eldorado a couple of times during that summer.

Blanche came from Georgia to see her mother for a few days when I was there in 1992. I was quite busy re-plumbing my house for water and gas, a major job. I was also still painting. All this work took me about two months, so staying at Nancy's was a big help.

I brought a man from McCamey to help do the plumbing. His name was David Thompson, but when he was a boy his father called him *Jackass Andy*. He changed his legal name to "Jackass Andy." He even had this name on his Social Security card and drivers license. It was just to spite his dad, I think.

Jackass Andy's son had a big problem when he joined the Army. When asked what his father's name was, nobody believed him. He ended up in the guardhouse until proof was supplied that his dad's official name really was "Jackass Andy." "Jackass was later bitten by a rattlesnake while working in the oil field. Some time after that, he was driving a truck long haul. While finishing a meal, he rose and turned to leave, dropping dead within a couple of steps. Andy was Indian and his funeral service was conducted on the side of a mountain around McCamey where his ashes are scattered to the four winds.

Blanche took her mother home for a visit. I assured them I would continue to look after her house and yard. It was another month before I finished working on my house. I still had to test the new gas lines and re-cover them with dirt. Jackass quit while we were leveling the bedroom floor, so I had to spend a few more days finishing that.

A family in Sonora wanted to buy my house. We came to an agreement and closed the deal and he began moving in. I had to rush to finish things up, including leveling that back bedroom floor, a challenge for one person.

There were enough things waiting to be done at home in McCamey, after all the time spent working on the house in Sonora. I needed to move my store inventory and supplies left in storage after closing the store. I had no place to go with so many accumulated items. Most of this was no longer useful and had to be discarded. I gave away some of it, sold some of it and dumped the rest. I also had a few items stolen. It is disheartening to have to destroy so many new parts that have become obsolete. All this represents upwards of 10,000 dollars, most unrecoverable. I sold some of the testing equipment for "peanuts" and gave away much of the rest.

The next Hump Pilot Reunion was to be in Atlanta, Georgia. When I told Blanche she offered to put me up to save me a $450.00 hotel bill. I decided that, with those savings, I could now afford to go. Blanche's daughter, Resa, and her children were living with Blanche at the time, but there was plenty of room for me in her Fayetteville, Georgia home she told me... Nancy had returned to Sonora after a long visit in Georgia.

Blanche had plenty of room, but Faegene didn't want to go. I thought this a good opportunity for me to see Atlanta, so I bought an airline ticket.

Thank goodness Blanche met me at the unloading gate of the airline at Atlanta. I found out that Atlanta was the second busiest airport in the world. Later it became the busiest.

When I arrived I told Blanche where the Hump Pilot's meeting took place. She said "Ouch. That's all the way across Atlanta." Well, we drove that distance every day of the reunion, about 40 miles of heavy traffic, each way. Blanche had taken a week of vacation and joined me in all the activities, including a visit to the Aviation Museum at Warner Robins Air Force Base in Macon, Georgia.

Blanches' next-door neighbor drove us to the Museum near Macon, Georgia, as he wanted to see the opening of the new exhibit of the Hump Pilot's organization. Riding in their car was more comfortable than riding in the bus. We spent an enjoyable day at the museum, including a nice meal in the Officers' Club. We viewed all the airplanes and the Hump Pilots display at the Museum.

The Banquet and dance at the hotel on the last day, Saturday, wound up a great meeting with my China comrades.

I was amazed at all the tall trees and heavy population of this part of Georgia. I wasn't used to being unable to see the horizon and even got a little disoriented from time to time when there was a cloud cover.

After the Hump Pilot meeting was over, Blanche drove us down to Warm Springs, Georgia, to visit the "Little White House" used by President Franklin Roosevelt where he went to take treatments for his Infantile Paralysis. There I found that he loved being around the warm friendship of the common people. On display were his little home, his special built car made so that he could be able to drive it, and a museum. I thoroughly enjoyed visiting this place and came to admire President Roosevelt.

When Blanche took me to the airport to board my plane, she helped me through the various stages, including finding the airport train. She led me to my gate through which I would board my airplane. That was extra trouble for her, but I appreciated the help very much. After I got home I received a nice note from her, telling me that after I left the airport the train broke down and she had to walk all the way back to her parking area. When she stopped her car when leaving the parking area, she discovered her purse was locked in the trunk. She was "hemmed in" at the pay station and had to drive up a little to get her money from her purse she had put into the trunk, to pay for the parking.

- Major Changes in My Life

Faegene and I had been saving our money for years in hopes of finding a nice home to move into. We finally located a possible buy next door to Sherry and Jack. I made an offer for the nearly new three-bedroom house, and my offer was accepted September 1996.

I hired a painter to re-paint the walls while I re-painted all the woodwork inside the house. My son-in-law, Jack, began painting the outside without saying anything to me. There are not many sons-in-law like that. The house looked like a brand new one when we finished. I installed a new dishwasher and had the carpet steam-cleaned. Oh yes, I had the house treated for termites. That is something you MUST do around McCamey.

I began watering the lawn and it looked so nice I wanted to move right in. The hard part now began, deciding what to throw away from the old house, and what to move into the new one.

- Faegene Ill With Leukemia.

Faegene had not felt well for some time, and when she started getting things ready for our move by January, she was having more and more trouble, tiring out quickly. She just seemed unable to get much done, try as she might. I took her to the doctor for a check-up. The doctor took a blood test and found that she had acute leukemia. He re-checked her blood two days later and confirmed his diagnosis.

The next day my daughter and I took Faegene to a cancer specialist in Odessa, who confirmed she had acute ALL Leukemia and only a few weeks to live. After the doctor suggested intense radiation treatment in the hospital, we asked how long it would take and what could we expect. We were told there was no guarantee that treatment would give even one day of remission, with the possibility it could give from a few days to a few months. Faegene refused the treatment, saying she wouldn't want to go through the pain and discomfort and be in a hospital. She just wanted to go home.

Sherry realized we had to get her mother moved to the new house immediately. There was no way we could take care of her in the old house.

They moved our king size bed, the stove and refrigerator. Faegene and I moved in then while they moved everything else. What a wonderful help they were. This day was Sherry's birthday, January 30, but she used it for moving us. Shelley and her family came on the weekend and helped us, including Lisa and Chris. The family really needed to be together at this time. They even cleaned and installed the beautiful chandelier Faegene had bought several years ago, and moved our piano in.

I began cooking breakfast each morning, and made Faegene as comfortable as possible. Sherry stayed with Faegene one afternoon while I went to Odessa to buy a king-size mattress. We padded it with three inch rubber matting making it more comfortable.

When I visited the doctor, he said he was worried about me because I planned to take care of Faegene instead of putting her in the hospital. He indicated it would be too hard on me. I later found out what a difficult task I had taken on, but was determined to be with her and keep her as comfortable as possible.

As the disease progressed she weakened daily. Sherry suggested we might get some help from the Home Health group, a program designed to help people like Faegene. I'd never heard of them. We contacted them and received immediate action. They had their own doctor examine her and ordered the necessary medicine for pain. One trained nurse and a nurse assistant came every day for an hour, to bathe her and give her a nice rubdown. This was really and truly an hour of pure bliss for her. The nurses were pure angels from heaven. They were always cheerful and helpful.

Through this Home Health program we were able to get from Medicare any equipment that we needed to support her, quickly. What a wonderful, wonderful program it was.

In the meantime Faegene was getting sicker and more nervous, especially at night. I was taking care of her almost all of the time and all night. Sherry came over each morning about nine o'clock, after breakfast, so I could rest a little. I tried unsuccessfully every morning to sleep an hour. I at least rested and a few times I slept part of the hour. After the hour of rest I would drive to town for the mail and buy groceries. I did most of the cooking for her, with help from Sherry, who brought special foods she thought her mother would like.

Nighttime was hardest for us both. She never slept over a few minutes at a time. All night long I was busy with her, holding her, taking her to the bathroom and sitting on the bathtub waiting for her, rubbing her back, giving her water, etc. As she weakened, things were becoming more physically difficult and we began using the portable units. I still had to lift her, though. One night I did doze off for only a few seconds and how difficult it was to force myself up at once and help her. I then began to appreciate what the doctor meant when he said he was worried about me.

My average sleep was less than an hour each day and night for the thirty-five days and nights I nursed her. She would sit up in the bed and rock back and forth, and say in desperation "Help me, help me." My heart just felt like it was breaking in two. I would hold her in my arms and try to comfort her, feeling some of the desolation and desperation she must have felt. She just couldn't sleep very long at any time, but especially not at night.

No matter how hard it was, I was determined to do all I could for her. I knew how it would have been in the hospital, as years ago I had spent nearly twenty days and nights with her father in the Odessa Medical Center. He never went to sleep until about three o'clock in the morning and then I could sleep. I always awakened when two hours later the nurses brought medication and bathed him. I was busy nearly all the rest of his waking hours giving him drinking water, taking him to the bathroom, feeding him, etc. Even though there were nurses available they were too busy to give the close care he needed. I knew from that experience that if Faegene had been in the hospital the nurses would not have time to care for her as I could here at home.

At times I would think: "Why can't the medical profession have a cure for cancer?" Faegene was dying, as we all shall some day and there will be only a memory left behind for the loved ones. I am not smart enough to understand the reasons and ramifications of death. How does one deal with it? There were so many questions in my mind, such as to why or how this happens. We have no choice but to accept death as inevitable. My feeling is a deep regret that Faegene will have no more happiness and joy in this world. Why am I attempting to write about this tragic time of our lives? Perhaps it is because I think it might help me to share with others as well as giving empathy to others in handling their grief under similar circumstances.

- Faegene Dies

Kenneth and Faegene Babcock

When I was looking outside the window the next day after Faegene, my wife of 56 years, had died, I wondered why I was spared and she had to go? I had the meager satisfaction that I had done all I could for her during those thirty-five days and nights, and deeply regretted I had not been able to do more. I felt the doctors and I had let her down by not finding the cancer earlier, when there may have been a possible cure.

I felt her loss deeply, wishing I had made her happier while she was alive. I hoped that, perhaps, I might be able to help others to live a fuller, better life. God expects me to share His love with others. I can honor Faegene's life by living mine to the fullest, sharing love with others. Memory of her will always be in my heart. She left me a wonderful daughter, wonderful grandchildren and great-grandchildren. I tell myself: "Rejoice and be thankful for the lives God has given us."

- Hip Surgery

I turned now to the future, thinking, "I cannot go through the rest of my life with these worn out knees that hurt with every step." My knees had been really bad for some time now due to Osteo-Arthritis, which is a wearing out of the cartilage in the joints. Bone rubbing against bone. I well remember how my father went through excruciating pain with both his knees in his later years. There was no alternative for him.

I asked Sherry to go with me to Lubbock to check with Dr. Gill, an orthopedic surgeon specializing in joint replacements. I'd heard favorable information about his ability. Sherry had good hearing and would help me to hear, as I was somewhat hard of hearing even with the hearing aids. I was quickly X-rayed and in only a few minutes was in conference with Dr. Gill.

The X-Ray showed that I needed to replace my left hip joint before doing the knees. I was surprised at that, as I'd had no pain or problems with my hip. I decided to go with his judgment and arranged for the replacement.

On May 20, 1997, I was rolled into the operation room at six a.m. for my hip replacement operation. It sounds simple, doesn't it? That's when it's you, not me. Well, it was quite an operation as far as I was concerned. I had a scary recovery. I had to fight hard for several minutes to start breathing again.

After the operation I lay on my back in my bed with my left leg hooked to a revolving machine that kept my hip and left leg moving twenty-four hours a day, except when the therapists cajoled me into walking. Being on your back all day and night was tiring and there was constant pain, thankfully decreasing from day to day.

Sherry was in the room with me most of the time and how I appreciated her being there. She was there for all the little things I thought I needed. More important it was a comfort for me to know she was there.

Blanche called from Georgia. What a delightful lift for me. After that I looked forward eagerly to her calls. She had the ability to say exactly the right things to cheer me up.

Getting up and walking was a tough challenge. The therapists were nice and capable, but insisted that I must walk, walk, walk. I tried my best to walk more from day to day. It wasn't long until I was walking farther than they asked and on Friday they had me going up and down stairs with either crutches or a walker.

My hip operation had been on Tuesday morning. Saturday morning I was rolled out of the hospital to go home. I was ready. Dr. Gill had first given me orders for special exercises and walking. I was determined to always add a little more than he prescribed each time I exercised or walked. My orders were also not to drive a car for the next six weeks.

Those six weeks alone, not being allowed to drive, was an unbelievably lonesome time for me. My telephone bill was quite large.

My good friend Wally Scott, living in Odessa, Texas, drove the 52 miles to McCamey to take me for a walk on the flat top of King Mountain, five miles north of town. What a lift that gave me. We had memories to share of our instructing Army Primary cadets days in Fort Stockton, Texas, about fifty years earlier, and I enjoyed every step I took. Wally was a deceptively quiet gentleman, having set a World record of shooting an arrow 641 yards. That record was held for twenty-five years. He had become interested in gliders after WW II, logging over 7,000 hours and over 300,000 miles of cross county flying, IN HIS GLIDER. He had won the Barringer trophy for the longest flight twenty nine times in the past thirty-five years of competition. His records go on and on, but few people other than flying enthusiasts knew about him. He held the World Record longest distance flight for a short period. His wife, Boots, would drive their van and follow him in order to bring him and the glider back to Odessa. The distance was hundreds of miles. They have been close friends of mine for years. Wally died just last year. What a tragedy.

My friend Doug Hopkins would also come to visit me and drive me away from the house for a little while. We quite often drove to Odessa or Midland to eat out. My son-in-law would take me with him to get the mail, or a cup of coffee. The help these wonderful people gave me was priceless and appreciated. The boredom of being alone was so hard for me to accept, after almost 56 years of marriage. I guess I'm a "people person." I love associating with other people.

When my six weeks of not being allowed to drive was over, I made up for it by driving the 200 miles to Lubbock for the required check-up on my hip. Getting to drive felt like getting out of jail. I had freedom again.

Dr. Gill was quite pleased with my progress and set October twenty-first for my double knee replacement. After leaving the doctor's office I drove about ten blocks and had a tire go flat in the residential section of Lubbock. I managed to pull off the road, get out of the car, and stood wondering how I could manage to change that tire. Dr. Gill's orders prohibited me from kneeling on my knees. I heard someone say "Hey." A man was coming from across the street. He said, "I've got a hydraulic jack, I'll run get it." He didn't wait for an answer, just hurried back across the street. A police car drove up, and the policeman was ready to help. They didn't realize I couldn't do much because of my new hip. Almost before I could say "Jack Robinson" they had that wheel off and my spare on. The police called a tire supplier and told them I was on the way to buy a new tire so to wait for me, as it was already their closing time. How about that western hospitality.

- On the Road Again

In a few more days I drove the 1300 miles to Fayetteville, Ga. to visit Blanche. We drove to the Road Atlanta Car Race Track north of Atlanta to visit with her daughter Nanetta and her husband, John. John is an outstanding race driver and came in second, although he usually comes in first. After walking all day at the racetrack I fully realized how much I needed my knees replaced. I was glad I had that appointment for October twenty first, with Dr. Gill.

After two weeks visiting Blanche and her family, I drove through Tennessee to Oklahoma City to visit my old childhood pal and former roommate at the University of Texas at Austin, Texas, Dr. Jay Talmadge Shurley, "Jayter" to me.

After a nice visit with Dr. Shurley, I left for Henderson, Kentucky to visit with Dick Alves, my first Army Aviation cadet student whom I taught to fly at Gibbs Field in Fort Stockton, Texas in 1942.

Dick Alves was thrilled to see me and showed me around the immediate area near Henderson. He showed me several oil wells he had shut down because of low production and expensive requirements of the environmentalists. He also owned some nice farmland growing a good crop of tall grain.

Dick told me how much he had enjoyed the time he spent in Fort Stockton. It was the best time of his life, he said. He thoroughly enjoyed learning to fly, and told me of some of the fun he had while in Fort Stockton, Texas. He voiced his appreciation of the support given the cadets by the Fort Stockton people. I told him about my time in China during WW II and showed him a commercial videotape, "Flying the Hump" in which I had been interviewed.

A couple of days later I drove on to Columbus, Ohio, to visit my niece, Peggy, and her husband, Rick Kaplan. Peggy and I went biking, and later went swimming. That was the first time for me to swim in a long time, and I sank like a rock. Peggy was quite a fine swimmer. She swam a solid thirty minutes back and forth in the Olympic pool while I tried to keep from drowning in the other.

They had a beautiful dog and we drove to a special place for "Breakfast on the sidewalks. Bring your pet." We had breakfast with the dogs. That was really fun and unusual. There were many flower window boxes filled with lovely flowers all along the streets, and dogs galore. Peggy is extremely active in pet rescue in Ohio.

We played my videotape "Flying the Hump". Peggy and Rick enjoyed seeing me in it and were quite impressed.

Next day I drove back to Henderson, Kentucky to help Dick Alves and his wife, Nancy, celebrate his eighty-first birthday. I gave him a copy of "Flying the Hump" for his birthday gift. He called me a hero, and I said: "Yes, I am, by risking my life teaching you to fly." That got a laugh. He was really a fine student.

The next stop on my trip was the headquarters of the Hump Pilots' Association in Missouri. I had a nice visit with Jan Thies, executive secretary for the HPA, and her husband, Bill.

I left them in time to arrive in Branson during daylight and checked into a nice little motel. I spent two nights there, seeing several shows. As I was alone I was often put right on the front row. I got to shake hands and talk with some of the stars. I'd like to have stayed longer but felt I needed to get home. Maybe I could return another time.

I drove through the Ozark Mountains, getting a good look at Arkansas, and continued on across Arkansas to Shreveport, Louisiana, where I called Gordon Wendell, my Hump Pilot friend and a fellow instructor I had known at Randolph Field. I spent the night with Gordon and Betty, his wife, talking about old times. What lovely hosts they were. They made me feel just like family. I hated to leave. We'll get together later, hopefully.

My next stop was a visit with Richard Bloomer, my ex-roommate in China, and his wife. Richard now lives on Lake Travis in a lovely home overlooking the lake. It was a nice visit, and we caught up on some of the things we'd been doing since the war. We had never found anything about our other roommate that survived the war, Earl Rolloff, of Chicago. Both of us had tried but were unsuccessful.

I stopped by to visit Edith May's friend, Jean Cory, who lived in the same neighborhood as Richard. This was the first time I'd seen her since the 1930s. We enjoyed remembering our past life in Sonora. She showed me her dad's diary, a remarkable book. I corrected my memory of the date we had climbed Mr. Emery. It was in 1933 instead of 1931.

I had been wondering around visiting people I wanted to see, and succeeded in keeping my mind busy. I now planned a trip to Colorado Springs, Colorado, to attend the Hump Pilot's Reunion in September. When I called our old friend Fern Munro in Colorado Springs she invited me to stay in her large apartment. That made it possible for me to go early and visit a distant cousin I'd never met.

When I got my business in order I left the early part of September and drove to Colorado.

Fern had always been a "cut above" most of us, intellectually. In McCamey, during 1940 and 1941, she had organized the "Footlight Fanatics", a volunteer group Faegene and I joined, to put on plays to generate income for the benefit of the Volunteer Fire Department of McCamey. She successfully directed several plays to large audiences; at least for McCamey they were large. It was great fun and we raised substantial money for the Volunteer Fire Department.

This group of actors and actresses also went on three or four weekend trips, sleeping and cooking out, having a ball. What pleasant memories did these trips bring to us, such as going to the Carlsbad Caverns, a fishing weekend on Spring Creek, another weekend to the Chisos Mountains in the Big Bend of Texas, now a National Park.

When I arrived in Colorado Springs, Fern showed me her new book about Winnie the Pooh, a satire on philosophy. Because her eyes were bothering her, I began reading to her out of that book. There were many big words, and my pronunciations weren't always correct, so she would immediately correct me. I was amazed at her knowledge and her understanding of the words and book. We enjoyed the implications and suppositions of philosophy the book brought out, giving us many laughs. What a time we had with it. Fern thoroughly enjoyed having someone to share this book, and with her insight and our discussions the book came to life.

Fern's apartment was on the fourth floor facing west with Pikes Peak in full view from her lovely balcony. We could see a small river below the apartment building just west of us, with walking trails along it. I rode my bicycle up and down those trails nearly every day, enjoying the high altitude of 7,000 feet and the cool fresh air of the mountains.

Fern was older than me. She was having problems with vision and had sold her car, so I took Fern out to eat several times, which she thoroughly enjoyed. We also attended a special picture show at the college with Doctor Jim Hieberger, her good friend and medical adviser. One day I took her on a drive into the mountains, to see the fall colors and beautiful scenery.

One day I drove over to Westminster, a part of Denver, to visit my cousin Dean Knoll and his wife Lovejoy. They drove me to the little town of Hygiene, Colorado, showing me the Shaker Church where my mother and Dean's father had attended church. Many of the Knoll ancestors were buried in the Shaker Church Yard. Mother was born in 1885 and her family attended this church during her youth.

Leaving Hygiene we drove through Estes Park and up over the 11,000-foot divide in Rocky Mountain National Park. The paved road was quite different from the road my family took back in 1932.

Standing there looking down on the rest of the world was thrilling and cold. Ravens were sailing all around just a few feet from our heads. I told Dean I hadn't known crows flew at such altitudes, and he explained, "These birds are Ravens. Notice that they don't flap their wings like the crows, but sail on the currents of air." They sure were sailing, within ten feet of our heads.

Looking down several thousand feet we spotted a few elk grazing near some lakes. I tried walking while at that altitude and was glad I was able to do so without getting too breathless. When I was a small boy my family had brought me to these mountains and it always gave me a thrill just as it did that day. My father and mother had spent their childhood in Colorado, and were familiar with this part of the state.

Dean then drove us down the other side of the divide, the road running alongside the Colorado River. When we came across several cars parked along the road, we stopped and found out there was a bull moose resting across the river from our road. It sure had large horns. This was another thrill for us. Dean said he had read that two Moose had recently been moved into this area.

We drove around the Grand Lake area, a famous recreation site, and found an interesting little café for our dinner. I was thoroughly enjoying myself, seeing sights I'd not seen since I was a child. Driving through Berthoud Pass in a tunnel was a surprise and certainly different than going over the old Berthoud Mountain Pass.

Driving down the highway toward Denver we passed by the Silver Plume mine, then down to Georgetown. Those were mining towns my father had worked in when he was in college.

Daddy worked at the Silver Plume mine in the early 1900s, and in 1932, when I was thirteen, we visited the mine. It was a working mine even at that time, and I saw the settling tables running. Those shaking, settling tables separated the different minerals by weight, such as gold, silver, lead and zinc.

I suggested to Dean and Lovejoy we ride the train over the Georgetown Loop, a famous train linking the two areas. It was not far and it passed over a famous rebuilt bridge across the canyon. What a thrill that was to get to re-live some history my father had helped make, back in 1905. I remember seeing the original bridge in 1931 that was made of wood. The replacement was made of metal, but impressive nevertheless.

Dean and Lovejoy also took me on a drive up to Mount Evens, another trip my family took in 1931. This was also a thrill for me. The lake at the foot of the peak was a small frozen lake in 1931, but now was not frozen and was much larger. We took some great pictures of the mountain sheep and mountain goats. What a great time I had, thanks to Dean and Lovejoy.

Next day I left them to drive out to Sterling, in North East Colorado, on the flat North Plains, to visit Deans' sister, Viola Bringelston. I spent an enjoyable hour or so with Viola and her daughter. Viola was my older sister's age and they had been good friends when we visited Colorado back in the 1920s and 1930s. We reminisced about the olden times, particularly about 1931 or 1932 when Viola, Gretchen and Gertrude went swimming in the mountain stream close to the Moffet tunnel. They swam less than one minute. It was just too cold.

Viola was suffering with arthritis and depended upon her daughter for her shopping. It had been about sixty-six years since I'd seen her, and it was so nice to meet her daughter for the first time.

The drive back through Denver became interesting when I took the wrong road in the night. I finally found my way after seeing some parts of Denver I wasn't really interested in seeing.

In Colorado Springs I called on Barbara Lobdell, a cousin I'd heard about from my sister, Edith. Barbara was the great granddaughter of my mother's brother, Colonel Dallas Knoll. I was impressed that Barbara had attended West Point and her husband Doug was ex-military and also a West Point graduate. He was working in the field of technology for the government at that time, I believe, close to Colorado Springs. I had dinner with Doug and Barbara, their four well-behaved children and also her sister, Nancy Knoll.

In 1929 Uncle Dallas Knoll had come back from the Philippines where he had been serving under General McArthur and visited us in Sonora. He told us at that time we'd have to fight the Japanese some day. He gave us children some Chinese metal coins with a square hole in them.

I called Deans' older brother in their new home in Estes Park. He invited me to come up so I drove back to Estes Park. He lived on Kinnikinnic Ct., a street named after a ground-covering weed by that name. Ralph and Nancy Knoll showed me their progressive pictures of the building of their home from the ground up. What a beautiful home and what a wonderful place to build, with such fantastic views in all directions. I saw some deer and elk near their home when I drove up.

Both Dean and Ralph and their wives had visited Faegene and me in Texas a few years earlier. How nice it has been to get a little better acquainted with my kinfolk.

Ralph drove me up to the mountain pass on the same gravel mountain road I'd traveled in 1931. This was the old road leading to the 11,000 ft. pass, the same pass Dean and Lovejoy had driven me to on the new highway. Driving over that old road was a real thrill for me, bringing back memories of my first trip so many years ago. Ralph pointed out a recent large slide of rock just above the old road, which had wiped out a dam.

Ralph and Nancy were so nice to be around, just like his younger brother and Lovejoy. They made my trip to Colorado another wonderful memory, inspiring me to want to return someday. I spent another day with them and then had to rush back to pick up Blanche at the Colorado Springs airport.

Blanche was due to arrive next day as she was flying in to see her daughter and son-in-law, Nanetta and John, who was racing his car at the Pikes Peak Race Track. They were to be there for three days, and I had invited Blanche to join me for the next week's Hump Pilot Reunion being held in Colorado Springs. We enjoyed being together at the races and were able to be with the racers on the parking ramp. We were watching and helping John when and if we could. Blanche joined them in the pit stop to hold the fire extinguisher ready if needed. Thank goodness there were no problems. We also helped in the timing of the laps.

We were all set for Blanche to stay for the three-day Hump Pilot's Reunion the next week. I had paid for all the prearranged tours for the two of us. Unfortunately Blanche's daughter, Resa, back in Georgia, developed a blood disorder involving blood clots, and was rushed to the hospital in Newnan, Georgia. Blanche had to fly back to Georgia Sunday to be with her. The HPA reunion would begin the next day.

Fortunately Resa's doctors managed to get the illness under control. I was happy for that, but sure missed getting to share the programmed tours with Blanche. Like the old saying: "Sometimes the best made plans of mice and men go astray" applies to this type of situation.

A few days earlier Blanche and I had become acquainted with Mrs. Jackie Acker and her eight-year old daughter, Maggie, at Seven Falls Park. Jackie's father had served in the CBI during WW II, and she approached Blanche and me when she saw the CBI Hump Pilot emblem on my car bumper. I was able to tell Jackie about the operation of the war in that Theater. She had little knowledge about her father's service in that theater. He had passed on without explaining much about his experiences in the CBI, so she was seeking more information about his service there.

When Jackie heard Blanche had to return to Georgia on Sunday she felt sorry for me and offered to go on the tours with me, with her husband's approval.

She and Maggie, her eight-year-old daughter, turned out to be actual tour guides. Our group was so fortunate to have them with us. The two of them went on the tours and quickly became the guides for our bus. Bob, her husband, was also a competent guide, I found out later.

Jackie and her family became such good friends, and helped me so much to enjoy the reunion, although I was still disappointed that Blanche couldn't be with me. All of the Hump Pilots enjoyed them being with us. The first tour was of The Garden of the God and Jackie ended up leading that tour as well as most of the others.

On one tour we rode the train up to the top of Pikes Peak, finding a freezing wind blowing snow, sleet and ice on the Peak. Even through that weather we could see the panorama of Colorado Springs and surrounding area far below. The large store and sandwich bar located right on the apex of Pikes Peak certainly was welcome. No one was dressed for that freezing cold wind outside. I warmed up a little with a cup of hot coffee.

Jackie also attended the banquet and dance as my guest. By then most of the members knew who she was. I felt as if Jackie was representing her father.

After the reunion I had to leave, having an appointment with Doctor Gill in Lubbock, Texas in only a few days. I drove across Colorado, planning to go through Ouray and Silverton on the way to Pinos Altos, New Mexico, to visit Mrs. Evelyn Yates, widow of my good friend, Thurman. He had been with me at Fort Stockton, Randolph Field and Berry Field at Nashville, Tennessee. He was stationed in the Assam Valley of India. Thurman had passed away only a year earlier.

I was delayed several hours at Ouray, waiting for the snow to be cleared from the mountain pass. When I crossed it at an altitude of 11,000 feet the temperature was twenty-four degrees and the snow was about eight inches deep off the road.

Passing down the mountain slope I left the snow behind. The fall colors began to show up in the aspen trees. When I reached Silverton, elevation 9,000 feet, I drove through the town, remembering my visit there a few years earlier with Marilyn and George Cragin. Faegene and I had flown up from El Paso with them in their plane and had spent the weekend in the home Marilyn owned.

It was night when I arrived at the little pioneer town of Pinos Alto (High Pines), New Mexico. I went into the post office, which was also a general store, to ask the way to Evelyn's home.

Evelyn lived in a rustic old home with plants of all kinds on the front porch, and the back yard contained a small garden. The little town must still be much like it had been in the early nineteen hundreds. Just a few miles away I heard there was an Indian cave dwelling. This little town was several hundred feet higher than the town of Silver City, an old silver mining town a short distance away. I would guess the altitude of Pinos Alto at about 7,000 feet. It was apparent to me that Pinos Alto had changed little during its lifetime. It was a real, old-time town.

The next day Evelyn wanted me to see western New Mexico and her ranch in the mountains, so we took a long ride through central western New Mexico to Springer, Arizona, then turned north several miles through the little town of Datil and then on to "Pie," New Mexico. Evelyn's ranch was about fifteen or twenty miles away from Pie. She told me years ago she baked pies and sold them in "Pie town". She didn't say the town was named because of that, but I wondered. This part of New Mexico was sparsely populated with lots of flat land without trees. Her ranch, though, was in a pine forest on a mountain ridge. This ridge bordered the west side of a broad flat valley. It had rained lately, so we couldn't get all the way to the ranch house.

Coming out of the mountains we jumped a large bull elk grazing in the forest right beside the road. What excitement that was, to see that big bull elk so close. She said that was the first time she'd seen an elk in that area or that close to the road.

The next day we made a short visit to the Mimbres Canyon, where the artifacts from the Mimbres Indians are found. Some of the Mimbres Indians may still live in that area. They were famous for making clay pottery with unique designs with black coloring.

Reluctantly I left Pinos Alto the next morning, destination Roswell, New Mexico, to visit another of my old army buddies and former fellow instructor at Fort Stockton. He had also flown the Hump and had been stationed in Sookerating, in the Assam Valley of India. J. C. Foster and his wife, Claudette, took me out to dinner and we had a real nice visit. They were busy and seemed to be happy and doing quite well.

Well, the next stop for me would be at my doctor's office in Lubbock, Texas. This drive was my first time to cross the rolling prairie of New Mexico. There were many signs of oil production, and I could picture ranching in that rolling hill country, searching for livestock in the small rises and dips of the prairie. It looked like good cattle country if water was available.

I did make it on time to my appointment with Dr. Gill, in Lubbock, and he confirmed my operation date of October 21, 1997, a week later. He planned to replace both knees at the same time.

- A Double Knee Replacement

The next Monday Sherry and I drove the 200 miles to Lubbock. I needed to find and mail a birthday present for Blanche. I found her a birthstone ring, an Opal, which Sherry mailed her the next day.

Early the next morning I was in the hospital only a short time before being rolled by cart into the operating room. I had warned the Anesthetist, a lady doctor, about the problems I had with breathing after the hip operation. She investigated the records and assured me things would be all right this time. Even so, I still had some breathing problems after being brought out of the anesthesia, but not nearly as bad as before. It was afternoon before I was returned to my room, and there I was, flat on my back with two machines, working my knees up and down. It seemed to me only a few minutes later that two physical therapists came to my bed. I knew what they wanted. Before they asked, I told them I couldn't do it. They insisted, "Just for a few seconds." I knew I had no choice.

With them holding me up I reluctantly eased off the bed onto my feet. As my weight came down on my knees there were no words I could find to define the pain. I nearly passed out with the nurses holding me up. They quickly helped me back up on the bed again until I came around. They assured me this sometimes happens when a person's blood pressure drops suddenly. I lay down, exhausted. I had always heard the worst pain you could have was during childbirth. I felt as if I'd had twins.

A few short hours later here they came again. I was still hurting from their last visit. Did they have no pity? Again I knew there was no other choice. Off the bed I was practically dragged, onto both legs again. Surprise. It only hurt about 99% as badly as the first time. Well, maybe only 95% as much. They cajoled me and lied to me, telling me that if I walked with their help to the first door, they would let me turn around and go back to bed. They didn't let me stop there, of course, encouraging me to walk to the second door and back, supporting me some all the way. One carried a chair right behind me, just in case. Did I hurt? What a foolish question. I couldn't imagine anything hurting worse. To be completely honest it wasn't quite as bad as the first time.

They managed to get me back onto the bed, and I turned up the little pump that controlled the pain medication. This little pump supposedly put more pain killer right into my blood. I then realized this system only made me think it was killing the pain. It must have been only a psychological action with no painkiller in it at all. I don't care what the nurses told me, I didn't believe them. Ha.

The next day was somewhat easier for me to walk. They didn't want me trying it alone just yet. Being in bed or walking I was still uncomfortable. The constant pain was just something one had to endure, but it was hurting slightly less each day.

By Saturday morning, though, I was walking with only the help of a metal walker, and feeling better than I thought possible to feel ever again. I was sent home. I didn't expect it to be that quickly. Maybe the staff wanted off for the weekend. For the first time since checking in to the hospital, I was put in a wheelchair and then pushed out of the hospital. They wanted me safely out of there.

My wonderful daughter Sherry was right there with me the whole time when I needed her most. Somehow her presence enabled me to go through all that pain and discomfort. Just her presence and a comforting word strengthened me. Blanche also called every day from Fayetteville, Georgia. That always lifted my spirits. I looked forward to that call each day. I realized I was not "an island unto myself." I needed the love and care from others for me to feel a whole person. My pastor Jodie had driven up from McCamey to see me in the hospital. She fed me some of the spiritual food I needed.

On the road home we stopped twice to let me walk and stretch a little.

The first week home I stayed with Sherry and Jack and really needed their help. The time spent that week was like a continuous nightmare. It was Halloween and I heard every knock on the front door and the murmurs and calling of excited children. The voices of the witches and goblins sounded quite real to me.

Jack elevated the foot of the bed about six inches, as the doctor instructed, but I slept very little, I was so uncomfortable. Getting into and out of bed was no fun. I fitted pillows around me most of the night just trying to be a little more comfortable. What nightmares those first nights at "home" were.

My sister had offered to keep me for a few weeks, so after I had been with Sherry a week or so, they came by and drove me home with them. They lived in a beautiful home on Lake LBJ. I was hurting less by then, so I hoped I'd be little trouble for Edith and Bob.

I needed to walk a lot and did. Every day I went out walking several times. It felt good to be able to do so with lessoning pain. The deer in the lake area were numerous and fun to see. I counted up to fifteen in the largest group. I also saw four swim across the inlet close to the house.

The lady doctor there found that I was anemic, and started me on iron pills. From that time on I took no more pain pills and I began feeling much better. My little sister was an excellent cook, especially when making hot cakes from scratch. This was my first opportunity to spend time with Edith and Bob. I knew mother had taught her to cook, so it was no wonder she was such a good one. Everyone knows our mothers are the best cooks in the world.

Edith had been about twelve when I left for the University in 1936. Three and a half years later I moved to McCamey, 120 miles west of Sonora, only a short time before she entered college. Although I caught some rides to Sonora from time to time to visit, Edith was away in college. Then came WW II. After the war, she married Dr. Bob Kokernot and moved to South Africa for six years. Then they moved to Cali, Columbia, in South America for two years, coming back to Champaign, Illinois while Bob taught medicine. After that they were living in Houston, 600 miles from my home in McCamey, when they divorced. Now, at last, we were able to be together for a couple of weeks while I was recuperating.

Edith's current husband, Bob Grinnell, liked the same kind of music I did, and kept his player busy playing many of the Big Band Music songs of the 1940s that we loved. That was so nice.

When I took a Southwest Airlines flight to Midland to be home in McCamey for Christmas I had already discarded the walker. In McCamey, my friend Doug Hopkins came to my rescue again, joining me for long rides out in the country or driving to Midland for supper. This again relieved some of my intense boredom of staying home for the rest of those six weeks being restricted from driving. When my six weeks of abstinence from driving was over I returned the favor to Doug by driving him in my car for long rides in the country.

My phone bills were higher than normal, too, as I contacted friends and especially Blanche. She knew what I had been going through, and encouraged me as usual. I was eager to learn more about her life, and felt that I wanted to become a part of it.

I tried not to be a burden to Sherry and Jack, but they never complained. They were just wonderful to me, sharing their food and just being there. I was glad my home was next door.

- The Wedding Of Chris and Kristin

My grandson Chris and his bride to be, Kristin, planned to be married in January of 1998, giving me barely time to recuperate from my double-knee operation.

What an occasion this wedding turned out to be. Of course I had to go. Although my knees were still a little sore I could walk much better than before the operations. My daughter told me we were flying to Dallas on such and such a date, and once there we'd rent a tuxedo and get a room in a hotel, etc. That's exactly what we did. Jack and I became "Stuffed Shirts" over-night, and spent "X" amount of dollars. I supported my grandson in his getting married. He had found a lovely, intelligent young lady to turn him into a husband. I would be amiss if I didn't tell about that wedding.

I was a loose end so they had me lead it off by being first to march down the aisle. Then Sherry followed me down and we each lighted a candle. The ceremony proceeded with changing pictures of the two of them from the time they were babies to the present on two large movie screens in the church. Lisa, Chris's sister, sang two beautiful songs and the wedding ceremony proceeded.

Being the last one to walk out alone up the aisle again, at the end of the ceremony, honored me. All my family was proud of my being able to walk. I was pretty proud of "me," myself.

The wedding was so beautiful. We were all proud of our children. "If only Faegene could have been there," I thought. She at least had been able to attend and enjoy Shelley and Cary's wedding a few years back.

During the reception there was wonderful food and a beautiful wedding cake. Then we ended it with dancing. Kristin's father and mother really could jitterbug. I found I was able to dance some. I thought how close I had come to missing this wedding. Somehow it all had worked out. It was fun to be able to dance again with little or no pain.

Chris and Kristin have been so loving and happy and now have three wonderful daughters, my great grandchildren. They are an addition to my first three great grandchildren given me by my granddaughter Shelley and her husband Cary Shackelford. What a wonderful gift.

- Reminiscing About the Past

After the wedding was over, I phoned the cadet I had worried about in 1943 at Fort Stockton, because of his airsickness. F/O Murphy lived in Garland, Texas, a suburb of Dallas. He was excited when I called him, and drove to my hotel to take me to his home for a visit. I got to see and talk with his wife, Betsy. He and I both were piano players, so we took turns playing.

It's always great to share common memories from the past. We recalled his learning to fly in Fort Stockton and the difficulties he overcame. Then we discussed seeing each other in Chengkung, China, in February, 1945. He was appreciative of my efforts I made in Fort Stockton by talking him into staying in the flight program. He pointed out how different his entire life would have been had I not encouraged him successfully to continue flying.

Isn't it wonderful, sometimes, that we are able to influence or try to influence others. Because of his continued flight training his life had been much fuller and more exciting. This is an excellent example of only a little extra effort.

One of Murphy's sons came by and I was happy to meet him. I found out Murphy had several children, and his life has been blessed by his wonderful wife and children.

Chapter 18

A New Beginning

My knees continued to improve daily. I had continued the specific exercises even after the 6-weeks of regular exercises. With Valentines Day coming up I called Blanche. She told me she had been thinking of that day, too. She had read an advertisement in the newspaper of a Valentine's Day special dance at the Calloway Garden's complex, about fifty miles south of Fayetteville. I said, "Why don't you make the arrangements and I'll come up for it. You said it will be Big Band music?"

"Sure did."

"Okay. Let's go for it."

I prepared my car and made arrangements to be gone for several weeks. I then left on the 1230-mile trip to Fayetteville, Georgia.

The dance at Calloway Gardens was just as nice a dance as one could wish for. We just felt wonderful and the music was terrific. Everyone seemed to be with their sweethearts, smiling and dancing, dining, and sipping wine (furnished).

The price included entrance into the Calloway Gardens, so we spent a lovely time viewing this wonderful spot of beauty in Central Georgia. It contains lakes and seven golf courses, rustic trails and bridges, a very ancient Chapel and nature trails. The Gardens sponsor a vegetable garden national T. V. program in the spring every year.

Many times we have thought back to that perfect time at Calloway Gardens. How nice to have wonderful memories to share with each other.

Now that I was in Fayetteville I realized I could be a help to Blanche. I looked after her mother during the day while Blanche slept after coming home from her all night job at the Post Office Distribution Center. I helped with the clothes washing, cooking, etc. Rhonda and her two young children were also living with Blanche. Rhonda was attending Georgia State University in Atlanta and helping with the care of her grandmother. When Blanche invited me to stay longer, I was happy to do so. We wanted the opportunity to get better acquainted and this made it possible.

My knees were doing great, so I began to help Blanche, Resa and her husband build a privacy fence around Blanche's large back yard. Blanches' daughter, Resa, and her husband planned to build a wooden fence at their home later.

Blanche had been working in her back yard for over a month in her limited spare time, clearing out the vines, small trees and bushes. It had to be cleared enough to find the edge of her property where she wanted the fence. This land had never been cleared even when they moved in, in 1975. Clearing a pathway was a difficult job, but together we got it done.

We finally rented a hole-digger and dug all the holes for the 4x4 posts. We had the 4x4s and seven-foot palings delivered and went to work carrying all those 4x4s to their holes and cementing them one at a time into the holes we had drilled. It was necessary to use the level to install them straight up and down.

We rented a power-hammer to nail on all the palings, so they were able to do that while I went back to Texas for a few days. Thinking back I just can't believe the four of us did so much so quickly. Blanche and Resa had continued to work every night at their jobs in the Post Office at Atlanta. Everybody was worried about me because of my new knee replacements, but I got along fine. I felt I was working about as hard as the others. They were especially worried I might trip and fall, and by golly, I did. I caught my toe under a vine one day and was immediately lying flat on my face, with nothing hurt. Didn't even bend my nose.

When we finished the fence I sprayed the preservative onto the entire fence surfaces, front and back, with a hand sprayer. The fence looked really great, and Blanche was so proud of it. We made a great fence-building team, but we're not looking for any more work of that nature.

Nancy, Blanche's mother, knew me from Sonora. She trusted me and was happy to have me there. Although at eighty-eight she needed little help, I was able to cook some meals and care for her while Blanche was at her job with the Post Office Distribution Center. Blanche would get home about 6:00 each morning and pile right into bed. Rhonda had about all she could do to keep up with her studies and caring for her children. She and I shared the cooking, although she was much faster and better than I. I also helped wash and fold clothes from time to time. I tried to fit in where needed.

As Nancy loved to go places I would take her with me whenever I drove. I drove here and there getting more familiar with the roads and towns in this area. Directions were sometimes confusing to me in this strange area so full of high trees and wooded areas and clouds. One time I drove south on Redwine Road ten miles and ended up in Peachtree City, west of Fayetteville. I drove into downtown Peachtree City, turned east and drove the seven miles back to the house. Interesting.

Although Blanche and I had little time together, we enjoyed the time we did have. I was busier and happier by far than if I had stayed in Texas. Blanche had felt she would be asking too much of me to help care for her mother, but I was glad to do so. To me Nancy was no problem.

Blanche and I felt our friendship was something special for us both. We also felt a blessing that her father had wanted us to meet. I wanted to know more about her children, Resa and Rhonda, both living in Fayetteville, and Nanetta in Sealy, Texas. Rhonda and her children were still living in the house with Blanche and Nancy.

I was buying some of the groceries to help pay my way and tried to keep the vehicles gassed up. When I had the chance I visited jewelry stores alone from time to time during the year, finally finding a pretty diamond ring that I liked, and hoped Blanche would. Although it would stretch my budget, I bought it. We had now been together off and on for the past two years. I felt sure we were compatible. I had known for some time that I loved her. She had indicated she felt the same for me, but that's as far as we'd talked. I realized I was sort of an intruder in her family, an unknown factor to her children. I was hoping they could accept me if Blanche did.

One day I felt it was time to make a move. While holding the ring box, I handed it to her and said: "I love you, Blanche, will you marry me?" I'll always remember her expression of surprise and delight. Then she said "yes."

The next day Blanche made the remark that we couldn't get married until she replaced the carpet in her house. I admit it needed replacing. Another "fly in the ointment" was the dark painted trim inside the house. It needed to be painted white before re-placing the carpet.

"Well" I thought, "I'd better get started." I went out after breakfast, bought paint, some roller paint supplies, brushes and started to work. For the next few days I painted about seven hours each day. A year earlier Rhonda had already painted the kitchen and when I first arrived we had also helped paint Nancy's (Mom's) room.

I installed floor trim in the kitchen and back hall and painted it white. I also painted the rest of the walls and all of the trim in the rest of the house.

My knees and hip weren't bothering me but the doctor had told me to never get down on my knees. I therefore sat on the floor and painted. I rode my bicycle about fifteen miles a day with our neighbor, Carlton Williams, early each morning, except Sunday.

Just before I finished the painting, Blanche and I picked out a nice carpet and linoleum design for both bathrooms and Nancy's room and had it installed. Less than a week later all was completed, and we set the date for our wedding.

In the hustle and bustle of planning our wedding, we were surprised and pleased when Blanche's daughter, Rhonda, and Michael Weatherup announced they were getting married on December 31, 1999, two weeks before our wedding date. Blanche suggested she thought it would be a nifty idea' to have a double wedding ceremony. Rhonda didn't agree with her mother's sense of humor, so among close friends and family Rhonda and Michael were married in the beautiful outdoor setting, close to the pyramid house Michael had built. I even played the wedding march for them on a synthesizer.

- …Wedding Bells are Ringing, For Me and My Gal …

Blanche and I had planned to have a small wedding, just our families and close friends. There was no way. It quickly became apparent our families expected a full wedding, reception and all. The church charge was $750.00 just for the ceremony—that is, if you were a member. We felt we couldn't afford that, so we checked on a little chapel, but it was too small.

We checked with the City Hall about the rejuvenated Railroad Station. It was already rented. The lady at City Hall in charge of the Railroad Station building called the Holiday Inn, which had facilities. She must have done some tall talking in our favor (Blanche was 66 and I was 80). The manager told the lady to send us to see him.

In talking to the manager, we agreed on the room and asked the price. The answer: "No charge." We knew their usual charges was $100.00. The manager explained it would be good public relations. Our date was set for January 15, 2000. I still wonder what that clerk had said to him when she called him.

I asked Rick Massengale, the Church Organist and Music Director, if he would or could play for us and he answered, "I'd be glad to." I was happy about that.

Things were working out well for us. With a lot of help from our families the room was decorated and we arranged for a caterer who did a fabulous job. Blanche's son in law, John Phillips, from Sealy, Texas, consented to walk her to the altar.

Being members of the "Biking for Life" Bicycle Club, Blanche and I decided to ride off on our honeymoon on our bicycles after the wedding. Everything was set, people notified, and plans completed. All our immediate families planned to attend.

The support of our families could not have been better or more cooperative. All of our families coming so far for our wedding made us feel honored. In our minds we had underestimated this and were happy and pleased. On the day of the wedding people just kept on filing into the room until every seat was taken. What a memorable wedding it made for us.

I made the only booboo during the entire wedding ceremony. I was calm and collected, or so I thought, but when putting the ring on Blanches' finger, I said, "With this 'wing', I thee 'red'". Suddenly the laughter rang out and I realized then what I had said.

After the Ceremony we danced down the aisle to the tune of "Anniversary Waltz," with Lisa, my granddaughter, and Rhonda, Blanches' daughter, singing it for us. All the grandchildren served in the wedding party in one way or another. Everyone enjoyed the food, especially the wedding cake, as it was decorated with two bicycles on top.

After visiting some with the crowd Blanche changed her dress. We went out to leave on the bicycles, and found them adorned with balloons and cans tied behind, with two "Just Married" signs. Streamers were hanging all over. The wedding bouquet was tossed, and we mounted our bikes and rode off in a sea of bubbles (in place of rice) turning off into the traffic. We naturally met a red light when we started out. Actually we only rode a couple of miles and were picked up as pre-arranged. We didn't actually go on our honeymoon until several weeks later.

Regeon - Babcock

The bride and groom, members of the
Fayette Biking for Life Club,
left for their honeymoon riding their bicycles!

Kenneth Babcock and Blanche Taylor Regeon were united in Holy Matrimony with a double ring ceremony at 2:00 p.m. Saturday, January 15, 2000, at the Holiday Inn Express in Fayetteville, Georgia. The Rev. Bobby McMahan performed the ceremony and Rick Massengale provided the music. Vocalists were Rhonda Weatherup, daughter of the bride and Lisa Thurman, granddaughter of the groom. Her son-in-law John Phillips gave the bride away.

A reception for friends and family followed the wedding. Family included Mrs. Nancy Taylor, mother of the bride from Sonora, Texas, the bride's daughters, Nanetta and John Phillips with their daughters, Jessica and Jamie from Sealy, Texas, Resa Regan with her daughters Jesse and Jodie from Senoia, Georgia, Rhonda and Michael Weatherup with children Chelse and Zachary from Brooks, Georgia, Edith, groom's sister and Bob Grinnell from Horseshoe Bay, Texas, Sherry, groom's daughter and husband, Jack Phillips, from McCamey, Texas with their children, Shelly Shackelford from Wink, Texas, Lisa Thurman from Fountain Valley, CA., Chris and Kristin with baby Mikah, the groom's great granddaughter from Cedar Creek, Texas.

We were so proud that Blanche's mother, Nancy, was in attendance. We were also trying to find someone to stay with her when we went on our longer honeymoon planned for later as Rhonda had married and moved to Brooks, Georgia. Our immediate plans were set for March to take a short cruise from Ft. Lauderdale, Florida, and on to Nassau.

On the eleventh of February, Nancy died suddenly. We buried her beside her husband Cashes Taylor, in the Sonora, Texas Cemetery. This, of course, was quite devastating to us. We were happy she lived to see us married and grateful we had her as long as we did, nearly 90 years. We still miss her. What a wonderful mother-in-law she was, even for such a short time. Nancy was such a nice person. She never said a derogatory word about anyone. I even tried to get her to, but not a negative word would she say about anyone. I can still hear her say: "Bless his (or her) little heart."

We now took our mini-honeymoon planned for March, with Blanches' daughter, Resa, and her new husband, Steve Phillips. We flew to Miami, where we rented a car. We drove to Ft. Lauderdale for two days before boarding the cruise ship to Nassau. We were nearly three days on the ship. At Nassau there was a boat to take us scuba diving at a small reef a few miles away. There were some beautiful and bright colored fish swimming close to a small reef where we scuba dived for the first time. I wasn't too comfortable doing that, as I seemed to have trouble with the floppy flippers on my feet, but I was awed at the beauty of those fish.

After Scuba diving we explored the Island where the Gilligan's Island TV series was filmed. It was quite interesting. Just offshore was also a small pen of stingrays to watch.

When we got back to the ship late in the afternoon, and entered our stateroom, there was a "Pooch" sitting on my bed. The room attendant had made it out of the folded towels. What a surprise. My sunglasses were sitting on its nose. The dog was standing on my bed. How cute and clever. I naturally tipped him extra when we finished the cruise.

Next morning we steamed into the bay at Ft. Lauderdale and that afternoon we were on the beach and in the ocean. There were several waterspouts around the area. Several were pretty close to us and looked just like little tornadoes.

We went through Disney World and enjoyed the dolphin and killer whale acts. We were careful to sit high enough so the whales couldn't splash us with water. Then later there was a really big fireworks display.

In town we spent an hour or so in an interesting "Ripley's Believe It Or Not" house. Next day it was time to board the airplane for Atlanta.

My life has been so wonderful here with our children. All of Blanches' children have made me feel so accepted and I love them all as my own. I miss my Texas family and only get to see them from time to time when we return to Texas or they come here. As a close-nit family Blanche and I visit frequently with our Georgia children and celebrate all birthdays together. I am so thankful to be so blessed with so much love. I am living a new life.

Chapter 19

Back To China, Year 2000

The first honeymoon had been rather short, but this one was planned to the other side of the planet, China. It was scheduled for May and June. The Beijing Retired Pilots association had invited us Hump Pilots to join them in Kunming, China, for a joint meeting and re-dedication of the Hump Pilot Marker on the 10,000-foot Mountain beside Kunming.

When the time to leave for China arrived, we had every requirement completed and were ready. We had looked forward to seeing San Francisco (our choice of airport to leave for China) that afternoon. After landing at the airport and reaching our hotel, we realized San Francisco was too far away for us to visit. We just decided to rest up for the long flight the following morning.

Next morning we were rested and ready to board our big Boeing 747 airline. We found ourselves sitting in seats two and three, in the middle aisle. On taking off we watched for San Francisco but never saw it. By the time we reached cruising altitude all the persons on the window seats had already closed the curtains and seemed to be going to sleep. Those curtains remained closed all the way to China, about twelve or thirteen hours. Why in the world did they want those window seats if they weren't going to use them?

I was eager to see all that I could and had especially been looking forward to seeing some of Alaska, as well as Siberia. I looked around and found one window in the pantry to share with three others persons on the right side of the plane. We could look out two at a time, while crossing over the Aleutians, and managed to get a view of the mainland. There was snow on all the mountains. I took a few pictures of some ice floes and snow covering the lowlands along the northern shore of the straits.

One of the magazines in the airplane had a map with which we could follow along our flight. What a panorama of ice and snow we flew over. We could see a lot of it from thirty six thousand feet. There were markings going down the banks along the ice floes, but no other sign of life. Those markings could have been made by boats or kayaks being shoved up or down on the banks by Eskimos. I wondered.

Clouds were thickening below and became a solid layer under us. I was grateful I had seen as much of Alaska as I did. We landed in Beijing, China, about an hour before dark. What a way to travel. What a difference in today's travel and that during WW II. Go back even farther into the 1800's and it was a matter of months to cover the distance that we had covered in twelve hours that day.

Well, there I was in China again, with Blanche to share it with me. We were fed some supper and went right to bed. Next morning after breakfast we were flown in two China National Airway Jets to Kunming. It was cloudy, as usual, like it had been so much of the time in 1945. I saw little more of China until we were landing at Kunming.

The airport was in the same area as it had been some fifty-five years ago. There was the lake and the scarred bluff, which a bomb-loaded B-24 had flown into in 1944 after taking off from Chingkung airport across the lake. I could also see the little hill east of the airport where my two roommates had been buried.

I had been told Kunming was changed. "Boy," was it. In the 1940s Kunming had been a small city of perhaps 25,000 people, with an additional population of perhaps 25,000 refugees. There were only two or three buildings with more than one story back in 1945.

China in the Year 2000

A Memorial Ceremony - April 24, 2000
At the Hump Flying Monument,
which was built in 1993 to commemorate
the WW II Airlift (Flying supplies and men
over the Himalayan Mountains into China.)

The Qin Shi Huang's Terra Cotta Warrior and Horses
Qin Shi Huang (259-210 B.C.), the first Emperor of the Qin Dynasty,
was named Ying Zheng. He became king of Qin at a tender
age of 13 following the death of his father

The Great Wall - Ken and Blanche walked
along a portion of this 3700 mile marvel
Sino-American WW II Reunion 2000 in Kunming

Chinese Ingenuity!

215

The new airport in Diquing, built in 1999 with a 13,000 foot runway

Diquing is located in the northwest of Yunnan Province, near Burma and Tibet. This is the city of the legendary Shangri-La. The Hump Airlift route was over this area during 1942-1944. There are about 470 snow-covered mountains with elevations of 13,000 feet in this area. A lot of Hump aircraft crashed in these mountains. Shangri-La in Tibetan language means "You are coming, my friend," but this word used in other languages means "a mysterious fairy land" or "a Heaven of Peace in a secluded land."
When General Doolittle bombed Tokyo in 1942, the reporter asked President Roosevelt where our bombers took off from. The president answered, Shangri-La.

The Great Wall - May 3, 2000 - Sino-American WW II Reunion 2000 in Kunnming
(Ken and Blanche are in the center, second row)

We were driven by bus to the King's World Hotel, and given a room on the 17th floor. I was told there were about two hundred hotels such as the King's World in Kunming. There were even more floors above us.

This city of more than four million people held little or no similarity to the Kunming of the 1940s. We visited Chennault's 14th Army Air Force headquarters building, which was now being repaired as an historic site. That small part of Kunming was the same as in 1944, but the main streets were now wide, paved, with bicycle lanes on both sides of the streets. There were bicycles by the thousands as well as trucks, buses, cars and people crowding the downtown streets.

They even had intersections with stop and go lights. Somehow all conveyances seemed to get along with each other, seldom being involved in accidents. We observed the same traffic congeniality in all the large cities of China we visited. There were many near misses, though, but everyone just went on their way, taking it all in stride. We saw three-wheel bicycles loaded with stacks of products as high as ten feet. Once in a while the rider had to get off and push.

When we left the hotel for a trip to the "Rock Forest," some hundred miles of paved road to the south, our caravan of buses was led by police cars, their sirens were going full blast, and there were trucks loaded with soldiers accompanying us. We were considered by the Chinese people as the heroes of WW II in China. Everywhere we went we were treated as heroes. Our presence during WW II had kept the western part of China free from an invasion by the Japanese. These people appreciated us risking our lives for them, and they knew many had died for their freedom. Even China values freedom highly. Our trip to the Rock Forest was through a countryside I had seen from the air back in 1945. We drove within only a few miles of my old WW II home base at Luliang.

Every bit of tillable land was under cultivation as farms or small gardens and the farms seemed to be hanging on the sides of the mountains. No wonder there were water buffalo for working their fields; tractors were unable to climb those mountainsides. Farms were located everywhere that could be cultivated. There were few weeds, if any, only crops or vegetables. There was no room for weeds.

The Rock Forest is hard to describe, bare rocks sticking up like thousands of sentinels. These spires had been buried in the ocean, deteriorating for millions of years by water dissolving all but the hardest rock. Only a small part of these formations were contained in the park. Pathways wound around through those rocks and trees in the park, and we needed guides to keep us from getting lost in the "forest".

When we returned to Kunming we were driven directly to a museum. We were a little late getting back to the museum, which had just closed its doors. When the Museum director learned we were "Flying Tigers" he immediately opened it up just for us. Sometimes it pays to be a hero.

There was also a Hump Pilots museum right in the center of the city. All writing in the museum was in Chinese, but shortly there arrived interpreters, all with Wal-Mart nametags. There obviously was a Wal-Mart close by which we had not recognized due to our inability to read Chinese. We spent about an hour there, thanks to the Wal-Mart clerks that spoke English. There was a listing of all known airplane crashes posted on a wall. There were pictures of places and people along with some airplane parts recovered from the Himalayan Mountains.

That afternoon Blanche and I took a walk, by ourselves, into the business district. We heard not one word of English, except our own. It felt strange for us, as well as feeling a little nervous. What if we needed help of some kind. No one would have understood us. There were many sales offered in the stores, jade pieces and other jewelry and hundreds of cell phones on display. The only communications were the figures the salespersons flashed with their little hand held computers. We felt safer when we got back to the hotel, but even there no Chinese could speak more than a few words of English.

During the time between WW II and today, the cities of China have made unbelievable progress. Apartment houses were being built in every city we visited. Streets were paved. It was interesting to note, though, that some things were still being done the same way as in the 1940s. Although there was some heavy equipment, there were also thousands of workers moving dirt in baskets on their heads or on poles across their shoulders. My thought was that the government was helping to solve the unemployment problem by using these old methods.

There were numerous street sweepers at their job twenty-four hours a day, both men and women, carrying their homemade brooms and a large dustpan. Most had a type of homemade wheelbarrow or a three-wheel bicycle with a bed in the back, for carrying off the sweepings.

The white-collar workers in the city wore clothes quite similar to those we wear today in the U.S.A. A large majority of those workers rode a bicycle with fenders to work, rain or shine. We saw men in suits, women in nice long dresses, riding their bicycles to work in the rain, covered with a plastic rain cape. It seemed strange to us, early in the morning, to be seeing hundreds of bicyclists riding toward their jobs. There were bikes parking by the hundreds in the parking fence along the road. I wondered how they would ever find their own bike.

There was now an airplane trip on our travel plans to fly us to Tibet, an area called Shangri-la. The Chinese name was "Diqing," The elevation was 11,000 feet. The plan was to fly over Lake Tali, along the "Hump Route," then turn north to Shangri La. Unfortunately it was too cloudy to see much until we reached Shangri La. We landed at Diqing airport in a light rain, on a broad plane between mountains.

There were pretty girls wearing beautiful ceremonial dresses who greeted us by putting lovely dainty white silk shawls around our necks.

Looking around at the almost treeless broad valley, smooth enough for extensive farming, we could see a wide shallow river meandering through the valley. A few scattered homes, several of them two stories, could be seen nearby.

We were guided into the administration building where souvenirs were for sale. The mayor of the area gave a talk in Chinese, with an interpreter who told us why the two-hour bus trip had been cancelled. It was pointed out that most of us were 80 years old or older and might not be able to "handle" that high altitude. I felt fine, and not one of us was complaining. We were disappointed. At least we were able to see this unusual place located high up in the middle of the Himalayan mountain range. There were a lot of peaks surrounding the area with snow on them.

We were reluctant to leave, but had to get back to Kunming in order to catch an airplane for Chengdu, our next scheduled point of interest.

China Airways then carried us to Chengdu from Kunming. Chengdu was where most of the B29s had operated from during WW II. I think the place we landed that afternoon was the location of the air base called A-5 back in 1945. There had been several other bases built near Chengdu for Army Air Force use for the B-29s, and had concrete runways in 1944.

This field was now under expansion, and we had to tote our own luggage about 300 yards to board the buses to take us to our downtown hotel. Chengdu was a good size city, larger than Kunming. Rich farm land and irrigation water were contributors to the economy.

Our hotel was in the middle of town where we could watch the Chinese workers passing by on thousands of bicycles coming and going all day long. From time to time we would see people on the sidewalks doing their form of exercising called tie-chi, moving their bodies while staying in place.

We had come here to see an ancient dam and irrigation canals built in the mountains over 2,000 years ago, still operating. Our bus carried us on a modern highway, passing through a large industrial city under construction. The highways were also under much construction. Most of the area was farming country. As we traveled, we tried to guess what was being farmed. Much of the crop was probably rice. I saw some weeds and asked about them. All that the guide could tell me was that what looked like weeds were valuable crops to these people. Being early spring it was difficult to identify all the crops. The homes and communities opened our eyes to how farm families lived. Many apartment buildings were under construction, the tall scaffolds built of bamboo tied together reaching to the top of the many-storied buildings.

In about an hour and a half we reached the mountains from which we could look down to see the Irrigation dam below us, dividing the large river flowing down the valley between the heavily wooded mountains. The original design of two thousand years ago was to the expertise of the Chinese people, which gives us food for thought. What else did they accomplish? Their high degree of engineering so long ago could probably compare favorably with our engineering ability of today.

There were temple buildings built right up the side of the steep mountain above the dam and swinging bridge. We had been unloaded on the side of the mountain above the temple buildings. To reach the river we had to climb down these paths from temple to temple. Between the temple buildings were statues and lighted incense burner pots. We realized these temples were under use currently. There were incense trays burning all along the trail.

The pedestrian hanging bridge across the river was made of bamboo, and well built.

Seeing so many accomplishments of the ancient world of China forces a realization of the civilization thousands of years ago that we know so little about. Most of the inventions were used long before there was a United States. I thought, "What a powerful nation China would have already been today had it been a democratic nation."

We were told the mountains we had just come out of were the home to the Panda Bears. We didn't see any, of course, until we visited the Beijing Zoo a few days later.

After visiting the dam site we were driven to a beautiful building in the town just below the dam where we had dinner. There was a wedding dinner being held in the same room in which we were eating. I noticed their meal was more elaborate than ours. We were told that it was customary for the groom to furnish an elaborate meal to finalize the marriage ceremony. We were all invited to join in a toast to the happy couple.

As usual there was a heavy glass Lazy Susan on our table, upon which all dishes of food were placed. We would serve ourselves by rotating the Lazy Susan. As usual there was soup, baked chicken or duck, cut up, a whole baked two-pound fish (carp) served with head and tail intact, as well as Mongolian beef and other dishes of vegetables and rice. Some dishes I couldn't identify. For desert there were small slices of watermelon. We didn't dare drink the water. Most of us drank a mild beer, served from a quart bottle. We had chopsticks, with regular knives and forks available to us.

I liked the fish, which was surprisingly delicious. I had to dodge the small bones, of course. Sometimes when fish was served, the waiter removed the head. We had chicken foot soup, and I took a picture of the chicken foot. Can you believe it—no one ate any!

We were only served Chinese food on our trip. Absolutely no American food was served. We saw several McDonalds in the large cities, but the bus wouldn't stop. We would gladly have paid five dollars for a hamburger.

Whenever we were to leave by plane on the next leg of our tour, we were instructed to place our bags in the hallway of the hotel by a certain given time, usually ten or eleven o'clock.

Getting back to the hotel after the daily trips, tired or not, we had to comply by packing then placing the bags at the designated place in the hall by the specified time.

In the Chengtu hotel, as in each hotel we stayed in, I made sure the master door latch was locked, and the safety latch in place. Next morning we noticed the door was partly open, but the safety latch had held. Someone had attempted to break into our room that night. They had to have had a master magnetic door opener. Had I not used the safety latch???

Our next stop would be Hsian, an old, old city of the North, where there was a huge wall around the old part of the city, and we climbed up the steps to the top, some seventy-one in all. The top of the wall was about 30 to 70 feet wide. I think it must have been at least sixty feet high. There were even some buildings built on top of the wall.

Seeing old Hsian brought back a vivid memory of my first visit here. During the summer of 1945 I had flown a small load to Hsian late in the afternoon, and planned to spend the night. We had been flying off and on for two days and nights without any sleep. I had heard you could buy a steak in downtown Hsian. The airfield was at the edge of the city, so the co-pilot and I hired some rickshaws pulled by coolies, who ran the seven miles to that café in the middle of town. After eating those thin steaks that were delicious, we had climbed into our rickshaws and those men ran every step of the way back. We gave each of them a dollar tip.

Now back to modern China. We finally came down from the city wall and went to the Goose Pagoda. I remember one huge bell being on display there. Other bells were used high up in the pagoda. It just seemed like a glorified bell tower to us, but this really was a magnificent building, with several huge bells installed at different levels.

We were now scheduled to ride the bus several miles from town to see the famous Terra Cotta soldiers and other displays, all still standing inside the excavations. There were literally hundreds of terra cotta soldiers, each with a different expression carved or molded on their faces. Horses were also made so life-like, and there were even some carriages. How such a large area was excavated and so many soldiers molded in place is still somewhat of a mystery. It seemed the soldiers were for protection of the Emperor in the afterlife. The Chinese people were replacing or repairing these ancient figures, as there had been an effort to destroy these not long after the Emperor died.

There were other mounds to be seen, apparently not opened to the public yet, but the Chinese seemed to know who or what was buried in them.

We were now allowed to take pictures, which we did. There were so many tourists it was difficult to get all the pictures we wanted. Being the first week of May coincided with the China workers' yearly holiday of the first six days of May. The Chinese were taking advantage of their holiday to see the famous Terra Cotta Soldiers. Among the tourists were Koreans, Germans, Americans and many, many Chinese.

These archeological sites were well protected by the buildings built over them. These were about twenty miles from Hsian, and our bus driver kept us a little nervous by taking a short cut returning to Hsian. This gave us a close view of the farmers, their homes and the small villages along the old dirt road. We were glad when we reached the paved highway without getting stuck.

Our next and last place to visit was the capitol of China, Beijing, and the Great Wall. Beijing was a city of about eleven million people, and still growing. At the edge of town apartment buildings were under construction for several miles.

From our bus on the long ride out to the Great Wall we could see many orchards, farms, and much road construction. Small farming communities were scattered alongside the large new highway. As in the rest of China we could see no wasted space. No farm plot too small. Undoubtedly China will be taking her place in this world as an important industrial nation and in the near future will be considered one of the leaders.

Our main point of interest now was the Great Wall, several miles north of Beijing. It seems the Wall has become a major attraction for all tourists, both local and foreign. There were huge crowds of tourists from all over the world, with whom we mingled. People crowded on the steps of the Great Wall, just climbing up and down. There were Germans, North Koreans, Chinese, Americans and who knows how many other nationalities.

Car and bus traffic was quite crowded, so it was some time before our bus could find a parking place. We were in a narrow valley where the Great Wall crossed. The day was clear and visibility perfect, so we could see miles of it going up and down and winding around the mountains east and west of us, like a huge serpent. In many of the Chinese restaurants in the United States are beautiful large pictures of this section of the Great Wall.

This part of the Wall had been repaired and replaced until it looked to be almost original. The gate at the bottom of the valley was a pass-way under a 40-foot bridge, and it appeared to me to be the original road. We took pictures of the floor and walls of this large tunnel, which passed underneath the Great Wall, showing the deeply-worn wheel tracks in the blocks of stone placed on the road underneath the Wall. Some vague carvings of figures were on the walls.

Blanche and I climbed pretty far up on the wall, up one side of the valley. Step after step it went, on and on. The steps varied in height, so we had to be careful. We decided not to go the whole two thousand miles at that time, as we didn't want to miss our flight to the U.S. two days later. We also have a videotape that shows that we were there.

Visiting the Great Wall took most of the day. When we finally got back to Beijing, we were taken to a restaurant for a "Peking Duck" Dinner. About everything was usual except we had duck instead of chicken. The duck had been cooked then chopped up in small chunks.

We also had fish, complete with head, which a waitress expertly removed, along with the bones. The drink was a mild beer and the soup was that delicacy, chicken foot soup, including the foot.

After supper we were then driven to what was called a Chinese Opera. It was fun to watch, but no similarity to our idea of Opera. There was acrobatic dancing instead of the high-pitched soprano singsong voices I'd expected. When walking down a street in Kunming in 1945 I heard a loud recording of a female voice in a high flat pitch that resembled fingernails scratching on a slate. Thankfully there was no such singing at this Opera.

There were tables for four, with nuts and mixed flavored Chinese condiments placed to munch on while watching the Opera. The orchestra consisted of some string and percussion instruments to accompany the gymnastic dancing.

The next day we toured an aviation museum, built under a mountain. A huge tunnel was filled with lines of aircraft on both sides and down the middle. Some aircraft on display were some of the fighter planes used against us in the Korean War. Some Russian, American, and German planes were included in the exhibit. Both modern and ancient airplanes were on exhibit.

That night we attended a Chinese Symphony Orchestra made up of 26 pieces, strings and percussions instruments, popular in China for some hundreds of years. Most of the string instruments were similar to our guitars and harps. It was interesting and sounded uniquely pleasing.

The second half of the program was performed by beautifully clothed women, dancing with scarves or ribbons, to a smaller orchestra. This program was the most beautiful and impressive of anything we had seen in our entire trip to China. We heard one man say it was alone worth the price of the trip. I agreed with him as the beauty and grace of the costumes and silk scarves and the dancing were just fantastic. Their lovely use of the colored cloths, graceful bodies, the rhythm and timing of the dancing and the tinkling music were an unbelievable effect. What a fitting finish to our trip to China. This touch of romanticism and exotic dreams seemed to float out of the mysterious China of past centuries, just for us.

Back to earth and in the hotel, we were told to have our luggage in the hall by eleven o'clock that night. We would be leaving China early tomorrow. Our trip of a lifetime was about over. How could we remember so much of our experiences? We had a few excellent books for us to take home as reminders, and many rolls of film, which will help us to remember.

A true evaluation of China and its people would require studies of the thousands of years of the previously isolated Chinese civilizations. What was its imprint on the present Chinese? In spite of the cruel murderous Mao regime after WW II, and the ancient Emperors and rulers, the Chinese seem to have changed little. China is still China. In the past, travel by water to China took weeks or months, isolating China from other civilizations. No foreign people were welcome in China. Today China is only hours away from any civilized country in the world, and now is being forced into major changes. Trade and commerce with the rest of the world will probably affect these people, whether it is wanted or not.

I personally believe there are many unknown facts about China and it's past that we will never know. For one thing it is such a vast country, with more mountains than any other and beliefs different than those of the rest of the world. There are many different ethnic groups making up the population. It is completely Eastern in ideas.

We boarded our plane with mixed feelings. Although looking forward to a good old Fayetteville, Georgia, Dairy Queen hamburger, there was still a feeling of regret to be leaving the China we had barely touched. A description of China might be summed up in two words, "Vast, Mysterious."

Flying back to the United States we made a one-hour stop at the Shanghai airport to pick up more passengers. Although I had landed at this same airport in 1945, it no longer resembled what I had seen back then. This terminal was quite modern and large, just like those in the USA. We had to disembark, sitting in the Shanghai terminal until told to re-board. I was thinking how much of China we had not seen, including Shanghai itself, where I once spent three days.

I was disappointed that, by the time we passed over Japan on our homebound flight, it was too dark to see anything of Japan other than a few lights.

The airliner, from time to time during the night, put information on the television screens giving our ground speed (maybe we should say "water speed.") We were averaging 628 mph. We had a tail wind of over one hundred miles an hour. It took only 9 hours to reach San Francisco. I thought of how a horse, when heading home after a days work, went faster and faster. Maybe the airliner was anxious to get home.

To compare transportation today with that of the early 1940s and with the 1700s, one has to have a deep appreciation for progress during the past 300 years. In 1944 during my journey from Miami to Casablanca I saw and experienced so many things of interest. I have missed all that. I like the speed of traveling, but certainly miss seeing all the amazing sights passing thousands of feet below.

Our trip ended so early in San Francisco, because of the tailwind, that there were no gates available to unload us. We waited in the airplane nearly an hour before we could deplane. We had left Shanghai late evening in daylight and flown west into night, into daylight again, all in only nine hours. It gets confusing trying to keep up with the time when you travel so rapidly from country to country in today's high performance airplanes.

Flying from California the next day I was able to see out my window, viewing sparse areas of population with no cities, just vast areas of dry rangeland and few forests. It staggers the imagination to picture oxen-powered schooners and wagons, people on foot and horseback, traversing such barren country over 150 years ago. We have read sayings like "only the strong survived." Perhaps we should say: "Only the strong-willed and desperate survived." Was it fate or destiny?

Eastern New Mexico and the plains of Texas appeared, dotted with oil wells, farms, roads and communities. In a few hours I could see numerous lakes and streams in Southeastern U.S.A, displaying what the west didn't have. What a diverse and rich country we live in, and how little of it we have seen, compared with what there is to see.

Our trip to China had covered so much area too quickly for us to really appreciate the size of our world, much less that of the United States. I still wonder at the lack of curiosity of the other passengers. Perhaps they had flown the high-flying airplanes so much they were just oblivious to the sights that could be seen. Nearly all had the shades down during all the flights, even in the daytime.

Arriving back at Hartsfield Airport in Atlanta, we were looking forward to being home again. Our terrific honeymoon was behind us, to be held forever in our memory. We were looking forward to getting our film developed so we could share our trip with relatives and friends. Now we could show off our souvenirs from China. We knew we were home when our friend Gail Pope graciously picked us up at the airport at 10:00 that night.

Again I think of what a different world we live in today compared with the world of my youth. Our friends and relatives showed little interest in our fantastic trip. Before the world had "shrunk up" with the advent of jet-powered airplanes, everyone would be quite excited to see and learn about foreign countries. Today it seems to be of little consequence.

Blanche and I were certainly awed by our trip, seeing so much of China and the progress the Chinese were making, yet with evidence of the old China still very much present. I have been fortunate to have lived in China in the 1940s, and now having visited the new China, I am able to compare the life-styles and changes of the past fifty-five years.

- There's No Place like Home, and Love Makes the Home

In thinking back to my lifetime experiences of my first eighty-five years, I am now living in a different physical environment, having moved from Texas to Georgia. I am enjoying the new environment of Georgia, with its trees, flowers and rain. I am happy to be married to such a wonderful wife, who joins me with the new opportunities that have opened for us, which becomes more effective to our life. Together we share our happiness with others and spread our love to the many friends we have.

Many times, after telling people I recently moved to Georgia from Texas, I am asked, "Why did you move here from Texas?" My answer is: "I always thought it would take a team of mules to drag me away from Texas—until I met Blanche." Now that is the Gospel truth.

I could not have written this book without her help and encouragement. I've told Blanche many times how smart I was for marrying her.

The thought hit me that I needed to join the Toastmaster's Club and improve my communication abilities, as I may have to sell some of my books when they are published. What fun it has been since joining the Toastmaster Club and meeting so many wonderful people. We are all trying to improve our speaking and it's quite effective.

I am so happy Blanche's father, Cashes, went to the trouble to introduce us. Otherwise, I doubt we would ever have met. We both agreed on two principles when we were married: to always be truthful with each other; and to communicate. That sounds so simple, but sometimes it isn't, is it? We are sticking to our promises, though.

Blanche and I like to do things together; we both belong to the American Legion or its Auxiliary, the Toastmaster's Club, the Writers' Club, and the Biking For Life Club. Every Wednesday morning Edna Chennault, daughter-in-law of General Claire Chennault, joins Blanche and me at the Christian City Hospital where I play the piano and Blanche sings the songs of the WW II era for the patients on the Alzheimer's floor. Edna shares her love with all. What fun we have. Some of the patients sing with us, some even dance. The music of the bygone eras really *reaches* these people, bringing many wonderful memories back to them. We feel great when we hear them laugh and see them smile.

At home together, we *take a break* and eat popcorn, drink cokes and play dominoes. Our friends, Marshall and Betty Doster, love to play 42 with us when we can both work it into our schedules.

Another of my passions—Entertaining

Ken Babcock - Piano Recital - Fayetteville, Georgia - 2002

Volunteer Time at Christian City, Union City, Georgia

High Noon Toastmaster Kenneth Babcock, Fayetteville, Georgia
Ken's speech, "Be Your Own Doctor", September 23, 2003
Since joining Toastmasters in 2001, Ken has been awarded the CTM (Competent Toastmaster) award

- Work on house in Sonora and Taylor Reunions

Even before we were married, Blanche had wanted to remodel the inside of her mother's house in Sonora. She located a contractor for estimates and he sent us his estimate. The painting alone of the inside wood in the house was estimated at $7,000.00. I insisted I could do it for a fraction of that. So I got the job.

Away we went to Sonora, carrying paint, brushes and accessories. The contractor was already installing ceiling tile, wall paneling, light fixtures and ceiling fans.

Well, we began painting all the doors, window panels, floor trim, and kitchen cabinets. We first did the sanding with a small wood sander and painted up to three coats on all the inside wood. It took us three weeks of hard work and we are proud of the results. I could now better appreciate the estimate given us by the contractor on the painting. Blanche helped with the painting as well as doing other necessary work. We now have a nice two-bathroom home in Sonora, and are quite proud of it.

"Busy bees don't rest." That's a personal quote about Blanche. She took on a job, to write a little history book of the Taylor family. She had already done some genealogy work on the Taylors and her cousin Mattie Mae suggested they should have a Taylor reunion next spring in Sonora. Blanche said she would produce a book about the Taylors and their ancestors.

That little idea ballooned into quite a production. Blanche and I gathered material, received write-ups of personal lives and general information. I copied an entire book that Cousin Mattie Mae McKee had located that was written in 1937 about the Altizer side of the Taylor family living in early Virginia. All of this culminated in two 8 ½ by 11 inch books containing about 400 single spaced written pages each. These pairs of books contained writings and pictures of the present and past of the Taylor Families and their descendents.

Blanche performed this miracle, with a small amount of help from me, in only six months. She spent all her time day after day, working until the wee hours, going through boxes and boxes of pictures, picking out the best ones to use in the book. Research, writing, organizing pictures and assembling all the information about each individual family was a monumental task she had unselfishly undertaken. She was determined to have it ready for the deadline of June the eighth and we did.

We had befriended a nice cooperative lady in a local printing shop. In the last week before the re-union in Sonora we called upon Blanche's daughter, Resa, to help us at the printing shop, and we went to work there, printing. At six o'clock Friday, we finished and the lady at the shop glued and installed the covers of the two books.

The next morning about 10:00 we left the house headed for Texas, our van loaded to the "gills". We could not have carried all those books in a regular automobile.

When the families at our reunion in Sonora, Texas, saw those books, they couldn't believe it. Our actual cost per set was slightly over $57.00 (about 1000 pages). That was reasonable, we felt. This was our first experience at publishing and writing books, and we are proud of ourselves. We're now involved in writing the history of my life that began in 1918.

Blanche made am excellent speech about "the book" and the Genealogy of her family. I was quite proud of her.

- HUMP Pilot Reunions (later years)

I took some of my manuscript this past summer to the ATC Hump Pilots reunion in Dayton, Ohio to get their opinions. One of the men was reading a few pages and began laughing. I had misspelled *Emmelman*! We visited the famous Aviation Museum as well as the Bicycle Shop run by the Wright Brothers, where the first airplane that could take off and fly was designed and built.

About two months after returning from our reunion Marshall and Betty Doster, fellow members of the Toastmaster club and close friends, invited us to accompany them to Virginia for Marshall's Navy reunion of the USS ELDEN. We accepted his invitation, and it was a thrilling trip for us. We took our time driving two days to get to Charlottesville, Virginia.

Although I am an airplane pilot, these shipmates of Marshall's accepted me just like one of their own. Those men and their wives treated us like we were one of them. Blanche and I felt honored.

The USS Elden was an Escort Ship used to protect convoys from enemy submarines, airplanes and destroyers. They were well equipped to locate and destroy enemy submarines, and their multiple guns were able to help protect the convoy from enemy air attack.

With fifteen officers and 180 enlisted men sharing quarters for two years on a ship with a length and beam of only 290 feet by 35, these men became as close as brothers. That is amazing. Being in constant danger may have tightened the bond between them.

Marshall told about missing his ride back to the ship after riding their whaleboat ten miles to shore at Yokasuka in the South Pacific. He was the movie operator in his ship and went ashore with his helper to exchange some films to be shown on the ship that night.

"Although we had taken the island, it had not yet been secured." The two of them decided to look over the captured Japanese Navel Station dug into a mountain. They sneaked past the Marine guard at the entrance of the first level where there was a factory setup for building two-man submarines.

On the second level they found a hospital, and then on the third level found the headquarters for the Japanese Navy. Wow.

They took time to find a few souvenirs then rushed back to their boat, but the whaleboat was already gone. How to get back to the USS Elden, ten miles out on the bay? The Elden was leaving for the USA the next morning. They hardly noticed the wind was whipping up white caps while they searched desperately for a way to their ship.

A typhoon had come up causing their whaleboat to leave early. As they searched the dock area they ran across a whaleboat from the Cantrell, one of the other ships in their own division. They caught their ride.

The whaleboats were sixteen feet long with ballast tanks on each side for helping to stabilize the boat in rough water. They were no match for a typhoon, though, and were still prone to capsize. Fortunately, the typhoon had died down somewhat and they made it safely back to the Elden.

Stepping aboard in the darkening afternoon they were met by the ship's captain, who, after reprimanding them severely, told the sailors that if they kept their noses clean this "event" would be purged from their record. Marshall informed me there was no one with cleaner noses on that ship than his helper and himself. The captain kept his promise and took it off the record.

This story has a surprise ending. Marshall didn't know for about fifty years that the Elden's whaleboat they had missed was swamped by the typhoon and those boys in it were lost. What a shock to Marshall. He then was certain his Guardian Angel had been with him all the time.

While in Charlottesville we visited Monticello, home of Thomas Jefferson. We were certainly impressed by the advanced plans and actions designed into the building of his home. A passageway passing under his house was used as a cellar as well as a passage from the kitchen to a small elevator to carry the food up to the dining room. Other innovations throughout his plantation were just amazing. He was a fine man to have as president in those early days. He promoted the building of the University of Virginia, which we also visited. Both the University and his home were built in the 1700s.

Being in the country where her ancestors had lived long ago, Blanche and I were able to easily picture her ancestral grandmother whom we had read about, who had "Killed a Bar" with rocks. When she was ninety-two years old, another ancestral grandmother broke through the ice in the river and drowned. She was riding a horse carrying a sack of feed for some livestock when the ice gave way.

The trip to Charlottesville and back by automobile was thrilling as well as historical. We saw the land settled so long ago by white men and pictured in our minds the farms and trails hacked out of the forests, the "log- rolling" and the house building. We could imagine the smoke rising from the burning of the stumps and trimmings from the downed logs as they had been cleared from the land for farming.

Since Blanche and I have married, we've attended several Hump Pilot and ATC Pilots' reunions, meeting old friends and making many more. Some of the war stories we share may be forgotten. We have never had to embellish these stories, however, as the truth is stranger than fiction. Many stories were ended in the high mountains and forests of the Himalayan "Hump" years ago, never to be told. Blanche and I have attended reunions in Boston, Irvine, (California), Arizona, Dayton, Washington D.C., Atlanta, Mobile, New Orleans and Colorado Springs. There won't be many more, though, as our ranks are thinning rapidly.

In Boston we learned to speak Bostonian—don't pronounce the "r's".

In Washington we saw many things, yet somehow missed seeing the President.

In Atlanta we saw Underground Atlanta, CNN, and the Hump Pilots section of the Aviation Museum at Warner Robbins. We talked to General Scott, author of "God is my Co-Pilot." He is quite proud that he served in the CBI Theater.

In Dayton we saw the Aviation Museum, the grave of Erma Bombeck (a big rock was her tombstone), and the famous bicycle shop where the Wright Brothers built the first airplane and the first wind tunnel.

All things have to end in this life, and each year the meetings of the ATC and the Hump Pilots organizations have been rapidly declining in numbers. We have attended the ATC and last official reunions. Both organizations had only a few attending, and several years ago the members decided to officially disband in the year 2005. A few of us will continue to get together from time to time, on our own initiative.

Blanche and I will continue enjoying our busy lives together. My memories are still vivid, and sometimes at night I re-live my China experiences while trying to go to sleep. My desire to share all my experiences with you has been the motivation for writing this book.

~ ~ ~

Epilogue

To Sum Up My Life

Many people have asked me about the China War, so I decided to share my life story with them. I intended to give my readers a mental picture and the feeling of being in the airplane with me while flying in China. My intent was to include the way we felt, the food we ate, and some insight into the Chinese people.

We must remember that each of our airfields in China was operating under a different commander. Some had more or less foods like meat or vegetables. Combat groups, I noticed, had such things to eat as hot cakes, bread, meat as well as rice and eggs. It so happened I was never in such great surroundings and lived only on rice and "egguses", as scrambled eggs were called in China.

It would have been nice if one could have chosen places in China to explore, but I never had that opportunity.

My entire story is really a story of the many people I was in contact with from time to time as I journeyed around the world. People make living more exciting. Without someone to share it with, our lives would be dull and without luster.

My life is made better by sharing with you this true narrative. My journey through life is an historic event as well as containing many adventures. There were mountains to climb, challenges to meet and opportunities to learn.

Unexpected opportunities came, such as learning to fly airplanes, which changed my life. After teaching Aviation cadets for two years, 1942 and 1943, I became an officer in the AAF and flew in the Air Transport Command in the States, North Africa, India, and then China until the end of WW II.

Released from the Army, I opened a retail and repair store in electronics, then in 1949 through 1979 operated thirty years as a crop-duster.

During those thirty years of crop-dusting I also instructed flying, and continued instructing for another ten years.

I officially retired in 1982, applying for social security. I continued my exercise regime of riding a bicycle and traveling with my wife when we could. I also continued some contract flying.

How fortunate I've been to have had one full life and now another. Love of my fellow man is a wonderful gift God has given me and that love just keeps on growing.

There were other decisions to be made. I gave myself some time to think and visit some friends, relatives and Blanche Regeon. A year went by, during which I visited those friends and relatives, and especially Blanche. She and I were brought up in the same little town of Sonora, Texas and I had gone to school with several of her close relatives.

Blanche turned out to be a most understanding and intelligent person. Our backgrounds being so similar helped us to understand each other. We both were alone and happy when together. Now that we are married we are seldom apart, as we like to do things together.

We love meeting people and being active. I had never thought I'd enjoy living away from Texas and the friends of a lifetime. But here in Georgia I have many new friends, have a bigger family and live 1300 miles from the town I called home for 65 years. I left a new house in Texas, fully equipped, to come to Georgia to marry Blanche. I've never regretted it.

Our yard here contains a hundred trees well over 60 feet tall. In Texas I had four miniscule trees. How different it is to live around so many trees, heavy traffic, rain, light wind and lakes scattered everywhere. The wonderful people are friendly and accept us as we are. There are so many accomplished people living here, writers, actors, musicians and outstanding speakers. We appreciate being around such people. There are many opportunities for us here that were not available out in West Texas. Of course I miss the friends and country I had known so closely for so long, but I am quite happy here.

I am glad to conclude this book with such a happy ending. Blanche and I enjoy our large family and our many activities. We have a swing on the front deck, if we ever get old enough to use it.

Index of Names

Name	Pages
Ackers, Bob, Jackie and Maggie	204
Adams (Mertzon, TX)	24
Adams, Coach	24
Alaniz, Tony	181
Aldwell, Roy	26
Alford, Lt.	68
Allred, Val Jean	43
Alves, Richard	60-61, 200
Archer, Francis	8
Archer, George	8
Ashenhurst, A. C.	156
Babcock, Blanche L. Taylor Regeon	159, 182-186, 193-196, 199, 200, 203, 212-214, 217
Babcock, Edith Stella Knoll	6, 21, 27, 29, 31, 37, 187
Babcock, Faegene Eddleman	11, 45-46, 49, 52-55, 57-58, 62-64, 69, 74-78, 130, 132, 134, 136-138, 153, 162-165, 167, 172, 182, 186-190, 192-198, 201-204, 208
Babcock, Frank & Kay	42, 43
Babcock, Kathryn	191, 193
Babcock, Orville Gorman (O.G.)	7
Bailey, L.H., MD	23
Blackstock,	160
Bloomer, Richard	103-105, 115, 181, 187, 201
Boughton, I. B. MD	31
Boughton, Rique, Alain, & Josette	31
Bradford, George	91
Brantley, W. B.	11
Bringelston, Viola	203
Britt, Superintendent	15
Brown, "Brownie"	54-55
Campbell, Mrs.	168
Campbell, Sir Malcolm	50
Carlsguard, Glenn	141
Carpenter,	16
Carter, Mary	55
Chenault, Rex	58, 59
Chennault, Claire, General	98, 100, 217, 224
Chennault, Edna	224
Chiang, Kai-shek	100, 101, 121
Comstock, Chick & Wanda	135-136, 146, 150-151
Connelly, John	51
Connelly, Tom	31
Cooper, James, Md.	136-137
Cooper, Jodi	212
Cory, Jean	201
Cory, Victor	35-36
Cottler, Lt.	80
Cox, Wyatt	101
Cragin, George & Marilyn	204
Cranford, Aaron	145
Crawford, Bill	109, 123
Darby, Twoie	162
Day (Melvin, TX)	24
Dietrich, Colonel	84
Doster, Marshall & Betty	226-228
Draper,	33
Drommerhousen, Dan	125
Eagleton, Effie	186
Eaton, John	32
Eddleman, C.L. and Edna	53, 56, 64, 77, 130
Eddleman, Merel	53, 133
Eddleman, Mrs Roy & Mary Ann	192
Eddleman, Otho	56
Ernster,	118
Estes, Billy Sol	146
Fambrough, Les	21
Farmer, Chelse	212
Farmer, Zachary	212
Fisher,	177-178
Foster, J. C. and Collete	208
Gable, Clark	31
Gardner, Henry	172, 181
Gardner, Lefty	172-173
Gil, G.S,, Md., Surgeon	198-200, 204-205
Gilmore, Bob	141
Gilmore, Ted	11-12, 56
Glasscock, Lonnie	69
Glasscock, Wilburn and Bertha	21
Goodnight, Charles, Colonel	13-14, 22
Graciano, Gordo	181
Grinnell, Bob	20, 207, 213
Hall, Ed and Mary	134
Hall, Leslie	134
Haren, Leland	151
Hieberger, Jim, Md.	202
Henderson, Rex	164
Hensley (Melvin, TX)	24
Higgins, O. B.	24
Hines, Frank	56, 142-144

Name	Pages
Hodgkins, Dudley & Marcia	107, 187
Holland, Roberta	27-28
Hopkins, Doug	199, 207
Houston, Jake	42
Hubbard, Cleo	14
Hudspeth, Roy	39
Hurd, Martin	105-107, 115, 122-124, 187
Hurt, Colonel	43
Jackass Andy	194-195
Janelle	17
Jennings, C. J.	45
Jobe (San Angelo, TX))	24
Johnson, Elmo	8, 35
Johnson, Lynden B.	31
Jones (San Angelo, TX)	24
Jungk, Dorthy	12
Jungk, Fred	12
Jungk, Pat	12
Kaplan, Rick & Peggy	200
Keval, Cpl.	126
Knoll, Colonel Dallas	203
Knoll, Dean and Lovejoy	16, 202-204
Knoll, Gretchen	202
Knoll, Ralph and Nancy	203
Knoll, Sussana Bashor	9
Knoll, Viola	202
Kokernot, Bob MD.	29, 207
Kokernot, Walter	187
Kring, Ikey	31
Lane, Monte	56
Lemay, Curtis, General	101
Lindamood, Jesse	212
Lindsey, Abbie	137-138
Littlefield, Coach Clyde	24
Lobdell, Barbara and Doug	203
Lovell, Maryann	192
Locker, Leon	158
Logan, Emma Lee & Emma Lou	28
Looney, Pete	146
Loving	14
Mann (Brady, TX)	24
Mao (China)	101-102, 222
Massengale, Rick	211
Mauldin, Jimmy	142
Maynard, Steve	182
McKee, Mattie Mae	226
McKinney, Tony	164
McKinney, Bob	134-135
McKinney, Lloyd and Freddie	147, 162
McKinney, Bobby	162
McMahan, Robert	212
Metz, Myrtle	49
Miegel, Bill and Marie	105-106
Milam, Ben	172
Miller, Florine	7, 9-11
Miller, Garnet	11
Miller, Lamont	11
Miller, Mr. Mrs. T. L.	11
Mills, J. O.	39-40
Mitchel, Elmo	33
Monroe, Sam	165
Morris, Vernon	24
Morris, Mr. & Mrs. H. V.	24
Munro, Fern	201-202
Murphy, Joe and Betsy	62, 94, 208
Nemzek, Robert	120
Nevill, Harrell (Ironhead)	151
Nevill, Marshall	151
Neville, Wanda Rape	8
Parham, Bob, Opal	130
Penick	31-32
Peterson, Carl	157-158
Pfiester, Beulah	12
Phillips, Chris	167, 192, 207
Phillips, Jack	186, 203
Phillips, Jamie	212
Phillips, Jessica	212
Phillips, John A. III	211-212
Phillips, Kristin	185, 207-208
Phillips, Nanetta L. Regeon	200, 203, 210
Phillips, Resa R. Regeon	195, 204, 212-213, 226
Phillips, Sherry Babcock	167, 185-186, 196-198, 205-208, 212
Phillips, Steve	213
Pickle, Jake	51
Pietsch, Barbara	107-108, 77,
Pietsch, Horace	78, 80-82, 95, 104-106, 112
Pope, Gail	223
Rand, Sally	11
Rape, Jack	7
Reeves, Mel	137
Regeon, R. Royce	193
Ridley, Chilton	6
Ridley, Floyd	6
Ridley, Kenneth	6-7

Name	Pages
Ridley, Mrs.	7
Robinson, (Robbie)	160
Roloff, Earl	105
Roosevelt, Franklin	196
Roosevelt, Teddy	78
Rosemary	163
Sandidge, Ernie, MD	181-182
Saunders, Alan	7
Saunders, Harold	7
Saunders, Richard	7
Scott, Jr., General Robert Lee	228
Scott, Wally	199
Seals, Mr.	139
Seals, Dan	139
Sewell, R. V.	40-41
Shackelford, Cary	208
Shackelford, Gil	185
Shackelford, Lacy	185
Shackelford, Mellissa	185
Shackelford, Shelly Phillips	185, 212
Sharp, Roy	165
Sheard,	126-127
Shepard, Charlie	156
Shoemaker, George	98, 188
Shurley, Ira & Jewel	45
Shurley, Jay Talmadge	43, 45-46, 200
Shurley, Ruth Tipton and Edgar	26, 34
Smith, Floyd and Florence	188
Smith, Johnny	58
Smith, Lacy	39
Smith, Olin	151, 165
Sofge, Cora Belle Taylor	193
Stacy, Carlene Peeples	42, 49, 194
Stelling, Colonel	99, 117, 122
Stokes, S. H.	39
Sylvester, Major	98
Taylor, Basil	13
Taylor, Billie W.	161
Taylor, Cashes W.	41, 148, 159, 193, 213
Taylor, Jimmie	13, 56, 159, 193
Taylor, Nancy A.	13, 24, 193-195, 210-213
Taylor, Mr. & Mrs. Robert Eli	7, 13, 39
Teaff, Bob	18, 26
Teagarden, Jack	23
Thies, Jan and Bill	164
Thompson, Bob	139
Thurman, Lisa	185, 197, 208
Tipton, E.D.	26, 76
Tipton, Gertrude Babcock	26, 29, 76, 191, 194, 203
Trainer, Joseph	32
Tunner, General	114, 116
Turnbull, Bill	122
Valliant, Martha	207
Walkey, M/Sgt.	128
Waller, Jim	174
Walters, Milo	143
Vanderstucken, Joseph	145
Warren, Darrel	138
Ward, Bob	11
Ward, Colonel Roy	68
Ward, Sr., John	42
Warner, Al	161
Watkins, Marie	36, 39
Watson, Florine Miller	11
Weatherup, Michael	206
Weatherup, Rhonda G. Regeon	204-207
Webb, Spider	33
Wendell, Gordon and Betty	68
West, Blanche D.	207
White, Ted	21
Wiggington, Miss	8
Williams, Bill	124
Williams, Carleton	206
Wimmer, Ed (Barlow)	104, 107
Winckler, John	120
Yates, Thurman and Evelyn	57-59, 62, 67, 187, 204
Yost, George	102

1-800-418-1078
pivotrim 19.95